Business and Society

T0353319

Business and Society

A Critical Introduction

Second Edition

Edited by
Sonya Marie Scott, Kean Birch, Richard Wellen
and Audrey Laurin-Lamothe

BLOOMSBURY ACADEMIC
LONDON • NEW YORK • OXFORD • NEW DELHI • SYDNEY

BLOOMSBURY ACADEMIC
Bloomsbury Publishing Plc
50 Bedford Square, London, WC1B 3DP, UK
1385 Broadway, New York, NY 10018, USA
29 Earlsfort Terrace, Dublin 2, Ireland

BLOOMSBURY, BLOOMSBURY ACADEMIC and the Diana logo are trademarks of
Bloomsbury Publishing Plc

First published by Zed Books in Great Britain 2017
This edition published 2023

A catalogue record for this book is available from the British Library.

A catalog record for this book is available from the Library of Congress.

ISBN: HB: 978-1-3503-5707-5
PB: 978-1-3503-5706-8
ePDF: 978-1-3503-5709-9
eBook: 978-1-3503-5708-2

Typeset by Deanta Global Publishing Services, Chennai, India

To find out more about our authors and books visit www.bloomsbury.com and sign up for
our newsletters.

Contents

Illustrations

Contributors

Kean Birch is the director of the Institute for Technoscience & Society and an associate professor in the Science & Technology Studies (STS) Graduate Program and Faculty of Environmental and Urban Change at York University, Canada. He is the co-editor of the leading international STS journal *Science as Culture*, published by Taylor and Francis, and founder and series editor of the *Technoscience & Society Book Series* at University of Toronto Press.

Caroline Shenaz Hossein is Canada research chair of Africana Development & Feminist Political Economy and associate professor of Global Development at the University of Toronto Scarborough and appointed to the graduate program in the Department of Political Science at St. George. She is the interim director of the Institute for Inclusive Economies and Sustainable Livelihoods at U of T. She is founder of the Diverse Solidarity Economies (DISE) Collective. She is author of multi-award winning *Politicized Microfinance* (2016), editor of *The Black Social Economy* (2018), co-editor of *Community Economies in the Global South* (2022) by Oxford University Press and co-editor of the *Encyclopedia of the Social and Solidarity Economy* (2022) for UNRISD. Dr Hossein is working on her forthcoming book, *The Banker Ladies.* Follow her on Twitter @carolinehossein

Audrey Laurin-Lamothe is an associate professor in the Business and Society program at York University, Canada. Her research focuses on financialization, economic elites, and their impact on wage stagnation and economic inequalities. She is the author of *Financiarisation et élites économiques au Québec* (2019, Presses de l'Université Laval).

Salewa Olawoye is an assistant professor in the Business and Society program at York University, Canada. She has a PhD in economics and social science consortium (University of Missouri—Kansas City, 2016). Her research focuses on heterodox approaches to sustainable economic development through natural resources and monetary theory. Her research mainly focuses on these issues in the Sub-Saharan African region. She co-edited the book *Monetary Policy and Central Banking: New Directions in Post-Keynesian Theory* (2012) and is editor of *COVID-19 and the Response of Central Banks: Coping with Challenges in Sub-Saharan Africa* (2023).

Mark Peacock is a professor in the Business and Society program at York University, Canada. His research interests include the philosophy of economics and the theory and origins of money. He is the author of the books *Introducing Money* (2013) and *Amartya Sen and Rational Choice: The Concept of Commitment* (2019).

Alberto Salazar is an associate professor in the Department of Law at Carleton University, Canada. He obtained his PhD at Osgoode Hall Law School, York University (Toronto, Canada) and served as a MacArthur fellow at the University of Oxford and as a CAPORDE fellow at the University of Cambridge. His recent publications have appeared in the *Berkeley Business Law Journal*, *Virginia Journal of International Law*, *McGill Journal of Sustainable Development Law*, and *American Journal of Comparative Law*.

Sonya Marie Scott is an assistant professor in the Business and Society program at York University, Canada. Her areas of research include economic subjectivity, the mathematization of economics, business cycle theory and contemporary responses to crisis. She is the author of *Architectures of Economic Subjectivity: The Philosophical Foundations of the Subject in the History of Economic Thought* (2013) and editor of *Languages of Economic Crises* (2021).

John Simoulidis is an associate professor in the Business and Society and Interdisciplinary Social Science programs at York University, Canada. His research interests include political theory and political economy, food as commons and cooperatives. He is co-editor (with Robert Albritton) of *New Dialectics and Political Economy* (2003).

Richard Wellen is an associate professor in the Business and Society program at York University, Canada. His recent research deals with the political economy of digital transformations in business, higher education systems and scholarly publication. His books include *Making Policy in Turbulent Times: Challenges and Prospects for Higher Education* (2013, co-edited with Paul Axelrod, Theresa Shanahan, and Roopa Desai-Trilokekar).

1 | A critical introduction to business and society

Kean Birch, Audrey Laurin-Lamothe and Sonya Marie Scott

Introduction

This book is about the relationship between *business* and *society*. As such it's concerned not only with how different business forms, practices, and knowledges shape society *and* how different social forms, practices, and knowledges shape business, but also with how this mutually constitutive relationship has changed over time. Contemporary capitalist societies, for example, are going through a profound shift in the way that businesses account for natural resource use and pollution (Jackson 2009). Specifically, capitalist societies have moved from treating the environment as a 'free' gift to incorporating pollution as an economic cost; this has happened alongside growing social awareness and action to address the implications of harmful environmental changes – we discuss this in more detail in Chapter 16. In this context, business and society cannot be isolated from one another in their treatment of environmental problems, since they are so entangled with one another that it makes no sense to posit a simple one-way causative relation (i.e. societal values forcing changes in business practice, or vice versa).

Definition: Business

The term 'business' is a generic term we use to mean any organization that engages in for-profit activities, no matter how those profits are subsequently distributed. That means that business covers a range of organizations, including public corporations (see later), private firms, partnerships, family firms, sole proprietorships, state-owned enterprises, worker cooperatives and consumer cooperatives.

Definition: Society

The term 'society' is a generic term we use to mean a collective group of people who share a common set of social institutions (e.g. law, money, government, citizenship, language), social norms (e.g. beliefs, conventions) and geographical space (e.g. territory). We do not assume that societies are homogeneous, static or consensual in that every society – every social group really – involves diversity, change and conflict.

Business plays a major role in our lives as many scholars have noted (Bakan 2020). Most of us either are employed by businesses or run our own businesses; most of us depend on businesses for the basic services and infrastructures we take for granted (e.g. phones, energy, mobility); almost all of us are reliant on businesses for our daily subsistence (e.g. food); and much besides. Many of us are excluded from the benefits of business (e.g. employment, products and services) as the result of societal prejudice and discrimination – an issue we address in Chapter 20. Outside of the economic sphere, businesses dominate public debate through lobbying and other influences on politics (Birch 2007), discussed in Chapter 10; they dominate policymaking and regulation, discussed in Chapter 18; they dominate our cultural life through the production of art, film, music, games and so on (McChesney 2000); on top of this, the ubiquity of advertising, marketing and branding means that business representations of themselves and of consumers no longer register on our consciousness (Ewen 1976). Lastly, the internet is clearly a public network which nobody owns, yet our access to its vast informational and networking capacity is shaped, organized, filtered and exploited for profit by powerful businesses that provide search and social media services.

We can see that today business and society are largely inseparable; business is society, and society is business. It's hard to imagine a world in which private business doesn't exist, or doesn't dominate our lives in quite the same way it does now. What's more, this domination has become a truly global issue, as we outline in Chapters 13, 14, 15 and 16. However, a world without business as we currently know it did once exist, so it is important to remember that private business and capitalism more generally are not 'natural' or even inevitable (see Chapters 2, 3 and 7). Moreover, there are alternatives, as we outline later in this book (see Chapters 21 and 22).

In the rest of this introduction, we open with a discussion of the importance of markets and of business to society reflecting a key debate in the social sciences – and elsewhere – on the rise of 'neoliberalism' (see later). We do so in order to raise a key question in the next section: Why is business still important in society if markets supposedly reign supreme? We then present our approach to understanding the relationship between business and society. Finally, we conclude with a survey of the characteristics of three different types of society – traditional, modern and postmodern – and how they relate to the many themes addressed in this book.

The market triumphant?

Nowadays, it often seems like the 'free' market has won; it's presented by pundits, politicians, and policymakers as the solution to all sorts of social problems, from crime to climate change. We discuss the theoretical basis for these claims and the criticisms of them in Chapters 4, 5 and 6, especially the influential idea that *the market* leads to a social order that benefits everyone. Collective, political or social action, on the other hand, whether undertaken by governments or charities or international organizations, has seemingly failed to deliver on the promises made to us of a better world. Instead, the market has become the *de facto* institution for managing our societies. According to many critical scholars, activists and politicians, however, this has meant that our politics, societies and economies are now dominated by something called neoliberalism, a concept they frequently use to describe a range of nefarious and egregious policies, ideas and behaviours ranging from corporate tax evasion through rising student debt to environmental deregulation. For an introduction to neoliberalism as a concept see the works of David Harvey (2005) and others (e.g. Crouch 2011; Mirowski 2013; Birch 2015a, 2015b).

Key concept: The market

Markets mean different things to different people. Mainstream economics textbooks, for example, frequently only provide a vague definition of markets (or 'the market') as a mechanism that brings together buyers and sellers who wish to exchange goods and services with one another. Generally speaking, these types of market are associated with the rise of capitalism from the fifteenth century onwards, although it is important to remember that every human society has had some form of market in order to exchange things. Modern capitalist markets, then, entail other characteristics, including private property, contractual relations, competition between producers, prices determined by interactions between supply and demand, the use of money as the basis of exchange, and the compulsion people face to sell their labour for a wage in order to survive. Furthermore, the benefits of capitalist markets arise from their role as a determinant of prices, which often leads to the market being described as a price mechanism. Prices are supposed to provide people with information and incentives that promote the 'efficient' allocation and distribution of resources in society, especially by promoting specialization or the division of labour (e.g. each of us specializes in what we are good at and then trades with one another).

Source: Aldridge (2005)

In his book *A Brief History of Neoliberalism* the geographer David Harvey (2005) defines neoliberalism as the deliberate extension of markets as the main, if not only, institution to organize society and ourselves – see Chapter 4 for more on this view. Neoliberalism is based on an analytical perspective that emphasizes individual preferences, individual responsibility and individual choices – what many refer to as *homo economicus*, which we discuss in Chapter 5 – as the best and only way to understand human nature and human organization.

This view of the world has become so dominant in countries like the USA, UK and Canada that it has become 'common sense'; for example, when we ask our students if humans are naturally or inherently selfish, most students say 'yes'. Instead, there is a need to unpack the role played by our personal relationships, our family lives, our cultural values, our religious or non-religious beliefs, our social institutions and so on because all these things complicate the notion of inherent self-interest or selfishness. It is important to remember that we can be selfish, we can be altruistic, we sacrifice for the greater good and so on, and often do so in complicated, inconsistent and contradictory ways.

The triumph of the 'free' market – and we will explain those scare quotes around 'free' shortly – is manifested in many ways. Here, we want to present the example of *free trade* treaties like the North American Free Trade Agreement (NAFTA) signed by the United States, Canada and Mexico, which came into force in 1994, and then was subsequently modified in 2020. This North American treaty is now named the USMCA (the United States, Mexico, Canada Agreement) in the United States, the CUSMA (Canada, United States, Mexico Agreement) in Canada and the T-MEC (Tratado Mexico, Estados Unidos, Canadá) in Mexico. Despite these somewhat nationalistic changes of name the agreement remains largely the same – indeed some dub the new agreement NAFTA 2.0 (see Chapter 14). Supporters of these trade and investment agreements argue that they will promote trade by reducing trade tariffs (i.e. customs duty on imports and exports) and other non-tariff barriers to trade (e.g. country-specific product regulations), thereby promoting economic growth. However, critics point out that these outcomes are far from certain or likely to happen. One reason that these outcomes may not happen – and the reason we use scare quotes around 'free' – is that few people outside each country's negotiating team ever get to see copies of the draft agreements before they are formally signed. Consequently, it is difficult for citizens and subjects to review these sorts of treaty before they come into effect.

Definition: Free trade

Imports and exports can be taxed by national governments. Such tariffs, as they are called, can be imposed for different reasons. For example, tariffs have been used throughout history by various countries to support domestic producers against overseas competitors (e.g. the United States imposed tariffs on imports throughout the nineteenth century). Globalization advocates argue that tariffs restrict trade and, thereby, reduce economic efficiency by supporting inefficient producers; these advocates therefore argue that the world's economy would be better off without tariffs.

This lack of transparency is a problem because of the potential implications such treaties could have on things like access to medical and pharmaceutical treatments, a concern raised by organizations like Médecins sans Frontières (MSF). In particular, MSF argues that these deals often create strengthened intellectual property restrictions that reduce the availability of affordable generic drugs in poorer countries (Samarasekera 2022).

Contradictorily, then, such 'free' trade agreements can actually reduce market competition as IPRs protect against competition (Sayer 2015). Since these agreements are made without public input or even review of the treaty process or its provisions, it is hard to see how markets are in and of themselves liberating, despite what some scholars have argued (e.g. Friedman 1962).

Whether or not the market is a liberating force is beside the point, however. If we examine the perspectives of market critics (e.g. Harvey 2005) or market supporters (e.g. Friedman 1962), both sides in this debate overlook, to a large extent, the place of business in our societies. While the market may represent an ideal to which many thinkers and politicians aspire, it is business that dominates everyday life – that is, it is an organizational entity and not the market mechanism that shapes our world. How we govern business, how we ensure that business is responsible and how we ensure that business does not dominate society are all important issues, and ones we address in this book – see Chapters 8, 9, 10 and 12.

Why business and society?

Understanding the relationship between business and society is critical for understanding contemporary society. On the one hand, business is a major institution and organization in all our lives, although in different ways. Most people work for private businesses, frequently for large *(public) corporations*. According to Deakins and Freel (2012), for example, between 35 and 50 per cent of private employment in the United States, the UK and Canada is in large enterprises, whether corporations or not. Moreover, across a number of countries in the Global North, small business represents a significant proportion of total private business entities and total private employment; such small enterprises are often individually owned operations, family businesses and such like. Other people, fewer in number but growing, work for charitable, voluntary and community organizations, which often adopt private business practices and methods (e.g. accounting), or social economy organizations like cooperatives, mutual associations, credit unions and so on (Amin et al. 2002; Birch and Whittam 2012) – see Chapters 20 and 22. A final group of people work for the state, often in government bureaucracies (e.g. civil service) but also in state-owned business and arms-length corporations. Business is, in this sense, incredibly diverse, and it is too simplistic to equate business with a faceless, pathological corporation of popular opprobrium (e.g. Nace 2003; Bakan 2004).

On the other hand, business has had a rocky relationship with society throughout history; for example, business has been the frequent target of social critique and anti-business social movements for one reason or another. As the corporate revolution – which we discuss in Chapter 7 – matured in the United States, for example, the concentration of corporate holdings into larger and larger organizations led to significant resistance against monopolies like Standard Oil at the end of the nineteenth century. The political theorist Scott Bowman (1996) notes that this led to growing criticism of business corporations by scholars and thinkers of the time (e.g. Thorstein Veblen), as well as popular movements against corporate power. More recently, similar criticism has been directed at banks and other financial businesses after the 2007–8 global financial crisis (van Staveren 2015), especially because many of these banks are deemed 'too-big-to-fail' (Birch 2015a) – for more on resistance and alternatives to corporate power, see Chapter 21. Finally so-called "Big Tech" firms like Alphabet/Google and Amazon have been accused of creating an expanding sphere of private control over the informational and transactional infrastructure of our societies which allows them to harvest data about our lives and use it to strengthen their market power (see Chapters 12 and 23).

Key organization: The (public) corporation

In this book we use the term 'corporation' to mean a for-profit business that has a distinct ownership and governance structure. A corporation has shares – also called stocks – that are owned by investors (also called shareholders) who can trade those shares on a public stock market like the London Stock Exchange or New York Stock Exchange. These shares make up the equity investment in a corporation and provide investors with a claim on the value of the assets of the corporation and on the profits made by the corporation (called a dividend). The value of a share – or share price – is determined by the demand for it on the stock market; that is, the more demand there is for a share the higher the share price. Demand is usually driven by the expected future earning potential of a corporation, although there are numerous examples of share price bubbles throughout history. The total number of shares multiplied by individual share price equals the total market capitalization of a corporation, which is often used as a proxy for the total value of the corporation. Corporations are governed in particular ways as well, which we discuss in Chapter 8, and have particular legal and social responsibilities, which we cover in Chapter 9.

In light of these issues, it is helpful to remember what institutional economists like Herbert Simon (1991) and Geoffrey Hodgson (2005) point out; namely, a significant proportion of economic activity takes place *within* business organizations and *not within* the market. So, whatever our attitude to business – whether positive or negative – we are still left with an important question: If markets are the dominant institution in society, how come business plays such an important, if not central, role in our societies and economies, both today and historically? According to many mainstream or orthodox economists, the existence of business simply reflects a situation in which economic activity is more efficiently organized collectively than through market transactions (e.g. Coase 1937; Jensen and Meckling 1976). However, returning to Hodgson (2005: 551), he points out that in order to understand business and the relationship between business and society we have to look at business as a 'historically specific entity that has arisen in a historically specific legal framework' – we cannot simply treat it as an analytical given – see Chapter 7. Capitalism, for example, has always involved some form of business organization, although this has often varied between countries (see Chapter 13); in fact, business organization, including the corporate form, actually emerged prior to capitalism in medieval societies (Barkan 2013). Consequently, it is more apt to argue that business underpins capitalism and capitalist markets, rather than reflects the failure of capitalist markets to function properly.

Our approach to business in this book

Throughout this book, we take a critical approach to the study of business. Our aim is to problematize the idea that business and business practices are wholly positive forces in society, in our lives. This approach and aim is underpinned by a commitment to political economy as a way to understand 'economic' life, although we do not think it is helpful to distinguish and separate the *political* from the *economic*, or both of these from the *social* for that matter. Our approach is framed by the view that economic, political and social matters are thoroughly entangled with one another, meaning that to understand business and the relationship between business and society entails understanding the economic, political *and* social aspects of that relationship. Consequently, it means (1) analysing the functioning of markets as a price mechanism (i.e. economic), as well as (2) analysing the historical origins and evolution of business forms and other institutions such as money (i.e. political) and (3) analysing the cultural and ethical values of people in different societies towards money and business, as well as the family, friendship, love and so on.

Although our approach is framed by a concern with political economy, we do not come from one theoretical tradition or another; rather, we bring together a number of traditions in this book in order to present a range of alternatives to the mainstream, orthodox economic position that dominates much scholarly, political and social debate about business, the economy and society more generally. As such, we bring perspectives from critical political economy, institutional economics, human geography, sociology, political science, feminism, postcolonial studies and political ecology among others, all of which contributes to the pursuit of interdisciplinary social science. Despite our heterogeneity, though, our approach in this book is underpinned by several key analytical concepts. These can be summarized as follows:

- *Production and systems of value*: most social scientific traditions of political economy, outside of neoclassical economics at least, engage in one way or another with Karl Marx (1867 [1976]). While our perspective is not Marxist, it is strongly influenced by his critique of political economy and several key processes he highlighted. In this book, we take it as axiomatic that the economy is historically contingent, it is not 'natural' or 'inherent' – the market is not waiting for us to find it. Rather we organize it as we live it. Capitalism emerged as an economic system as the result of certain social processes, often violent and inhumane ones. In order to understand the relationship between business and society, then, we have to analyse how (economic) value is produced, how it is distributed, and how this production and distribution are legitimated as part of historically and geographically contingent *systems of value*. As such, this necessarily entails challenging dominant, Western perspectives on the global development of capitalism and modernity (Amin 1977, 2013; Rodney 1982).
- *Politics, ethics and social values*: as we noted, the economy is not a distinct thing separate from the rest of our lives. All of our lives are bound up with the configuration of the economy, especially in the form of business, but also more broadly in seemingly non-economic activities. As many writers in the eighteenth-century Scottish Enlightenment noted, including Adam Smith (1759) in *The Theory of Moral Sentiments*, commerce and business are not neutral objects of enquiry; the same contention applies today as much as it did then. First, over the last half century a number of thinkers in the Global North have posited a transformation from industrial capitalism to a *knowledge-based* or *cognitive capitalism* (e.g. Boutang 2011). While these ideas have various bases in reality, they also represent visions of future society to which we can aspire. In this sense, the political, ethical and social values inherent in such visions function to legitimate certain policies and practices. Second, housework, childcare and other caring activities are ignored in many political-economic analyses because they are unwaged and, therefore, seen as uneconomic (Bezanson and Luxton 2006). Obviously, this does a massive disservice to the role women have (often) had in society. What these examples illustrate is that economies do not exist *outside* of human actions and decisions; instead, it is important to remember that we are the ones who *make* our economies and, hence, this is why they are so diverse (Roelvink et al. 2015).

- *Institutions and organizations*: perhaps the greatest conceptual influence on our book has come from the ideas of various institutional theorists, especially the work of Karl Polanyi (1944 [2001]). In particular, Polanyi's discussion of land, labour and money as *fictitious commodities* helps to ground our analyses of other social institutions (e.g. money, law, corporate governance) as constituted by geographically specific political, social and economic action and decisions – again, not natural givens. Aside from Polanyi, our perspective is also grounded in the work of thinkers on business organization; these include (old) institutional economists like Thorstein Veblen and more recent ones like Geoffrey Hodgson (2005), as well economic sociologists and others who work on organizational theory (e.g. Fligstein 1990; Simon 1991; Roy 1997). An important part of this is acknowledging and analysing the importance of non-conventional economic systems and organizations, including the *social economy* (Amin et al. 2002) and *informal economy* (Hann and Hart 2011).

- *Constitutive discourse*: a final conceptual angle is the notion that knowledge and knowledge claims (or *discourse*) are constitutive of the world, although this position is tempered by the need to relate discourse to the socio-material system. Drawing on work in postmodernism, anthropology, cultural political economy, and science and technology studies (e.g. Gibson-Graham 1996; Callon 1998; Muniesa 2014), we stress the need to take ideas seriously, especially as they relate to claims about the economy. Neoclassical economics, for example, is powerful not because it *represents* the world accurately, but because it is *performed* by many powerful social actors.

As the discussion of these key concepts illustrates, how we analyse and represent the economy matters in an everyday context. A final example might help demonstrate what we mean here. As we mentioned previously, the idea that people are selfish is often treated as a 'common sense' assumption. However, the notion of individual ownership of private property as we currently understand it – which represents the pursuit of personal self-interest – is not inherent to our lives. Private property is not a natural desire born of selfishness, nor is it a natural right; rather, it is a cause and effect of the specific political-economic system in which we live, capitalism. If we take a critical look at ownership and property rights – which we do in Chapter 21 – we can identify (a) what types and forms dominate, (b) their relation to broader socio-political contexts, and (c) the underpinning ethical and moral discourses that legitimate their current structure – issues we address in Chapter 14. On the last point, for example, a number of radical thinkers, especially anarchists and socialists (see Chapter 6), have argued that private property is by definition the same thing as theft; or, more succinctly, 'property is theft'. They make this claim based on the argument that any form of individual, private ownership of something – for example, land, commodities, knowledge and so on – necessarily leads to the exclusion of others from its common use, thereby inhibiting any further adaptation or changes except by the owners. Meanwhile, owners benefit from the collective investment in the property made over many generations. It is such questions that motivate our arguments in the rest of the book.

Key concept: 'Property is theft'

There is a famous aphorism coined by Pierre-Joseph Proudhon, an anarchist from the early nineteenth century, in which he stated that 'property is theft'. What he meant by this was that all things in all societies are, inherently, the products of that whole society, all of its peoples, throughout its history, in its socio-economic context and so on, and *not* the products of individual people working alone. Consequently, any claims to private property by an individual are claims to expropriate (i.e. take) the something that is the product of everyone's work, now and in the past. In that sense, private property is a theft.

Source: Frase (2013)

Our approach to society in this book

So far, we've looked at ways in which business and society might interrelate. But before we continue the rest of this journey throughout the book we'll need to define and explore what 'society' means. It's a word that we use often – it makes sense to us intuitively – but rarely do we really have a clear definition of just what society is. In this final section we will explore the main features of three different types of society: traditional, modern, and postmodern. Keep in mind that we're not going to be looking at any specific society *per se*, but rather at *ideal types* – or models – which serve to illustrate characteristics and tendencies, showing us in general terms what defines these different forms of social organization.

Traditional Society. From the fifth century to the eighteenth century, Europe was organized according to the features of what is termed a traditional society. This description does not apply to this period in Europe alone, however. Imperial China (2nd century BCE–early 20th century CE), Mayan civilization (2000 BCE–16th century CE), Ancient Rome (8th century BCE–5th century CE), among many other civilizations, were traditional societies as well.

If we start with a description of traditional society in Europe, we find a predominantly rural and agricultural society organized around the supreme authority of a monarch. This historical period is called feudalism (see Chapter 2), a social structure in which the political, religious and juridical systems were controlled by a crown (i.e. monarch), who is understood to be the incarnation of God's will. We can imagine the structure of feudal society as a pyramid with the monarchy on top, the clergy making up the next level, the nobility under them, knights or soldiers under that, and the vast majority of the population as serfs or peasants on the bottom. Social mobility in traditional society was not possible, one stayed in their class based on birthright, and those on the bottom had little control over their activities, being indebted to the rulers – the feudal lords and kings.

But what did European society of the Middle Ages have in common with Imperial China, Mayan civilization, and Ancient Rome? In other words, what are the sociological characteristics of a traditional society apart from the pyramidal class positions that we saw earlier? Here we'll describe three main features of traditional societies.

1) Family as determinant of social position. Each individual in a traditional society is born into their position. Families have different ranks and bloodlines can mark distinctions in occupation and status. Most interactions are contained within family and the surrounding community, and group well-being is generally understood to be more important than that of any person.

2) Traditionalism and conservativism to maintain status quo. Traditional societies tend to be organized around religious beliefs and generational wisdom. Influences that challenge the legitimacy of the social order or worldview are threats to the whole and are not typically tolerated.

3) Limited division of labour in an embedded economy. Traditional societies tend to have populations that are capable of subsistence – that means that almost everybody knows how to maintain their way of life through cooking, making clothes, crafting instruments and tools, engaging in agriculture, among other things, though generally these activities are divided along gendered lines. This means that there is a strong reliance upon the natural environment, and factors like weather and other natural events have a big impact on quality of life.

Modern Society. The Age of Enlightenment in seventeenth- and eighteenth-century Europe is closely related to the transition from feudalism to modernity. The philosophical and intellectual movement labelled the Enlightenment encompasses ideals centred on reason, freedom, and progress, among other cardinal principles of modernity. We should note that many ideas that are now considered 'modern' were also being developed in other parts of the world, some long before these arose in Europe (see Chapter 6). The philosophical story of Hayy ibn Yaksan – written by Islamic philosopher Ibn Tufayl in the twelfth century, and considered to be the first philosophical novel – even influenced important figures in the European Enlightenment such as philosopher and advocate of the scientific method Francis Bacon (Tufayl et al. [2009]). In the European tradition, however, a key moment came with the publication of the *Encyclopedia* – a volume edited by philosophers Denis Diderot and Jean le Rond d'Alembert. Originally published in 1751, this was the first encyclopedia of its kind, and is a fitting symbol of the movement, as it intended to achieve the most advanced knowledge in a variety of fields in human history without the interference of the Church, which had previously held a monopoly over knowledge and learning. According to sociologist Anthony Giddens, the novelty of modernity has no precedent in any other period history in terms of the pace and scope of change and the unprecedented social institutions developed (e.g., the nation-state): "The modes of life brought into being by modernity have swept us away from all traditional types of social order, in quite unprecedented fashion" (1990: 4).

We should delineate the three main features of a modern society, which can be generally understood to begin in seventeenth-century Europe and continue until the 1950s throughout Europe, and later North America and other parts of the world as well.

1) *State as social organization.* Modern society is organized around the power of the state, instead of around the power of a monarch or religious leader. In this social configuration there is room for the coexistence of multiple ideologies such as liberalism, socialism, communism, and fascism. Religion becomes a private matter rather than the organizing principle of the social whole.

2) *Urbanization and individualism.* Modern societies tend to be predominantly urban and industrialized, and depend upon the nuclear family and institutions of socialization such as schools. The collective spirit of traditional societies is replaced with the spirit of individualism, where each person can make life choices according to their own sets of values and priorities.

3) *Capitalism as economic organization.* Modern society is organized through the exchange of goods by means of money. Capitalism replaces feudalism, and owners of the means of production (i.e., factories) hire workers who sell their labour for a wage (see Chapter 6). As a result we see a greater division of labour, greater social interdependence, the development of technologies which drastically change ways of living and producing, and telecommunication and transport that accelerate the connection between different populations and parts of the world.

It's important to note that science plays a major role in a modern society, and the discoveries that it renders possible are generally welcomed because of their logical and experimental demonstration as well as the benefits that they bring. Science also aims to understand social aspects of the human condition in areas that eventually became independent disciplines such as sociology, economics, political science, linguistics, psychology, anthropology, and so on. The social sciences emerged from this broad context as a way to understand the past, the world, and the new social order. Sociology in particular emerged in the late nineteenth century as a way to understand the transition from feudalism to modernity in Europe. Throughout this book we will ask ourselves many of the same questions that sociologists are asking themselves: How do societies change? What are the roles of industrialization, the division of labour, the development of the nation-state, bureaucracy, individualism, capitalism, and urbanization in these processes of change? How do they affect business, economic relations and our very outlook on the world? We will address these foundational ideas in the early sections of this book, using the work of sociological thinkers such as Max Weber (Chapter 2), Karl Marx (Chapters 2 and 6), and Karl Polanyi (Chapter 2) as some of our guides.

Postmodern Society. You may have heard people talk about postmodern society or even just call a certain TV series or piece of art 'postmodern'. Does this mean that postmodern society is something entirely new that exists outside of the modern? In fact, many of the economic, political, and social features that we find in a postmodern society are quite similar to those of modern society. The bureaucratic state still exists, along with representative democracy, a division of labour, capitalism, and a predominantly urban way of living. However, we know that we live in a different world than the one that prevailed in Europe or North America in the 1920s. So: what's changed?

The two world wars (1914–18 and 1939–45) left profound wounds in our ability to believe in the promises of modernity, such as progress and improve-ment for all. The invent of aerial and carpet bombing, the nuclear weapons used during the Second World War, the horrors of the Holocaust which saw two-thirds of Europe's Jewish population—over 6 million people – murdered in concentration camps and by Nazi forces, and the overall destruction and pain caused by war, led many to question the reasonableness of technologies and their utility in achieving progress. Philosophers Max Horkheimer and Theodor Adorno even argued that the pinnacle of the Enlightenment was the total domination by humans over nature, a mentality which could have terrible consequences such as the Holocaust and other forms of fascism and social oppression (1991). More broadly, the success, or even existence, of modern ideals such as progress, justice, and reason are questioned in postmodernity. While works by French philosophers such as Jean Francois Lyotard (1979), Jacques Derrida (1998), Julia Kristeva (1984), and Luce Irigaray (1992) may have been the first to begin to name and articulate the condition of postmodernity in our society, it's also reflected in popular ways, such as in fear of or apathy towards the future, or disillusionment with the ruling elite and the democratic institutions they tend to control. The general feeling of someone who has a postmodern attitude is a feeling of the futility of the democratic vote, and the belief that technologies and science will not fundamentally increase our well-being and reduce inequalities. The road from the past to the future is no longer a straight line of progress, but rather a constellation of narratives. Above all, it is difficult for individuals to believe they can make any significant systematic change in the social order. Rather, people try to control what they can, like individual success, working out, psychological support, fruitful social interactions, and so on.

Finally, while the economy has long been organized at a global level (see Chapter 3), in the postmodern configuration this implies that the production and the distribution of commodities has become increasingly complex, involving massive and intricate global supply chains (see Chapter 13). The state is now integrated in a global network and in institutions of global governance (see Chapter 14), which does not prevent capitalism from facing more profound and expanded crises (see Chapter 17). Neoliberalism, the ideology behind the transformation of the state in 1970s, questioned, reformed, and privatized the social welfare associated with the preceding period of modernity (see Chapters 9 and 21). Within the domestic economy, where there is decrease in industrial production there tends to be an emergence and growing importance of the third sector of the economy – the service sector – both in terms of wealth created and the proportion of employment. The economy tends to rely increasingly on information, knowledge, and culture as a main form of capital, as opposed to the automotive industry, the extraction and transformation of raw materials, and heavy industries, though of course these heavy industries persist, often to our environmental peril (see Chapter 16). Despite increasing automotive and technological advances, work conditions tend to be more precarious, with an important part of the active population not benefiting from a permanent job. Lastly, in contrast to modern societies, postmodern ones are characterized by information and communication technologies that include platforms driven by digital data and digital surveillance (see Chapter 23).

Conclusion

In this chapter we've introduced several of the frameworks that will be used in this book. Not only will we be considering business from a social perspective, but we'll also consider the social from the perspective of business. We've analysed the importance of markets and the rise of neoliberalism, articulated our approach to business, and surveyed different types of societies. Each of these themes will play out in different ways in each of the chapters, all showing how crucial it is to understand the complex relationships between business and society.

Bibliography

Aldridge, A. (2005) *The Market*, Cambridge, Polity Press.

Amin, A., Cameron, A. and Hudson, R. (2002) *Placing the Social Economy*, London, Routledge.

Amin, S. (1977) *Imperialism and Unequal Development*, New York, Monthly Review Press.

Amin, S. (2013) *The Implosion of Capitalism*, New York, Monthly Review Press.

Bakan, J. (2004) *The Corporation*, London, Random House.

Bakan, J. (2020) *The New Corporation: How Good Corporations are Bad for Democracy*, London, Random House.

Barkan, J. (2013) *Corporate Sovereignty*, Minneapolis, University of Minnesota Press.

Bezanson, K. and Luxton, M. (2006) *Social Reproduction: Feminist Political Economy Challenges Neo-Liberalism*, Montreal, McGill-Queen's University Press.

Birch, K. (2007) 'The Totalitarian Corporation?' *Totalitarian Movements and Political Religions*, Vol. 8, pp. 153–61.

Birch, K. (2015a) *We Have Never Been Neoliberal: A Manifesto for a Doomed Youth*, Winchester, Zero Books.

Birch, K. (2015b) 'Neoliberalism: The Whys and Wherefores … and Future Directions', *Sociology Compass*, Vol. 9, pp. 571–84.

Birch, K. and Whittam, G. (2012) 'Social Entrepreneurship', in D. Deakins and M. Freel (eds), *Entrepreneurship and Small Firms* (6th Edition), London, McGraw Hill, pp. 105–23.

Boutang, J.-M. (2011) *Cognitive Capitalism*, Cambridge, Polity Press.

Bowman, S. (1996) *The Modern Corporation and American Political Thought*, College Park, Pennsylvania State University Press.

Callon, M. (ed.) (1998) *The Laws on the Markets*, Oxford, Blackwell Publishers.

Coase, R. (1937) 'The Nature of the Firm', *Economica*, Vol. 4, pp. 386–405.

Crouch, C. (2011) *The Strange Non-death of Neoliberalism*, Cambridge, Polity Press.

Deakins, D. and Freel, M. (2012) *Entrepreneurship and Small Firms* (6th Edition), London, McGraw Hill.

Derrida, J. (1998) *Of Grammatology*, Baltimore, Johns Hopkins University Press.

Diderot, D. and d'Alembert, J.L.R. (1751–1777) *The Encyclopedia*, 21 volumes, https://quod.lib.umich.edu/d/did/ (accessed August 2022).

Durkheim, É. (1893 [2014]) *The Division of Labor in Society*, Translated by S. Lukes, New York, Free Press.

Ewen, S. (1976) *Captains of Consciousness*, New York, Basic Books.

Fligstein, N. (1990) *The Transformation of Corporate Control*, Cambridge MA, Harvard University Press.

Frase, P. (2013) 'Property and Theft', *Jacobin*, September, www.jacobinmag.com/2013/09/property-and-theft/ (accessed May 2015).

Fraser, N. (2017) 'Crisis of Care? On the Social-Reproductive Contradictions of Contemporary Capitalism', in T. Bhattacharya (ed.), *Social Reproduction Theory: Remapping Class, Recentering Oppression*, London, Pluto, pp. 21–36.

Friedman, M. (1962) *Capitalism and Freedom*, Chicago, University of Chicago Press.

Gibson-Graham, J.K. (1996) *The End of Capitalism (As We Knew It): A Feminist Critique of Political Economy*, Oxford, Blackwell Publishers.

Giddens, A. (1990) *The Consequences of Modernity*, Cambridge, Polity Press.

Hann, C. and Hart, K. (eds) (2011) *Markets and Society: The Great Transformation Today*, Cambridge, Cambridge University Press.

Harvey, D. (2005) *A Brief History of Neoliberalism*, Oxford, Oxford University Press.

Heilbroner, R. and Milberg, W. (2002) *The Making of Economic Society* (11th Edition), New York, Prentice Hall.

Hodgson, G. (2005) 'Knowledge at Work: Some Neoliberal Anachronisms', *Review of Social Economy*, Vol. 63, pp. 547–65.

Horkheimer, M. and Adorno, T. (1991) *Dialectic of Enlightenment*, New York, Continuum.

Ibn Tufayl, M. ibn 'Abd al-M. and Goodman, L.E. (2009) *Ibn Tufayl's Hayy Ibn Yaqzan: A Philosophical Tale*, Chicago, University of Chicago Press.

Irigaray, L. (1992) *Speculum of the Other Woman*, Ithaca, Cornell University Press.

Jackson, T. (2009) *Prosperity without Growth*, London, Earthscan.

Jensen, M. and Meckling, W. (1976) 'Theory of the Firm: Managerial Behavior, Agency Costs and Ownership Structure', *Journal of Financial Economics*, Vol. 3, pp. 305–60.

Kristeva, J. (1984) *Revolution in Poetic Language*, New York, Columbia University Press.

Lyotard, J.-F. (1979 [1984]) *The Postmodern Condition: A Report on Knowledge*, Manchester, Manchester University Press.

Marx, K. (1867 [1976]) *Capital: Volume 1*, London, Penguin.

Marx, K. and Engels, F. (1848 [1985]) *The Communist Manifesto*, London, Penguin Books.

McChesney, R. (2000) *Rich Media, Poor Democracy*, New York, The New Press.

Mirowski, P. (2013) *Never Let a Serious Crisis Go to Waste*, London, Verso.

Muniesa, F. (2014) *The Provoked Economy*, London, Routledge.

Nace, T. (2003) *Gangs of America*, San Francisco, Berrett-Koehler.

Nolan, P. and Lenski, G.E.. (2009) *Human Societies: An Introduction to Macrosociology* (11th Edition), Boulder, Paradigm.

Polanyi, K. (1944 [2001]) *The Great Transformation*, Boston, Beacon Press.

Polanyi, K. (1957) 'Chapter XIII: The Economy as Instituted Process', in K. Polanyi, C.M. Arensberg and H.W. Pearson (eds), *Trade and Market in the Early Empires: Economies in History and Theory*, Glencoe, Free Press and Falcon's Wing Press, pp. 243–70.

Rodney, W. (1982) *How Europe Underdeveloped Africa*, Washington, DC, Howard University Press.

Roelvink, G., St. Martin, K. and Gibson-Graham, J.-K. (eds) (2015) *Making Other Worlds Possible*, Minneapolis, University of Minnesota Press.

Rossides, D.W. (1990) *Comparative Societies: Social Types and Their Interrelations*, Englewood Cliffs, Prentice-Hall.

Roy, W. (1997) *Socializing Capital*, Princeton, Princeton University Press.

Samarasekera, U. (2022) 'UK–India Trade Deal Could "Jeopardise" Generic Medicines', *The Lancet*, Vol. 400, No. 10364, pp. 1667–9.

Sayer, A. (2015) *Why We Can't Afford the Rich*, Bristol, Policy Press.

Simmel, G. (1896 [1991]) 'Money in Modern Culture', *Theory, Culture & Society*, Vol. 8, No. 3, pp. 17–31.

Simmel, G. (1900 [1978]) *The Philosophy of Money*, London, Boston, Routledge & Kegan Paul.

Simon, H. (1991) 'Organizations and Markets', *Journal of Economic Perspectives*, Vol. 5, pp. 25–44.

Smith, A. (1759 [1976]) *The Theory of Moral Sentiments*, Oxford, Oxford University Press.

Turner, J.H. (2010) *Theoretical Principles of Sociology, Volume 1: Macrodynamics*, New York, Springer.

Van Staveren, I. (2015) *Economics After the Crisis*, London, Routledge.

Weber, M. (1920 [1949]) *The Theory of Social and Economic Organization*, Translated by T. Parsons and A. Morell Henderson, Glencoe, Free Press.

Weber, M. (2019) *Economy and Society*, Translated by K. Tribe, Cambridge, MA, Harvard University Press.

2 | The emergence of capitalism in Western Europe

Mark Peacock

Introduction

Today our lives are dominated by capitalism as the economic organizing system for our societies and the global economy. However, capitalism has not always existed, which raises the questions of how, where, and why capitalism emerged.

There are many approaches to explaining the development of capitalism. We will start with a brief presentation of mainstream approaches derived from Adam Smith's work and then focus on two opposing views that draw their inspiration from Karl Marx and Max Weber respectively. Mainstream approaches see the evolution of capitalism as a 'natural' process, whereby the apparently natural desire of human beings for wealth and money is allowed to flourish freely, something which results in the creation of capitalist markets as the main mechanism of economic exchange (see Wood 2002 for a critical analysis of these mainstream claims).

In the eighteenth century, Adam Smith (1776 [1976]: I.ii.1) wrote of a 'propensity in human nature . . . to truck, barter, and exchange one thing for another', by which he meant that, if left unhindered, humans would instinctively enter into market exchanges with one another. This has led some historians, like Henri Pirenne (1956) and Fernand Braudel (1979 [2002]), to look for the origins of capitalism in urban centres of trade in medieval Europe, in cities such as Florence, Venice and Milan. Mainstream approaches account for the absence of capitalism through the existence of restrictions or restraints on commerce imposed by rulers. Without these restrictions, according to mainstream approaches, capitalism would have developed earlier, but restrictions on commerce prevented its emergence.

Key thinker: Adam Smith

Adam Smith (1723–90) was professor of moral philosophy at the University of Glasgow. His most famous work, *The Wealth of Nations* (1776), is often used as a defence of capitalism which was emerging in Britain in the eighteenth century. The book includes the key notion that humans are, by nature, selfish, an idea which has had a lasting impact on economics as a discipline (see Chapter 5 of this volume). In his *The Theory of Moral*

Mainstream approaches leave important questions unanswered which are addressed by alternative accounts of the development of capitalism. This chapter presents two such alternative accounts: one is a Marxist perspective, the other a Weberian one. They are non-mainstream because neither sees anything natural, let alone, inevitable, about the development of capitalism. Instead, both theories see capitalism unfolding only after major social upheavals.

Key discussion questions

- What is feudalism?
- What were the enclosures?
- In capitalist society, workers are propertyless. What does this mean and what are the implications for workers' freedom?
- What significance does Protestant religious doctrine have in Max Weber's accounts of the origins of modern capitalism?
- What does Weber mean by economic traditionalism?
- Name a key difference in Marx's and Weber's approaches to explain historical change.

Marxist approaches

Marxist perspectives draw on the work of the nineteenth-century thinker Karl Marx. They are characterized by the contention that *social classes* are the key agents of historical change because different social classes have conflicting or antagonistic interests. The conflict between classes gives rise to *class struggle* as a driving force in historical change. To understand the emergence of capitalism from a Marxist perspective, we must first understand *feudalism* in England, the country in which capitalism first developed. It's important to note that feudalism varied greatly at different times and places in Europe. What follows is a generalized account of feudalism in England which does not necessarily apply to other parts of Europe.

Key thinker: Karl Marx

Karl Marx (1818–83) was a German activist and one of the most influential thinkers of the modern world. He spent much of his life in British exile, having been expelled from his native Germany, and his ideas were fundamental to the formation of the international communist movement. His three-volume work *Das Kapital* provides a monumental diagnosis of the capitalist mode of production.

Definition: Feudalism

Feudalism was a political-economic system which dominated Europe during the medieval period. In a feudal society, peasants made up the largest part of the population and they were obliged to work on the land of their lords. Some features of feudalism still exist, for example monarchies, aristocracies and laws of land ownership.

In feudal society, the majority of the population were peasants who lived on a lord's manor. The lord possessed the title to land and peasants were required to work for the lord. The land cultivated for the lord's use was called the *demesne* which could be one continuous tract of land or be divided into fields (strips). Peasants lived in cottages located in a hamlet or village located on the demesne. They, too, had access to land, in the form of strips – fewer in number and perhaps of lesser quality than the lord's – which they cultivated for their subsistence needs. Most peasants were unfree (*villeins* or *serfs*); their serf status came with various obligations to the lord which we associate with *serfdom*. Serfdom defines the relationship between the two central classes in feudal society: landlords and peasants.

Serfs had to work on the lord's land for a certain number of days per week, referred to as *corvée labour* (Postan 1971: 311–16). This was one of the 'complex of payments' – taxes, tithes, fines, being others – that Marxists refer to as feudal rent (Postan 1971: 552–3). This form of surplus appropriation depended on the presence of extra-economic force. The number of days varied from manor to manor and was fixed by custom. These labour services were sometimes commuted into money payments, but whichever form they took, these obligations were a source of enrichment for the lord. Lords appropriated wealth from serfs, with as much as half the value of a peasant family's annual harvest going to the lord (Postan 1971: 603). Although they were subject to the lord's impositions, peasants did enjoy *customary rights*, for example, they could use common land to graze their animals and they had the right to glean fields after a harvest, collecting any leftover crops that would otherwise rot on the land (Neeson 1993).

Not all peasants were serfs. Some were *free*: like serfs, free peasants possessed land but were not subject to the levies of the lord. Whether free or serfs, peasants who did not own sufficient land to subsist on their own produce worked as wage labourers either on the lord's demesne or for wealthier peasants, who themselves had holdings of land. Perhaps half of the peasants had to supplement their own cultivation through wage labour, especially when feudal obligations were commuted from labour services to money payments, for monetary payments to lords presupposed that peasants acquired money, either through selling their agricultural produce or their labour time in exchange for cash (Postan 1971).

The contentious relationship between lords and peasants gave rise to class conflict about the appropriation of the peasants' product – who got how much. Those peasants who possessed enough land could attain a high degree of *self-sufficiency*; they were neither dependent on their lord for survival nor did they have to work for wages because they produced most of the goods (mainly food) that they consumed. Lords were parasitic; their exactions contributed nothing to agricultural output. Lords' interventions in peasants' lives were thinly disguised attempts to appropriate as much as they could from peasants. Some peasants fled from one lord to seek tenancy with another, although such attempts were not technically legal because they were not legally free to relocate. Unsurprisingly, medieval history is punctuated by episodes of peasant resistance or full-scale 'revolt' against landlords, for example the Peasants' Revolt of 1381.

Now that we have an idea of feudal society, let's trace some English history from the fourteenth to the eighteenth centuries. After the Black Death of 1348, which, in England, claimed one-third to a half of the population, lords acquired vacant lands. Serfs could not bequeath land to their heirs without the lord's permission, so, upon the death of a serf, the lord could claim the land. Lords rented their newly acquired lands to those able to pay what the market would bear; and as population increased, demand for land and rents rose. Renting land became a lucrative option for lords who rented larger parcels of land to each tenant, thus increasing the size of farms (Brenner 1976, 1985). The development of a market for land meant that peasant tenants had to compete for land at the market rate. This led to measures which raised the productivity of farming; for those tenant farmers who were the most productive could afford to pay the highest rents (Brenner 1985: 301). As agricultural efficiency rose, the need for agricultural labourers declined. These developments provided the context of a process known as *enclosure*, to which we now turn (see Marx 1867: Chapters 26–8).

Enclosure involved the privatization of manorial land. It refers to the physical and legal *enclosing* of land by landlords, who erected fences around land previously accessible to peasants, as well as the extinction of common and customary use rights (Wood 2002). This spelled the beginning of the end of the so-called 'open field system' of agriculture, as peasants were denied access to their farming strips and to common land. Peasants' means of survival was thus under threat as their customary rights were removed. Enclosure was an attempt to dispossess peasants of land, and it did not go uncontested (see Chapter 21). But by the end of the seventeenth century, England's lords had laid claim to three-quarters of the country's agricultural land (Brenner 1976).

The lords' aim in enclosing land was often to convert it to pasture, usually sheep farming. Supporters of enclosure argued that enclosure would end the independence peasants enjoyed by virtue of possessing land (Neeson 1993: 34). Without access to land, peasants became less self-sufficient and increasingly reliant on wage labour, which was needed for commercial farming. Enclosure is therefore associated with the creation of a class of people whose survival depends on their ability to find work and the emergence of the tenant or 'capitalist' farmer who paid a market rent, as opposed to customary rent, to landlords (Wood 2002). But the transition from a country of peasants, who were relatively independent of the need to work for a wage, to a country of workers, who had no option but to seek wage labour if they were to survive, was not smooth. The immediate effect of enclosure was the creation of a mass of people who possessed no land. These people were faced with a choice between working for a wage or dying. Two opportunities for earning wages presented themselves (1) labouring on farms in the countryside or (2) working in craft or manufacturing in urban centres. But dispossessed peasants were not free to choose between these options. In England, legislation restricted peasants' freedom and hindered the creation of a labour market.

Before we review this legislation, note that enclosure engendered a law and order problem. First, peasants resisted enclosure, for many saw their survival under attack. Peasant 'enclosure riots' became common from the sixteenth century, despite being outlawed (Manning 1988). Peasants who were unsuccessful in stopping the enclosure of land and who did not find work as farm labourers were left with the option of finding work in towns and cities. This caused a second threat to law and order, to which we now turn.

Unable to find sufficient work, migrants who left the countryside for towns resorted to begging or thievery. Such people were known as 'masterless men' because they were without employment and thus without oversight by a lord or master who might keep them in order. Legislators reacted to the hoard of masterless men with 'vagrancy laws' (a 'vagrant' being a person without dwelling or job). These laws varied 'from the savage to the merely repressive' (Manning 1988: 159): whipping, branding, mutilation and hanging were among the punishments for vagrants (Marx 1867: chapter 28). Vagrancy made legislators aware of a more encompassing problem: the poor. The problem of the poor concerned not only their swelling numbers but also the question of what to do with them. *Poor Laws* were conceived to address this problem. A poor person ('pauper') was assigned to the parish in which he or she was born and would become part of the 'sedentary poor' and thus a recipient of poor relief financed by local taxes. Vagrants received no relief. If they did not work or could find none, they were considered criminals, but being 'able bodied', they were expected to work (Beier 1985: 9). Indeed, they could be forced to work under Elizabethan legislation known as the *Statute of Artificers* of 1563.

The *Statute of Artificers* regulated the employment of labour. Under the Statute, the unemployed could be compelled to work in certain trades or in farming at wages set by local magistrates. It was an offence under the *Statute of Artificers* to quit one's job and leave the place in which one lived without permission of the local authorities (Beier 2008; Tawney 1914). The Statute thus hindered the development of a national labour market in England because it denied three freedoms:

- freedom to decide where to work;
- freedom to quit one's job;
- freedom of employers and employees to negotiate wages.

This was an era of wage labour without a labour market (Beier 2008), and the absence of these three freedoms slowed the development of capitalism. It was not until the 1830s that these restrictions to the formation of a labour market were removed (Polanyi 1944 [2001]).

The foregoing account of the rise of capitalism is a Marxist account because it focuses on social classes and their struggles as factors driving historical change. Note that the class which Marx associates most strongly with capitalism – the capitalist class or 'bourgeoisie' – was not the driving force in the creation of capitalism. Though there existed a merchant or commercial class, particularly in English urban centres like London, the transition to capitalism was initiated in the countryside and its main driver was the class of landlords. Some of these lords became capitalist farmers in the process, just as some peasants became tenants of those lords and ran their increasingly large plots of land as commercial farms. It was through the clash of lords' and peasants' interests that capitalism and the classes of capitalists and workers came into existence. Table 2.1 summarizes the key features of feudalism and capitalism according to Marxist perspectives.

TABLE 2.1 Comparison of Feudalism and Capitalism

	Feudalism	Capitalism
"Ruling" class	Landlords	Capitalists
Subordinate class	Peasants	Workers
Status of subordinate class	Unfree (serfs)	Free and (legally) equal
Relationship of subordinate class to means of production	Customary, direct access to and possession of land	Propertyless (no ownership or possession of means of production)

The class divide in feudal society is between peasants and lords. In a capitalist society, it's between capitalists (those who own the means of production) and workers. In order to better understand the class dynamic involved, it's helpful to contrast the two subordinate classes – serfs in feudalism and workers in capitalism. Feudal serfs were unfree; they were not allowed simply to throw off their obligations to lords; insubordination from peasants could be answered by lords using military or legal power. On the other hand, peasants had direct access to the means of production – they could use land through which they could provide themselves with the means of subsistence; in theory, they could survive independently of lords. For workers in capitalist society, it's the other way around. Workers are free: they may choose which job to pursue and may quit their job if they wish. Unlike feudal serfs who, by their very status as serfs had obligations towards the ruling class of lords, workers have no obligations to the ruling class of capitalists by virtue of being a worker. Therein lies workers' freedom. The only way workers become obliged to the capitalist is by accepting a job – the capitalist cannot compel the worker to work without the worker's consent. On the other hand, workers in capitalist society are propertyless; they have no access to the means of production with which to produce the means of subsistence. Only capitalists own these, and workers are dependent on them for a wage. Unlike feudal serfs who possessed land, workers in capitalist society cannot produce anything unless they are given access to the means of production by a capitalist.

This sheds a different light onto workers' freedom. In the previous paragraph, it appeared that workers were advantaged *vis-à-vis* feudal serfs because they are free. Only if they want to work, do workers have to work; they are free to choose whether or not to work and free to choose their occupation. Feudal serfs had no such freedom to choose whether to work for a lord. But for workers in capitalist society, the choice between working and not working is really a choice between earning the means to survive and starving, for if a worker does not work, she cannot produce anything from which to live by virtue of being propertyless. For this reason, the capitalist does not have to force or coerce workers into accepting a job; workers who do not work for a capitalist will simply die. It's therefore from *economic necessity* that workers sell themselves on the labour market; and it's their lack of ownership of the means of production which compels them to work for a capitalist.

Marx (1867: 874) expressed this point by noting that workers in capitalist societies are 'free' in a 'double sense': (1) workers in capitalist society are free to seek whatever work they wish and they owe nobody anything by virtue of their status; only by entering a work contract of their own free will can workers oblige themselves to work for a capitalist, and workers are even free not to work if they choose not to do so; (2) workers are also free in a second sense, free, that is, from ownership of 'any means of production of their own'; workers, that is, are 'unencumbered' by means of production; they own nothing except themselves. This 'unencumberedness' makes the freedom in the first sense hollow: workers are formally free in the sense that nobody can compel them to work. But in reality, the choice whether or not to work is a choice between staying alive and dying – not much of a choice at all.

Aligned with the Marxist thesis, Karl Polanyi (see Chapter 1) emphasized the unprecedented process of commodification intertwined with capitalism's development. *Commodification* is a process by which a person, an activity, a social relation, a good, a service, or anything else is transformed into a commodity, that is, offered as a product for sale on the market. Polanyi was particularly interested in three commodities: labour, land, and money. Each of these bears a specific type of price (wages, rent and interest), and all three are qualified as 'fictitious'. He called them fictitious because while they are necessary for production, they exist independently of the commodity form and were not created simply to be sold on the market: "labor and land are no other than the human beings themselves of which every society consists, and the natural surroundings in which it exists" (Polanyi 1944 [2001]: 75). Finally, he argued that when a society has created markets in which these fictitious commodities circulate, it becomes a society that does not simply contain market mechanisms but is a 'market society' where social organization is fundamentally determined by the structure and dynamics of the market itself.

The history of the transition from feudalism to capitalism in England which we have traced in this chapter is the history of the expropriation of the 'immediate producers' (Marx 1867: 875). The immediate producers began this transition as peasants who lived off the land and had access to the means of production. They ended it as propertyless workers with one survival option – wage labour. This history, Marx writes, 'is written in the annals of mankind in letters of blood and fire'. This was not a history many peasants would have chosen had they known what lay at the end of it, yet it's a history that has determined the fate of most of the world's population who became propertyless workers.

Key Concepts: Commodification and Fictitious Commodities

A commodity is often defined as an item produced with the intention of selling it on the market. If one made a table for personal use, for example, it would not be a commodity. But if one makes it in order to sell, it is a commodity. Capitalism is characterized by com-modification, that is, a process through which ever more of the things we consume are commodities. Have you ever produced your own food, clothing, wrist watches or USB sticks? Probably not, we acquire these things from other people who produce them for sale; they are all commodities. People's income in a capitalist society derives from selling commodities. For most of us, this means selling our labour time.

In order to explain how something like one's own time might be considered a commodity, political economist Karl Polanyi (1944 [2001]) produced a theory of *fictitious commodities*. There are three fictitious commodities: (1) labour time; (2) land and (3) money. What makes these commodities 'fictitious'? Let's illustrate with the example of labour. Human beings' capacity to labour is part of what it is to be human, it "goes with life itself" (Polanyi 2005 [1957], 75). But neither people nor their labouring activity come ready-made as commodities. To commodify labour, a deep social transformation is required, whereby people become separated ("free") from the means of production (see Chapter 1) and must therefore sell their labour time in order to survive.

Land is the natural environment; it existed long before humans trod the Earth. Prior to capitalism, there was no market in land. In European feudal society, for example, land could be inherited, given as a gift by the monarch to a lord but could not be freely bought and sold. The creation of a market in land required the dismantling of these legal and customary restrictions. Enclosure, as described earlier in this chapter, was a prerequisite of the commodification of labour and land. But what about money? Money is "a token of purchasing power" (Polanyi 2005 [1957], 75) and becomes commodified through the creation of a money market on which financial assets can be bought and sold (see Chapter 11). *Qua* token of purchasing power, money must be managed by banking institutions and the state. Today, central banks have the task of maintaining the stability of purchasing power by attempting to keep inflation low.

The commodification of land, labour and money is essential to a capitalist society, but Polanyi notes that these are not ordinary commodities. A normal commodity, like a pair of boots, can be bought, sold, worn or discarded without difficulty. But treating land, labour and money as commodities creates social dislocation. If human beings cannot find an employer, then, if their fate were left to the market, they might simply starve. If nature were used merely as a tool for making profit, this would lead to deforestation and pollution of waterways, while green spaces would be covered by shopping malls and factories. The effects of the commodification of money were experienced during the financial crisis of 2008 (see Chapter 17), whereby the deregulated market for financial assets led to a collapse of the international financial system. Only far-reaching state intervention was able to rescue the capitalist economy.

Establishing the fiction that land, labour and money are commodities, rather than leading to their free-market allocation, has, in fact, led to its opposite, namely, state action required to avert the dire consequences of commodifying land, labour and money. One sees this in state welfare policies which protect workers through periods of unemployment, environmental protection which restricts land use or limits pollution and monetary policy through which the purchasing power of money is carefully managed (Polanyi 2005 [1957]: 76). Only by limiting the effects of commodification, Polanyi argues, is society saved from disintegration.

Max Weber and the Protestant ethic

We now turn to a contrasting perspective on the emergence of capitalism, one associated with the German economist and sociologist Max Weber. According to Weber, *modern* capitalism, as we know it and as Weber knew it in the early twentieth century, has not always existed. Throughout history, Weber argued, in epochs which pre-date modern capitalism, types of behaviour also found in the modern capitalist world are not uncommon. These types of behaviour include profiteering, greed and acquisition (Weber 1920: 20–1). Such behaviour, be it among Chinese mandarins or Roman aristocrats, is bound by a 'frame of mind' alien to modern capitalism. Weber calls this pre-capitalist frame of mind 'economic traditionalism' (22). He illustrates this frame of mind by examining 'traditionalist' attitudes among labourers and business people.

> **Key thinker: Max Weber**
>
> Max Weber (1864–1920) was a German scholar whose ideas are often presented in contrast with those of Marx. He is known for his pessimistic diagnosis of modern life in which, he thought, individuals were trapped in a dull, impersonal and bureaucratized existence which stultified human freedom. His *Protestant Ethic and the Spirit of Capitalism* (first published in 1904–5) is still widely debated.

First, consider agricultural labourers who are paid 'piece rates', that is a wage rate for each unit of crop harvested. At harvest, if landowners wish to increase the productivity of labourers in order to get crops harvested promptly, they could increase labourers' wage rate. Landowners would do this in the hope that labourers would increase their hours of work rather than reduce them. Instead of working the usual twenty hours at $20 per hour (and earning $400 per month), labourers could work sixty hours and, at the increased wage rate of $40, they would each earn $2,400 – as much as they would usually earn in six months. However, workers who have a traditionalist frame of mind, Weber tells us, will work less when the wage rate increases. Why? Instead of asking: 'If I produce as much as possible [at the higher wage], how much money will I earn each day?', the traditionalist labourer asks: 'How long must I work in order to earn the [same] amount . . . I have earned until now and that has fulfilled my *traditional* economic needs?' (22–3).

Traditionalist workers are uninterested in increasing their income and improving their standard of living because they have become accustomed to a given standard of living. They see no need to increase this standard, especially if they have to exert themselves to do so. Weber thus concludes that '[p]eople do not wish "by nature" to earn more and more money' (23); contrary to Smith's view, they are not naturally acquisitive.

A traditionalist frame of mind also affects the way in which businesspeople conduct their affairs. Weber recalls a time when business owners had an 'easygoing' life, working 'perhaps five or six hours a day and occasionally considerably less' (28). Competition existed among businesses but was not fierce. 'There was time for long daily visits to the taverns, early evening drinks, and long talks with a circle of friends. A comfortable tempo of life was the order of the day' (28). This is a far cry from the more ruthless form of business we know today. So how did we get from the world of economic traditionalism to modern capitalism? Something 'upset' the 'ease and comfort' of traditionalist business life.

Those with a traditionalist frame of mind lack the *spirit of* (modern) *capitalism*' (27). To exemplify this 'spirit', Weber (14–15) quotes the American politician, inventor and entrepreneur Benjamin Franklin (1706–90), who issues advice on the acquisition of money. Franklin extols the virtues of thriftiness and industriousness and instructs people to save, for squandering money not only represents a loss of the principal but also of the interest one could have earned by saving money one spends. Buying on credit is bad, for one pays interest on loans and thus loses this amount. Wasting time is also bad, for idleness represents a loss of money one could have earned had one not been idle.

Franklin, argued Weber, proposes that the increase of personal wealth is a *duty*. Franklin was not describing what one should do if one happens to have a taste for becoming rich and living an extravagant lifestyle; rather, acquiring money is an 'end in itself' (16–17). In fact, Franklin advised his readers to *reduce* expenditure on goods at any opportunity and to save instead. Striving to make money and yet more money becomes a moral duty to be carried out through the single-minded pursuit of a task – as a worker or a business owner – which Weber called a 'calling'. This is the spirit of modern capitalism and it has, Weber contends, not existed prior to the modern epoch.

In contrast to the Marxist view that the origins of capitalism are to be found in economic class relations, Weber argued that the spirit of modern capitalism originates in a frame of mind 'that strives systematically and rationally *in a calling* for legitimate profit' (27). Three features of this characterization are noteworthy. First, striving for profit is 'systematic' and 'rational'; it becomes the central organizing principle in one's life, and it is a rational pursuit, which one plans and calculates meticulously. Second, profit is pursued in a calling, a single economic activity towards which one directs one's efforts methodically. Third, one strives for legitimate profit; making money is to be done in an honest way. Who was responsible for introducing this frame of mind to business?

Weber gives us hints about the source of this spirit both in the title of his book and with the religiously connoted word calling. A calling is one's God-given task, or one's place in the social division of labour (i.e. whether one is a carpenter, tanner, sheep farmer etc.) (39, 107). Calling is a biblical concept, but the idea of one's calling becomes especially significant during the Reformation in Europe, in which Protestant reformers, such as Martin Luther (1483–1546), criticized Catholicism and paved the way for Protestantism. For Luther the pursuit of one's calling was 'the highest expression that moral activity could assume' (39). Prior to this, pursuit of work was deemed ungodly; Christianity in its pre-Protestant forms is exemplified by monks who withdraw from the world and shun what Weber called 'this-worldly work', that is, work as an activity in the world outside of a religious institution like a monastery (40). With Protestantism, one's profession or job acquired religious significance (41). This doctrine was radicalized by John Calvin (1509–64).

Calvin preached the doctrine of predestination, which teaches that, prior to one's birth, God determines each individual's fate in the afterlife: we are either destined for salvation in heaven or doomed to eternal death in hell. God's decision about our fate is unalterable. Worse still, nobody knows whether she belongs to the chosen few destined for heaven or whether she will be damned (55–9). This leads, Weber tells us, to an *angst*-ridden life for Protestants, who constantly ask themselves whether they have been 'elected' by God to go to heaven after their death (64). To assuage their fear, Protestants were advised by religious leaders to work tirelessly in a calling, for this was 'the best possible means to *acquire* the self-confidence that one belonged among the elect' (66). Success in one's worldly calling was not a means of *acquiring* salvation but it was an *indication* that one stood in God's favour. The pursuit of one's calling had a second role, for it was through this pursuit that people achieved 'good works' which increased the glory of God on earth. God, as Calvin understood Him, did not require merely sporadic good works but continual striving after such works; the only way to honour God was through the systematic pursuit of one's calling (70–1).

Success in one's calling led to the amassing of wealth, and it was also a much-wanted sign of God's blessing. This posed a problem for Protestants, for their religion forbade the consumption of luxuries and frowned on a life of comfort and extravagance. Hence, the Protestant was expected to strive methodically in his calling, and, if successful, he would become wealthy, but he was not allowed to consume this wealth; his life was to be *ascetic* (115–16). Instead of consuming their wealth, they reinvested it in their business in the hope that they would meet with further business success which would strengthen the sign of their posthumous salvation.

Protestantism therefore ushered in a new attitude to making and using money. Previously, Christianity had frowned on wealth because it led to a life of luxury which was anathema to honouring God. The ascetic monk had been the highest symbol of piety prior to Protestantism. Protestantism, however, 'shatter[ed] the bonds restricting all striving for gain' and conferred legitimacy on the accumulation of wealth (as long as it was done honestly). It simultaneously proscribed the use of wealth for the purpose of living luxuriously (115). The result of the duty to accumulate wealth in one's calling and the prohibition of consuming one's wealth on luxuries led to '*the formation of capital* through *asceticism's compulsive saving*' (117, 29). This is precisely the behaviour one requires of a capitalist whose business is to thrive and persist. There thus arose a new business ethic among Protestants: the businessperson felt empowered to pursue economic gain in their calling, while Protestant workers 'attached themselves to their work' with a zeal which removed the hindrances to increased labour productivity once posed by economic traditionalism (120).

The changes that Protestantism brought about date to the sixteenth century, but what does it have to do with our lives today? We do not associate success in business with people who are deeply religious. Weber notes that, at the start of the twentieth century, businesspeople were already 'indifferent, if not openly hostile, to religion' (31). So if his thesis about Protestant influence on the development of capitalism is correct, Weber must explain a transition from an early phase of modern capitalism, in which the growth of enterprise was driven by Protestants for religious reasons, to a subsequent stage, in which religion plays little or no part in the motives of businesspeople.

To understand this transition, consider a small town in which a few Protestants, imbued with the capitalist spirit, had set up a business. Other businesspeople still adopted the easygoing rhythms of economic traditionalism. Which businesses survived market competition? Obviously, Protestant-run businesses that employed Protestant workers had an advantage because of their rigorous work ethic. Other businesspeople would have had a choice between keeping up with the Protestant businesses (by adopting a similar work ethic) or going out of business (29). In this way, a new business ethic spread to non-Protestant communities. To compete with Protestant businesses, non-Protestants had to adopt an ethic of hard work and single-minded dedication. With regard to contemporary businesspeople, Weber writes that the Protestant '*wanted* to be a person with a vocational calling; today we *are forced* to be' (123). Today, if one wishes to pursue business, one has to adopt an ethic like that of Weber's early Protestants if one is to succeed. Similarly, if one seeks a job, one must adopt an ethic of hard work, reliability, loyalty to one's employer and so on, for if one lacks this ethic, one will be fired. Few of us nowadays adopt this ethic for religious reasons; rather we have no choice but to adopt the ethic of hard work from necessity. The alternative is bankruptcy or unemployment.

Contemporary society, having become secularized, has also shed its disapproval of luxury and consumption. Today, few frown on those who amass fortunes and spend them on holiday homes, yachts and private jets.

Consumerism has triumphed over asceticism, and over 100 years ago, when Weber (124) was writing, the acquisition of material goods was no longer frowned upon. Modern capitalism thus survives without the religious undergirding of Protestantism which called it into life; and it also survives without the asceticism which was essential to its early development.

Marx, Weber and historical materialism

Marx and Weber are often seen as opposed in their accounts of the development of capitalism. There are, however, some similarities in their work. First, both saw capitalism as something radically new in history, neither a mere extension of what went before nor as something which would inevitably come about if certain obstacles to the development of capitalism were removed. Second, both agreed that capitalism, in its earliest form, was not associated with either the rich commercial class in cities or with industrialism. For Marx, the site of early capitalist relations of production was the countryside, and the main agents of change were landlords. For Weber, small-scale Protestant businesspeople first carried the seeds of the capitalist spirit. One much-discussed difference between Marx and Weber concerns their approaches to historical change. This is a *methodological* difference, one which pertains to the difference in their approaches and methods to human history, to which we turn in closing this chapter.

Weber alluded to 'naive' *historical materialism*, the view that ideas, including religious beliefs, are a 'reflection' of the economic structure of society (1920: 19). Some form of this view, which Weber rejected, is supported by Marxists who believe that social change stems from economic factors and that ideas adjust themselves to economic factors but are not the driving force of historical change.

Key methodological issue: Historical materialism

In the 'Preface' to *A Contribution to the Critique of Political Economy* (1859: 211), Marx wrote:

> In the social production of their existence, men inevitably enter into definite relations, which are independent of their will, namely relations of production appropriate to a given stage in the development of their material forces of production. The totality of these relations of production constitutes the economic structure of society, the real foundation, on which arises a legal and political superstructure and to which correspond definite forms of social consciousness. The mode of production of material life conditions the general process of social, political and intellectual life. It is not the consciousness of men that determines their existence, but their social existence that determines their consciousness.

This is a statement of historical materialism, the view that the dominant feature of a society is its economic structure which conditions other aspects of society.

Weber's remarks on historical materialism can be interpreted as a reaction to the 'vulgar' forms of Marxism of the late nineteenth century which interpreted Marx's writings in a rigidly 'economistic' sense (Giddens 1971: 193). Beliefs and ideas (like Protestantism), according to 'vulgar' Marxists, are secondary phenomena with no causal impact on the development of history. Few Marxists today see this as an adequate representation of Marx's ideas, and it is not fruitful to conceive Marx and Weber in an opposition according to which the former sees the key to historical change lying in the economic sphere while the latter sees it in the sphere of ideas. Weber's study of the development of capitalism illustrates how ideas can be causal forces in historical development (1920: 48), but he did not hold that ideas are the only or main driving force of historical change; nor did he think that, without the Protestant Reformation, modern capitalism could not have evolved.

Conclusion

This chapter has examined two approaches to the development of capitalism in Western Europe, those of Max Weber and Karl Marx. Despite their differences, both authors challenge the view that capitalism flourishes in Western Europe because markets are unfettered, allowing the supposedly 'natural' tendencies of human beings – to invest, innovate, produce, and exchange goods – to freely flourish. Instead Marx and Weber identify profound and disruptive social changes which create the conditions for the development of capitalism. It's important to note that Marx and Weber focused primarily on Western Europe where they lived. This focus might mislead the reader into thinking that the early phases of capitalist development were exclusively concentrated in Western Europe. This was not the case. Indeed, there are arguments in favour of the view that, since its earliest stages, capitalism was a *world system* (Cox 1964, Wallerstein 2004). The following chapter examines capitalist development in other parts of the world with which Western Europe has been related since the capitalist system first developed.

Suggested readings

- Ch. 26–8, Marx, K. (1867 [1976]) *Capital: Volume 1*, London, Penguin.
- Ch. 6, Polanyi, K. (1944 [2001]) *The Great Transformation: The Political and Economic Origins of Our Time*, Boston, Beacon.
- Ch. II and V, Weber, M. (1920 [2002]) *The Protestant Ethic and the Spirit of Capitalism* (2nd Edition), Los Angeles, Roxbury.
- Ch. 1 and 5, Wood, E.M. (2002) *The Origins of Capitalism: A Longer View*, London, Verso.

Bibliography

Beier, A. (1985) *Masterless Men: The Vagrancy Problem in England, 1560–1640*, London, Methuen.

Beier, A. (2008) '"A New Serfdom": Labour Laws, Vagrancy Statutes, and Labour Discipline in England, 1350–1800', in A. Beier and P. Ocobock (eds), *Cast Out: Vagrancy and Homelessness in Global and Historical Perspective*, Athens, Ohio University Press, pp. 35–63.

Braudel, F. (1979 [2002]) *Civilization and Capitalism, 15th–18th Century*, London, Phoenix.

Brenner, R. (1976 [1985]) 'Agrarian Class Structure and the Development of Capitalism', in T. Ashton and C. Philpin (eds), *The Brenner Debate*, Cambridge, Cambridge University Press, pp. 10–63.

Brenner, R. (1985) 'The Agrarian Roots of European Capitalism', in T. Ashton and C. Philpin (eds), *The Brenner Debate*, Cambridge, Cambridge University Press, pp. 213–327.

Cox, O.C. (1964) *Capitalism as a System*, New York, Monthly Review Press.

Giddens, A. (1971) *Capitalism and Modern Social Theory*, Cambridge, Cambridge University Press.

Manning, R. (1988) *Village Revolts: Social Protest and Popular Disturbances in England, 1509–1640*, Oxford, Clarendon.

Marx, K. (1859 [1994]) 'Preface', Translated by S. Ryazanskaya, in L. Simon (ed.), *Karl Marx: Selected Writings*, Indianapolis, Hackett, pp. 209–13.

Marx, K. (1867 [1976]) *Capital: Volume 1*, London, Penguin.

Neeson, J. (1993) *Commoners: Common Right, Enclosure and Social Change in England, 1700–1820*, Cambridge, Cambridge University Press.

Pirenne, H. (1956) *Medieval Cities: Their Origins and the Revival of Trade*, New York, Doubleday.

Polanyi, K. (1944 [2001]) *The Great Transformation: The Political and Economic Origins of Our Time*, Boston, Beacon Press.

Postan, M. (1971) 'Medieval Agrarian Society in its Prime: England', in M. Postan (ed.), *The Cambridge Economic History of Europe*, Volume 1, Cambridge, Cambridge University Press, pp. 548–632.

Smith, A. (1759 [1976]) *The Theory of Moral Sentiments*, Oxford, Oxford University Press.

Smith, A. (1776 [1976]) *An Inquiry into the Nature and Causes of the Wealth of Nations*, Volume 1, Oxford, Oxford University Press.

Tawney, R. (1914 [1972]) 'The Assessment of Wages in England by Justices of the Peace', in W. Minchinton (ed.), *Wage Regulation in Pre-Industrial England*, New York, Barnes & Noble, pp. 38–91.

Wallerstein, I. (2004) *World-Systems Analysis: An Introduction*, Durham, Duke University Press.

Weber, M. (1920 [2002]) *The Protestant Ethic and the Spirit of Capitalism* (2nd Edition), Los Angeles, Roxbury.

Wood, E.M. (2002) *The Origins of Capitalism: A Longer View*, London, Verso.

3 | The spread of capitalism

Kean Birch and Caroline Shenaz Hossein

Introduction

Early capitalist proponents like Adam Smith – who we introduced in Chapter 1 – thought that capitalism originated in cities and the urban, civilized and modern life they represented. Capitalism appeared as a bulwark against the *ancien regime* of feudalism; it challenged and eroded irrational and narrow beliefs, stultifying hierarchies and the limits of tradition and parentage. From this perspective, capitalism stimulated the Enlightenment and Scientific Revolutions which brought us new insights and technologies; it also promoted democratic and liberation movements, enabling people to break free from absolutism and tyranny (Slater and Tonkiss 2001). Consequently, the emergence of capitalism from the fifteenth and sixteenth centuries onwards – as outlined in the previous chapter – totally transformed European societies and economies and continues to transform other countries around the globe. It's easy to see, then, that when capitalism first emerged, it was perceived as a step towards progress, a way to develop society. The preceding feudal system in Europe exploited some groups and privileged a very small elite class (Jenkins and Leroy 2021). Life was socially tiered, and certain groups were viewed as lesser than others, whether it was the Slavs and Jews, or later, African peoples. It was this logic of inferiority that permitted the ruling classes to dominate, to exploit labour and to rule both in the feudal and capitalist systems of today (Robinson 1983).

In contrast, there are still many today who argue that capitalism's subsequent diffusion has led us into the modern age in which the expansion of wealth and well-being go hand in hand. For example, the work of journalist Thomas Friedman (1999, 2005) lauds the promise of development offered by capitalism – we come back to this in Chapter 13 – while the historian Niall Ferguson (2011) puts Europe's ascendancy down to 'six killer apps', including competition. While some of this may reflect historical changes, it's far from the total picture; in particular, these claims hide a *dark side* to capitalism.

Capitalism has a dirty history, not only in the poetic terms evoked by William Blake's image of the 'dark Satanic mills' of industrialization, but in the dust, blood and tears of millions of people trampled, enslaved and massacred as a result of its spread around the world. The idea that capitalism emerges in one place (e.g. Europe) and then spreads around the world misses the point; capitalism only emerged in Europe *because* the rest of the world was forced

– through war, slavery and colonialism – into a subservient position. Large parts of the world were turned into European colonies and dependencies, shipping their raw materials to the capitalist heartlands in return for goods and services they were no longer allowed to produce. What this illustrates is the fact that capitalism was a world-wide transformation; it was not limited to one country or one continent. As a result, all parts of the world are now entangled with capitalism, whether people like it or not. The view that capitalism is a world-wide system has a long history. For example, early Marxists like Rudolf Hilferding, Michael Bukharin and Vladimir Lenin argued that imperialism was another stage in capitalist development (Brewer 1990). Their ideas influenced later thinkers and theories; these include dependency scholars such as Oliver C. Cox (1959, 1964), C. Y. Thomas (1974) and Immanuel Wallerstein (1979b), who all wrote about dependency and *world-system theory*. We will return to these ideas later.

The starting point for this chapter is the idea that capitalism can't be explained as a simple, progressive story of modernity being spread around the world by enlightened European explorers, travellers and merchants. This is what we call the *linear story* of capitalism in which it's assumed that countries move from underdeveloped backwaters to modern, advanced capitalist economies through a number of intervening steps as they adopt capitalism. We problematize this notion by presenting a *non-linear* or *circular* story of capitalism's world-wide spread; it's a story told by a number of scholars including those mentioned earlier (e.g. Cox, Thomas, Wallerstein) as well as other thinkers like Giovanni Arrighi (1994 [2010]), Samir Amin (1977, 2013), Walter Rodney (1982) and Andre Gunder Frank (1969, 1972). In *Worldmaking after Empire*, Ethiopian-born political theorist Adom Getachew (2019) excavates the ways in which Caribbean and African state leaders – including Williams (prime minister of Trinidad and Tobago 1962–81), Nyerere (president of Tanzania 1964–85), Manley (prime minister of Jamaica 1972–80, 1989–92), Nkrumah (president of Ghana 1960–6), along with many other Black intellectuals – were engaged in ideas of decolonization and self-determination while under colonial rule. First, we outline the linear narrative of European progress and exploration; that is, the idea of Europe bringing modernity to the rest of the world. Second, we challenge this linear story by discussing how European capitalism was and is based on the underdevelopment of other countries around the world.

Key discussion questions

- What is development?
- What is wrong with the linear story of capitalism?

- In what ways did capitalism have violent roots in colonialism and slavery?
- Why is dependency theory helpful in explaining the spread of capitalism?
- Is capitalism a world-wide system?
- How are joint-stock companies related to the spread of capitalism?

Mainstream perspectives

The linear story of capitalism Histories of the spread of capitalism often follow a linear format. It goes something like this. Prior to the emergence of capitalism the world economy was not integrated. Aside from a few long-distant and time-consuming merchant voyages or trips – for example, Marco Polo's travels from Europe to China in the thirteenth century – trade was mostly limited to neighbouring or nearby countries. For Europeans, the long trade routes to East Asia and the wealth it held were risky because of the 'threat' from countries like the Ottoman Empire to European traders. In this climate, and up until the fifteenth century, Europe was a relative backwater in global terms; this claim contrasts somewhat with the history most of us in Anglo-American and European countries learn at school. China and India had much larger economies as a result of the size of their populations (Dicken 2011: 15), and were more technologically advanced in many ways (Scott 2011). In contrast, until the emergence of capitalism only a few European cities were centres of wealth and technology, especially the independent Italian city-states like Milan, Florence, Genoa and Venice. These cities were major centres of population, banking, industry and trade – relative to the rest of Europe, at least – dominated by a merchant class, rather than the aristocracy.

All this changed, however, in the fifteenth century when European monarchs started to finance explorations of the rest of the world, the most famous being Christopher Columbus and the 'discovery' of the Americas in 1492. The rationale behind these journeys was to find alternative routes to China and India that would bypass the hostile Ottoman Empire, which had captured Constantinople in 1453. This so-called Age of 'Discovery' was dominated by a small number of European countries: it started with Portugal in the early fifteenth century; followed by Spain in the fifteenth and sixteenth centuries; and then the Netherlands, England and France from the sixteenth onwards (Slater 2005). Each of these countries sought to dominate particular spheres of the world and world trade through direct means – like conquest, subjugation of indigenous populations, slavery and colonization – and indirect means – like control over trade routes. The expansion of trade and conquest brought an enormous amount of the world's wealth (literally gold and silver) flowing into Europe where it helped stimulate economic, scientific, technological, cultural and political revolutions. As exploration turned to colonization from the seventeenth century onwards, other parts of the world were brought into the orbit of Europe's early capitalist system, leading to the integration of the world economy and the gradual development and modernization of non-European countries.

Key concept: Age of 'Discovery'

Starting in the fifteenth century, a number of European countries sought to find alternative routes to East Asia that bypassed the Ottoman Empire. Some countries, like Portugal, sought to find sea routes around Africa, while others, like Spain, sought sea routes directly West over the Atlantic. The search for trade routes resulted in Europeans travelling to the Americas and other parts of the world with which they had had no (or only limited) previous links. Following exploration, European countries sought to invade, conquer and/or colonize the Americas, Africa, Asia and Oceania, driven by religious fervour (e.g. spreading Christianity), mercantilist capitalism (e.g. extracting wealth) and territorial ambitions (e.g. building empires). Over several centuries, millions of people around the world were subjugated, enslaved or killed as the result of war, famine and disease.

Source: Slater (2005)

The global expansion of Europe led to frequent conflicts between European countries, both in Europe and in other parts of the world, especially as they started to establish colonies from the seventeenth and eighteenth centuries. This resulted from disagreements about control over land and trade, and was driven by a particular way of thinking about trade and trading relations called *mercantilism*. The assumption underpinning mercantilism was that trade is a zero-sum activity in which one country's gain led to another country's loss; for example, if one country won control over trade to East Asia then it would benefit from all the wealth coming from that trade to the exclusion of all other countries (Marx 1867 [1976]). For most European countries then, mercantilism was an extension of territorial ambitions and inter-state competition; that is, increasing your wealth at the expense of another country gave you a major bonus when waging war. Mercantilism led many European countries to establish large trading companies with exclusive trading rights to different parts of the world – we return to this issue later when we discuss the English/British East India Company (Robins 2006). However, mercantilism did not last. In 1776 Adam Smith criticized the mercantilist form of capitalism in his book *The Wealth of Nations*. He argued that competition and trade could lead to a gain for both parties through the benefits of a division of labour; this theory was based on the notion that it was more productive to specialize and trade with others than to try and do everything yourself. Eventually, Smith's and other *classical political economy* theories came to dominate the policies of European countries and their governments, especially Britain, in the nineteenth century (Hobsbawm 1997).

Key thinkers: Classical political economy

Stretching from Adam Smith to Karl Marx, classical political economy covers all those eighteenth- and nineteenth-century thinkers who based their theories of capitalism on the labour theory of value. The labour theory of value is based on the idea that the value of a commodity is derived from the labour needed to produce that commodity. Classical political economy went into decline with the 'marginal revolution' in the late nineteenth century and is no longer a mainstream theory of capitalism. This is discussed in more detail in Chapter 5.

Modernization theory and the Western project. In the twentieth century, this view of the spread of capitalism was increasingly associated with other concepts, like modernization, which emerged in 'Western' countries – today it's exemplified by people like Thomas Friedman (1999, 2005) and Niall Ferguson (2011). From this 'modern' perspective, Western values, practices and knowledges are characterized as universal examples of social and economic development. Earlier modernization theorists believed they had the prescriptions to 'develop' poor, non-Western countries by forcing them to imitate Western countries' experience with capitalism. According to political scientist Samuel Huntington (1971), for example, modern science and technology gave humans greater control over the natural and social environment whereas traditional or communal knowledge led to inferior standards of living. These ideas led Western elites to define people in the so-called Third World as primitive and in need of saving. For example, David Apter's (1965) *The Politics of Modernization* begins with the claim that modernization theory represented a 'special kind of hope'. For many modernizers, the project of colonialism itself can be seen as a modern exercise in 'we know best'. The modernist assumptions were that the Western concepts of nation, state, civil society and representative government could be easily transplanted across the rest of the world.

Modernization was conceived as a top-down, global, lengthy, phased, homogenizing, irreversible, progressive, complex and revolutionary process that included industrialization, urbanization, social mobilization, secularization and democracy. The best-known argument for modernization was put forth by the American economist W. W. Rostow (1960) in *Stages of Economic Growth: A Non-Communist Manifesto*, where he argued that the transition from underdevelopment to modern development came through five successive stages influenced by economic development: transition society, preconditions for take-off, take-off, maturity and, finally, mass-consumption. Rostow's ideas reflected the broader geopolitical context in which he was writing. In the 1950s, and after the Second World War, the capitalist United States emerged as a global superpower opposed by the socialist USSR.

Modern capitalist development, as espoused by the likes of Rostow, was based on certain assumptions. Specifically, Rostow's (1960 [1991]) theory was built on the analysis of the British Industrial (and capitalist) Revolution, which led him to assert that all societies pass through this single, linear path where each stage is a prerequisite for the next.

However, many Western countries took quite different developmental pathways than those outlined by modernization theorists like Rostow; as we discuss in Chapter 13, there is more than one form of capitalism. Although modernization theory initially contributed to a problematic understanding of the Global South, revisionist modernizers have also attempted to consider the issues that occur within countries in order to understand the diverse and varied modernities that can result from diverse historical, political, social and cultural experiences.

To conclude this section, it's possible to summarize the linear story as premised on certain assumptions about the spread and evolution of capitalism around the world (see Chang 2008). These can be simplified as three basic ideas:

- *Exploration*: capitalism originates in Europe and then spreads outward from there as European countries explore and colonize the rest of the world, exporting capitalism as they extend European influence. As more countries are dominated by European countries they become integrated into a widening global economy which ties together colonial homelands (in Europe) with overseas colonies (in other parts of the world).
- *Development*: the spread of capitalism outwards from Europe was built on the back of new production processes (e.g. factories), new industries (e.g. cotton), new technologies (e.g. railways) and new ideas (e.g. science), all of which have subsequently contributed to the economic and social development of other places and their peoples around the world.
- *Modernization*: European countries modernized and developed as a result of capitalism, leading to rising living standards and other benefits (e.g. higher life expectancy). Other countries that followed the European example did and will benefit from the same outcomes.

In what follows we problematize this linear narrative, its underlying assumptions and the assumed benefits of capitalism and modernization.

Critical perspectives

There is a non-linear view of the spread of capitalism. It emphasizes the need to think about the interdependent relationships between different parts of the world; that is, to think of capitalism as a global economic system, rather than individual countries trading with one another. It's particularly important to think about how different parts of the world were integrated into a global economy as a consequence of colonialism and imperialism. To do this requires us to understand the international division of labour and international patterns of production and consumption. While Adam Smith – see Chapter 1 – analysed specialization in individual factories and how this leads to productivity gains, similar arguments can be made about specialization between different countries in a global economic system like capitalism (e.g. Frobel et al. 1980). Usually this type of thinking is based on the idea of comparative advantage developed by the nineteenth-century political economist David Ricardo. His ideas justify claims about the benefits of free trade, supporting the view that unrestricted trade between countries will benefit everyone because each country can focus on what it's best at producing and then trade for everything else it needs (Krugman 1996). However, there are other, more critical, ways to understand global capitalism, and we examine some of these next.

Key thinker: David Ricardo

Ricardo was a British political economist who lived in the eighteenth and nineteenth centuries. He wrote an influential book called *Principles of Political Economy and Taxation* (1817), in which he laid out the theory of comparative advantage. This theory sought to conceptualize the positive benefits of 'free' trade. While his arguments have been very influential, especially in legitimating free trade in the nineteenth century and again in the late twentieth century, they have also been criticized by a range of people.

The non-linear, or circular, story of capitalism. Modernization theory was and is clearly limited by its Western lens. Although its perspective of the Global South was shrouded with ahistorical, homogenizing, linear, apolitical, ethnocentric and simplistic understandings of very diverse people, it was premised on improving the conditions of those who were faced with severe poverty, inequality, violence and instability. However, modernization theorists omitted several important elements in the development story: namely, the historical experiences of slavery, imperialism and colonialism. Modernization was not just about building roads, educating people, providing electricity and expanding trade, it was about the expansion of geopolitical power. Examining the world 'simply as it was' according to Western assumptions meant that modernization theory did nothing to challenge prevailing power relationships as well as institutions through which power was organized to sustain the *status quo*.

Modernization theory was criticized on these grounds by a number of 'dependency theorists'. Dependency theory critiques dominant ideas about the linear story of capitalist development (Isbister 2006). It arose out of the Global South, principally from Latin American and Caribbean scholars such as Cardoso (1977), Thomas (1974) and Rodney (1982), as an alternative explanation of underdevelopment and the spread of capitalism. Whereas modernization theorists argue that underdevelopment is a *condition*, dependency theorists argue that it's an ongoing *process*. According to dependency theory, underdevelopment is not simply a failure to develop; it's also an active process of impoverishment. In *How Europe Underdeveloped Africa*, for example, Walter Rodney (1982) argued that imperialist capitalism involved European extraction of riches and engagement in the slave trade in Africa and the Americas in order to finance Europe's industrial development – in this sense it had nothing to do with modernity or promoting modernization. Consequently, it makes no sense to talk of developed countries as being 'underdeveloped' in the past, although they may have been 'undeveloped' at one point. Another notable and prolific thinker from the dependency school is the late Egyptian-born and Senegal-based Samir Amin (1977), who has critiqued the bias embedded in modernization theory. According to Amin, the root cause of poverty and underdevelopment in the South is the result of capitalist development. In other words, countries of the Global South found themselves in positions of underdevelopment because of the operation of capitalism (Amin 2013).

Generally, dependency theory makes four claims: (1) underdevelopment is a process, not a condition; (2) poverty in the Global South (e.g. in former European colonies) is a result of Europe's industrial prosperity; (3) international and historical factors are key to understanding underdevelopment; and (4) a global capitalist system undermines economic development in the Global South. The impoverishment of the Global South did not result from so-called primitivism, but rather from the colonial and imperial activities of European countries which fuelled their economic growth at the expense of their colonial possessions (Amin 2013; James 1989; Cardoso 1977; Williams 1944 [2004]). As such, the process of underdevelopment of the Global South was deliberate (Brohman 1995).

Dependency theory is distinct from modernization theory because it focuses on the *global* capitalist system. Unlike modernization perspectives, dependency theory seeks to examine the relations between core/metropole countries and periphery/satellite countries (see Figure 3.1). As such it's based on the idea that capitalism involves core countries (e.g. European

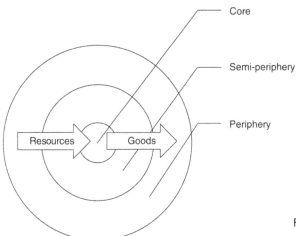

FIGURE 3.1 Core-periphery relations.

colonizers) extracting raw materials from peripheral countries (e.g. European colonies). This global capitalist system is conceived as decidedly non-linear. In particular, Trinidadian sociologist Oliver C. Cox (1959, 1964) was the first academic to describe the world system as a racist system, which alienated countries in the Global South (see Hunter and Abraham 1987). Cox's work was sidelined for a very long time because his assertion that development theory wasn't neutral was deemed by many mainstream thinkers to be too 'radical'. Brazilian dependency scholar Cardoso (1977) argued that world systems were not understood to be legitimate in academia until they were accepted by US-based scholars, despite the fact that they had gained widespread appeal among thinkers in the Global South. Crucial to this legitimation in the Global North was the work of Immanuel Wallerstein (1979a), who also characterized capitalism as a world system involving a chain of production and consumption relationships between cores and peripheries.

Rather than a linear process of economic development under capitalism then, it's more accurate to conceptualize the spread of capitalism around the world as a circular process in which countries were drawn into capitalism as a world system, especially through slavery, colonialism and empire. This process of uneven and unequal development goes back to at least the sixteenth century with the emergence of capitalist world economy in which the colonial powers (i.e. the core) were able to industrialize based on the agricultural and mineral primary goods extracted from the colonies (i.e. periphery) (Isbister 2006). Consequently, the present underdevelopment of the Global South is better thought of as the result of its centuries-long position in global capitalism, especially its experience with slavery, colonial exploitation and imperial conquest.

Capitalism, slavery and colonization. We now want to examine the dark side of capitalism; this is most evident in the relationship between capitalism and slavery. The slave trade was started by Europeans in Africa and can be dated to the Portuguese explorations in the fifteenth century. In the Americas, the major colonies receiving slaves were Brazil and the Caribbean. According to the *Voyages* project (see Figure 3.2), for example, most of the 35,000 slave voyages from Africa went to these places (Eltis and Richardson 2010). These countries formed part of the so-called Triangular Trade which linked Europe, Africa and the Americas in an international flow of enslaved people, raw materials and manufactured goods.

A key player in this triangular trade was the British Empire. It gained direct control of a number of Caribbean islands and territories in South America. Moreover, the 1713 Treaty of Utrecht granted enormous power to the British Empire under the *Asiento* contract in which Britain became the authorized slave distributor for the Atlantic (Black 1965) – the British government gave this contract to the South Sea Company, a joint-stock company (see later). The *Asiento* was a contract that the Spanish crown had established in 1595, giving a monopoly on the supply of slaves to Spanish colonies in Central and Southern America. When the *Asiento* was given to Britain in 1713, white indentured servants at the time, such as the Portuguese and Irish, moved into plantation management as African slaves were sold to plantations in British colonies as well. Even after it lost the *Asiento* in the mid-1700s, the British continued to support the plantation system in its own colonies of Barbados, Jamaica, Grenada and Trinidad because the earnings were so lucrative (Williams 1944 [2004]).

Millions of Africans lost their lives as a result of slavery. Slavery meant that African people were considered and treated as legal property (Olusoga 2015); enslaved people were brutalized, tortured and raped without recrimination. The profits made from the slavery of African people in the Americas financed Britain's Industrial Revolution. As such, it's possible to argue that the Industrial Revolution, which transformed the quality of life of so many British people through economic development, was rooted in the immoral, inhumane and racist practices that resulted in the deaths of millions of African people. European countries, like Britain, became rich through extracting resources with the enslaved labour of Africans in colonies.

Even though slavery began to be abolished by European countries from the end of the eighteenth century, Eric Williams (1944 [2004]) argued that the abolition movement was rooted in economic decisions rather than humanitarian ones. The institution of slavery was first abolished in France in 1794; it ended in the British Empire in 1833 with the Slavery Abolition Act; and in the United States in 1865 soon after President Abraham Lincoln's Emancipation Proclamation was enacted. Ending slavery was resisted by slave owners because of the

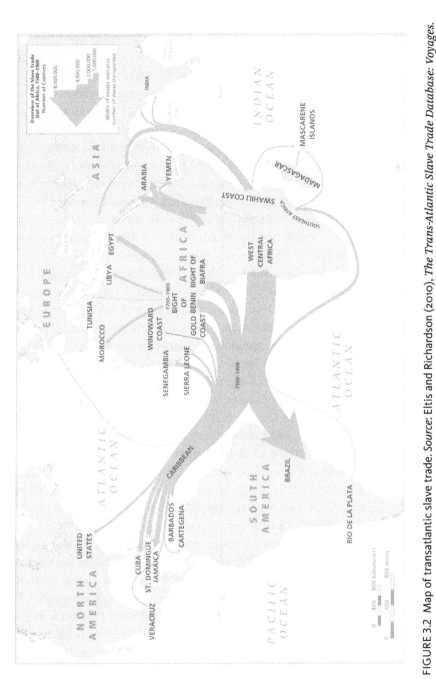

FIGURE 3.2 Map of transatlantic slave trade. *Source:* Eltis and Richardson (2010), *The Trans-Atlantic Slave Trade Database: Voyages.* New Haven: Yale University Press. (Reprinted with permission from the publisher).

great profits generated; in some cases, owners were compensated for losing their 'property', representing one of the largest transfers of wealth from the government to private individuals in British history (Olusoga 2015).[1]

Slavery illustrates that the use of enslaved African labour in the Americas and the extraction of resources from the Global South were not a free exchange of goods and services among partners, but rather goods and people were obtained through brutality and violence. Plantations and the trans-atlantic trade were important to securing Europe's superior positioning in the world system (James 1989; Cox 1964). After abolition, colonial plantations were not sustainable without forced labour and neither were plantations economical with the constant insurrections by the slaves. In response, the British Empire enacted legislation to carry out an expansive indentured worker system in a number of its colonies, such as Guyana, Trinidad, Mauritius and, to a lesser extent, Jamaica. With subsidies from the British state, for example, the British East India Company transported thousands of poor (often low-caste) Indians from Calcutta, India to the British West Indies (Caribbean).

These indentured workers lived in the exact same slave dwellings and undertook the same work that African slaves once carried out under similar conditions. The Guyanese academic Walter Rodney (1982) made a compelling point that slavery, as an institution, did not in fact end in the colonies until the early twentieth century because the indentured worker system of Indians and Indo-Caribbean people continued into the 1900s. A plantation economy controlled by the British continued for many years after official emancipation in these Caribbean colonies. Colonization under British direct rule had a lasting and detrimental effect on the Caribbean. British male administrators managed the affairs of the colonies and local people were organized in ways that best suited the Crown. Resources such as bauxite, gold, silver and diamonds were pilfered; local people were given a Western Christian education; and all things African were banned. Of the local population those who were mixed-race (white and African) were somewhat privileged because the colonizers would cherry-pick among the locals who had access to resources under a strategic plan of 'divide and conquer'. Mixed-race persons often inherited the wealth of the white colonizers (Thomas 1988). Within a number of Caribbean societies, a class structure tied to race emerged in which mixed-race persons had the right to vote and dark-skinned persons of African heritage did not (Rodney 1982).

Today, the richest families in the Caribbean can easily be traced to the colonization period. Those with a white lineage clearly benefited economically from this historical legacy. Colonies that experienced enslavement and colonization have local elites (born out of the colonizing project of miscegenation) and they have (mis)used their financial resources to sustain unequal structures in the Caribbean society, a legacy that continues today.

Case study

Reparations for slavery

A contemporary and collective movement of the African diaspora has started to agitate for dialogue on the slave trade, slavery and colonization by slave-trading countries in Europe and to make a case for compensation for the pain, suffering and losses endured by the descendants of African slaves in the Americas.

Slavery and colonization have had dire repercussions for the development of African countries and their diaspora. It is not that African countries and their diaspora cannot 'modernize' but that persons of African descent have been subject to centuries of gross human indignities and intense exploitation by racist colonizers – a part of the story that is often conveniently overlooked. The shameful past of slavery has been largely ignored by Europe. The socio-economic oppression encountered by millions of persons of the African diaspora is rooted in the experience of enslavement and colonialism. The underdevelopment of the Caribbean (and Africa) is the direct effect of the slave trade, indentured servitude and colonization.

Caribbean states, academics and civil society organizations in the region and the diaspora have started to mobilize a reparations movement. For example, a University of West Indies (Cavehill campus, Barbados) professor, Hilary Beckles, leads a task force for reparations from former European slave-trading nations such as Britain, France and Spain. The reparations movement seeks recognition from colonizer countries that they owe their industrial development to the wealth accumulated from the slave trade, slavery and colonization. As highlighted earlier, the minority whites in the Caribbean own most of the riches because they amassed huge fortunes from plantation slavery and also received compensation by the British state for the loss of their 'property'. No Black person was ever compensated for the violence perpetrated against them as a people under enslavement (or colonization). In November 2021, the Caribbean country of Barbados officially became a republic and has cut formal ties with the British monarchy (Guardian 2021).

Empirical example: The British Empire

The British Empire dominated the world capitalist system for over a century (Arrighi 1994 [2010]). On the one hand, the Empire was based on colonialism, slavery and indentured servitude in the Caribbean and North America, as we have outlined earlier; on the other hand, it was based on international trading routes and large, semi-private trading companies in India and the Far East.

Aside from direct colonial control, large parts of the British Empire emerged from trading networks centred on joint-stock companies (JSC) like the East India Company (EIC), Royal Africa Company and South Sea Company. These JSCs were a form of business organization chartered by the Crowns of various European countries, including England/Britain, the Netherlands and France (Micklethwait and Woodridge 2005; Robins 2006). Their purpose was to undertake long and dangerous voyages to other parts of the world in order to engage in trade, especially the spice trade. In order to share the risks of these journeys, JSCs were structured so that many people shared ownership (i.e. shareholding). In general, JSCs were characterized by the following aspects:

- Created by a charter from by Crown for certain period of time (e.g., twenty-one years); this could be renewed at the end of each charter period. The charter gave the JSC monopoly privileges on trade with particular parts of the world; for example, the EIC had monopoly rights to trade with 'East India' – that is, India, Indonesia, Malaysia and so on. Consequently, no other English/British JSC could trade with East India.
- Independence from the Crown, in that the monarch and their government did not direct the actions of the JSC or own the JSC. Instead, the JSC was owned by many shareholders who could trade their shares in share markets; this was in order to spread the risk of failure among many investors.
- JSCs had separate legal identities from their shareholders, so that a JSC's existence did not depend on the lifespan of its investors. Shareholders were given limited liability protection, which meant that investors were not responsible for the actions of the JSC.
- JSCs were given sovereign rights to wage war, print money and make treaties, since they operated in parts of the world many months away from their home countries.

Despite these JSCs being semi-private, independent entities, they were deeply implicated in English/British colonialism, although their activities were driven more by the commercial goals of private business (i.e. profit).

> **Key organization: Joint-stock company**
>
> The main examples from England and Britain include Muscovy Company (est. 1555), East India Company (est. 1600), Hudson's Bay Company (est. 1670) and South Sea Company (est. 1711). Other countries also had similar JSCs; for example, the Netherlands (est.1602), Denmark (est. 1616), Portugal (est. 1628), France (est. 1664) and Sweden (est. 1731) all had East India Companies with monopolies of trade to East Asia. Of these, the two most important were the Dutch and English/British EICs.

The English/British EIC had a long history of operations, lasting from 1600 until 1874, and played an important role in establishing the British Empire in the Indian subcontinent. According to Robins (2006), who has written a history of the EIC, it was established at the end of 1600 by Queen Elizabeth I and was originally chartered to engage in the lucrative spice trade with places like Indonesia. However, by 1667 it was driven out of the spice trade by the Dutch EIC and shifted its attention to Bengal, in the Indian subcontinent. The EIC initially traded gold and silver bullion in exchange for textiles, since Bengal was a major textile manufacturing hub; for example, India had a 25 per cent share of world textile manufacturing in 1750 (Robins 2006). In 1757 the EIC waged war on the local Bengali rulers and was subsequently granted rights to collect taxes by the Mughal emperor in Bengal. This led to the EIC assuming a direct governing role which it used to destroy the Bengali textile industry.

The EIC slowly declined in importance during the nineteenth century as it lost trading rights and as the British state took over responsibility for the running of India as a colony. However, in the century and half that it dominated the Indian subcontinent it managed to do significant social and economic damage. This included the destruction of the textile industry; turning India into a primary commodity exporter (e.g. cotton), causing huge famines through speculating on food prices – for example, 10 million people died in Bengal as a result of the 1772 famine caused by artificial food shortages (Robins 2006); and exporting opium to China. The EIC gained such a bad reputation that even people like Adam Smith criticized its monopoly privileges and the speculation of its employees and lack of remedy for these abuses. For example, one 1773 British Parliamentary Committee concluded:

> In the East, the laws of society, the laws of nature have been enormously violated. Oppression in every shape has ground the faces of the poor defenceless natives; and tyranny in her bloodless form has stalked abroad. (Quoted in Robins 2006)

Conclusion

In this chapter we sought to do a number of things. First, we presented the dominant and linear narrative of world history taught in the Global North about the spread of capitalism and civilization after the European 'discovery' of the world in the fifteenth century. Second, we presented theories of a world system to problematize the linear story of capitalism. We made sure to tell this story by citing thinkers who offer a critical understanding of colonization and the spread of capitalism. These theories of development show how the world economy is an integrated system in which the position of some countries at the core of capitalism has meant other countries are relegated to the periphery. This is not the natural or automatic outcome of capitalist forces and pressures like competition and innovation, but instead results from the violent domination of world markets, trade and production by European countries through conquest, slavery, colonialism and imperialism. We sought to present this dark side of capitalism so that there are no illusions about its impacts, and that the countries upholding capitalism used violence against human beings to do business. Third, we discussed this dark side as a necessary underpinning of world capitalism in that it drove the expansion and spread of capitalism, rather than simply being a by-product. Fourth, we illustrated our claims with the example of the British Empire and its leading role in the Atlantic slave trade and in the destruction of India's manufacturing capacity and its people through a famine. Overall, our aim has been to show how capitalism is not a natural force spreading around the world producing benefits wherever it goes, rather, it's driven by the decisions and goals of different peoples, countries, businesses and governments.

Suggested readings

- Ch. 1, Getachew, A. (2019) *Worldmaking after Empire*, Princeton, NJ, Princeton University Press.
- Slater, T. (2005) 'The Rise and Spread of Capitalism', in P. Daniels, M. Bradshaw, D. Shaw and J. Sidaway (eds), *Introduction to Human Geography* (2nd Edition), Essex, Pearson, pp. 36–61.
- Ch. 5, Rodney, W. (1982) *How Europe Underdeveloped Africa*, Washington, DC, Howard University Press.
- Ch. 1, Robinson, Cedric J. (1983/2000). *Black Marxism: The Making of the Black Radical Tradition.* London, Zed Press.
- *The Trans-Atlantic Slave Trade Database: Voyages. www.slavevoyages.org/* (accessed September 2022).
- *Legacies of British Slave-ownership project. www.ucl.ac.uk/lbs/* (accessed May 2016).

Note

1 Legacies of British Slave-ownership project: www.ucl.ac.uk/lbs/ (accessed May 2016).

Bibliography

Amin, S. (1977) *Imperialism and Unequal Development*, New York, Monthly Review Press.

Amin, S. (2013) *The Implosion of Capitalism*, New York, Monthly Review Press.

Apter, D. (1965) *The Politics of Modernization*, Chicago, University of Chicago Press.

Arrighi, G. (1994 [2010]) *The Long Twentieth Century*, London, Verso.

Black, C.V. de Brosse (1965) *Story of Jamaica: From Prehistory to the Present* (revised Edition), London, Collins.

Brewer, A. (1990) *Marxist Theories of Imperialism*, Florence, Routledge.

Brohman, J. (1995) 'Universalism, Eurocentrism, and Ideological Bias in Development Studies: From Modernisation to Neoliberalism', *Third World Quarterly*, Vol. 16, pp. 121–40.

Cardoso, F.H. (1977) 'The Consumption of Dependency Theory in the US', *Latin American Research Review*, Vol. 12, No. 3, pp. 7–24.

Chang, H.-J. (2008) *Bad Samaritans*, London, Bloomsbury.

Cox, O.C. (1959) *The Foundations of Capitalism*, New York, Philosophical Library Inc.

Cox, O.C. (1964) *Capitalism as a System*, New York, Monthly Review Press.

Dicken, P. (2011) *Global Shift* (6th Edition), New York, Guildford.

Eltis, D. and Richardson, D. (2010) *Atlas of the Transatlantic Slave Trade*, New Haven, Yale University Press.

Ferguson, N. (2011) *Civilization: The West and the Rest*, London, Penguin.

Frank, A.G. (1969) *Capitalism and Underdevelopment in Latin America. Historical Studies of Chile and Brazil*, New York, Monthly Review Press.

Frank, A.G. (1972) *Lumpenbourgeoisie: Lumpendevelopment: Dependence, Class, and Politics in Latin America*, New York, Monthly Review Press.

Friedman, T. (1999) *The Lexus and the Olive Tree*, New York, Farrar Straus Giroux.

Friedman, T. (2005) *The World Is Flat*, New York, Farrar Straus Giroux.

Frobel, F., Heinrichs, J. and Kreye, O. (1980) *The New International Division of Labour*, Cambridge, Cambridge University Press.

Getachew, A. (2019) *Worldmaking After Empire: The Rise and Fall of Self-Determination*, Princeton, Princeton University Press.

The Guardian. (2021) 'At the Stroke of Midnight, Barbados Becomes the World's Newest Republic', https://www.theguardian.com/world/2021/nov/30/at-the-stroke-of-midnight-barbados-becomes-the-worlds-newest-republic?CMP=Share_iOSApp_Other.

Hobsbawm, E. (1997) *The Age of Capital: 1848–1875*, London, Abacus.

Hunter, H.M. and Abraham, S.Y. (1987) 'IV: A World-Systems Perspective on Capitalism', in H. Hunter (ed.), *Race, Class, and the World System: The Sociology of Oliver C. Cox*, New York, Monthly Review Press, pp. 223–6.

Huntington, S. (1971) 'The Change to Change: Modernization, Development and Politics', *Comparative Politics*, Vol. 3, pp. 283–322.

Isbister, J. (2006) *Promises Not Kept: Poverty and the Betrayal of Third World Development* (7th Edition), West Hartford, Kumarian Press.

James, C.L.R. (1989) *The Black Jacobins: Toussaint L'Ouverture and the San Domingo Revolution* (2nd Edition revised), New York, Vintage.

Jenkins, D. and Leroy, J. (2021) *Histories of Racial Capitalism*, New York City, Columbia University Press.

Krugman, P. (1996) *Pop Internationalism*, Cambridge, MA, MIT Press.

Marx, K. (1867 [1976]) *Capital: Volume 1*, London, Penguin.

Micklethwait, J. and Wooldridge, A. (2005) *The Company*, New York, Modern Library Chronicles Book.

Olusoga, D. (2015) 'The History of British Slave Ownership has been Buried', *The Observer*, July 12, www.theguardian.com/world/2015/jul/12/british-history-slavery-buried-scale-revealed (accessed August 2015).

Ricardo, D. (1817 [2001]) *On the Principles of Political Economy and Taxation*, Kitchener, Batoche Books.

Robins, N. (2006) *The Corporation That Changed the World*, London, Pluto Press.

Robinson, C.J. (1983 [2000]) *Black Marxism: The Making of the Black Radical Tradition* (2nd Edition), London, Zed Press.

Rodney, W. (1982) *How Europe Underdeveloped Africa*, Washington, DC, Howard University Press.

Rostow, W.W. (1960 [1991]) *The Stages of Economic Growth: A Non-Communist Manifesto*, Cambridge, Cambridge University Press.

Scott, B. (2011) *Capitalism*, New York, Springer.

Slater, D. and Tonkiss, F. (2001) *Market Society*, Cambridge, Polity Press.

Slater, T. (2005) 'The Rise and Spread of Capitalism', in P. Daniels, M. Bradshaw, D. Shaw and J. Sidaway (eds), *Introduction to Human Geography* (2nd Edition), Essex, Pearson, pp. 36–61.

Thomas, C. (1988) *The Poor and the Powerless: Economic Policy and Change in the Caribbean*, New York, Monthly Review Press.

Thomas, C.Y. (1974) *Dependency and Transformation: The Economics of the Transition to Socialism*, New York, Monthly Review Press.

Wallerstein, I. (1979a) 'The Rise and Future Demise of the World Capitalist System', in I. Wallerstein (ed.), *The Capitalist World Economy*, Cambridge, Cambridge University Press, pp. 1–36.

Wallerstein, I. (ed.) (1979b) *The Capitalist World Economy*, Cambridge, Cambridge University Press.

Williams, E. (1944 [2004]) *Capitalism and Slavery*, Chapel Hill, University of North Carolina Press.

4 | Markets and economic order

Mark Peacock

Introduction

All societies have some sort of economic mechanism through which people acquire their means to survive; the market is one such mechanism. All of us today rely on the market to acquire our means of survival. Few of the goods and services which a typical individual person consumes are made by that individual. Although market exchange has existed for much of human history, dependence on the market as we know it is a relatively new phenomenon. In Chapter 2, we saw how dependence on the market was brought about through the transition from feudalism to capitalism in England. But what sort of mechanism is the market? When does it work reasonably well and produce something we might call *economic order*, and when does it descend into something nearer to chaos?

Many theories of the market speak of the market producing *order* or *equilibrium*. Another way of putting this is that markets are *self-correcting* or *self-regulating*: if things start to go wrong or become disordered, the market will automatically or spontaneously correct such errors itself. This self-corrective capacity of the market has an air of mystique about it and we investigate what is meant by it in this chapter. To understand the gist of the idea of self-correction, consider a ship at sea which has gone off course. The ship's course can be corrected, but the ship is not *self*-correcting; it is rather the captain who steers the ship back onto its true course. Those who believe the market to be self-correcting do not conceive the market as a ship, for the market has no captain who steers the market; the market somehow steers itself.

Whether and to which extent the market is self-correcting has policy implications. If markets generate order without external influence, this will have a bearing on our view about how much government intervention is required to correct for the market's failings. If the market generates order effectively and provides for people's needs quite well, the role of government in economic life might be minimal; if the market does not produce order, or does so imperfectly or slowly, the role of government might be considerable. Economic theories which one may call 'mainstream' and policymakers who are influenced by orthodox economics hold that markets are efficient and produce order in ways which require little government intervention in order to produce good outcomes for society (see Chapter 5). This view is not shared by all economists as we discuss in Chapter 6 on 'heterodox economics'. However, before we look at the market economy, let us examine an economic system which might be deemed its opposite, one that is, like the ship depicted earlier, steered by a captain. This type of economy is called a *centrally planned economy*.

Key economic system: Centrally planned economy

Many 'socialist' societies in the twentieth century, like the Union of Soviet Socialist Republics (USSR), were centrally planned economies. Economic activity in such societies is planned by the government. While there were some remarkable achievements of central planning, for example, the industrialization of the USSR within a couple of decades prior to the Second World War (far quicker than the more market-oriented industrialization of Western European), central planning has a poor record of meeting consumers' needs. Typical phenomena in such economies were shortages of desirable goods and the production of low-quality goods. The model of central planning is rarely supported as a viable economic model today, although some authors have recently argued that big data and artificial intelligence systems used to manage the operations of firms like Amazon and Walmart show that such a system might be efficient in ways not possible under earlier management systems.

Sources: Bleaney (1988); Dyker (1992); Phillips and Rozworski (2019)

Key discussion questions

- Why are centrally planned economies sometimes called 'command economies'?
- What is the criterion of success in business and how might it guide people to make intelligent decisions about their avenue of work?
- What does it mean to say the markets produce order *ex post* or *a posteriori*?
- In which respects does market competition resemble the playing of a game?
- Outline Marx's distinction between the division of labour in society and the manufacturing division of labour (the latter is referred to as the 'internal division of labour' below).
- What do our views on the market's ability to bring about economic order imply for our views on government policy?

Different economic orders

Centrally planned economies With the following thought experiment we can ask how one would centrally plan an economy. Imagine that a team of politicians – the Politburo – was charged with the task of 'running' the economy, rather like a CEO runs a corporation. How would they go about this? Presumably by following something like these steps:

- First, the politicians would ascertain what sort of goods the people require and in which quantities.

- Second, they would set up factories to produce these goods, hopefully using inputs that are efficiently supplied (e.g. raw materials, machines, workers), and they would instruct a certain number of workers to build cars, others to make clothes, grow food and so on.
- Once the goods had been produced, they would distribute these goods to people. Perhaps, as was the case in actually existing 'socialist' countries, workers would be paid money wages and they would decide which goods to buy.
- At the end of the year, the politicians might discover that too many of some goods and not enough of others had been produced. This would lead them to adjust production targets in the following year.

Put like this, the task of central planning seems straightforward. Yet the history of planned economies tells a different story. While everyone had a job in centrally planned economies, production was inefficient and incentives to be efficient were few (Dyker 1992). There was a chronic shortage of basic consumer goods, and centrally planned economies proved ineffective at meeting consumers' needs. Few people today support the type of planning which characterized countries like the USSR and today still characterizes aspects of China, Cuba and Vietnam.

One difference between a centrally planned economy and a market economy is that, in the former, the state usually owns the economic units of production – for example, factories, machines, raw materials and so on. There is no *private property* in the means of production in a centrally planned economy, something which reflects the socialist values of the countries which used central planning. A second difference between a market economy and a centrally planned one is that, in the latter, people are instructed what to do to a far greater degree. For this reason, centrally planned economies are sometimes called *command economies*: the government commands people to do certain things in accordance with its central plan (e.g. what to produce, how much, which production techniques to use, how much to pay the workers).

In a market economy, by contrast, people are free to decide what to do. If a group of people decides to form a business which manufactures USB sticks, it is not because the government instructs them to do so. In a market economy, people are free to decide what to produce or which career to pursue. If some people decide to produce USB sticks, they themselves determine the number of USB sticks they produce per year, at what price they are to be sold, how much to pay the workforce, from where the materials for making USB sticks are sourced and so on. But if people are free to decide what to do in a market economy, how can we be assured that the right number of USB sticks is produced and at what price? This brings us to the issue of the market's ability to 'self-correct'.

Markets, order and self-correction. In what follows, we concentrate on one market, namely the labour market, and we ask how order is produced in this market and how the labour market might be said to correct disorder. We start with what Karl Marx calls the *social division of labour* (Marx (1867 [1976]: 476). This term refers to the distribution of producers to different branches of production in society. Let us take a snapshot of the social division of labour in a country like Canada in the year 2021.

In 2021, about 20 million people had jobs in Canada. Of these, more than 1.8 million worked in manufacturing, nearly one million in natural resources, more than 1.5 million in construction and about one million in accommodation and food services (Statistics Canada 2023a).This is not a full breakdown of the Canadian social division of labour as there are many other branches of production. Moreover, the branches of production just mentioned can be further subdivided; for instance, the natural resources sector is divided into forestry, mining, fishing, oil, quarrying and gas. Our question is: How does this social division of labour come about in a market society?

Let us first say how this social division of labour does *not* come about. The distribution of people to jobs is not centrally planned. That is, the government does not tell so many thousands of people to become miners, others to become arable farmers, others still to become computer programmers and so on. Instead, individuals make up their own minds about which job they wish to pursue. Hence, the first step in the determination of the division of labour in a market society consists in the decisions of millions of people who use their freedom to decide which job to pursue. Marx (1867 [1976]: 476) wrote that this first step in the determination of the social division of labour follows 'the play of chance and caprice'. With this phrase, he tries to capture both the freedom people have to decide what to do and the uncoordinated or decentralized nature of the process of allocating people to jobs: people usually decide which job to look for independently of other people's decisions.

We all know, though, that getting a job as a carpenter or an architect is not simply about deciding to become a carpenter or an architect. Even people who are qualified to take on these jobs do not manage to find a job. Indeed, with an unemployment rate of about 7.5 per cent, over a million people in Canada were unable to find work in 2021 (Statistics Canada 2023a). This might lead us to think that the market is not working very well – at least not for those people without work. Let us consider an example.

Assume a person, let us call her Béatrice, wishes to set up a business as a watchmaker. Her decision to manufacture watches is the way she tries to become part of the social division of labour. Before commencing business, Béatrice will probably make a business plan which will contain answers to the following questions:

- How many watches should I produce per year?
- Should I aim at a particular market segment – for example, luxury, budget, women's watches and so on?
- How should I advertise my watches?
- From which suppliers should I acquire the component parts – for example, batteries, leather for the straps, steel for the watch faces and so on?
- At which price should I sell and how much profit do I aim to make?

There are many watchmakers in an economy, and, unlike in a centrally planned economy, the government in a market economy does not issue instructions which say: 'the country's watchmakers should produce 25,000 watches next year'. In a market economy, *nobody* plans or knows how many watches are to be produced in total; the number of watches produced results from the *decentralized* and uncoordinated decisions of many individuals who have decided to become watchmakers. But if every watchmaker decides how many watches to produce independently of other watchmakers, how can we be sure that the right quantity of watches is produced? How, in other words, from Marx's 'play of chance and caprice' can something like economic order emerge in the market?

Assume that Béatrice produces 1,000 watches in year 1 of her business. Is this the right amount, too many or too few? At the beginning of year 1, Béatrice expects to sell 1,000 watches to retailers, and this is the number she makes. At the end of the year, however, it transpires that she has only sold 200, and hence she has 800 unsold watches and a lot less profit than she had hoped. Something has obviously gone wrong, and Béatrice knows this because her expectations have been disappointed. Perhaps she underestimated how many people rely on their iPhone to tell the time and stopped buying wristwatches.

What should Béatrice do to ensure that year 2 might go better? There are many options:

- Béatrice might reduce the price of her watches so that more are bought; economists would say that, by reducing the price, more watches will be demanded, and so the supply of and demand for your watches will come into 'equilibrium' and, if Béatrice gets the price right, she will sell her entire stock. Lowering the price, however, will reduce her profit on each watch sold, and she might end up making a loss if she does not produce in a cost-efficient way.
- Alternatively, Béatrice could maintain the current price and embark on an advertising campaign, in the hope that more people will buy her watches.
- Instead, Béatrice might look at what her competitors are doing and copy their business strategy; have they found cheaper sources of components, for instance?

Béatrice could combine these strategies or try out others, but whatever she does, it will be a matter of *trial and error*. Béatrice has no guarantee that her change of business plan will lead to success, and, if it does not, she will, eventually, confront the ultimate option of admitting failure and closing down her business.

Let us assume that other watchmakers are in a similar position to Béatrice at the end of year 1, and the unsuccessful businesses (including Béatrice's) all close down. Next year, in year 2, there will be fewer watches on sale; the market, one might say, has 'corrected' the oversupply of watches in year 1. This would be an example of 'self-correction'. What that means is that a number of suppliers have withdrawn from the market because of their unfavourable experience in year 1. The total number of watches produced in year 2 shrinks. Once again, this correction was not instructed by the government but is the result of the independent decisions of many separate watchmakers. The story does not end there. Imagine that market conditions in year 2 are different from those in year 1. During year 2, consumers buy more watches than they did in year 1, perhaps because wristwatches have become more fashionable. In year 2, then, there will be greater demand for watches, and retailers will be looking for additional supplies of watches to sell to their customers. But the supply of watches has fallen in year 2 because Béatrice and other watchmakers shut down their businesses at the end of year 1. The increased demand for watches in year 2, together with the reduction in supply, means that watches have become scarcer, and this will increase their price. These higher prices in year 2 signal that watchmaking has become lucrative. Extant watchmakers will work overtime and produce more watches, and other producers will enter the market in the hope of making a profit.

Let us continue the story and assume that, following a period of unemployment after Béatrice closed her watchmaking business at the end of year 1, she re-enters the watchmaking business in year 3, having seen the watch business boom in year 2. In year 3 she gets lucky: she sells enough watches at high enough prices to make her desired level of profit. Something has gone right for Béatrice and she knows this because her expectation of sales, prices and profits have been met (possibly exceeded). The market, one might say, has corrected for the unexpected increase in demand in year 2 by indicating to producers, via price signals, that they should enter the watchmaking business. To Béatrice's disappointment, however, the spike in the demand for watches in year 3 is temporary; in year 4, people stop buying watches and watch manufacturers – including hers – cannot sell their stock at the profitable prices. Béatrice's business goes bankrupt again. This is another example of 'self-correction'; watches have become less scarce because there are too many watchmakers and not enough people to buy them in year 4. This leads some watchmakers to close their businesses. The story could go on and on, but we will take our leave of it here and pose and answer some questions about the scenario we have portrayed earlier.

Do markets create social order?

How does the social division of labour come about? We started with Marx's 'play of chance and caprice', that is, with the decentralized employment decisions of millions of people in an economy, including Béatrice's decision to become a watchmaker. Not all these decisions transpire to be practicable, and the social division of labour which results depends not only on Béatrice's decision to produce watches but on the decisions of other producers, who are in competition with Béatrice, and of consumers, who might but might not buy her watches. Once she has tried her hand at watchmaking, Béatrice will receive feedback from the market and this will guide her future decisions. If watchmakers' plans or expectations are not realized (e.g. if many do not make their desired level of profit), they will react by changing their business strategy. This might, but will not necessarily, move the market in a direction in which order is attained – fewer watchmakers making fewer watches. In our example, the exit of watch manufacturers from the market after their disappointment of year 1 is an instance of this. All this really means is that watchmakers react to the 'information' the market gives them, and if this information is not welcome (because their plans are disappointed), they will change their market behaviour. The social division of labour which exists at a given time is a product of the feedback which market competition provides to economic agents and their reactions to this feedback. What emerges is a pattern or order which reflects all these changes and movements in the market. The order which is thereby produced in the market is sometimes described as being created *ex post*; that is, *after* the process of competition has taken place.

How does anyone know whether becoming a watchmaker is a good idea, better than becoming a chef, a wine-taster or a manufacturer of USB sticks? A person like Béatrice might already possess watchmaking skills, and she might know things about the watch market that give her a certain competence in watchmaking. But despite all she knows about watchmaking, before she starts her business, she does not know whether it is a good decision to become a watchmaker. Even the most detailed and well-researched business plan will give you no guarantee that your business will succeed. The only way Béatrice can find out whether becoming a watchmaker is a good idea is to become one and to see if she is successful. Becoming a watchmaker and entering into market competition with other watchmakers is how she *discovers* whether becoming a watchmaker is a good idea. Some economists, like Friedrich Hayek (1976), talk of the market competition as a 'discovery procedure'; a person discovers whether it is a good idea to become a watchmaker by becoming one and seeing whether her expectations are fulfilled. Market competition is like a game which each player is trying to win. Before the game starts, nobody knows who will win, and only by playing the game does one find out who wins. And like a game, not only is the outcome of market competition unpredictable, but it is possible that someone with less skill, competence or knowledge than another player will win. The outcome of market competition, like the outcome of a game, is partly determined by luck.

Key thinker: Friedrich Hayek

Friedrich Hayek (1899–1992) was a highly influential proponent of the capitalist market economy. Although his support of the market is shared by mainstream economists, Hayek might be termed a 'heterodox economist' (see Chapter 6) because his theory of markets does not rest on the assumptions about rationality, knowledge or 'equilibrium' held by mainstream economists (see Chapter 5). In 1947, Hayek co-founded the Mont Pèlerin Society, a group of (neo)liberal intellectuals who aimed to solve the 'crisis' of civilization posed by increasing state power, the erosion of the rule of law and antipathy to the free market (Mirowski and Plehwe 2009). The ideas behind the Society were inspired by Hayek's popular classic, *The Road to Serfdom* (1944). Hayek was described as the 'guru' of former British prime minister Margaret Thatcher, and he is often described as a major inspiration for 'neoliberalism'.

Will there be enough watchmakers in your economy, too many or too few? Before people try their hand at watchmaking, nobody knows what the right number of watchmakers is. A sign that there are too many is that some of them will be unprofitable because they do not sell enough watches. One response to this market signal is that watchmakers will close down their businesses. But things are not quite so simple. If many watchmakers are unprofitable, it might not be because there are too many watchmakers in the market; rather it might be that they are making the wrong sort of watch. The best strategy for a watchmaker like Béatrice at the end of year 1 might not be to close down her business but to make a different type of watch, one which might be more attractive to consumers. What is the 'correct' strategy – close down, change the type of watch one produces or something else again? Nobody knows for sure, and the only way to find out whether a strategy is successful is to try it and see what happens. As we noted earlier, this is a process of trial and error.

What determines whether your watchmaking business is successful? Your business is successful if your hopes and expectations are realized (i.e. if you sell a certain number of watches and make the profits you hoped to make when you started your business). If these expectations are realized or surpassed, a watchmaker can, for the time being, say that it was a good idea to become a watchmaker. Before one starts one's business, though, there is no guarantee of success, as we noted when answering question two. Ultimately, whether a watchmaker's business is successful depends on whether the business is useful for other people. So the question each watchmaker must ask themselves is: 'Will I produce something of use for other people at prices which those people find acceptable?' The people to whom one has to be useful are consumers. As we saw earlier, there are many other factors beyond a watchmaker's control which also determine whether a given watchmaking business is successful. Consequently, the success of a business is partly a matter of luck, just as success in playing a game is partly a matter of luck (e.g. against whom is one playing, which cards is one dealt, how the die falls when it is rolled?) (Hayek 1976). For instance, Béatrice's business might fail because she launched it in 2008, on the eve of a world-wide recession, a time when people are unlikely to buy new wristwatches. This is analogous to people working in the accommodation and food services industry in 2019 on the eve of the Covid-19 pandemic. The employees working in that industry did nothing wrong, but their chance of becoming unemployed more than tripled within the course of one year (Statistics Canada 2023a). Similarly, the launch of Béatrice's business might coincide with the launch of a new line of well-marketed watches from a large international corporation, and Béatrice might be unable to compete against this corporation. Had she launched her business five years earlier, it might have succeeded, but market conditions have changed and Béatrice has the bad luck of starting her business at the wrong time. This is not her fault because she could not have predicted these market conditions, it was simply bad luck.

Does the market ever establish an order or reach an 'equilibrium' at which everything settles? Theoretically, it is imaginable that an equilibrium is reached at which every producer's and every consumer's expectations are realized such that nobody has an incentive to change her or his actions. In practice, though, market activity is too dynamic and subject to disturbances for this to happen. Entrepreneurs create new products, technicians and scientists invent new production techniques, consumers' tastes change, and shocks to the market, such as pandemics, terrorist attacks, financial crises and wars, are forever upsetting the market system (see Chapter 17). Nevertheless, if individuals who operate in the market react to the market signals they receive, there will be movement towards the creation of order and there is some chance that people's plans and expectations will come into line with those of other people to a certain extent. But simply because people's plans and expectations are realized this year does not mean that the same will happen next year, and so economic agents must constantly react to feedback in the form of market signals and change their plans accordingly, in the hope that they can maintain whatever success they have had hitherto.

The internal division of labour

We have examined earlier two types of economic order – that which is centrally planned and is associated with command economies, and that which is decentralized and is associated with the free market. As we saw in the context of a market economy, a social division of labour arises as a result of the decisions of many independent producers like Béatrice. Not everyone, though, is an independent producer, that is, an entrepreneur who owns their own business. In fact most people are not self-employed. In 2021, there were 2.65 million self-employed people in Canada (nearly two-thirds of whom were men and one-third women) (Statistics Canada 2023b). So the vast majority of people employed in Canada in 2021 were employed in businesses not owned by themselves. These people are workers or employees. This gives rise to a second element to the division of labour, which Marx (1867 [1976]) calls the manufacturing division of labour. The manufacturing division of labour refers to the way labour is divided within a single workplace or business, not within society as a whole. I will refer to this as the *internal division of labour*, to make clear that this refers to the way in which labour is divided *within* a single business. For example, if a person, let us call him Egil, works for a car manufacturer, he will be responsible for perhaps one task only; for example, fitting doors onto the car's body or testing the car's safety features (e.g. brakes, seatbelts or airbags). Or if we consider a bank, the internal division of labour consists of all the positions the bank has: branch managers, tellers, personnel staff, customer advisors and so on. The people who fill these positions all share a single employer, the bank. Once Egil is employed by a business, he and his fellow employees are what Marx calls 'part' or 'detail' workers (*Teilarbeiter*); each worker is responsible for perhaps a minute part of the corporation's activities, for example, mounting doors onto the body of cars, or advising customers of a bank about their retirement savings plans. Normally the manager of the business assigns tasks to individual workers in the workplace. As a car worker, Egil is not free to choose what to do; he must obey the commands of his boss, and refusal to do so could result in him being fired.

There are some important differences between the social division of labour and the internal division of labour:

- As an independent producer, like the watchmaker Béatrice, one produces a commodity – watches – which, when she has made them, belong to her; they are Béatrice's property and hence they are hers to sell if she wishes. As a detail worker in a car factory, Egil does not make a commodity of which he is the owner; what he makes does not belong to him – it belongs to those who own the factory, the capitalists.

- The social division of labour is regulated through the market *ex post* or *a posteriori*. That is, *after* individuals have made their decisions about which job to pursue, market competition determines how many producers survive in each branch of business. Nobody plans or determines in advance of market competition how many taxi drivers, watchmakers or computer programmers there should be in a society; it is only by observing the results of market competition that we know how many producers survive market competition in each branch of production. Within a business, by contrast, the division of labour is determined according to a plan. The business owners (also called capitalists), or a representative of the owners in the person of a manager, formulate the plan. The plan stipulates who works at which task within the business, how many workers are required in each activity and so on. The plan is conceived *ex ante* or *a priori*, that is, *in advance of production*. The manager's plan helps create the internal order of the business, for the manager not only creates the plan but has the authority to enforce it (recalling that refusal to obey the manager's commands can result in a worker being disciplined or fired). Adam Smith (1776: I.i.3) described the following internal division of labour in pin manufacturing:

> One man draws out the wire, another straightens it, a third cuts it, a fourth points it, a fifth grinds it at the top for receiving the head; to make the head requires two or three distinct operations; to put it on is a peculiar business, to whiten the pins is another; it is even a trade by itself to put them into the paper; and the important business of making a pin is, in this manner, divided into about eighteen distinct operations, which, in some manufactories, are all performed by distinct hands.

- The division of tasks within a factory is not chosen randomly and does not result from the 'play of chance and caprice'; rather it is worked out methodically and determined *a priori* by the manager whose will is backed up with the threat of discipline towards those workers who either disobey the manager or carry out their plan inadequately.
- Any worker who works for a business is therefore part of an internal division of labour, and is subject to the authority and commands of the owners of that business. Workers stand under the command of a boss and if they do not carry out their boss's instructions, they may lose their jobs. A business is a hierarchical order with sanctions for insubordination and not – as we saw in the discussion of Coase in Chapter 7 – a market where each input provider is making their own production decisions and deciding where and how to

allocate their efforts. Marx (1867 [1976]: 477) described the hierarchy of the business as a 'despotism', whereby the boss is the despot and the order within the business is imposed on workers. The economic order brought about in the social division of labour, by contrast, is characterized, Marx tells us, by 'anarchy', for, as we saw with Béatrice, our watchmaker, nobody dictates to people what jobs they are to pursue; watchmakers, like all other people in a market economy, are free to set up whatever business they like (within the bounds of the law). There are, of course, sanctions in the social division of labour, for market competition will tell a person whether their choice of occupation was good or bad. But these sanctions are not imposed by a boss, like they are within a business.

There are many debates about why the 'firm' is organized hierarchically according to a system of command and whether this is a fair form of organization (e.g. Ciepley 2013). Mainstream positions hold that hierarchically organized firms are efficient because they reduce the 'transactions costs' of production (see Chapters 7 and 8). Non-mainstream positions, by contrast, draw attention to the relations of authority within business entities and question whether it is legitimate that owners or managers have the power to command workers (Marglin 1974). These are not topics we pursue here, but ones which should be considered before one takes the relations of authority within a business as natural or given.

Types of economic order: From society to the business organization

We have considered the social division of labour and the internal division of labour. The latter, we observed earlier, is hierarchical; there is a chain of command from the business owners who, in many, particularly large, public corporations, employ managers. Managers are responsible for running the business or corporation for the purposes of furthering the interests of its owners, which usually means making as much profit for them as possible. To this end, managers issue commands to employees whose tasks are likewise organized with the aim of making profits for the owners.

One may ask whether the order created by the internal division of labour is fair. That is, what justifies the power of capitalists (or managers) to issue commands to workers? One answer might be that workers are never forced to work for a particular business; a worker, like everyone else in a market economy, is a free individual over whom a business has no authority unless the worker decides freely to work for it. Nobody can be compelled to work for Amazon, Walmart or Microsoft against their will; workers who work for these or other businesses freely choose to do so. If people decide to work for Walmart, their work contract will place them under the command of a manager, but if the workers do not find the terms and conditions of the job acceptable, they can look for employment elsewhere. But recall what we said in Chapter 2 about workers and the freedom they enjoy. Workers are propertyless in that they do not own the means of production and, to become productive in any way, they rely on a capitalist to give them work. Without work, the worker has few options for survival, and so one might say that, despite their freedom to turn their backs on a given employer like Walmart, workers, in truth, are compelled to work as employees and thus to submit to the dictates of some business or other. If they do not work for a business, workers might starve. Hence the circumstances in which workers find themselves do not give them effective freedom to avoid the hierarchy of command in a business, even if the worker finds the conditions of their workplace harmful, degrading or dangerous. All workers are free to set up their own businesses, as Béatrice did, but, as we saw when discussing the social division of labour, there is no guarantee of success, and, if one's business fails, one might have few or no options other than submitting oneself to the dictates of a business owner and thus becoming a worker.

Adam Smith was one of the keenest critics of the effects of the internal division of labour. He noted that by being assigned 'to a few very simple operations' in the workplace, the worker 'becomes as stupid and ignorant as it is possible for a human creature to become' (Smith 1776: V.i.f.50). The division of labour, Smith argued, can lead to the moral and intellectual deformity of workers, and this could have grave consequences for the society in which we live. Today, still, people undertake jobs in which the tasks allow for little exercise of creativity and allow for no personal fulfilment. What effect does this have on such people and what is the role of people who consume the products they make and thus play an essential role in the perpetuation of harmful working conditions? There is good reason for consumers to be informed about more than the price and nature of the goods they buy; an essential part of what we buy includes the conditions under which goods are made. If we wish to be ethical consumers, we must pay attention to the conditions under which goods are produced and to the effects of consuming them (e.g. the effects on the environment and on the workers who produce the goods).

Case Study

Gig Economy Work: Liberation through the Market?

The growth of gig economy in recent years means that more workers are considered to be 'independent contractors' operating their own businesses, rather than direct employees. This is because the platform business – like Uber Eats – argues that it does not 'employ' the worker but merely helps them find customers who need their services. In

---

the past most couriers worked for a company specializing in delivery services or directly for a restaurant or retailer as part of their delivery staff. Today, however, online delivery platforms like Uber Eats, Deliveroo or Instacart have designated more workers as 'independent contractors' in fields where work might have previously been performed by employees with a long-term position within the internal division of labour of the business. Increasingly the work of graphic designers, cleaners, repair specialists or translators can be coordinated through digital platform technologies which have lowered the transaction costs for searching and contracting for individual tasks from workers who are not employees of the business (Oranburg and Palagashvili 2021).

While technologies allow increasing numbers of workers to make a living providing individually priced services on a short-term, 'on-demand' basis, it is not clear that this means the market has liberated these workers from the dictates of business firms. It is true that these workers are operators and owners of their own business much like Béatrice in our foregoing discussion. It is also true that research shows that at least some gig workers—especially in more professional fields – see a benefit in the flexibility provided by these opportunities to work outside of the traditional employment relationship (Dua et al. 2022). However, gig work platforms like Uber Eats in many ways still direct their work and determine the price that the workers can charge customers, *even though the workers are not employees of the platform as such.* Since these platforms do not have to treat their workers as employees, they therefore typically do not have to provide supplies, equipment, training, benefits, sick pay, or vacation time (see Chapter 23). In recent years there have been advances in gig workers' rights in some jurisdictions, notably in Ontario Canada where Foodora delivery workers were deemed 'dependent contractors' to reflect the dependence on the app and policies set by the company as they carry out their work (Hastie 2021; Gebert 2021). Despite these important legal gains, the contradictions of the online gig economy show that many of its workers remain subordinate to businesses that control their work even as they formally operate as independent agents in the market.

Conclusion

We have looked at different types of economic order and how they are created. We have seen that the self-correcting features of markets really means little more than that individuals in the market react to the signals they receive and ask themselves: Can I do anything to improve my economic situation such that the hopes I have of earning a living can be realized better than they are being realized at present? Only if what one does on the market proves to be useful to other people will one have any success either in getting a job or in running a business. We have also seen that order does not imply a movement to a stationary point from which nothing will change; rather, order is constantly in the making if individuals in the market react to market signals accordingly, but order is constantly disturbed and individuals in the market will constantly have to change their plans and seek new opportunities for making money.

There are many questions raised in discussions of economic order and these have implications for government policy and regulation. Consider again Béatrice, who at the end of the first year of business went bankrupt and became unemployed. Should the government support her financially while she is unemployed? Or is it the best thing not to support her so that she sets about finding new employment as quickly as possible? Those who have faith in the market's ability to correct for disorder might say that unemployed people should adjust their expectations about which jobs they can get and at which rates of pay. Proponents of the market might say that if Béatrice finds herself without work, she is free to seek work in catering, cleaning, prostitution or another low-wage sector. If her watchmaking business closed, that might have been bad luck, but does she deserve state support while she is unemployed? Others would say that, precisely because Béatrice's lack of success as a watchmaker was bad luck, it would be harsh, perhaps inhumane, not to have a safety net which supports people like her while they are unemployed.

Suggested readings

- Ch. 10, Hayek, F.A. (1976) *Law, Legislation and Liberty*, volume 2, London, Routledge and Kegan Paul.
- Ch. 1, Heilbroner, R. and Milberg, W. (2002) *The Making of Economic Society* (11th Edition), New York, Prentice Hall.
- Ch. 4, Section 4, Marx, K. (1867 [1976]) *Capital: Volume 1*, London, Penguin.

Bibliography

Bleaney, M. (1988) *Do Socialist Economies Work?* Oxford, Blackwell.

Ciepley, D. (2013) 'Beyond Public and Private: Toward a Political Theory of the Corporation', *American Political Science Review*, Vol. 107, pp. 139–58.

Dua, A., Elingrud, K., Hancock, B., Luby, R., Madgavkar, A. and Penberton, S. (2022) *Freelance, Side Hustles, and Gigs: Many More Americans have Become Independent Workers* (Issue August), https://www.mckinsey.com/featured-insights/sustainable-inclusive-growth/future-of-america/freelance-side-hustles-and-gigs-many-more-americans-have-become-independent-workers.

Dyker, D.A. (1992) *Restructuring the Soviet Economy*, London, Routledge.

Gebert, R. (2021) 'The Pitfalls and Promises of Successfully Organizing Foodora Couriers in Toronto', in J. Drahokoupil and K. Vandaele (eds.), *A Modern Guide To Labour and the Platform Economy*, Cheltenham: Elgar, pp. 247—289.

Hastie, B. (2021) 'Platform Work and Labour Law Challenges: A Comment on *CUPW v. Foodora*', *Canadian Labour and Employment Law Journal*, Vol. 23, pp. 121—140.

Hayek, F.A. (1944) *The Road to Serfdom*, Chicago, Chicago University Press.

Hayek, F.A. (1976) *Law, Legislation and Liberty*, Volume 2, London, Routledge and Kegan Paul.

Heilbroner, R. and Milberg, W. (2002) *The Making of Economic Society* (11th Edition), New York, Prentice Hall.

Marglin, S. (1974) 'What do Bosses do? The Origins and Function of Hierarchy in Capitalist Production', *Review of Radical Political Economics*, Vol. 6, pp. 60–112.

Marx, K. (1867 [1976]) *Capital: Volume 1*, London, Penguin.

Mirowski, P. and Plehwe, D. (eds.) (2009) *The Road from Mont Pèlerin: The Making of the Neoliberal Thought Collective*, Cambridge, MA, Harvard University Press.

Oranburg, S. and Palagashvili, L. (2021) 'Transaction Cost Economics, Labor Law, and the Gig Economy', *Journal of Legal Studies*, Vol. 50, No. S2, pp. S219–37.

Phillips, L. and Rozworski, M. (2019) *The People's Republic of Walmart: How the World's Biggest Corporations are Laying the Foundation for Socialism*, London, Verso.

Polanyi, K. (1944 [2001]) *The Great Transformation*, Boston, Beacon Press.

Smith, A. (1776 [1976]) *An Inquiry into the Nature and Causes of the Wealth of Nations*, Oxford, Oxford University Press.

Statistics Canada (2023a) 'Labour Force Characteristics by Industry', https://www150.statcan.gc.ca/t1/tbl1/en/tv.action?pid=1410002301 (accessed March 6, 2023).

Statistics Canada (2023b) 'Employment by Class of Worker', https://www150.statcan.gc.ca/t1/tbl1/en/tv.action?pid=1410002701 (accessed March 6, 2023).

5 | Economics, capitalism and business

The orthodoxy

Sonya Marie Scott and Mark Peacock

Introduction

In the previous chapter, we looked at markets and economic order, but the 'theory' of market order was kept deliberately in the background. In this chapter, we examine an economic doctrine which dominates university curricula the world over and which was developed to understand markets. This mainstream doctrine goes under the name 'neoclassical' or 'orthodox' economics.

This doctrine is increasingly challenged by economists, as is evident in student-led movements such as Rethinking Economics and the International Initiative for Pluralism in Economics. It is nevertheless the dominant mode of thinking among economists and policymakers around the world. What we consider later are only some aspects of this orthodoxy, most of which concern *microeconomics*. Microeconomics deals with individuals, their behaviour, decisions and motivation. It is based on a number of assumptions concerning human beings and deduces from these assumptions various theories about markets and the economy. We do not deal with *macroeconomics*, which concerns aggregate phenomena such as unemployment, economic growth and inflation.

In this chapter, we explore the origins of mainstream economics, and we consider whether it provides an accurate depiction of the way human beings act and make decisions. It is important to consider such matters because of the dominant position the orthodoxy holds in university curricula and in public policy. After examining mainstream economics in this chapter, the next chapter focuses on economists who dissent from the mainstream.

> **Key discussion questions**
>
> - What is mainstream economics?
> - What are the differences between Smith's notion of self-love and Bentham's principle of utility?
> - What are the characteristics of *homo economicus*?
> - What does the term 'Pareto improvement' mean and how is it supposed to provide a normative foundation for market exchange?
> - Why do economists use the term 'preference' to describe the underlying process of choice?
> - What are interpersonal comparisons of utility and why might it be difficult to make them?

The mainstream perspective

When we talk about mainstream economics we are referring to the dominant form of economic reasoning today. It involves a set of ideas, methods and conceptions of human nature that guide economists. These ideas constitute an *orthodoxy*, or core set of principles, which form the basis of mainstream economics. If you were to take an *ECON 101* course at the vast majority of universities in the world, you would be taught mainstream economics and nothing else.

Most historians of economic thought trace one principle of mainstream economics to the work of Adam Smith (1723–90), who was a major figure in the Scottish Enlightenment. Smith is an important political economist because he developed his ideas at the time when modern industrial capitalism was coming into existence in Britain. In 1776 he published *Nature and Causes of the Wealth of Nations*, which described the emerging capitalist economic order. Smith was concerned with understanding people's economic lives. Just as the structure of the economy was changing with the development of capitalism, so too was the way in which people lived and organized their lives. The shift from feudalism to capitalism – described in Chapter 2 – meant a whole new way of thinking. Instead of living rurally and engaging in agricultural labour, people moved in great number into towns and cities and organized their lives around jobs in factories. Within this emerging economic order, Smith grouped people into three classes – landlords, capitalists and workers. Each group, he explained, had a particular way of surviving: landlords lived by charging rent on land, capitalists by making profit and workers by earning wages from capitalists.

We might step back from history for a moment and ask how we would define ourselves as economic beings. Are you a scrupulous saver? A big spender? A workaholic? A philanthropist who donates to good causes? An investor with financial savvy and a keen sense of the market? For us the answers depend on our individual identity. For Smith, by contrast, the answers depend on the bigger question of 'human nature', itself a highly contentious notion.

Smith explained that capitalism depends upon a collection of people working in cooperation with one another, even if we are not aware of it, or not closely related with the majority of the people making the goods and services we buy. According to Smith, one distinguishing feature of contemporary civilization – and by this Smith meant Europe of the late eighteenth century – is the interdependence of human beings through the *division of labour*. More and more people in society come to rely on one another because no one person can produce all they need on their own. What had previously been a *subsistence* economy became an economy of mutual dependence. In this context, money became more and more necessary, so that individuals could buy those things they did not produce themselves.

We might think that this emerging society would be based upon a collective spirit of cooperation and goodwill because of this vast mutual dependence. Smith, by contrast, believed that capitalist society does not and does not need to depend upon goodwill. Rather it is our *self-interest*, or each person's desire to look after themselves first, that motivates us and is fundamental to our human nature. In a famous passage Smith wrote:

> It is not from the benevolence of the butcher, the brewer or the baker, that we expect our dinner, but from their regard to their own interest. We address ourselves, not to their humanity but to their self-love, and we never talk to them of our own necessities but of their advantages. (1776 [2000]: I.ii.2)

This statement seems to make a lot of sense. With it, Smith suggested that people respond to incentives; they are motivated by self-interest (or 'self-love' as Smith called it), rather than by selflessness; they are most likely to cooperate when it is to each person's advantage to do so.

At about the time that Smith was writing about the nature of capitalism, the British philosopher Jeremy Bentham (1748–1832) developed an ethical theory called *utilitarianism* based on the idea that human beings are driven by the pursuit of pleasure and the avoidance of pain (see Chapter 19). Bentham (1780 [2011]: 111–12) famously proclaimed:

> Nature has placed mankind under the governance of two sovereign masters, *pain* and *pleasure*. . . . They govern us in all we do, in all we say, in all we think: every effort we can make to throw off our subjection, will serve but to demonstrate and confirm it.

On the surface this looks like Smith's claim that human beings are motivated by self-interest. However, Bentham was making an entirely different point. He did not believe that we are selfish pleasure-seekers motivated by self-interest; instead he understood our motivations as a part of a broader social and moral theory. Indeed, as seekers of pleasure and avoiders of pain, each person should not act in his or her own interest alone; rather morality dictates that each of us act in the best interest of the *common good* – to seek the greatest good for the greatest number in society. This quest to seek the greatest good for the greatest number is called the *principle of utility* and it underpins utilitarianism (see Chapter 19). The principle of utility is not a description of self-interest but is rather a form of universal selflessness. For example, it may be important to sacrifice our immediate pleasure by giving up some of our income and paying taxes. As an individual we are contributing to the greatest good for the greatest number by allowing government to invest in public services like health care and education. If this sacrifice leads to an increase in happiness in society,

Bentham would support it; that paying taxes is to an individual's personal disadvantage is not a good reason for tax evasion.

So while Smith believed that self-interested individualistic behaviour was part of human nature and leads to social cooperation and interdependence, Bentham believed that conscious and calculated sacrifice of individual self-interest for the greater good was morally required. For example, Bentham argued that:

> an action may be said to be conformable to the principle of utility (meaning with respect to the community at large) when the tendency it has to augment the happiness of the community is greater than any it has to diminish it. (1780 [2011]: 113)

The same applies to the actions of government, and to the rule of law, which ought, as a matter of principle, to promote the greatest good for the greatest number. This idea is important in economic terms because it gives us a way to begin to measure the relationship between individual action and the welfare of the whole, as well as the role of the government in the economic affairs of the state.

Homo economicus. Smith's idea of self-interest, is a central principle of mainstream economics. It defines what economists call *homo economicus* or 'rational economic man'. *Homo economicus* is the economist's characterization of a human being as:

- a free individual (assumed to be a man) who
- pursues 'his' own self-interest,
- knows what 'his' self-interest is, and
- can measure 'his' own self-interest in economic terms (e.g. in terms of price or cost) and act accordingly.

Whether we think these traits of *homo economicus* are plausible or not, even some mainstream economists believe that it is not always possible to behave like a *homo economicus*. For instance, we do not always have sufficient information to determine what is in our self-interest (Hill and Myatt 2010). When we make decisions about purchases it can be hard to know if a product is defective, if a house has hidden problems, or if the new model of a phone or laptop is actually worth the money. Another problem comes in the form of uncertainty about the future. Many people believe that it is in our self-interest to make financial investments, but knowing how to invest can be tricky given all the ups and downs of stock markets, house prices, and so on. An investment that might appear to be in your interest at the time you make it can actually result in a loss of savings, perhaps bankruptcy, as was the case for many in the financial crisis of 2008. Hence, real human beings are not always able to act like a *homo economicus*.

Key critique: Going beyond 'rational economic man'

Many feminist scholars hold that mainstream economics is biased towards men (see Chapter 6). They argue that the use of 'man' in the expression 'rational economic man' was intended specifically to refer to men, who were, at the time it was developed in Europe, considered to be the more rational, intelligent and moral gender. While economics and philosophy have come a long way since the eighteenth and nineteenth centuries, and while women have gained many formal equalities in contemporary Western society, it is crucial to note the way in which this originally gendered conception continues to hold sway today. Attributes traditionally associated with men are still perceived to be the 'natural' and 'superior' characteristics of economic life – such as competitiveness, rationality and power. These assumptions play out both in economic writing and in the work world, where women face many systemic challenges, including a systemic under-valuing of women's work (e.g. low pay for work associated with women, such as caring, nurturing and emotional support) and a relative absence from positions of power in the business world and in the economics profession.

Source: Ferber and Nelson (1993); Folbre (2009).

In order to understand mainstream economics better, we can ask questions like: How are we to understand this *homo economicus*? Does 'he' correspond to our true nature or is 'he' an absurd caricature of real human beings? Does 'he' represent the way we ought to behave as rational economic individuals, even if we fall short of 'his' standards in our less well-thought-through decisions? We suggest that *homo economicus* is not 'the truth' about what human nature really is, but is a device necessary for making economics into a 'science'. This assumption was popular in the late nineteenth century, when many thinkers began to render what was once called *political economy* into the modern 'science' of *economics*. This change was accomplished primarily through the use of mathematical models and reasoning. For example, assuming that most human beings are rational economic beings who possess the attributes of *homo economicus* makes it easier to fit them into mathematical models. This is why economics textbooks seem more like the study of mathematics than anything else; most mainstream economists assume that human beings think of their advantage and self-interest in terms of quantity and price, and since price can be measured, we can then start to think about economics in mathematical terms.

These mathematical models are based on *homo economicus* and the economic decisions 'he' makes about buying and selling. In other words, the 'people' who inhabit the mathematical models of economics are primarily consumers who wish to maximize their own utility. One of the most fundamental concepts of economics is *marginal utility*. This idea, developed in the 1870s and associated with the Marginalist Revolution in economics, helps to explain how individuals make decisions about what to buy or sell at different prices. Although Smith established many orthodox assumptions about human nature, he can be classified as a classical political economist. The Marginalist Revolution, on the other hand, was a paradigm shift that defined the study of the economy as a science. In other words, while classical political economists were focused on the process of production and sources of wealth in a given country, marginalists were asking questions from the point of view of a consumer engaged in exchange relations.

Definition: Political economy and economics

Before the development of the modern discipline of economics, *political economy* was the common term for the study of economic phenomena. The term included 'political' because economic life was understood as part of a broader social and political reality. Today many scholars continue to do political economy, but they are not generally considered to be part of mainstream economics, and they often reject orthodox principles and focus instead on the role of power, class relations and institutions. *Economics*, on the other hand, is the study of market relations without the same concern for social and political power structures. Its development as a separate science in the late 1800s depended upon the use of mathematical models. The primary questions asked by economics as a science have to do with price, utility, market stability and supply and demand.

Source: Phillips (2003)

In order to illustrate what marginal utility means, it is helpful to consider an example. Imagine that a young athlete has injured her leg in training and cannot walk without a leg brace. A leg brace would be very valuable to her, and she might be willing to pay as much as $100 for it. But, if she were to be presented with a second leg brace, it would not be worth nearly as much, as a person can only use one brace at a time, and her problem would have already been solved. At $100 the athlete might not be willing to buy a second, but perhaps if there were a sale (buy one get the second 75 per cent off) she would consider buying the brace for $25 so that she had a back-up. Now consider the purchase of a third brace. What price would the athlete be willing to pay – $15? $10? Or perhaps she would be unwilling to buy a third brace at all. When we reason in this way we are reasoning at the margin, determining the subsequent value of each good as it satisfies our utility. This perspective can apply to any type of good or service. What is the next T-shirt worth? The next cup of coffee? The next loaf of bread? The next computer? This idea has become another key principle in mainstream economics as a way of assessing consumer demand and evaluating the appropriate level of prices.

We saw earlier that Bentham thought the principle of utility was a moral imperative which, through universal selflessness, aimed to achieve the greatest good or greatest *utility* for the greatest number. The assumptions which underpin mainstream economics, by contrast, are based on a different idea of utility; in mainstream economics, *utility* represents not the good of all people in society but the good of the individual whose decision is under examination. Utility can be understood as a synonym for preference and satisfaction. Hence, each economic agent or *homo economicus* asks not how 'he' should act to maximize utility in society at large but how 'he' should act so as to maximize 'his' own utility. Utility maximization, in mainstream economics, is a *behavioural postulate*. According to this postulate, people are self-interested and they pursue their self-interest in a calculating and rational way.

Case Study

Economics in Medieval Islam

Although most historians who study the development of orthodox ideas begin with classical thinkers such as Adam Smith, there have been important economic ideas which influenced orthodox economics dating back to Ancient Greece. In fact, once we move away from a Eurocentric conception of the history of economic thought, we can see that there are important economic ideas from almost every part of the world. Recently scholars have begun to examine the rich history of medieval Islamic thought, which contains many ideas and theories relevant to the contemporary mainstream. Historian Simon Yarrow has speculated that 'the conventional attribution of the discovery of natural economic laws to Smith would have galled medieval Arab-Islamic scholars such as al-Ghazali, Ibn Taimiyah and Ibn Khaldun, whose acute understanding of market forces matched his, even though they were articulated in different scriptural and moral frameworks' (2018, 217).

An early example of this medieval Islamic work comes in the form of texts called *mirrors for princes*, which served as guidebooks for those wielding both wealth and power. A good example is the *Qabus Nameh*, written by Persian prince Kay Kavus (1021–87) as a course on leadership and economic management for his son. In his work we find the concept of *utility*, a discussion of the value of commercial contracts, and commentary on economies of scale. Al-Ghazali (1058–1111) – a famed Persian theologian whose writings deal with a great deal of philosophical, religious, political and economic issues – wrote about economics and ethics, focusing on the human tendency towards greed and the acquisition of wealth, and the social mechanisms needed to temper such instincts. Dimishqui (1256–1327) – a merchant from Damascus (Syria) – wrote of the value of profit-seeking activity, and argued that the 'golden mean,' served as an equilibrium price, that is, a price that rendered profit to merchants without harming members of the community at large. There are many more examples in this tradition that is finally gaining recognition in the history of economic thought.

Sources: Hosseini 2003; Ghanzanfar 2014; Yarrow 2018; Wickham 2021.

The normative foundation of market exchange. In the previous chapter, we outlined how some thinkers believe that markets generate order. Here we pose a different question: What is so good about market exchange if we, for the sake of argument, take *homo economicus* as the starting point of our analysis? This is a *normative* question, that is, one which does not pertain to matters of fact but to what is good and what is bad (see Chapter 19). The answer to the question has far-reaching implications:

- Should we promote or restrict market exchange?
- If people are rational in the way described earlier, should we let them use their freedom unhindered to make whatever market transactions they wish?
- Should government ever intervene to restrict people from entering into certain market exchanges? If so, when?

First, though, let us analyse a simple market exchange. Consider two individuals, Ali, who wishes to sell his Chevrolet Sedan made in 1930, and Benedetta, who is a collector of classic cars. Ali and Benedetta will effect this transaction if they can agree on a mutually agreeable price. Let us say this price is US$15,000. Benedetta purchases the car in the belief that doing so will make her better off; she has a *preference* to have the car rather than keep the money. Similarly, Ali has a preference to relinquish the car and take the money because, by doing so, he expects to increase his utility. Ali and Benedetta *rationally* pursue their self-interest in this exchange; each, we may assume, wants to further their own self-interest, knows what is in their interest, and acts upon this knowledge through a calculation of the costs and benefits involved (each calculating what the value of possessing the car and what the value of having the money will be). As long as both parties are rational in this sense, we have good grounds for allowing them the freedom to decide for themselves what they wish to buy and sell in market exchange. There are, of course, exceptions to this such as when we believe that certain market transactions will harm the people making them. This is why the sale of narcotics is often illegal and also why we do not allow children to buy alcohol. But if it seems reasonable to assume that people know enough about themselves to buy and sell things such that their utility increases, we have little reason to intervene in their market affairs.

This illustrates a central normative principle of mainstream economics; what makes market exchange a good thing is precisely that neither Ali nor Benedetta is likely to be worse off as a result of Benedetta buying the Chevrolet from Ali for US$15,000. In fact, there is reason to believe that both are made better off; for example, if Benedetta thought the price were too high, she would have a preference for keeping the money and not buying the car. In the language of economic theory, the transaction leads to a *Pareto improvement*; that is, nobody is made worse off by the transaction and at least one person is made better off (Varian 2007). If we assume that this holds for each of the billions of market transactions made every day in the global economy, we can conclude that the billions of people who make these transactions are becoming better off every day through market exchange. And if every possible market transaction which led to a Pareto improvement were allowed to take place, we would reach a situation of *Pareto efficiency*, whereby there would be no way of increasing one person's utility through market exchange without reducing the utility of another person (Dixit 2014).

The market transactions which lead to a Pareto improvement include not only those we make as consumers (e.g. when we buy cars, electronic gadgets or cups of coffee); they include also the choices we make as producers, or as businesspeople and workers. Consider someone deciding to take a summer job at Walmart. If they are rational, they will calculate the advantages to themselves of earning the minimum wage for a certain number of hours a week; if they expect thereby to further their self-interest more than they would by, say, working on their BA honours thesis, then they should take the job – it increases their utility. Similarly for their employer. If Walmart's managers believe that Walmart will be better off (i.e. more profitable) by employing the prospective employee, they will offer them a contract. Once again, if each party is able to choose freely to enter into this contractual relationship, both parties improve their situation and nobody becomes worse off as a result.

Economists use the Pareto principle not only to judge market exchanges but also to judge public policy proposals. If a proposal is expected to make at least one person better off while making nobody worse off, it will be approved because it will bring about a Pareto improvement.

Individuals and preferences. In the previous section, we used the term 'preference' when discussing how people make choices. Consider, once again, Ali, who has two mutually exclusive options: x (acquiring \$15,000) and y (keeping his Chevrolet Sedan). If he thinks his utility will increase by acquiring the money, he *prefers* option (x) over option (y). One might think that saying 'Ali prefers option x to option y' is equivalent to saying 'Person A expects their utility will be higher if they choose x rather than y'. Even though the two formulations are similar, mainstream economists are more comfortable with the terminology of 'preference'. Here, it is necessary to discuss three characteristics of the notion of utility, as it is used by mainstream economists.

First, utility is subjective, a feeling of happiness which one derives from doing something pleasurable. This is not the sort of variable which can serve as a basis for a science of choice, as mainstream economists purport their discipline to be. We need something more objective, more easily observable for such a science. Preference, by contrast, is considered more objective because it is observable; we manifest our preferences in the observable choices we make, and this forms a better basis for what mainstream economists expect from their discipline, namely, that it be an empirical science. Second, talk of utility suggests that we derive an 'amount' of something which makes us happy when we pursue a pleasurable activity. Thinking of utility as a quantity of pleasure might lead to statements like: 'I get twice as much utility from x than I do from y'. Such judgements are of dubious exactitude (see Sandel 2009). It would be difficult, for example, to make utility comparisons between the following:

- a foot massage;
- a morning cup of coffee;
- watching a baseball game on TV;
- watching a baseball game live;
- reading a novel by Dostoevsky;
- learning a foreign language.

Can we state that a morning cup of coffee gives a person twice as much utility as a foot massage? And is the foot massage 2.7 times more pleasurable than watching a live baseball game? Answering these questions might be difficult, if not impossible. Luckily, mainstream economics does not assume that people can answer them; it suffices that people are able to say that they prefer x to y without any quantitative comparison beyond that.

Consider a trickier question which brings us to a third problem with the notion of 'utility'. Can a person ascertain whether the utility which Peter derives from drinking a glass of champagne is greater or less than the utility Petra derives from drinking it, or greater or less than the utility Joseph derives from going for an evening stroll? The difficulty involved here concerns making *interpersonal comparisons of utility*. Economists hold that such comparative judgements lack an objective basis, and some hold such judgements to be unscientific or even meaningless. How do we know how much utility Peter gets from the champagne and can we compare it to Petra's utility from drinking it? Mainstream economics does not actually rely on such comparisons, and economists have even declared that such comparisons are meaningless (Arrow 1963).

The terminology of preference allows us to move from some simple assumptions about human beings to the analysis one finds in *ECON 101* courses (e.g. indifference curve analysis and demand curves). The two main assumptions made about people's preferences are:

- *Completeness*: for any two options, x and y, a given consumer can rank x and y such that either x is preferred to y, y is preferred to x, or the two are equally preferred.

- *Transitivity*: if, for a given consumer, option x is preferred to option y, and option y is preferred to option z, then (by transitivity) option x is preferred to option z.

From the assumptions of complete and transitive preferences, the world of microeconomic analysis opens itself and *homo economicus* unfolds in all its glory. That, though, is something to explore in the pages of elementary microeconomics textbooks.

Critical perspectives

We have stated already that mainstream economics, however dominant it might be as a doctrine, is not without rivals and detractors. We present some of these 'heterodox' approaches to economics in the following chapter. In the remainder of this chapter, however, we focus on some limitations of mainstream economics.

Selfishness. 'Self-love', as Smith called it, has been a lasting legacy in economics, and although Smith's other great book, *The Theory of Moral Sentiments* (1759 [1976]), shows that he did not believe that individuals were motivated by self-interest alone, mainstream economists have been remarkably resistant to relinquish the assumption that people are, by nature, self-interested. But is everything we do motivated by self-interest? Many of our choices might be, but what about when one volunteers for a local community project or helps a friend move house? These do not seem to be self-interested acts. Helping others, however, does not contradict *homo economicus* as long as one's motive is to further one's own self-interest. Mainstream economists have become quite creative in explaining apparently 'selfless' acts in terms of *homo economicus* (see Becker 1974).

A particularly eloquent formulation of such explanations came long before mainstream economics came into existence. The English philosopher Thomas Hobbes (1588–1679), was once asked why he gave money to a beggar in London. Hobbes replied: 'I was in pain to consider the miserable condition of the old man; and now my alms, giving him some relief, doth also ease me' (Aubrey 1975: 166). Hobbes explained his act of charity in self-interested terms. Although the money Hobbes donated improved the situation of the old man, this was not Hobbes's motive; Hobbes gave the money so that he himself would feel 'eased'. As such, it was for the sake of increasing his own utility that Hobbes gave the money. Mainstream economists sometimes speak of the 'warm glow' effect one receives from acting in a way which increases the utility of others. So, one answer to the question of why we help our friends move house is that we derive a good feeling ('warm glow') from doing so; without this, the economist would have us believe, we would refuse to help.

The question is: Does *homo economicus* provide a plausible account of our motivation? Many people, including many non-mainstream economists, think not. One alternative explanation focuses not on whether one derives a warm glow from helping one's friend but on one *reason* for acting. If we are asked why we helped a friend move house, a perfectly natural answer is: 'Because I wanted to help her – it was a nice thing to do'. It would be odd if you replied: 'Because I wanted to receive a warm glow which would increase my utility'. We might actually receive a warm glow as a by-product of helping a friend, but this need not be the *reason* for our action. Once we acknowledge that one can have reasons for acting which do not have to do with self-interest, we can account for actions which pretty obviously do not maximize one's utility. Here are some examples: fighting in a war of independence at risk to one's own life might not be what maximizes your utility, but perhaps one feels a duty to fight; likewise, accompanying an aged relative in the last stages of their life might be a very arduous and painful experience, but one might do it nevertheless because one thinks it is right (see Sen 1977). But 'right', here, does not mean that we act in our individual self-interest; it might go against our self-interest because it pains us and means that we have to sacrifice other pursuits, for example our social life or university studies.

Key concepts: Freedom and coercion

Many scholars have asked whether we are truly free in our economic decisions. For example, a poor person is only as free as their financial resources allow; their socio-economic status determines the degree to which they are free to be truly rational economic actors. It may make sense to buy in bulk, because you can save on each unit in the long run, but if you don't have the money to buy twenty-four cans of soup at once, for example, then you will have to buy one at a time, paying the higher (and less rational) price. Another challenge to our freedom is the coercion we encounter in everyday situations. Some coercion is easy to see and understand. When we are under threat we might act in a way that is not of our free choosing. If one attends an outdoor music festival and suffers serious dehydration, one will likely pay $8 for a bottle of water because there is no other option. Some scholars have argued that even when we are not under direct threat, we behave in ways that are coercive because of social and cultural expectations. If we do not comply with these norms then we might be sanctioned – for example ridiculed, excluded or even held legally accountable. While we can easily see coercion in cases of emergency or threat, something like buying new clothing for one's wardrobe every season is rarely understood as part of a broader coercive circumstance dictated by the culture around us.

Source: Hanson and Yosifon (2003–4)

Are we really free to choose? The next question we address is whether maximizing your utility or choosing according to our preferences actually enhances our self-interest. Recall that *homo economicus* is conceived to be a *free* individual, free to make the choices 'he' thinks will further 'his' self-interest most. Is this always the case? As a thought experiment, imagine that, under hypnosis, a person is 'programmed' to believe that jumping up and down 100 times is in their best interest. The person remembers nothing about being hypnotized, but, sure enough, they find themselves jumping up and down several times a day for no apparent reason, other than that they think they are increasing their utility by doing so. We would probably say that the person has been manipulated and that their interests are not really served by jumping up and down. Their preference for jumping, one might say, is not their own preference but has been imposed on them externally and against their will.

This example might seem far-fetched, but consider another, made by heterodox economist John Kenneth Galbraith (1908–2006). What if our preferences are somehow created or constructed by others? Galbraith (1958) thought that businesses and corporations do precisely this through advertising; they make you want to buy certain products. If this is true, businesses and corporations produce not only the goods we consume but also the preferences which make us want to buy those same goods. These questions become even more urgent when we consider the fact that much of our consumptive activity now takes place via the internet – often using platforms and their apps – where companies collect and analyse our data to track and influence our habits and choices (see Chapter 23).

These examples raise the question of where our preferences come from. Many mainstream economists do not feel competent to answer this question and they assume, for simplicity, that people's preferences are simply given. Once we have our preferences – wherever they come from – economists think it is a good thing if our preferences are satisfied, because satisfying our preferences increases our utility. But if our preferences are not chosen freely by us but are, instead, the product of some kind of manipulation or indoctrination, it is not clear that satisfying our preferences is such a good thing. The point applies not only to our preferences for consumer goods but also for other aspirations and goals. Consider a female university graduate in the 1950s, the best student in her cohort. She has grown up with gender stereotypes imparted to her by family, school and media sources. The stereotype has drummed into her the view that pursuing a professional career is less important for a woman than for a man; if she wishes to pursue a career at all, an 'appropriate' career for a woman, she has been told, is elementary school teaching. She has been told that other careers, such as being a university professor, lawyer or politician, are not the sort of thing in which women should get involved. Our university graduate becomes a school teacher and she believes her choice was made freely, for nobody forced her to become a teacher. And she believes that she furthers her own interests best by becoming a teacher. The question is: Does her preference to become a teacher really represent her true interests? If not, we have reason to doubt whether acting on one's preferences always furthers one's interests. This calls into question the trait of *homo economicus* which holds that people know their own interests and act upon that knowledge.

Normative economics and the Pareto principle. We described earlier how mainstream economists adopt the principle of a Pareto improvement to justify market transactions. While this principle arguably provides some normative grounding for market transactions, it is limited when applied to public policy. Consider, for example, a government which is proposing a new tax. The tax would introduce a new top-rate tax on the super-rich, those earning an annual income over $5 million. With the proceeds of the tax, the government proposes to build affordable social housing in deprived urban neighbourhoods. Many people support this sort of redistributive measure (e.g. taxing the very rich to benefit the poor). According to the principle of Pareto improvement, however, the tax is not justified because the tax will make the rich worse off. However much better off the tax would make the poorest people in society, it cannot be justified as a Pareto improvement if it makes the rich even a little worse off. Even transferring a mere $10 from a multibillionaire to a pauper is ruled out by the Pareto principle. The adoption of the Pareto principle poses a limit to the normative reach of mainstream economics, and some economists are eager to transcend this limit (e.g. Sen 1987).

Conclusion

From a self-interested *homo economicus* through the principle of Pareto optimality to the determination of our preferences, in this chapter we have looked at how mainstream economics has sought to explain markets and prices on the basis that human beings are ultimately utility maximizers. Taking a critical perspective, we have questioned some of these assumptions: Are we always selfish in our motivations? Are we capable of knowing and acting upon our preferences? Does economic rationale like the Pareto improvement always lead to the greatest good for the greatest number?

Mainstream economic theory, which we have examined critically in this chapter, is highly influential. It is, as we have stated, taught in the vast majority of economics departments the world over, often to the exclusion of alternative economic theories (see the following chapter on such theories). Mainstream economics is also highly influential in policy circles, be it in shaping national governments' policies (e.g. 'austerity') or the policies of international organizations such as the IMF or the WTO.

Remarkably, though, mainstream economics does not dominate the study of business. Although mainstream economics boasts a 'theory of the firm', the syllabi of business schools are not dominated by the mainstream. For instance, theories of organizational behaviour draw on the work of Herbert Simon, himself an influential economist, though not one who falls into the mainstream. Simon's analysis of decision-making in administrative organizations, like firms, highlights limits to the rationality of decision-makers, as we did when discussing *homo economicus* earlier. Simon developed a theory of 'bounded rationality' to capture the less-than-perfect rationality of real human beings (Simon 1957, 1961). Furthermore, empirical studies of the firm have often found that decisions made by managers do not conform to the principles of mainstream economics; even profit maximization is not as clear a goal as some would believe. Studies of corporate power and concentration and of structures of property and ownership play an important role in understanding business, and these are themes traditionally neglected by mainstream economics.

So while it can be said that mainstream economics is not predominant when it comes to the study of business, it nonetheless shapes the economic policies and institutional frameworks within which business is conducted. Thus, we have introduced some principles of mainstream economics in this chapter so that the reader can understand policy debates and the economic analysis of global economic activity.

Suggested readings

- Ch. 2, Chang, H.-J. (2014) *Economics: The User's Guide*, New York, Bloomsbury Press.
- Ch. 1, Hill, R. and Myatt, T. (2010) *The Economics Anti-Textbook: A Critical Thinker's Guide to Microeconomics*, London, Zed Books.
- Ch. 10, Hunt, E.K. (2002) *History of Economic Thought: A Critical Perspective* (2nd Edition), New York, M.E. Sharpe.

Bibliography

Arrow, K.J. (1963) *Social Choice and Individual Values* (2nd Edition), New Haven, Yale University Press.

Aubrey, J. (1975) *Brief Lives*, London, Folio Society.

Becker, G.S. (1974) 'A Theory of Social Interaction', *Journal of Political Economy*, Vol. 82, pp. 1063–93.

Bentham, J. (1780 [2011]) 'Principles of Morals and Legislation', in *Selected Writings*, New Haven, Yale University Press, pp. 102–51.

Dixit, A. (2014) *Microeconomics: A Very Short Introduction*, Oxford, Oxford University Press.

Ferber, M. and Nelson, J. (eds) (1993) *Beyond Economic Man: Feminist Theory and Economics*, Chicago, University of Chicago Press.

Folbre, N. (2009) *Greed, Lust & Gender: A History of Economic Ideas*, Oxford, Oxford University Press.

Galbraith, J.K. (1958) *The Affluent Society*, Boston, Riverside Press.

Ghazanfar, S. (2014) 'Arab-Islamic Economics', in V. Barnett (ed.), *Routledge Handbook of the History of Global Economic Thought*, London, Routledge, pp. 202–15.

Hanson, J. and Yosifon, D. (2003–2004) 'The Situation: An Introduction to the Situational Character, Critical Realism, Power Economics and Deep Capture', *University of Pennsylvania Law Review*, Vol. 152, pp. 149–201.

Hill, R. and Myatt, T. (2010) *The Economics Anti-Textbook: A Critical Thinker's Guide to Microeconomics*, London, Zed Books.

Hosseini, H. (2003) 'Understanding the Market Mechanism before Adam Smith: Economic Thought in Medieval Islam', in S. Ghazanfar (ed.), *Medieval Islamic Economic Thought: Filling the 'great gap' in European Economics*, New York, Routledge, pp. 88–107.

Phillips, P. (2003) *Inside Capitalism: An Introduction to Political Economy*, Halifax, Fernwood.

Sandel, M.J. (2009) *Justice: What's the Right Thing To Do?*, New York, Farrar, Straus & Giroux.

Sen, A.K. (1977) 'Rational Fools: A Critique of the Behavioural Foundations of Economic Theory', *Philosophy and Public Affairs*, Vol. 6, pp. 317–44.

Sen, A.K. (1987) *On Ethics and Economics*, Oxford, Blackwell.

Simon, H.A. (1957) *Models of Man: Social and Rational*, New York, Wiley.

Simon, H.A. (1961) *Administrative Behavior: A Study of Decision-Making Processes in Administrative Organizations*, New York, Macmillan.

Smith, A. (1759 [1976]) *The Theory of Moral Sentiments*, Oxford, Oxford University Press.

Smith, A. (1776 [2000]) *The Wealth of Nations*, Toronto, Random House.

Varian, H. (2007) *Intermediate Microeconomics: A Modern Approach* (7th Edition), New York, W.W. Norton.

Walras, L. (1874 [1954]) *Elements of Pure Economics or the Theory of Social Wealth*, Homewood, Richard D. Irwin.

Wickham, C. (2021) 'How Did the Feudal Economy Work? The Economic Logic of Medieval Societies', *Past and Present*, Vol. 251, pp. 3–40.

Yarrow, S. (2018) 'Economic Imaginaries of the Global Middle Ages', *Past and Present*, Vol. 13, pp. 214–31.

6 | Political economy and critiques of capitalism

Heterodox perspectives

Sonya Marie Scott

Introduction

Now that we have discussed mainstream or 'orthodox' economics, we can turn to critical perspectives. While mainstream economics is widely accepted as the correct form of economic reasoning within universities today, there are other ways of doing economics and other valuable forms of economic knowledge. These different approaches can be grouped in the category of 'heterodox economics'.

Defining heterodox economics is not easy because so many different thinkers and schools of thought fall under its banner. Generally speaking, heterodox economics can be defined negatively; that is, in terms of what it is not. Some have even gone so far as to argue that 'the only widely recognized and accepted feature of all the heterodox tradition is a rejection of the modern mainstream project' (Lawson 2006: 485). It is safe to say that heterodox economics rejects some or even all aspects of mainstream economics. But why would anyone choose to reject the mainstream?

The reason people distinguish between mainstream and heterodox economics is both intellectual and political. In some cases it is a question of methodology – many heterodox economists disagree with the methods and models of mainstream economics because they believe that they are not useful in explaining or predicting economic reality. In other cases, the distinction is political – many heterodox economists believe that the mainstream economics entrenches existing power relations and gross injustices within capitalism. In this sense heterodox economics can serve as an alternative to the *status quo* (i.e. capitalism) and actively seeks to reshape our economy and society.

Now that we have seen some general indications of what heterodox economics is against, we want to note what it supports. Because of the great variety of heterodox thinkers this is not an easy issue to address. The goal of this chapter is to present the ideas of several key figures or theories in the heterodox tradition – both inside and outside of the classroom.

Historical heterodox perspectives

The Marxian critique of capitalism. Perhaps the most historically significant heterodox theorist is Karl Marx (1818–83). Chapter 2 dealt with some of Marx's ideas in detail, exploring his theory of the emergence of capitalism. In Chapter 4, we discussed the Marxian understanding of the social division of labour. Here we look at Marx from two perspectives. First, we explore his criticism of the mainstream rational economic man (*homo economicus*) and, second, we explore how this criticism develops into an indictment of an economic system based on exploitation and alienation.

Many people associate Marx with socialism and communism, and some even read him only in light of the many socialist regimes which have sprung up in the twentieth century, such as the USSR, Cuba and China. But Marx's work focused primarily on the capitalist system that was transforming the world and the lives of all those who came into contact with it in his time. In fact, Marx was mainly concerned with relationships that people experience in capitalism; he argued that despite the fact that 'economic' relationships look like rational and free-willed interactions between individuals as described by mainstream economists (see Chapter 5), they are actually class relations, because each individual is part of a larger group called a *social class*.

Class, for Marx, was defined by the way in which we relate to *capital*. Capital can be thought of, roughly speaking, as the money and resources needed to conduct and finance business (e.g. property, factories, equipment and money). But none of these things represent capital if they are not part of a social relationship or a structure of ownership and power. Those who own and control capital are members of the capitalist class or capitalists; Marx also referred to this class as the *bourgeoisie*. In nineteenth-century Europe they would have been the owners of factories and industry. Those who do not own and control capital, having only control over their own person and capacity to work, are the working class, or the *proletariat*. The bourgeoisie requires the proletariat to work in their factories and for their businesses in order to produce and return a profit. The proletariat requires work in the factories in order to receive a wage.

Marx criticized what he termed 'bourgeois economics' – or, the mainstream economics of his day – for basing its system of thought on the false claim that the individual is free. Instead, he argued that our position in the class structure of society – that is, as either worker or capitalist – is not the result of the superiority of one person's skill or work effort over that of another. This is due not only to the fact that the worker is bound by their class to agree to work for the capitalist, but also to the fact that paid work (or wage labour) is a special kind of relationship. An employee does not simply make an agreement of employment; instead they sell their own labour power, time and vital energies, as a commodity for the capitalist to use in the production process. This labour, when put into action in the production process, will produce surplus – goods worth more than the component parts that went into them in the first place. This idea is called the *labour theory of value* – and it is the foundation of Marx's economics. It is not simple exchange – buying cheap and selling dear – that produces profit in a capitalist system, but rather the labour of workers that does so, but they do not get to keep this surplus. At its heart, the fundamental relationship of capitalism is *exploitation* – the use of the worker's labour to make profit for the capitalist (Marx 1867 [1976]).

Within capitalism, competition is held to be of paramount importance. Many have argued that competition in perfectly free markets will promote creativity, innovation and efficiency (e.g. Smith 1776 [2000]; Hayek 1948 [1992]; Freidman 1962). Marx, however, attacked this belief, arguing instead that 'competition isolates individuals, not only the bourgeois but even more the proletarians, despite the fact that it brings them together' (Marx and Engels 1845–6 [1947]: 142). Even though people both live and work in close proximity, the relationship between people becomes more functional, instrumental and isolating. The feeling of isolation and anonymity that one can feel in a big city is a perfect example of this. Thinkers like Marx call this isolation *alienation*. According to Marx, there are four fundamental forms of alienation in a capitalist economy:

- *Alienation from the product of one's labour*: once workers exchange their labour for a wage, they *alienate* (or give up) their right to control the things they produce.
- *Alienation from the labour process*: the very process of working is controlled by employers (or capitalists). As a result Marx commented that workers often become an 'appendage of the machine', like tools to be used in the production process.
- *Alienation from oneself*: Marx believed that labour is the very essence of human nature. Thus, when we sell our labour to another we sell the most vital aspect of ourselves.

- *Alienation from others*: in a society divided by class, workers are rarely able to connect with one another in a meaningful way due to alienating working conditions, long hours and the isolation of modern life.

Given Marx's belief that *homo economicus* was a fiction which conveniently served the interests of the capitalist class as it justified an exploitative relationship by calling it 'free' or designating it merely a question of contract, and given that he believed that the fundamental structure of capitalism was based on exploitation and alienation, many have read Marx's work as a call to change an unjust system. In fact, few political or economic thinkers have had as much influence on the world, inspiring resistance and revolution against the capitalist system.

An American critique: institutional economics. In the late 1800s the United States underwent a significant social and economic change. As we discuss in Chapter 7, the United States experienced the rise of a new business model – that of the modern corporation. In the midst of these changes, some historians, legal scholars and economists started to insist upon the need to understand the economy historically, as part of a broader evolution. The development of neoclassical economics at the same time (see Chapter 5) took the individual as its starting point and did not consider historical context, instead tried to establish universal and objective economic laws. A number of *institutional economists* challenged this idea, focusing specifically on the role of institutions in the economy, hence the name 'institutional economists'. The institutional economist John R. Commons (1931: 649) defined institutions as follows:

> Collective action ranges all the way from unorganized custom to the many organized going concerns, such as the family, the corporation, the trade association, the trade union, the reserve system, the state. The principle common to all of them is greater or less control, liberation and expansion of individual action by collective action.

There are several important thinkers who are part of this tradition, most notably Thorstein Veblen (1857–1929). Veblen was famous for his critique of what he termed 'the leisure class' – those who lived by the labour of others and actively flaunted their wealth in order to maintain their status and power through leisure activities and lavish patterns of 'conspicuous consumption' (Veblen 1899). Commons was a labour economist concerned with the legal system and the way that law could influence the development of the economy and vice versa (Commons 1931). Both thinkers challenged the idea that the individual acts in such a way as suggested by mainstream economics. As humans, they claimed, we are embedded in social, historical and legal institutional contexts.

Key concept: 'Conspicuous consumption'

Veblen developed a theory of the leisure class at the end of the nineteenth century. This theory gives us insight as to how and why some of the most wealthy and powerful players in the US economy would behave in a way that appeared to be irrational and 'wasteful' of both time and resources. He argued that engaging in leisure activities, refraining from work and consuming luxury goods was not an activity of simple preference or personal indulgence. Instead consumption was a notably 'conspicuous', or publicly obvious, performance in order to establish social status and power:

> Since the consumption of these more excellent goods is an evidence of wealth, it becomes honorific; and conversely, the failure to consume in due quantity becomes a mark of inferiority and demerit. (Veblen 1899 [1994]: 74)

Lavish parties and galas, the finest furnishings and fashions, all were part of a social and political practice to demonstrate superiority over those who had to labour or merely had enough to survive. Given the importance of conspicuous consumption in the formative stages of US industrialism we might question what traces of these practices have affected mainstream consumer society today.

Source: Veblen (1899 [1994])

Common to these 'old' institutional economists (not to be confused with *new institutional economics*, which developed in the 1980s and has very different objectives) are six fundamental beliefs about how we should understand capitalism. These are listed in Table 6.1.

TABLE 6.1 Principles of 'Old' Institutional Economics

The individual	Economic behaviour is not independently self-motivated; it is shaped by the institutional environment of the individual.
History	History is evolutionary, economics is evolutionary as well. Change is what defines our society and economy.
Technology	Technological development is a crucial consideration when analysing the nature of the economy. Our technologies shape our history and are shaped by our history.
The market	The market is characterized by competition and conflict. It is not harmonious or self-regulating as the mainstream approach might suggest.
Institutions	Institutions can be shaped and altered to better serve the needs of people in society.
Economics	Economic analysis depends upon more than mathematical models alone. Instead, disciplines such as psychology, anthropology and law can be used to more fully understand human economic behaviour.

Source: Mercuro and Medema (2006).

Institutional economics has had a lasting influence on legal activism, the labour movement and on proponents of the welfare state. Perhaps the most important idea of its legacy is that economics is not an arena of human activity to be understood separately from other aspects of society, but rather that it is actively shaped, defended or changed through institutions, such as law and government regulation (see Chapter 18). Instead of self-regulating markets which will inherently take care of themselves and all of those who live in any particular economy, we have human institutions that can define and defend structures that respond to human needs.

A mainstream alternative: Keynesian macroeconomics. John Maynard Keynes (1883–1946) was a British economist who had a tremendous influence on the discipline of economics and on economic policy from the 1930s until the 1970s. In this section we focus on the way Keynes challenged many assumptions regarding our economic natures and the nature of the economy. He is notorious for challenging the mainstream belief that humans are fundamentally rational, and even more so for questioning many of the core principles of *laissez-faire* economics by promoting government investment in the economy during times of recession (Keynes 1936).

Unlike mainstream economists who tend to argue that we know and act upon our preferences when making economic decisions (see Chapter 5), Keynes claimed that our economic reality is marked by uncertainty (Scott 2013). Two undeniable aspects of the human condition are *time* and *ignorance*. Time, because decisions made today are usually made with certain expectations of the future, and ignorance, because we cannot be certain of what the future might hold. For example, a government may choose to dedicate its resources to investing in and promoting an industry like oil with the expectation that oil prices will remain high, but then face plummeting oil prices and its consequences (e.g. unemployment).

We are not simply the victims of the future, however, because we are constantly revising our expectations based on new inputs. As a whole, this makes for a rather complex system:

> the state of expectation is liable to constant change, a new expectation being superimposed long before the previous change has fully worked itself out; so that the economic machine is occupied at any given time with a number of overlapping activities, the existence of which is due to various past states of expectation. (Keynes 1936: 50)

With so much uncertainty and constantly changing expectations, what might prompt people to make economic decisions at all? The decision to buy this or that good might seem relatively harmless, but what about the decision to start a business, to invest, to take a risk? While Keynes did believe that individuals were free to make their own choices, he did not think that rationality was the sole driving factor behind our free economic choices. Instead an internal 'spontaneous optimism', what Keynes called our *animal spirits*, prompts individuals to take risks and make risky economic choices. This inherent characteristic of our economic nature is so important, he argued, that it is essential for the very operation of a capitalist economy (Scott 2018).

On a structural level, Keynesian economics differs from the mainstream, resting upon the fundamental belief that private decisions alone will not necessarily lead to the most successful or stable economy. Sometimes government decisions are required in order to temper market forces. As a result, the idea that government must borrow in tough times in order to increase productivity and maintain employment in the economy became standard across Western economies between 1945 and the late 1970s. The shift to neoliberal economic principles since the 1980s and 1990s unseated Keynes as the dominant macro-economic theorist, though the great financial crisis of 2008 (see Chapter 17) has reinvigorated support for Keynesian economic policy in some quarters (Krugman 2011).

Contemporary heterodox perspectives

The abovementioned approaches are all critical of capitalism and the mainstream economics that supports and promotes it. Some are anti-capitalist, such as Marx, while institutionalists and Keynes were working to make capitalism more equitable yet leaving its basic structure intact. The same range of positions can be found in more recent heterodox perspectives, which we turn to next.

Feminist political economy. Feminism is popularly associated within the Western liberal tradition with equal gender rights – that is, the right to vote, to hold office, to own property, to make decisions regarding reproductive health and so on. Yet many civil liberties struggles have extended well beyond the scope of political rights into the realm of economics. Feminist scholars and activists like Barker and Kuiper (2003), Ferber and Nelson (2009) and Fraser (2013) argue that despite women acquiring many political and social rights, economics remains a site of deep inequality within contemporary gender relations. This is primarily because formal rights – rights that see women and men as equal under the law – are of little importance if the economic situation of women does not practically allow for equal opportunity, education, freedom from domestic violence and financial security to raise children with dignity.

We should be careful here when we talk about 'women', and when we talk about 'gender equality'. As renowned activist and feminist theorist Angela Davis has written, 'Feminism involves so much more than gender equality. And it involves so much more than gender. [. . .] It has to involve a consciousness of capitalism, and racism, and colonialism, and post-colonialities, and ability, and more genders than we can ever imagine, and more sexualities than we thought we could name' (2016: 104). For example, the situation of women within the Global North varies with that of women in the Global South (Mohanty 2003; Walby 2009; Gibson-Graham and Dombroski 2020), as does the experience of women within each society (see Chapters 15, 20 and 22). In other words, the experience of women varies across countries, across classes, across ethnicity, race, sexuality and ability. Even in societies where women enjoy a high degree of formal freedom, women's experience may be highly dependent upon their socio-economic status. Women who are privileged are more likely to be educated, to have professional careers and to hire help to offset traditional women's labour such as housekeeping, cooking and child-rearing. Women who are marginalized are more prone to bear the uneven brunt of poverty, often obliged to work several jobs and take care of domestic labour. This disparity is further exacerbated when we consider the many social barriers posed by racism (Bullock 2013). Consider that within the Global North women of colour make up a disproportionate percentage of the most poorly paid and most precarious workforce (Fuller and Vosko 2008). Women in the Global South are responsible for more labour than their male counterparts but are rarely rewarded with wages, social prestige or political rights. In fact, the great majority of the 1 billion poorest inhabitants of the world are women (United Nations Womenwatch 2015), who are also the most likely to suffer the consequences of post-crisis economic recovery measures such as austerity programmes (Karamessini and Rubery 2014), and the negative impacts of climate change and global pandemics (UN Women 2022).

Part of the reason for the state of affairs is the structural history of *patriarchy* – which sees wealth and family lineage pass along the male line, and divides labour and worth accordingly. Not all societies have been patriarchal throughout human history, as there are instances of matrilineal and shared political regimes. Prior to European colonization, for example, the Iroquois/Haudenosaunee of North America had a matrilineal social structure, which saw kinship determined along the mother's line, and had shared responsibility for political power (Baskin 1982). Patriarchy, however, is the dominant form in most contemporary capitalist societies and was instrumental in shaping the labour relations between men and women as the Industrial Revolution unfolded.

Another reason for the persistence of gendered inequality has to do with the way that mainstream economics measures value. Marilyn Waring (1999) has brought the issue to public attention through her studies of national accounting practices. She argues that only certain types of activities and resources are given economic value; for example, when calculating the sum total of economic activity of a nation (i.e. GDP), only certain types of activity get counted. We can count goods bought and sold, along with wages paid, but the activities such as bearing and raising children, teaching them social skills and values, doing housework and caring for family members – what is called *social reproduction* – often remains invisible. In mainstream economic terms, these activities have 'no value' because they are not measured and accounted for. Some feminist scholars argue that patriarchy, like capitalism, created its own mode of production, rooted in the marriage relationship where women are exploited by their husbands (e.g. Delphy 1984). Other feminist scholars emphasize that capitalism relies on devalued, unpaid and invisible reproductive labour in order to generate and regenerate workers (e.g. Fraser 2017).

Key concept: Social reproduction

Social reproduction refers to the labour required to maintain people in our society. The term was specifically developed by Marx in order to identify the task of *reproducing* the working class so that they could *produce* for society. In feminist terms the concept of social reproduction then refers to the specific labour of raising and caring for people – raising and educating children, imparting social values and knowledge, providing a clean environment, food, shelter, clothing and care, and the emotional support needed to cope with daily life. This labour has traditionally been gendered labour – that is, labour carried out by women. It has also been (and continues to be) typically unpaid labour, carried out in the private sphere of the home instead of the public realm of the formal labour market.

Source: Bezason and Luxton (2006)

The invisibility of domestic labour is important for several reasons. First, it lies at the very heart of the mainstream economic method. As we saw in the previous chapter, mainstream economics became a mathematical 'science' by rendering economic phenomena quantifiable through price. Unpaid labour, since it has no price, is not considered part of the general economic activity of a nation. This may seem natural, as we have internalized the idea that things like cooking, cleaning, raising children and taking care of the elderly should bear no discernible cost. But this is a socially constructed and historically situated belief. Many feminists have argued that there is no scientific basis upon which one can assert that women are better at caring for and cleaning up after their families than men (Davis 1983; Guillaumin 1988). The notion that work involving 'caring' and other domestic tasks is 'unskilled' has led to the consistent undervaluation of work in traditionally female professions such as nursing, early childhood education and many jobs within the service industry (Fudge and Vosko 2001; Dunford and Perrons 2014).

The second reason this is so important is because the national accounting system helps to determine government objectives and national budgets. Because childcare is invisible, national governments often do not invest in affordable public daycare, meaning that women, especially those with low to middle incomes, cannot afford to go out and work in order to gain financial and personal independence. If the labour of women in the Global South is almost completely invisible, while war is extremely profitable, then why would wealthy nations focus on aid, fair trade and debt relief instead of war and military initiatives? Feminist political economists argue that we must redefine value and begin to make the invisible visible in order to change society (e.g. bell hooks 2000; Gibson-Graham et al. 2013; Seguino 2020).

Anarchist economics. Anarchism is commonly associated with political movements instead of economics (see Chapter 16). But, as with all heterodox economic traditions, anarchist thought involves a consideration of the state, the market and the nature of economic relationships. Emma Goldman (1869–1940) was an influential anarchist activist and thinker in the United States and Canada in the early twentieth century. She defined anarchism as the fundamental liberation from many of the constraints imposed by the capitalist system and the state:

> Anarchism, then, really stands for the liberation of the human from the dominion of religion; the liberation of the human body from the dominion of property; liberation from the shackles and restraint of government. Anarchism stands for a social order based on the free grouping of individuals for the purpose of producing real social wealth, an order that will guarantee to every human being free access to the earth and full enjoyment of the necessities of life, according to individual desires, tastes, and inclinations. (Goldman 1910: 68)

A common feature of anarchism, therefore, is the shared goal of freeing human society from the institutions which govern by hierarchy and power, such as the government, the system of unequally distributed wealth and the Church. Goldman was not the first to express such ideas. She was influenced by several important classical European anarchist thinkers such as Pierre-Joseph Proudhon (1809–65), Mikhail Bakunin (1814–76) and Peter Kropotkin (1842–1921).

Contemporary anarchist thought is quite diverse and overlaps with many other schools of thought. In the popular imagination it is most often associated with the 'alter-globalization' movement that began to gain considerable momentum in the late 1990s and early 2000s (see Chapters 13 and 17), and with other protest movements of the recent past, like Occupy Wall Street (el-Ojeili 2014), or the 'hacktivism' of groups like Anonymous and the 'leak activism' of groups like Wikileaks (Fuchs 2014; Goode 2015) and the Panama and Paradise Papers (Berglez and Gearing 2018). But anarchist economics are not fundamentally about protest movements. Instead, anarchist economics focuses on developing alternative models of social organization, production and distribution (Parker et al. 2007). While there are a great number of contemporary anarchist movements, including those that focus on questions of ecology and the environment (Bookchin 1986), and those that focus on freedom for traditionally marginalized groups such as women and people of colour (Dark Star Collective 2012), the most developed school of anarchist economic thought focuses on *participatory economics*, also known as *parecon*. People such as Michael Albert (1997) emphasize the importance of 'economic vision', which involves actively conceptualizing goals and values rather than simply conforming to current models or the *status quo*. Participatory economics relies on five basic principles in its plan to *transform* the economy into an economy that relies upon active participation of its members:

> 1) social rather than private ownership; 2) worker and consumer . . . councils rather than corporate workplace organizations; 3) remuneration for effort and sacrifice rather than for property, power or output; 4) participatory planning rather than markets or central planning; 5) participatory self-management rather than class rule. (Albert 2003: 84)

While no society runs upon these principles yet, some of these guiding ideals can be seen at work in cooperative organizations and worker-managed industries (see Chapter 22).

Common property resource economics. As we discuss in Chapter 16, environmental issues and sustainability are undoubtedly a part of our public consciousness today (Klein 2014). Here we take up the question of how ecological concerns interact with mainstream economic ideas, specifically by looking at the question of 'the commons' (also see Chapter 22), or common property resource economics.

Elinor Ostrom (1990), a Nobel Prize-winning economist and advocate of the institutional management of natural resources, famously wrote about ways in which to manage 'common pool resources' (such as forests, fisheries, water sources, oil reserves etc.) without relying strictly on the market or on government agencies. In other words, she sought to resolve what Garrett Hardin (1968) described as the 'tragedy of the commons'. Hardin used the example of a pasture that was open to all, where each individual would increase their own use to the detriment of others. The logic of individual benefit, unlike the theory presented by Adam Smith, is in fact what results in a detrimental impact on society:

Therein is the tragedy. Each man is locked into a system that compels him to increase his herd without limit – in a world that is limited. Ruin is the destination toward which all men rush, each pursuing his own best interest in a society that believes in the freedom of the commons. (Hardin 1968: 1244)

In contrast, Ostrom's studies, based on a new institutional approach, focused on the ways in which institutions can mitigate the logic of individual appropriation while not resorting to whole-scale state control. Much like the definition of institutions that we saw with the old institutional economists such as Veblen and Commons, this notion of institution is inherently evolutionary and does not provide a blueprint for the management of common public resources. The mixture of public and private solutions to the management of collective resources forces us to go beyond the belief that privatization can solve all problems, or that government is the only reliable manager of common goods. Institutions can thus be a source of economic order that escape the traditional market–state dualism discussed in Chapter 4. For example, Ostrom (1990: 185) argued that in many cases small communities can 'supply themselves with new rules, gain quasi-voluntary compliance with those rules, and monitor each other's conformance to the rules' in order to use and share natural resources in a sustainable and collectively beneficial manner. This can often influence larger-scale institutional change at the regional or national levels, but is fundamentally based upon the principle of actively making rules and living with the consequences of these rules (i.e. creating dynamic institutions) in an immediate and locally managed setting, with sustainability and renewability as goals instead of profit alone (see Case Study on the 'Land Back' movement in Canada and the United States).

Case Study

'Land Back' movement, Canada and the United States

In 2012, after the tar sands of Northern Alberta and Saskatchewan (see Chapter 16) became a hot-button issue in Canada and the United States, a popular Indigenous move-ment named 'Idle No More' arose to confront the logic of the private appropriation of land and natural resources (i.e. the logic of extractivism) in Canada. In particular, *Bill C-45* (2012) included revisions to environmental legislation and the *Indian Act*, redefining the way in which business is conducted, and making the use and acquisition of Indigenous territory and resources easier for big business. In their manifesto, Idle No More explain:

'The state of Canada has become one of the wealthiest countries in the world by using the land and resources. Canadian mining, logging, oil and fishing companies are the most powerful in the world due to land and resources. Some of the poorest First Nations commu-nities (such as Attawapiskat) have mines or other developments on their land but do not get a share of the profit. The taking of resources has left many lands and waters poisoned – the animals and plants are dying in many areas in Canada. We cannot live without the land and water. We have laws older than this colonial government about how to live with the land.'

The historical context of Idle No More's critique is very important, as the movement works to undo many of the assumptions of mainstream economics insofar as these assumptions drove the economic strategies of European settler-colonialism in the Americas. As Coulthard (2014: 152) has pointed out in his recent work on colonial relations in Canada, 'settler-colonialism is territorially acquisitive in perpetuity'. What this means is that the colonial relationship which began when European colonial forces settled North America in the seventeenth century was based on the acquisition of land and resources at the expense of the Indigenous populations and their ways of life. The appropriation continues today and often manifests itself concretely through the erosion of treaty rights that were historically established to secure certain pieces of territory and resources for Indigenous peoples, and through changes in environmental legislation regarding the use of natural resources.

Following 'Idle No More' a movement called 'Land Back' has blossomed. Spurred on by the controversial Keystone XL Dakota Access Pipeline Project that was set to cross Sioux Territory at Standing Rock (North and South Dakota), the #noDAPL (2016) movement that sought to block the pipeline brought the concept of 'Land Back' to the national stage in both the United States and Canada, and bore the slogan of 'Water Is Life' (Estes 2019). The land and water defenders – primarily Indigenous women and activists – shone a light on the ways in which extractive capitalism tends to benefit large corporations and their shareholders, while putting communities – primarily Indigenous and racialized communities – at risk of the consequences of this extraction such as pipeline leaks, refinery explosions, severe contamination from tar sands, seismic insecurity from fracking, among many other things.

The Land Back movement is complex, and while its hashtag (#landback) and mainstream media recognition are new, its origins stretch back along the entire history of Indigenous resistance to colonial power and its economic principles of extraction and accumulation (Estes 2017). Fundamental to the movement today are the principles of sovereignty, self-governance, cultural preservation and spiritual dignity:

'Land Back' is the demand to rightfully return colonized land – like that in so-called Canada – to Indigenous Peoples. But when we say 'Land Back' we aren't asking for just the ground, or for a piece of paper that allows us to tear up and pollute the earth. We want the system that is land to be alive so that it can perpetuate itself, and perpetuate us as an extension of itself. That's what we want back: our place in keeping land alive and spiritually connected. (Longman et al. 2020: 2)

Sources: www.idlenomore.ca; Coulthard (2014); https://www.standingrock.org; Estes (2017, 2019); Longman et al. (2020)

Taking the debate out of the classroom. There has been a growing popular and academic movement against mainstream economics since 2000. In 2000–1 French professors of economics and their students started a public campaign against university curricula requiring students to learn mainstream economics without allowing for alternative viewpoints or methods. This movement was called the 'post-autistic economics' movement and it critiques the inward-looking and dogmatic nature of the economics discipline. In one of their petitions, the French students explain the problem with the way mainstream economics is taught in universities:

> This approach is supposed to explain everything by means of a purely axiomatic process, as if this were THE economic truth. We do not accept this dogmatism. We want a pluralism of approaches, adapted to the complexity of the objects and to the uncertainty surrounding most of the big questions in economics (unemployment, inequalities, the place of financial markets, the advantages and disadvantages of free-trade, globalization, economic development, etc.).[1]

This movement gained popularity throughout many parts of Europe and North America, and the inclusion of heterodox economics is starting to take place especially in interdisciplinary departments and programmes. But this movement is only one side of a contemporary tendency to challenge the mainstream, one that has started in the place where the mainstream is most powerful, the university. Others have taken the case against mainstream assumptions out of the classroom and into the realm of public protest (Newman 2014). In Chapter 17 we will explore the effects that global economic crises have had on economic thinking, and the various popular protest movements that have come about as a result.

Conclusion

This chapter has explored some of the most historically influential proponents of heterodox economics. While we have shown that heterodox economics encapsulates a great variety of ideas and approaches, we also want to emphasize that it is united in its critique of mainstream economics. Contemporary movements are putting many heterodox ideas into practice, calling for other values, such as environmental sustainability, gender and racial equality, democratic accountability and the reduction of global inequality, to enter into public consciousness and policy debate. How these voices will impact future economic policy and our democratic landscape remains to be seen.

Suggested readings

- Ch. 10, Marx, K. (1859 [1990]) *Capital: A Critique of Political Economy, Volume One*, trans. Ben Fowkes, New York, Penguin.
- Ch. 4, Veblen, T. (1899 [1994]) *Theory of the Leisure Class*, New York, Penguin.

- Ch. 9, Fraser, N. (2013) *Fortunes of Feminism: From State-Managed Capitalism to Neoliberal Crisis*, New York, Verso.
- Ch. 1, Estes, N. (2019) *Our History Is Our Future: Standing Rock versus the Dakota Access Pipeline*, New York, Verso.

Note

1 Real World Economics: www.paecon.net (accessed August 2022).

Bibliography

Albert, M. (1997) *Thinking Forward: Learning to Conceptualize Economic Vision*, Winnipeg, Arbeiter Ring.

Albert, M. (2003) *Parecon: Life after Capitalism*, New York, Verso.

Barker, D. and Kuiper, E. (eds) (2003) *Towards a Feminist Theory of Economics*, New York, Routledge.

Baskin, C. (1982) 'Women in Iroquois Society', *Canadian Women Studies*, Vol. 4, pp. 42–6.

Berglez, P. and Gearing, A. (2018) 'The Panama and Paradise Papers. The Rise of a Global Fourth Estate', *International Journal of Communication*, Vol. 12, pp. 4573–92.

Bezanson, K. and Luxton, M. (2006) *Social Reproduction*, Montreal, McGill-Queen's University Press.

Bookchin, M. (1986) *Post-Scarcity Anarchism*, Montreal, Black Rose Press.

Bullock, H. (2013) *Women and Poverty: Psychology, Public Policy and Social Justice*, Chichester, Wiley Blackwell.

Commons, J.R. (1931) 'Institutional Economics', *The American Economic Review*, Vol. 21, pp. 648–57.

Coulthard, G.S. (2014) *Red Skin, White Masks: Rejecting the Colonial Politics of Recognition*, Minneapolis, University of Minnesota Press.

Dark Star Collective (2012) *Quiet Rumors: An Anarcha-Feminist Reader*, San Francisco, AK Press.

Davis, A. (1983) *Women, Race and Class*, New York, Vintage Books.

Davis, A. (2016) 'Feminism and Abolition: Theories and Practices for the Twenty-First Century', in A. Davis et al. (eds), *Freedom is a Constant Struggle: Ferguson, Palestine and the Foundation of a Movement*, Chicago, Haymarket, pp. 91–110.

Delphy, C. (1984) *Close to Home: A Materialist Analysis of Women's Oppression*, Amherst, The University of Massachusetts Press.

Dunford, R. and Perron, D. (2014) 'Power, Privilege and Precarity: The Gendered Dynamics of Contemporary Inequality', in M. Evans et al. (eds), *The SAGE Handbook of Feminist Theory*, Washington, Sage, pp. 465–82.

el-Ojeili, C. (2014) 'Anarchism as the Spirit of Contemporary Anti-Capitalism? A Critical Survey of Recent Debates', *Critical Sociology*, Vol. 40, pp. 451–68.

Estes, N. (2017) 'Fighting for Our Lives: #NoDAPL in Historical Context', *Wicazo Sa Review*, Vol. 32, No. 2, pp. 115–22.

Estes, N. (2019) *Our History is the Future: Standing Rock versus the Dakota Access Pipeline, and the Long Tradition of Indigenous Resistance*, London, Verso.

Ferber, M. and Nelson, J. (eds) (2009) *Beyond Economic Man: Feminist Theory and Economics*, Chicago, University of Chicago Press.

Fraser, N. (2013) *Fortunes of Feminism*, New York, Verso.

Fraser, N. (2017) 'Crisis of Care? On the Social-Reproductive Contradictions of Contemporary Capitalism', in T. Bhattacharya (ed.), *Social Reproduction Theory: Remapping Class, Recentering Oppression*, London, Pluto Press, pp. 21–36.

Friedman, M. (1962) *Capitalism and Freedom*, Chicago, University of Chicago Press.

Fuchs, C. (2014) 'Anonymous: Hacktivism and Contemporary Politics', in D. Trottier and C. Fuchs (eds), *Social Media, Politics and the State Protests, Revolutions, Riots, Crime and Policing in the Age of Facebook, Twitter and YouTube*, London, Routledge, pp. 88–106.

Fudge, J. and Vosko, L. (2001) 'Gender, Segmentation, and the Standard Employment Relationship in Canadian Labour Law, Legislation and Policy', *Economic and Industrial Democracy*, Vol. 22, pp. 271–310.

Fuller, S. and Vosko, L. (2008) 'Temporary Employment and Social Inequality in Canada: Exploring Intersections of Gender, Race and Immigration Status', *Social Indicators Research*, Vol. 88, pp. 31–50.

Gibson-Graham, J.K., Cameron, J. and Healy, S. (2013) *Take Back the Economy: An Ethical Guide for Transforming Our Communities*, Minneapolis, University of Minnesota Press.

Gibson-Graham, J.K. and Dombroski, K. (2020) *The Handbook of Diverse Economies*, Cheltenham and Northampton, Edward Elgar Publishing.

Goldman, E. (1910) 'Anarchism: What it Really Stands for', in *Anarchism and Other Essays*, New York, Mother Earth Publishing.

Goode, L. (2015) 'Anonymous and the Political Ethos of Hacktivism', *The International Journal of Media and Culture*, Vol. 13, No. 1, pp. 74–86.

Guillaumin, C. (1988) 'Race and Nature: The System of Marks: The Idea of a Natural Group and Social Relationships', *Feminist Issues*, Vol. 8, pp. 25–43.

Hardin, G. (1968) 'The Tragedy of the Commons', *Science*, Vol. 162, pp. 1243–8.

Hayek, F. (1948 [1992]) *Individualism and Economic Order*, Chicago, University of Chicago Press.

hooks, b. (2000) *Where We Stand: Class Matters*, New York, Routledge.

Karamessini, M. and Rubery, J. (eds) (2014) *Women and Austerity: The Economic Crisis and the Future for Gender Equality*, New York, Routledge.

Keynes, J.M. (1936) *The General Theory of Employment, Interest and Money*, London, Macmillan.

Klein, N. (2014) *This Changes Everything: Capitalism vs. the Climate*, New York, Simon and Schuster.

Kropotkin, P. (1902 [1939]) *Mutual Aid: A Factor in Revolution*, Harmondsworth, Penguin.

Krugman, P. (2011) 'Keynes was Right', *The New York Times*, December 29.

Longman, N. et al. (2020) '"Land Back" is more than the sum of its parts', *Briarpatch*, Vol. 49, No. 5, (Sept/Oct), p.2.

Lawson, T. (2006) 'The Nature of Heterodox Economics', *Cambridge Journal of Economics*, Vol. 30, pp. 483–505.

Marx, K. (1867 [1976]) *Capital: Volume 1*, London, Penguin.

Marx, K. and Engels, F. (1845–1846 [1947]) *The German Ideology*, Edited by R. Pascal, New York, International Publishers.

Mercuro, N. and Medema, S. (2006) *Economics and the Law: From Posner to Post-Modernism and Beyond* (2nd Edition), Princeton, Princeton University Press.

Mohanty, C.T. (2003) *Feminism Without Borders: Decolonizing Theory, Practicing*

Solidarity, Durham, Duke University Press.

Newman, J. (2014) 'Governing the Present: Activism, Neoliberalism and the Problem of Power and Consent', *Critical Policy Studies*, Vol. 8, pp. 133–47.

Ostrom, E. (1990) *Governing the Commons: The Evolution of Institutions for Collective Action*, New York, Cambridge University Press.

Parker, M., Fournier, V. and Reedy, P. (2007) *The Dictionary of Alternatives: Utopianism and Organization*, London, Zed Books.

Seguino, S. (2020) 'Engendering Macroeconomic Theory and Policy', *Feminist Economics*, Vol. 26, No. 2, pp. 27–61.

Scott, S. (2013) *Architectures of Economic Subjectivity*, London, Routledge.

Scott, S. (2018) 'Crises, Confidence and Animal Spirits: Exploring Subjectivity in the Dualism of Descartes and Keynes', *The Journal of Philosophical Economics*, Vol. XI, No. 2, pp. 1–28.

Smith, A. (1776 [2000]) *The Wealth of Nations*, New York, The Modern Library.

United Nations Womenwatch (2015) www.un.org/womenwatch (accessed September 2016).

UN Women (2022) 'Government Responses to Covid-19: Lessons on Gender Equality for a World in Turmoil', United Nations Entity for Gender Equality and the Empowerment of Women.

Veblen, T. (1899 [1994]) *Theory of the Leisure Class*, New York, Penguin.

Walby, S. (2009) *Globalization and Inequalities: Complexity and Contested Modernities*, London, Sage.

Waring, M. (1999) *Counting for Nothing: What Men Value and What Women Are Worth* (2nd Edition), Toronto, University of Toronto Press.

7 | The corporate revolution

Kean Birch and John Simoulidis

Introduction

As Chapter 3 has shown, the spread of capitalism is bound up with the actions and activities of the state *and* of business, and not one *or* the other. The spread of capitalism is also embedded in a series of so-called revolutions in the organization of ownership, work, production, and consumption – these stretch from the Agricultural Revolution discussed in Chapter 2, through the Industrial Revolution mentioned in Chapter 3, to the corporate revolution we focus on in this chapter. It's interesting to note that these revolutions, although related, did not necessarily follow from one another geographically or historically; for example, although the Agricultural and Industrial revolutions are most often associated with Britain, the corporate revolution happened, primarily, in the United States at the end of the nineteenth century (Cheffins 2008). The corporate revolution heralded the rise to dominance of corporations as the key business organization in capitalist countries, a trend which has lasted over a century and is still with us today. It has led to a range of debates about the responsibilities and roles of corporations in society (see Chapter 9), the expansion of corporate power (see 10 and 21) and the ethics of corporate decision-making (see Chapter 19).

The corporate revolution has its own peculiar origins and characteristics; we briefly outline them here, but we want to emphasize that different people have very different perspectives about these as well. Generally, most scholars and social commentators agree that the modern corporation has its origins in the joint-stock companies (JSC) that helped fuel the spread of capitalism – see Chapter 3. However, in countries like Britain and the United States the laws and regulations governing JSCs changed quite significantly during the nineteenth century, leading to the corporate revolution at the end of the 1800s. A number of thinkers, especially in economics and management studies (e.g. Chandler 1977), saw this evolution of the corporation as a part of a trend towards rising efficiency over time in the organization of business resulting from competitive market pressures. Others, especially in fields like sociology and law, have argued otherwise (e.g. Whitley 1999). We want to emphasize that it's important to avoid taking an economically determinist perspective when discussing capitalism: that is, we need to avoid assuming that there are economic imperatives or market forces (e.g. competition) beyond human control that direct our actions, decisions and behaviours. Rather, a critical approach to understanding the relationship between business and society necessitates an examination of the social actors involved, their rationales, their institutional context and the processes they constitute.

In this chapter we provide a brief outline of the corporate revolution from a more orthodox perspective and from more critical perspectives. We do this in order to challenge the assumption that capitalism necessarily drives our economies towards rising efficiency through market competition. We start with a brief history of the corporation and how the corporate revolution can be understood from an economically determinist perspective. We then present the critical perspectives that challenge this economic determinism, especially in relation to the legal, institutional and normative evolution of the corporation as a business organization. We finish with an example of the changes that happened in the UK and United States during the nineteenth century which led to the corporate revolution at the end of that century.

Key discussion questions

- What is a corporation?
- What was the corporate revolution?
- Are corporations the most efficient form of business organization?
- How have corporations changed over the nineteenth and twentieth centuries?
- What are the different legal conceptions of the corporation?
- Was the corporate revolution a revolution in efficiency or institutions?

Mainstream perspectives

A brief history of business and the corporation. Some people, like Micklethwait and Wooldridge (2005: 4–5), trace the historical origins of the modern corporation as far back as Ancient Rome. They argue that Romans created organizational entities with separate and distinct legal identities from their individual, human members – companies and guilds, in particular. From a modern perspective we may find it perfectly normal to consider an organization (e.g. corporation) to have an identity that is separate from its members (e.g. managers, workers, investors), but this notion of *legal personhood* has a complex legal history when it comes to corporations – see our discussion later for more. Broadly speaking, people have been creating (technically) non-business collective entities and organizations to carry out collective activities for hundreds of years, if not thousands. Examples would include things like religious communities, towns and cities, universities and so on. Legal personhood provides a number of benefits for undertaking these collective activities, including independence from the state or crown; long-life so the entity can survive the death of its founders; collective identity so individual members are not held responsible for collective decisions and actions; and the capacity to undertake major tasks in the public interest, which individual people cannot do by themselves (Cheffins 2008).

Definition: Legal personhood

Not every human person is treated equally before the law; for example, children are usually treated differently from adults. Moreover, the law also allows people to establish organizations with a separate legal identity from themselves, like a corporation. This does not mean that an organization is a 'person', just that they are treated like one when it comes to the law (e.g. they can sue and be sued, they can own property, they can hire workers).

When it comes to the history of the corporation, the key organizations – in a European medieval context at least – were the guilds and regulated merchant companies, according to Micklethwait and Wooldridge (2005). Regulated companies represented groups of merchants who were *granted a charter* by the Crown that gave them exclusive rights – known as a monopoly – to overseas trade routes with specific parts of the world. For example, the Russia Company was established in England in 1553 to trade with Russia, meaning that no other English company could trade with Russia (Cheffins 2008). The Russia Company was also the first joint-stock company (JSC) chartered by the English Crown, meaning that it was the first company owned by 'stockholders' and not those who managed the business – see Chapter 3 for more on JSCs and the rise of capitalism. Basically, people could buy shares (or stocks) in a JSC and benefit from any profit the JSC made from their trade voyages to far-off places without being liable for any debts incurred. Since these voyages were very risky (e.g. ships sank or were captured by pirates) it made sense to pool the risk among a number of investors and over several voyages (Micklethwait and Wooldridge 2005). The popularity of these JSCs waxed and waned in England (and then Britain) over the following century or so, until the late seventeenth and early eighteenth centuries when there was a rise in parliamentary charters leading to a stock market bubble and major stock market crash in 1720 – the South Sea Bubble, named after the company who, despite having a monopoly, failed to profit from it. Its stock price rose tenfold over the course of a year thanks to rumours of its extravagant success, rumours which were spread by the company itself. Then, after a speculative frenzy, the stock price crashed and bankrupted many who had bought on credit, as well as banks who issued loans backed by the stock (Cowles 1960). After the South Sea Bubble, JSCs were

TABLE 7.1 Joint-stock Company versus Partnership

Characteristic	Joint-stock company	Partnership
Established	By grant from the state	As contract between individual partners
Ownership	Owned by shareholders	Owned by partners
Lifespan	Renewed every few years; potentially forever	As long as lifespan of partners; dissolved when one dies
Liability	Shareholders not liable for debts of JSC	Partners liable for debts of partnership
Management	Shareholders elected directors who appointed overseas governors	Partners
Rights	Legal independent identity, own property, sue and be sued, etc.	Same as partners' individual rights

largely banned in Britain until the 1800s; this ban was in spite of the massive growth of manufacturing and trade resulting from the Industrial Revolution during the same period (Handlin and Handlin 1945). Instead of the JSC, the Industrial Revolution was dominated by partnerships as a business structure; this was a very different business structure compared with the JSC, as outlined in Table 7.1.

Key concept: Grant theory of the corporation

Before the mid-1800s, joint-stock companies (JSC) could only be established in England/Britain through the granting of a charter from the Crown or Parliament. This meant that JSCs – the forerunner of modern corporations – and other corporate entities (e.g. towns) could not be set up by anyone whenever they wanted; they required the political consent of the state. The charter laid out what the JSC could do, what privileges it had and for how long. For example, charters gave corporate entities the right to hold property, to sue and be sued, to an existence independent from its members, and to control and discipline the actions of their members (e.g. workers). JSCs were distinct from other corporate entities because they also had exclusive rights to specific trade routes, exploration and even territory. A corporate charter had to be renewed often (e.g. every twenty-one years), which meant that the state could take back their grant if they were unhappy with the actions of the corporation.

Source: Barkan (2013)

The corporate revolution: evolution towards efficiency? At the end of the nineteenth century, Britain was the dominant world economy, attracting a significant proportion of global investment and producing a significant proportion of the world's manufacturing output. This reflected the advantage provided by the Agricultural and Industrial revolutions that started in England and Britain. However, Britain's global economic dominance gradually shifted towards other countries after 1870, especially to the United States and Germany, where new forms of business organization enabled these countries to expand investment in manufacturing. This gave rise to what scholars have called the *corporate revolution* and *managerial capitalism* (Whitley 1999).

According to sociologist William Roy (1997), the corporate revolution resulted from the marriage between finance and manufacturing which provided corporations with greater access to investment capital through an expansion and distribution of the shareholder base. This was done by enabling more people to buy and trade shares, which meant that shareholding was no longer limited to wealthy individuals. As a result, the ownership of shares became increasingly widespread and distributed, and corporations were able to grow much larger than previously with this influx of capital. This capital enabled corporations to integrate vertically so that their operations ran from resource extraction through manufacturing to final sales. All of this happened at the end of the nineteenth century but led to a number of subsequent changes in the following century or so.

The phrase 'managerial capitalism' is used to describe the period following the corporate revolution. According to Whitley (1999: 8), managerial capitalism was 'dominated by large vertically integrated, and often horizontally diversified, firms run by salaried managers organized into authority hierarchies'. Managerial capitalism is characterized by the separation of ownership and control and is closely associated with the corporate revolution. At the start of the twentieth century, legal theorists like Berle and Means (1932 [1967]) argued that the corporate revolution had ushered in a clear separation between owners of and managers of corporations, which helped to transform the structure and strategies of corporations. This separation was the main way to distinguish business in the twentieth century from earlier business organizations. For example, business partnerships were popular before the corporate revolution, especially in the UK. In a partnership the owners (i.e. partners) also manage the business to ensure that it's successful. With a (public) corporation, however, the owners (i.e. shareholders) do not (usually) manage the business; instead, they leave it to professional managers trained in management techniques at business schools (Khurana 2007).

A number of scholars have argued that the corporate revolution and managerial capitalism result primarily from economic forces that reward economic efficiencies. First, the economist Ronald Coase (1937) argued that the firm (a less specific term than corporation) represented an important alternative to the market coordination of economic activity. Markets exist wherever agents or organizations involved in production buy inputs or services from outsiders or 'arms-length' suppliers rather than using a mechanism like a formal organization to hire and assign regular employees to make those inputs and services internally. By contrast, firms exist when it's more rational for an agent or organization to use its own resources and regular employees to 'make' rather than 'buy' from outsiders. Coase argued that the decision whether to 'make or buy' depended on what he famously called *transaction costs*. Although orthodox economic theory assumed that markets – conceived as transacting between independent agents who are free to set their own prices – are the most efficient way of coordinating production, it could not explain why so much production took place within organizations (i.e. not in markets). Coase's answer was that all market transactions involve some form of cost to them, including the cost of finding information, negotiating contracts and enforcing contracts. In this context, there are many risks and information deficiencies that people encounter when dealing with arm's-length suppliers or workers. For example, hiring and training workers for daily production runs can be very inefficient compared to hiring employees on long-term contracts. This is why it's often more efficient for production to be coordinated within firms and why Coase's theory could be used by so many later theorists as a model for explaining what the 'optimal' size of firms would be under certain conditions or in certain industries.

Along similar lines to Coase, the well-known management expert Alfred Chandler (1977) argued that the organizational coordination of economic activities provided significant benefits from economies of scale within businesses, as opposed to the market coordination of those same activities. Chandler argued that the former, internal coordination by management, represented the 'visible hand' of capitalism, as opposed to the 'invisible hand' of the market posited by Adam Smith in the late eighteenth century – see Chapter 4. Chandler argued that this internal coordination by management was more efficient than market coordination and, consequently, this explained why large corporations came to dominate American society – and then the rest of the world. Managers were able, for example, to take advantage of the size of corporations in their planning of economic activities, such as making long-term investment in corporate research and development departments which promised new products and services in the future. These sorts of investment were unlikely to happen if left to the market because market coordination is driven by short-term profit horizons.

Key concept: Invisible hand versus visible hand?

The metaphor of the invisible hand comes from Adam Smith in *The Wealth of Nations* (1776). According to Smith, in capitalism no individual seeks to promote the public interest (or the overall wealth of a country), nor could they know whether their actions did promote the public interest. However, this is not a problem because the competitive dynamic of market forces under capitalism is sufficient to ensure that resources are allocated in the most efficient manner. Capitalism is an economic system which is self-regulating, in which even if an individual 'intends only his [*sic*] own gain, and he is in this, as in many other cases, led by an *invisible hand* to promote an end which was no part of his intention'. In contrast, Alfred Chandler argued that managerial capitalism, in which managers planned and directed the administrative apparatus of large corporations, was based on the *visible hand* of management. The economic and professional leadership of the managerial class under capitalism – not the unguided play of market forces in Smith's model – is what allows the complex problems of the modern business system to be managed for the good of society.

Source: Chandler (1977)

From this brief discussion it's possible to highlight at least three ways that mainstream theories adopt an economically determinist view of the corporate revolution. This relates to assumptions about the following:

- *Legal structure*: they tend to assume that the legal structure of businesses and corporations necessarily follows economic pressures like market competition, transaction costs and economies of scale.
- *Organizational structure*: they tend to assume that there is one best way to organize business, and this reflects economic goals (e.g. profit). This assumption means that organizational structure is treated as the outcome of rational, self-interested action and decisions, which evolve towards more efficient structures over time.
- *Social structure*: they tend to assume that humans are individualistic and self-interested beings, which means that other considerations (e.g. ethics and social relations) do not need explanation or taking into account.

We take a critical look at these three issues in the following section as we problematize the notion that business organization necessarily evolves towards more economically efficient structures as the result of economic pressures.

Critical perspectives

From a critical perspective the corporate revolution shouldn't be read as a story of evolution towards economic progress and efficiency. The mainstream views we presented earlier imply that there was a gradual evolution of business organization from medieval JSCs to modern corporations with the assumption that the modern corporation, as the seeming endpoint of this evolution, is the most efficient way to organize business and, consequently, the best way to run the economy. This story of progress towards efficiency is inaccurate at best, as many scholars have stressed (e.g. Fligstein 1990; Roy 1997; Guinnane et al. 2007; Ireland 2010), and seriously misleading at worst. We want to highlight several aspects of the development of the corporation that need closer inspection in order to demonstrate how this notion of progress towards economic efficiency is deeply problematic on a number of levels.

- *Legally* corporations have evolved in relation to a range of forces, many of which have included political and social pressures and expectations as to the roles and responsibilities of large business organizations in society. Specifically, corporate structure and corporate personhood have evolved over time in response to these non-economic forces.
- *Empirically* corporations cannot be defined simply as business organizations responding to market signals and imperatives; they are social institutions that operate within broader social, legal and political contexts.
- *Normatively* the expansion of corporations has led to a number of problematic consequences which we briefly touch on here and come back to in later chapters.

We discuss each of these points in turn in this section, starting with the legal evolution of the corporation from the early nineteenth century onwards, focusing specifically on the United States. In running through these arguments, we want to stress that any form of economic determinism – that is assuming economic imperatives (e.g. profit) shape society – needs questioning wherever it appears.

Legal evolution of corporate structure and personhood. One of the critical things to bear in mind when discussing the corporate revolution is that legal concepts of the corporation have changed quite considerably over time, especially from the early nineteenth century to today – see Case Study. During this period of time, as the modern corporation emerged and rose to dominance, there have been at least four theories of the corporation that reflect a slow transformation of our understanding of corporate personhood and corporate governance. Here we draw on the legal work of William Bratton (1989), whose discussion largely focuses on the legal context in the UK and United States (see also Dewey 1926; Gindis 2009; Weinstein 2012).

- *Artificial entity and concession* (up to early nineteenth century): before *general incorporation* was introduced corporations were considered to be legal fictions created as a result of a concession (or charter) from the state. A (joint-stock) corporation was an artificial entity, created by the state, which provided its shareholders with *limited liability*.
- *Aggregate entity and contract* (late nineteenth century): as the UK and the United States introduced general incorporation laws during the nineteenth century, the perception of the corporation shifted. Corporations were no longer seen as a concession or grant from the state – because the state no

longer gave out charters – but as a contract between those people who owned shares in a corporation. Corporations were, therefore, seen as an aggregate entity representing all their individual members.

- *Natural or real entity* (post-1900 until 1970s): following the corporate revolution, the ownership and control of corporations was separated between shareholders and management respectively. The concept of a corporation in this period was dominated by the idea corporations are real entities with their own identity that are run by managers in pursuit of the corporation's interests, rather than shareholders. Shareholders can buy or sell shares in a corporation as they desire, but do not represent the corporation and do not control its assets. This view is based on the reality that there are no permanent owners (e.g. shareholders trade their shares constantly) and owners have become passive rather than active (e.g. shareholders do not get involved in day-to-day management).

- *Nexus of contracts* (post-1970s): the most recent legal conception of the corporation comes out of financial economics by economists like Jensen and Meckling (1976), who built on the earlier work of Ronald Coase. It's primarily based on the idea that a corporation is only a nexus (i.e. central connection point) of various contracting individuals (e.g. managers, shareholders and workers); in this sense, a corporation is merely another kind of market. This perspective stresses that shareholders are owners and need to be able to control managers, who are characterized as the agents of the owners. This means creating incentives for managers to only make decisions that increase shareholder value (and nothing else).

Definition: General incorporation

This term refers to laws that enable people to establish businesses, especially corporations. What this means is that anyone can set up a business by submitting the relevant legal documents and does not need to request a charter from the government anymore. These laws were gradually introduced during the nineteenth century in the UK, the United States and elsewhere.

Definition: Limited liability

This term refers to laws limiting the responsibilities of shareholders only to their monetary investment in a corporation. This means that shareholders are not responsible for the actions of corporations, including any debts incurred as part of their operations. Consequently, shareholders do not have to think about or oversee their investments to ensure that they are being used in a financially *and* socially responsible manner. It enables the separation of shareholding and management.

What these legal definitions of the corporation illustrate is that the law's treatment of the corporation is not consistent over time; it changes as a result of legal debate and disagreement. While the legal concept of a corporation may seem like an esoteric topic, it's important because these legal concepts impact the arguments and decisions that get made in court rooms, which then have implications subsequently for what corporations, shareholders, managers and others can do. Here we highlight one example of these impacts relating to managerial decision-making. The nexus of contract (NOC) definition of the corporation has become very influential since the 1970s, which has meant that most corporations are now run in specific ways (see Stout 2012). NOC is based on the idea that managers need clear incentives to ensure they *only* increase shareholder value, and not their own personal goals. One way to do this is to link managerial salaries to share prices, so that rising share prices lead to rewards for managers. This has involved giving senior managers (e.g. chief executive officers, or CEOs) share options that they can cash in when share prices rise; while this might sound sensible, a number of academics and others have pointed out several problems with this form of managerial remuneration. For example, it leads to managers focusing on short-term goals at the expense of long-term performance (Bratton 1989; Dobbin and Jung 2010; Stout 2012; Belanfanti and Stout 2018).

Case study

Company law changes in the nineteenth century

Britain

Bubble Act repealed (1825):

- The 1720 Bubble Act limited the creation of new JSCs for fear that new JSCs were being created for purely speculative purposes. The Bubble Act was only repealed in 1825, which opened the way for the granting of new JSCs by Parliament. However, the establishment of a JSC was still a difficult process because it required parliamentary consent.

Companies Acts (1844, 1856, 1862):

- The three *Companies Acts* progressively extended limited liability and general incorporation.
- The 1844 Act enabled general incorporation of companies; the 1856 Act extended general incorporation and limited liability to most businesses, excluding banks and insurance companies; and the 1862 Act extended general incorporation and limited liability to banks and insurance companies.

United States

State law:

- US company law was made at the state level.
- In 1811 New York state extended general incorporation to some corporations, and then to all corporations in 1846.

- By the end of the 1800s, almost all US states had some form of general incorporation law.

Key legal decisions:

- A lot of US company law reflects key legal decisions.
- In the 1818 *Dartmouth College vs. Madison* decision, the judge ruled that corporations should be understood as private contracts and not government charters.
- In the 1886 *Santa Clara vs. Southern Pacific* decision, the judge ruled that corporations have rights normally limited to people, including rights to due process and equal protection before the law.

Canada

Federal law:

- The Act of 1849 encouraged the formation of JSCs to build roads and other transportation infrastructure, and latter acts related to mining and manufacturing companies.
- The formations of corporations up to 1970 were governed by legislation derived from English company law.
- Canada Business Corporations Act (1970, 1975, 1985).
- A certificate of incorporation can be issued to an adult applicant by filling out a form and paying a small fee.
- Public outcry over the failure to hold anyone accountable for the Westray mine explosion in Nova Scotia in 1992 that killed twenty-six miners led to changes in the Criminal Code of Canada with the aim of holding corporate actors accountable.

Sources: Nace (2003); Stout (2012); Glasbeek (2017)

Corporation as social institution. A second critical issue to bear in mind when it comes to the corporate revolution is that changes in business organization evolve as a consequence of the broader institutional context and not simply because of economic pressures. This is illustrated in the work of economic sociologists who analyse the corporate revolution and subsequent evolution of corporations in the United States, as well as the wider world (e.g. Fligstein 1990; Roy 1997; Whitley 1999). What this research shows is that there is limited empirical support for the idea that the corporate revolution happened as a result of business organization evolving towards more efficient organizational structures. There have been several significant shifts in business organization and strategies, especially of corporations, in the last two hundred years of US history.

The changes in business organization before, during and after the corporate revolution are documented by William Roy (1997) in his book *Socializing Capital*. Roy argues that understanding the corporate revolution necessitates understanding corporations as social institutions and not just as business organizations – the difference between *organizations* and *institutions* is an important one to understand in the social sciences. The point Roy makes is that business structures and strategies are not independent of their social and institutional context. This wider context includes things like legal property rights and obligations, the changing social dimensions of those rights and obligations and the role of the state when it comes to property (Roy 1997). In this sense, if we want to understand the corporate revolution and the subsequent rise of corporations, we have to understand more than economic forces and pressures. We also have to understand law, society, government and so on. Another scholar who makes similar claims is Neil Fligstein (1990). He stresses that the historical evolution of corporate strategies results from different 'conceptions of control' and not economic determinism – that is, each conception of control emerges from the last, being dependent on previous strategies and structures rather than on an independent drivers like economic efficiency. There are, for example, other drivers of change, including the role and actions of the state (e.g. introducing new laws), changing managerial practices (e.g. avoiding competition) and so on (Fligstein 1990).

Key methodological issue: Organization versus institution?

Social scientists make choices about what they study all the time. Studying the relationship between business and society necessitates choices over whether to focus on specific entities (e.g. one business) or broader socio-political trends and patterns (e.g. a range of businesses). Social scientists make an important distinction between organizations and institutions in this regard. Organizations are generally defined as individual entities which have a specific collective purpose, structure and strategies; in contrast, institutions are generally defined as broader and less clear-cut social structures that influence people's behaviour. Institutions can be formal and include things like *the* family as a social arrangement, *the* state as a governmental arrangement, *the* corporation as an economic arrangement, and so on. They can also be informal and include things like social customs, habits and trust. For the purposes of this book, it is important to remember that an institution is more than an individual entity.

In order to illustrate our argument here, we draw on Fligstein's (1990) work in his book *The Transformation of Corporate Control*. He argues that corporations have moved through a range of different structures and strategies since the nineteenth century, each period building on the last. First, the United States' post-Civil War era, at least until 1890, was dominated by the rise of monopolistic strategies, especially through the formation of cartels and trusts according to Fligstein (1990). Cartels and trusts are formal and informal agreements between businesses to collude with one another in order to limit competition – as such, it was a *direct* form of control in a socio-legal context which lacked rules and regulations on business practice. Examples include businesses like Standard Oil. A trust is a legal device designed to vest control of assets in a trustee or group of trustees who act in the interests of the owners of these assets. By 1882, Standard Oil had consolidated forty companies, as no US state allowed 'holding companies' yet. The direct control evident in the late nineteenth century was supplanted by a new conception according to Fligstein, which was driven by new legal limits on monopolies, those resulting from the 1890 *Sherman Antitrust Act.* This Act led to a wave of corporate consolidation: between 1897 and 1904, 4,227 companies merged into 257 corporations. Despite dozens of lawsuits under this Act over the next decades, Rockefeller shifted to the holding company approach to centrally plan the industry: he would rationalize production at the most efficient units and close the least efficient. By 1904, 318 firms controlled 40 per cent of US manufacturing assets. This led to enormous concentrations of wealth: Rockefeller was worth US$1B when he died in 1937, while the US GDP at that time was roughly US$30B (McCraw 1997).

Second, from the late 1800s corporations adopted new organizational structures like the vertical integration of production; this meant incorporating all aspects of production from resource extraction through manufacturing to sales into one organizational structure. Examples here included businesses like General Electric that sold everything from electricity to electric products. Third, this evolved again in the 1920s as these large integrated corporations sought new avenues for growth through the introduction of things like marketing, branding and advertising. This change shifted focus from the production process to the product itself through an emphasis on brands and branding, leading many corporations to diversify into multiple product lines. Examples of these businesses included consumer product companies like Proctor and Gamble.

Fourth, in the 1950s these diversified corporations ended up as giant conglomerates with multiple product lines, competing in multiple markets. They were structured around a central headquarters and subsidiaries in different economic sectors and different countries. Examples here included most corporations in the post–Second World War era (until the 1980s at least). A final shift in corporate strategies has occurred relatively recently, since the 1980s, as financial accounting and finance departments in corporations have come to dominate corporate strategies. This has led to a focus on shareholder value and an emphasis on core competencies; hence, it has meant that many corporations have split up and sold off several of their divisions.

Critique of the rise of corporations. Whether we take the corporate revolution to mean an increase in economic efficiency or not, it's important to question the outcomes and effects of the revolution more generally. We return to a critique of corporate power in Chapter 10, so we limit ourselves to three observations here.

First, the ambiguity of corporate personhood and identity has meant that there have been and still are a number of problems with the way corporations operate and what they can get away with. For example, Veldman and Parker (2012) argue that this ambiguity has meant that corporations are able to claim human rights like the right to speech, even though they are not human. Claims to these sorts of human rights are problematic because corporations are not like humans in important ways; for example, they have a perpetual lifespan and enormous societal influence.

Second, the corporate revolution only happened because of specific changes in laws and regulations affecting corporations during the nineteenth and twentieth centuries, especially the extension of limited liability to a growing number of business organizations, not just corporations. Paddy Ireland (2010) highlights a key contradiction that comes with this shift. While the responsibilities of shareholders have been separated from the responsibilities of corporations, there have been contradictory pressures to ensure that corporations are run in the interests of shareholders. Consequently, shareholders benefit from the current situation without suffering the negative impacts from the actions of corporations.

Third, the evolution of the corporation from the JSC to the modern multinational conglomerate entailed important implications for the structure of the international economy. The multinational conglomerate is a much more powerful organizational form than the national corporation and has much greater power to integrate exchange, production and investment. With considerable foresight, Hymer (1970) warned us of the many social and political problems and economic inefficiencies associated with multinational corporations such as 'want creation, alienation, domination, and the relationship or interface between corporations and national states (including the question of imperialism), which cannot be analyzed in purely "economic" terms' (441).

Finally, the rise of managerial capitalism is also associated with the expansion of the power of corporations. As corporations have become larger and larger, their influence over society (through advertising, employment etc.), politics (through lobbying, donations etc.) and the economy (through size, market power etc.) has also grown (Bakan 2004, 2020). We come back to this discussion of corporate power in Chapter 10, but suffice to say here that the corporate revolution gave rise to growing concerns about the role of corporations in society.

Conclusion

In this chapter we sought to question the notion that the organization of business, including corporations, is determined by economic and market pressures or forces – that is, that business naturally evolves towards greater efficiency over time. First, we outlined the history of the corporate revolution and how corporations are understood from an economically determinist perspective. Second, we problematize economic determinism by outlining the legal, empirical and normative dimensions of the corporate revolution. In particular, we highlighted the evolution of the legal and organizational understandings of corporations. Third, we finished by outlining some of the normative issues with the corporate revolution, which we return to in subsequent chapters. Throughout we have sought to show that corporations have evolved historically in a number of ways that cannot be explained by one perspective.

Suggested readings

- Chs 2–4, Berle, A. and Means, G. (1932 [1967]) *The Modern Corporation and Private Property*, New York, World Inc.
- Conclusion, Chandler, A. (1977 [1993]) *The Visible Hand*, Cambridge, MA, Belknap Press.
- Ch. 1, Fligstein, N. (1990) *The Transformation of Corporate Control*, Cambridge, MA, Harvard University Press.
- Ch. 7, Nace, T. (2003) *Gangs of America*, Oakland, CA, Berrett-Koehler.
- Ch. 1, Roy, W. (1997) *Socializing Capital*, Princeton, Princeton University Press.

Bibliography

Bakan, J. (2004) *The Corporation*, London, Random House.

Bakan, J. (2020) *The New Corporation: How 'good' Corporations are Bad for Democracy*, New York, Allen Lane.

Barkan, J. (2013) *Corporate Sovereignty*, Minneapolis, Minnesota University Press.

Belinfanti, T. and Stout, L. (2018) 'Contested Visions: The Value of Systems Theory for Corporate Law', *University of Pennsylvania Law Review*, Vol. 166, No. 3, pp. 579–632.

Berle, A. and Means, G. (1932 [1967]) *The Modern Corporation and Private Property*, New York, World Inc.

Bratton, W. (1989) 'The New Economic Theory of the Firm: Critical Perspectives from History', *Stanford Law Review*, Vol. 41, pp. 1471–527.

Chandler, A. (1977 [1993]) *The Visible Hand*, Cambridge, MA, Belknap Press.

Cheffins, B. (2008) *Corporate Ownership and Control*, Oxford, Oxford University Press.

Coase, R. (1937) 'The Nature of the Firm', *Economica*, Vol. 4, pp. 386–405.

Cowles, V. (1960) *The Great Swindle: The Story of the South Sea Bubble*, New York, Harper.

Dewey, J. (1926) 'The Historic Background of Corporate Legal Personality', *Yale Law Journal*, Vol. 35, pp. 655–73.

Dobbin, F. and Jung, J. (2010) 'The Misapplication of Mr. Michael Jensen: How Agency Theory Brought Down the Economy and Why it Might Again', in M. Loundsbury and P. Hirsch (eds), *Markets on Trial: The Economic Sociology of the U.S. Financial Crisis (Part B)*, Bingley, Emerald, pp. 29–64.

Fligstein, N. (1990) *The Transformation of Corporate Control*, Cambridge, MA, Harvard University Press.

Gindis, D. (2009) 'From Fictions and Aggregates to Real Entities in the Theory of the Firm', *Journal of Institutional Economics*, Vol. 5, pp. 25–46.

Glasbeek, H. (2017) *Class Privilege: How Law Shelters Shareholders and Coddles Capitalism*, Toronto, Between the Lines.

Guinnane, T., Harris, R., Lamoreaux, N. and Rosenthal, J.-L. (2007) 'Putting the Corporation in its Place', *Enterprise and Society*, Vol. 8, pp. 687–729.

Handlin, O. and Handlin, M. (1945) 'Origins of the American Business Corporation', *The Journal of Economic History*, Vol. 5, pp. 1–23.

Hymer, S. (1970) 'The Efficiency (contradictions) of MNCs', *The American Economic Review*, Vol. 60, No. 2, pp. 441–8.

Ireland, P. (2010) 'Limited Liability, Shareholder Rights and the Problem of Corporate Irresponsibility', *Cambridge Journal of Economics*, Vol. 34, pp. 837–56.

Jensen, M. and Meckling, W. (1976) 'Theory of the Firm: Managerial Behavior, Agency Costs and Ownership Structure', *Journal of Financial Economics*, Vol. 3, pp. 305–60.

Khurana, R. (2007) *From Higher Aims to Hired Hands*, Princeton, Princeton University Press.

McCraw, T.K. (1997) 'American Capitalism', in McCraw (ed.), *Creating Modern Capitalism: How Entrepreneurs, Companies, and Countries Triumphed in Three Industrial Revolutions*, Cambridge, MA, Harvard University Press, pp. 303–48.

Micklethwait, J. and Wooldridge, A. (2005) *The Company*, New York, Modern Library Chronicles Book.

Nace, T. (2003) *Gangs of America*, San Francisco, Berrett-Koehler.

Roy, W. (1997) *Socializing Capital*, Princeton, Princeton University Press.

Stout, L. (2012) *The Shareholder Value Myth*, San Francisco, Berrett-Koehler.

Veldman, J. and Parker, M. (2012) 'Specters, Inc.: The Elusive Basis of the Corporation', *Business and Society Review*, Vol. 117, pp. 413–41.

Weinstein, O. (2012) 'Firm, Property and Governance: From Berle and Means to the Agency Theory, and Beyond', *Accounting, Economics, and Law*, Vol. 2, pp. 1–55.

Whitley, R. (1999) *Divergent Capitalisms*, Oxford, Oxford University Press.

8 | Corporate governance

Alberto Salazar

Introduction

In this chapter we critically review the models for governing for-profit corporations in modern capitalist societies. Governance generally refers to the mechanisms that control and direct the behaviour of individuals, groups or organizations. Corporate governance can be defined as the systems and processes that control and direct the conduct of corporations. It may involve legal and non-legal mechanisms that are used to govern corporations, their activities and the competing interests of shareholders, directors, executives, creditors, employees, consumers, suppliers, local communities, the environment, governments and society. The study of corporate governance is important because it helps us understand how and why corporations are regulated, the competing purposes of corporations, the extent to which the conflicting interests of corporate participants are balanced and whether the activities of the corporations have a positive or negative impact on the economy and society at large.

The current and dominant corporate governance model in liberal-market economies (see Chapter 13), such as the United States, the UK and Canada, is called the 'shareholder primacy' (SHP) model. The SHP model relies on the regulatory power of markets and legal and non-legal mechanisms to largely ensure that shareholders' interests are maximized. Such interests are typically measured by short-term and long-term share value, that in practical terms takes the form of firm profitability. Agency theory and nexus of contracts premised in neoclassical economics have provided the main rationale for SHP (see Chapter 7). Such theories treat shareholders as the highest risk-bearers and 'principals' whose interests should then be prioritized above all others. Directors and executives, therefore, are considered to be the agents of shareholders, who require monitoring to ensure that their behaviour aligns with the interests of shareholders. This chapter describes the SHP model and its problems, highlighting its current crisis of legitimacy. This crisis can be attributed not only to directors' and executives' increasing abuses and shareholders' excessive focus on short-term profits but also to the disregard of the interests of non-shareholder stakeholders, namely, workers, the environment, citizen-consumers, local communities, small businesses, creditors, governments and society at large.

After reviewing the contradictions of the SHP model, the chapter critically examines the alternatives, namely stakeholder-oriented models of corporate governance in liberal and coordinated market-economies (see Chapter 13). First, it analyses the strengths and weaknesses of the team production theory along with fiduciary duty paradigms in liberal-market economies. Second, it discusses the advantages of longstanding stakeholder models of corporate governance in coordinated market economies, especially in Germany and Japan. The chapter concludes with the example of low executive pay in Japanese corporations in order to illustrate modern departures from the SHP model.

Overall, this chapter suggests that the future of the corporation lies in finding effective and creative ways for integrating the interests of non-shareholder stakeholders while moderating the ideological commitment to profit-maximization, short-termism and elite wealth concentration. The renewed interest in stakeholder capitalism, the massive deployment of the new technology and the climate and global economic crises are already creating new pressures on companies around the world to depart from shareholder primacy models and to favour the incorporation of stakeholders' interest, long-term sustainability and the public interest while maintaining diverging corporate governance structures.

Key discussion questions

- What is corporate governance?
- What is the shareholder primacy model of corporate governance?
- What is the stakeholder-oriented model of corporate governance?
- Why is the shareholder model of corporate governance problematic?
- Does the stakeholder model of corporate governance offer a superior form of governance capable of resolving the challenges of governing modern corporations today?

The shareholder primacy model

Shareholder primacy and the agency problem. The shareholder primacy model is the dominant approach to corporate governance in many parts of the world. It is based on the idea that prioritizing shareholders' interest should take priority because they purportedly bear the highest risk as their investment is unsecured (i.e. they are the 'residual claimants'). Macey (1989: 175) argued that 'shareholders retain plenary authority to guide the fate of a corporate enterprise because, at the margin, they have the greatest stake in the outcome of corporate decision-making and not because they hold certain ill-defined property rights'. Whereas employees, creditors, consumers and managers enter into explicit contracts with fixed payments, shareholders rely on implicit contracts that entitle them to whatever remains after the firm has met its explicit obligations and paid its fixed claims (Easterbrook and Fischel 1991). Shareholders are thus described as 'sole residual claimants' to a firm's value or 'sole residual risk bearers' (Clark 1986: 17–18; Macey 1989: 186; Easterbrook and Fischel 1991).

SHP is underpinned by two concepts: (1) nexus of contracts and (2) agency theory (Verret 2010). The nexus of contract approach suggests that all participants are linked to the corporation through private contracts and organized under a single business plan. According to Jensen and Meckling (1976: 310–11), two key economists in these debates, the firm is considered a legal fiction which serves 'as a nexus for a set of contracting relationships' and 'as a focus for a complex process in which the conflicting objectives of individuals . . . are brought into equilibrium within a framework of contractual relations'. Moreover, the contractual relationship between shareholders and managers is also conceived as an 'agency problem'.

The notion of an agency problem originates in the separation of ownership and control in public corporations and represents a key issue facing shareholders ('principals') in the SHP model. Some of the earliest theorists in this area were Berle and Means (1932), who suggested that the separation of ownership and control resulting from the corporate revolution (see Chapter 7) facilitates opportunistic behaviour (i.e. mismanagement) by executives and managers ('agents'). They observed in the United States of the 1920s that the equity ownership of the largest firms had dispersed among numerous shareholders who often owned a small fraction of shares and, as a result, had little incentive to pay close attention to the internal affairs of their firms. These dispersed shareholders were rationally apathetic and were dependent on the recommendations made by executives and managers. According to Berle and Means (1932), control of public firms shifted from dispersed shareholders to executives and managers by default. Although the agency problem concerned Berle and Means, they also recognized that executives and managers should run the corporation to serve the interest of not just shareholders but also employees, consumers and the community.

Later in the twentieth century, Jensen and Meckling (1976) characterized the relationship between shareholders and executives and managers as an agency problem and cost. They based their arguments on the notion that public corporations represent a contract between principals (i.e. shareholders) and agents (i.e. executives and managers). This usually involves the delegation of control to agents in the performance of a service for the principal. Jensen and Meckling (1976: 308) argued that '[i]f both parties to the relationship are utility maximizers, there is good reason to believe that the agent will not always act in the best interests of the principal'. This potential for managerial misconduct was conceptualized as the agency cost problem and co-exists with the growing 'rational apathy' of dispersed shareholders that flowed from the logic of free-riding and a lack of skills and incentives (Clark 1986). In such a context, directors and executives become very powerful as they increasingly control corporate decisions and critical information, thereby further facilitating (1) the misalignment of their interests with the interests of shareholders and (2) managerial misconduct. This explains directors' and executives' decisions to engage in wrongdoings such as financial fraud, misreporting, excessive compensation or irrational risk-taking, according to agency theory.

Minimizing agency costs and monitoring agents thus became a central agenda for SHP approaches. Jensen and Meckling (1976) suggested that incentives for the agents to align their interest with the interests of principals (stockholders) can be established through contracts, law and other organizational forms. However, monitoring agents is costly, and so is devising incentives to align the interests of executives and managers with shareholders. Some of the incentives suggested in agency theory include using executive pay, corporate control transactions, managerial job competition and bankruptcy in conjunction with corporate law and policies (e.g. fiduciary duties of directors and executives and the expansion of shareholders' rights). These economic and legal incentives are expected to help align directors' and executives' conduct with shareholders' interests (Marks 2000). Additionally, corporate self-regulatory practices such as codes of conduct, disciplinary action by business associations and institutional shareholder activism have supplemented existent monitoring mechanisms. The protection of the interests of non-shareholder stakeholders, namely employees, consumers, creditors, local communities, the environment and governments, is believed to be better dealt with by private contracting or public policies (Bebchuk and Tallarita 2022).

Contradictions of the shareholder primacy model. The claim that shareholders are residual claimants as suggested by agency theory is problematic. The only time that shareholders may be residual claimants is when a corporation goes bankrupt. When a corporation is operating normally, shareholders are not necessarily entitled to whatever is left after the firm has met its explicit contractual obligations with employees, creditors, managers or consumers (Stout 2002). For example, Stout (2002) points out that the board of directors has considerable control over corporate earnings or profits and decides when and how profits should be distributed among shareholders. Moreover, other stakeholders can be described as residual claimants or high-risk bearers as they may also enjoy benefits or endure burdens beyond those that are provided in their explicit contracts (Stout 2002; Lazonick and Mazzucato 2013). For example, employees may receive a pay increase, bonus, longer job security benefits or suffer early layoffs or reduced working hours.

Furthermore, the persistence of agency cost problems continues to challenge the descriptive and normative power of the SHP model. The many mechanisms developed to control the conduct of executives and managers and align their behaviour with the interest of shareholders have been largely ineffective. Directors and executives continue to engage in many forms of mismanagement, including financial fraud, misreporting, excessive compensation or serving the interests of majority shareholders at the expense of minority shareholders and other non-shareholder stakeholders. For example, Oracle's Larry Ellison was the highest-paid CEO in the United States in 2012; he received $96.2 million that year, a 24 per cent increase, despite his company's share price falling by 23 per cent (Fairchild 2013). More revealing, nearly 40 per cent of the highest-paid CEOs in the United States have been bailed out, fired or arrested for illegal activities (Anderson et al. 2013). More recently, Theranos, a Silicon Valley 'unicorn' (i.e. a tech startup with a valuation of at least $1 billion), and its CEO Elizabeth Holmes, claimed that the company found a revolutionary way 'to scan for hundreds of potential diseases with a device called the Edison that could test just a few drops of blood taken with a finger prick' (Liedtke 2022). Theranos persuaded well-known investors and reached a near-$10 billion valuation in 2014. Reputable people such as retired general James Mattis, former secretary of state Henry Kissinger and former Wells Fargo chief executive Richard Kovacevich were involved as board members, which signalled to the public that the company was both reliable and successful (McCrum 2022). Later, it was revealed that Edison never worked, and the tests were faulty (Liedtke 2022). Both Holmes and former company president Sunny Balwani were charged with massive fraud in 2022 (Liedtke 2022).

Moreover, new agency costs have arisen with the shift in share ownership from dispersed individual owners to concentrated institutional investors or intermediaries such as asset management companies, pension and mutual funds and insurance companies in the last decades (Gilson and Gordon 2014). These institutional investors often invest on behalf of individuals and organization (the 'ultimate beneficiaries') that own the financial capital. For example, and as outlined in Table 8.1, investment intermediaries owned over 70 per cent of the stock of the largest 1,000 US public corporations around 2009, and the ownership of two dozen institutional investors was large enough to exert influence or control (Gilson and Gordon 2014: 6–7). This transformation in share ownership has been described by some academics as 'agency capitalism' (7) and has created new agency costs, that is to say 'institutional intermediaries engage in own-goal pursuit at the expense of ultimate beneficiaries' (7). Share ownership concentration has worsened in the last years with the rise of the 'Big Three' global asset management companies (i.e. BlackRock, Vanguard and State Street Global Advisors) that own most companies across different sectors

TABLE 8.1 Institutional Ownership of Largest US Corporations, 2009

Corporations ranked by size	Average institutional holdings (%)
Top 50	63.7
Top 100	66.9
Top 250	69.3
Top 500	72.8
Top 1000	73.0

Sources: Tonello and Rabimov (2010: 27 tbl.13); Gilson and Gordon (2013: 875).

and countries. Institutional investors or intermediaries appear to lack strong incentives to engage in shareholder activism, and there is an ongoing debate about the degree of their passivity or activism for or against stakeholders' interests. For example, some authors claim that the 'Big Three' are engaging in carbon emission reduction policies in companies in which they hold a significant stake (Azar et al. 2021).

Lastly, the SHP model has fostered a culture of short-term shareholder value while disregarding the interests of employees, consumers, creditors, suppliers, the environment, local communities and governments (Sayer 2015). Such an outcome has jeopardized the long-term sustainability of corporations, caused constant financial crises, widened the gap between executive pay and worker wages (Sayer 2015) and worsened the current climate crisis. This has contributed to creating further social and political instability. For instance, the gap between the rich and poor continues to grow faster, and only the wealthy are likely to invest in the capital market and then become shareholders and benefit financially, thereby worsening wealth concentration in society. Similarly, companies' carbon emissions have exacerbated global warming and the commitment of directors, executives and shareholders to climate change has been ambiguous. The SHP model appears to legitimize the rise of such shareholder class and its wealth accumulation priorities often at the expense of non-shareholder stakeholders' interests. Prioritizing and maximizing shareholder value in practice means organizing the corporation and the economy to serve the interests of the shareholder class (Ireland 2005).

Stakeholder models of corporate governance

The belief that corporations should focus on maximizing shareholder value has been questioned by various scholars, activists, journalists and others. These criticisms have pushed for a rethinking of existing corporate governance models and the need for integrating the interests of non-shareholder stakeholders. In the Anglo-American world, this debate began in the 1930s between Adolf Berle and Merrick Dodd. On the one hand, Berle (1931: 1049) supported the SHP model, arguing that 'all powers granted to a corporation or to the management of a corporation, or to any group within the corporation . . . [are] at all times exercisable only for the rateable benefit of all the shareholders as their interest appears'. On the other hand, Merrick Dodd (1932) contended that the purpose of a corporation was not confined to making profits for shareholders. In his view, a corporation also has a social service function and should provide secure jobs for employees, provide better quality products for consumers and contribute to the community.

More recently, the growing dissatisfaction with the SHP model has shifted the focus to stakeholder models of corporate governance, which are often associated with coordinated market economies (Hall and Soskice 2001). The following section reviews the alternatives to the SHP model.

Stakeholder models in liberal market economies. One influential stakeholder approach in the Anglo-American world with liberal-market economies (Hall and Soskice 2001) has been the team production theory. Margaret Blair and Lynn Stout (1999) developed this theory as an alternative to the SHP model. They recognize that employees, creditors, managers and governments contribute to the success of a corporation. They note that SHP may actually discourage non-shareholder constituents from making the types of firm-specific investments that are critical to a company's success (Blair and Stout 1999; Stout 2002). In their view, directors and executives should acknowledge and reward such contributions and should balance the multiple interests of shareholders, employees, creditors, suppliers, consumers and governments. As a result, the board of directors is vested with significant discretion to conduct the balancing act. The need to balance multiple interests is partially justified by the recognition that private contracting does not necessarily protect the interests and expectations of all corporate constituencies because of the difficulties in drafting complete contracts under conditions of complexity and uncertainty, contrary to the predictions of the nexus of contract approach (Blair and Stout 1999; Stout 2002).

Similarly, the broadening of the fiduciary duties of directors and executives and the emergence of the enlightened shareholder value model have altered the traditional SHP model to accommodate stakeholders' interests. The fiduciary duties of directors and executives have been expanded to permit or require them to consider the interests of employees, creditors, consumers, local communities, the environments and governments. The pursuit of shareholder value while considering or benefiting such stakeholders has been conceptualized as the 'enlightened shareholder value model'. In this model, directors and executives are also encouraged or obligated to pursue the long-term interests of companies. This has often been translated into the pursuit of long-term shareholder value (Bebchuk et al. 2022), thereby avoiding short-termism and instead favouring of the long-term sustainability of companies. The UK and Canada are good examples of jurisdictions which uphold the enlightened shareholder value model. For example, Section 172 (1) of the UK 2006 Companies Act states:

> [a] director of a company must act in the way he considers, in good faith, would be most likely to promote the success of the company for the benefit of its members as a whole, and in doing so have regard (amongst other matters) to (a) the likely consequences of any decision in the long term, (b) the interests of the company's employees, (c) the need to foster the company's business relationships with supplies, customers and others; (d) the impact of the company's operations on the community and the environment.

In Canada, Section 122 of the Canada Business Corporations Act was amended in 2019 to permit directors and officers to consider the interests of multiple stakeholders – including employees and the environment – when exercising their powers and discharging their duties with a view to the best interests of the corporation. While these are significant amendments to the SHP model, they have had only a little impact as these duties to consider stakeholders' interests have not been binding.

In addition to the unenforceability and the lack of practical effects of broader fiduciary duties of directors and executives, directors' suggested task of balancing multiple stakeholders' interests can be extremely problematic and unfeasible in the daily reality of corporate decision-making. In conducting the balancing act, directors and executives may instead serve their own interests (Bebchuk and Tallarita 2022). Stout (2002) recognizes that problem and admits that executives and managers in a team production context can also face significant agency cost problems. Even if willing, directors and executives are likely to face significant difficulties in measuring, implementing, assessing or disclosing their decisions to serve multiple stakeholders' interests (Bebchuk and Tallarita 2022).

Moreover, directors and executives are often under pressure from shareholders, particularly majority shareholders, to focus on shareholder value maximization, thereby hindering attempts to protect the interests of employees, creditors, suppliers, consumers, the environment and the community. Controlling or majority shareholders can put significant pressure on directors and executives to prioritize their interests even to the extent of capturing corporate boards to the detriment of non-shareholder stakeholders' interest (Coates 1999; Gold 2012; Millon 2000). This problem is further compounded when directors and executives are also shareholders. In such a case, they are unlikely to favour the protection of non-shareholder stakeholders as this may result in a reduction of shareholder value and thus a loss to their own interests as shareholders.

Ultimately, the limitations of the team production and fiduciary duty approaches in liberal-market economies reveal that relying solely on the goodwill, skills, discretion or even duties of directors and executives to build a stakeholder-friendly corporation is extremely difficult and ultimately insufficient. The abovementioned concerns, if unresolved, may undermine the value and feasibility of the team production theory and the expanded fiduciary duties of directors and executives. Given such objections, the SHP model, despite its problems, is preferred by some academics, policymakers and companies as it provides an easily observable metric for directors' and executives' accountability. That's to say, changes in share value can serve as primary or sole indicators of their performance and can be easily observed and used by shareholders to discipline directors and executives, thereby minimizing agency cost (Stout 2002). These apparent benefits of the SHP model are, however, dependent on the accuracy of share value, the availability of reliable firm performance information, the absence of managerial misconduct and the ability and activism of shareholders, among other things. The SHP model's disregard of the interests of stakeholders followed by instabilities and the lack of sustainability of companies and the economy also remains as a fundamental concern.

Nevertheless, team production mechanisms and multi-stakeholder fiduciary duties could create incentives for stakeholder activism, which can in turn put pressure on directors, executives, shareholders and companies as a whole to protect non-shareholder stakeholders' interests. For example, workers may see their interests recognized and legally permitted or required as part of directors' and executives' duties, which can prompt workers to become active to seek protection for their interests. Such activism may also help correct the problems of agency cost, excessive managerial discretion and controlling shareholder power. It may also encourage the adoption of some form of coordination or informal co-determination practices that may be responsive to stakeholders' interests, long-term sustainability and the public interest. Such informal coordination or co-determination is partially facilitated by the institutional incentives created by stakeholder-oriented fiduciary duties of directors and executives, and its effectiveness depends on the power struggles inside and outside boardrooms and courtrooms and beyond corporate law. From this perspective, team production theory and broadened fiduciary duties can potentially offer a superior alternative to the SHP model.

Stakeholder models in coordinated market economies. Important alternatives to the SHP model are found in the stakeholder models of corporate governance that are prevalent in coordinated market economies such as Germany and Japan. These stakeholder models do not rely solely on the ability of directors and executives to integrate the interests of multiple stakeholders as suggested by team production and fiduciary duty approaches. Instead, they grant decision-making power to multiple stakeholders, notably workers and creditors, and encourage strong forms of co-determination in which shareholders, directors and executives are not the sole decision-makers, but rather they coordinate their interests with the interests of creditors, workers, consumers and governments.

In Germany, corporate governance has been described as an insider-controlled and a stakeholder-oriented system (Franks and Mayer 2001; Schmidt 2004). It has two striking characteristics, namely, mandatory co-determination and a strong role for banks. Co-determination involves employee representation through a two-tier board system, namely, a management board ('Vorstand') and a supervisory board ('Aufsichtsrat'). The management board manages and represents the company, and the supervisory board appoints and oversees the management board of the company (Tungler 2000). Employee representatives sit on supervisory boards and often provide effective and highly informed monitoring of the management board (Fauver and Fuerst 2006). In addition to sitting on supervisory boards, employees also participate in the governance of German firms through works councils (Fauver and Fuerst 2006). These Councils represent employees' interest outside corporate boards and provide advice to management and are to be consulted on general working conditions.

Traditionally, banks have played a central role in corporate governance in Germany along with family investors and the labour force (Bessler et al. 2013). Banks have been long-term lenders and have owned large equity stakes in German firms (Bessler et al. 2013). Their equity stakes have enabled banks to sit on supervisory boards and to act on behalf of investors through voting proxies, thereby often controlling the majority of voting rights in German firms (Bessler et al. 2013; Jackson 2005). As a result, banks have exerted substantial long-term-oriented influence over corporate governance decisions, which is reflected in a modest market for corporate control and little shareholder activism (Bessler et al. 2013).

Despite recent changes to the traditional dominant role of banks (due to, for example, integration of German capital markets into European and global financial markets, reduced monitoring role and tax incentives to reduce shareholding), the German corporate governance system has been able to preserve its strong commitment to stakeholders' interest and long-term sustainability. Banks still hold a significant number of board seats in many German firms despite large sell-offs of their equity holdings; family investors continue to hold controlling stakes in a large number of listed small- and mid-sized firms; and workers and unions are still influential in corporate decisions due to mandatory co-determination and continue to bring significant challenges to hedge fund activism inside and outside supervisory boards (Bessler et al. 2013). For instance, section 90 of the Works Constitution Act, as amended in June 2021, requires employers to inform works councils about the use of artificial intelligence and works councils also monitor its implementation.

In Japan, corporate governance departs from the SHP models and favours a stakeholder model. Generally, the Japanese corporate governance model is characterized by main bank capital markets, *keiretsu* cross-holdings, and insider boards of directors (Higgins 2004; Basu et al. 2007). The *keiretsu* is an industrial group whose member firms are bound by long-term cross-shareholdings and maintain strong business and financial ties (Higgins 2004; Basu et al. 2007). The *keiretsu* system provides a strong monitoring mechanism, unlike the SHP model. By pooling voting rights, the *keiretsu* has control over member executives and managers, ensuring that none behave opportunistically (Basu et al. 2007). Firms that belong to the *keiretsu* are essentially bound together by a series of connected contracts, which maintain the crucial business relationships. Japanese boards have a hierarchical structure, and their composition depends on promotion from within the company with very little influence from 'outsiders' except for the main bank representatives (Higgins 2004). The extensive use of joint labour-management consultation allows employees to express their interests within Japanese corporate governance structures, unlike the more formal and legal participation of employees in German boards (Jackson 2005).

Banks were restricted in their use of cross-shareholding after the deregulation of the financial systems and corporate governance reforms in Japan. In 2003, the Commercial Code allowed Japanese firms to adopt a new board system with three committees (auditing, nomination and compensation) resembling the committee system that is found in the SHP model. The majority of the members of the new Japanese committees are expected to be outside directors (Hoshi and Kashyap 2010; Sakawa et al. 2012; Gilson and Milhaupt 2005; Jackson and Milhaupt 2014). However, some studies have shown that internationally exposed, more experienced and highly cross-held firms, with higher foreign ownership, are more likely to adopt the board model with three committees (Chizema and Shinozawa 2012). On the other hand, firms with larger proportions of bank ownership are to some extent negatively associated with the adoption of the committee system. As a result, the traditional monitoring of firms by banks seems to be declining (Chizema and Shinozawa 2012). These corporate governance changes may have an impact on the traditional Japanese model of governance. For example, Japanese corporations may be making a slow transition from the traditional approval of self-proposed executive compensation at the annual shareholder meeting to compensation committee determination (Sakawa and Watanabel 2013).

Empirical example: Executive pay in Japanese corporations

An important example of the difference between shareholder and stakeholder models of corporate governance can be found in the area of executive pay. Executive compensation practices in Japan illustrate such differences. Historically, Japanese corporations have developed a pattern of low executive pay in contrast to the excessive executive pay in liberal-market economies with a SHP model (see Chapter 13). As data in Table 8.2 shows, Japan has had lower executive pay levels than the United States since at least the late 1980s.

Even though CEO compensation in Japan has increased in the last years, it remains significantly lower than in the United States and Europe (Morita et al. 2020). In 2015, median CEO compensation in Japan was less than 10 per cent of comparable CEO compensation in the United States (Nikkei Asia 2016). In 2019, CEOs in Japan reportedly made one-ninth of their US counterparts (Kubota 2019). Contrary to Japan's executive pay tradition, the use of stock-based long-term incentive (LTI) plans to compensate CEOs in Japan has expanded in the last years, and that may partially explain the rise in executive pay (Morita et al. 2020). Yet, approximately 30 per cent of listed companies adopted stock-option plans in 2020 (Jacoby 2022:13) and 29 per cent of total CEO compensation was stock-based LTIs pay in 2019 versus 72 per cent in the United States (Morita et al. 2020). CEO compensation in Japan thus appears now more linked to share value and shareholders' interests than before. However, it's still not strongly tied to shareholder value as evidenced by the Japan-US executive pay gap, lower levels of stock-based pay and smaller financial rewards for meeting share value targets (Pan and Zhou 2018; Jacoby 2022: 13). The disparities between executive pay and worker wages further illustrate the extent to which Japan has diverged from liberal-market economies on excessive executive compensation. Jackson (2005: 292) notes that 'CEO pay was 7.8 times higher in Japan than the average worker, and 25.8 times

TABLE 8.2 International Comparison of Average Executive Pay (2001, US dollars)

Country	CEO pay (1988)	CEO pay (2001)	Percentage change 1988–2001	Ratio of CEO to worker pay, 2001	Foreign pay relative to US pay, 2001 US = 100	
					CEO	worker
Japan	$455,909	$508,106	11%	11.6	26%	93%
Canada	$383,999	$787,060	105%	23.2	41%	72%
USA	$730,606	$1,932,580	165%	153.7	100%	100%

Source: Mishel et al. (2003: 216).

TABLE 8.3 Ratio of CEO Pay to Average Worker

Country	Ratio (CEO to worker pay)
Japan	67:1
Canada	206:1
United States	354:1

Source: Macleans (2014).

in the United States in 1991, and this figure rose 11 times higher in Japan and an astounding 35 times larger in the United States'. The CEO-worker pay disparity worsened in the United States in the following years and has reached alarming proportions, particularly when compared to the Japanese ratio (see Table 8.3).

In Japan executive bonuses are also linked to workers' bonuses. If the latter is reduced in order to save labour cost and avoid massive layoffs in tough economic times, executive bonuses are also expected to drop (Abe et al. 2005). These corporate practices may be partially explained by post-war ideas of equality that have prevailed in Japan, which is an important cultural constraint both to control excessive executive pay and reduce the gap between the executive and employee pay (Kono 2016; Jacoby 2022: 15). This practice of informally tying executive pay to the salary of workers helps both lower executive compensation and narrow the pay gap between CEOs and average Japanese workers down to one of the lowest in the world (Salazar and Raggiunti 2016).

Thus, a central reason that accounts for lower executive pay in Japan has been the informal governance mechanisms that have protected the interests of workers, which in turn had an impact on executive pay decisions. Viewing corporate management as a collective effort has further encouraged the need to link CEO pay to worker salaries (Salacuse 2004). This is indicative of the central place that employee interests have in Japanese firms. This is also exemplified with Japanese corporations' traditional commitment to lifetime employment (Abe et al. 2005), although this has been declining in the last years (Kawaguchi and Ueno 2013) and has not been applied equally to male and female workers and the gender wage gap is still high (Nakamura and Rebein 2012). Nonetheless, the strong protection of worker interests is part of the larger commitment to promoting industrial citizenship of labour in Japan (Jackson 2001) and attests to Japan's stakeholder model of corporate governance.

Conclusion

This chapter has critically examined the two dominant paradigms of corporate governance, namely, the SHP model and stakeholder models. It reviewed the rationale for the SHP model and discussed its failures in light of evidence. The chapter then discussed stakeholder-oriented models in liberal and coordinated market economies. The last section examined the advantages of longstanding stakeholder models of corporate governance in coordinated market economies focusing on Germany and Japan. The evidence indicated that despite the pressure from global capital markets such models remain committed to serve multiple stakeholders' interest. The pattern of low executive pay in Japan was used to illustrate a stakeholder model of governance and its strong relevance in the divergence–convergence debate.

This short review has also shown that there are growing forces that are increasingly driving corporate governance systems around the world towards the interests of a broad range of stakeholders and long-term sustainability while maintaining diverging corporate governance structures. Corporate governance in liberal-market economies is under strong pressure to depart from the commitment to SHP and to consider stakeholder models amidst the exacerbation of climate crisis, financial instability, growing inequality, managerial misconduct and corporate corruption. The increasing interest of institutional shareholders in the sustainability of companies and the economy and the expansion of fiduciary duties of directors and executives illustrate some of the recent attempts to depart from SHP models. A movement towards more stakeholder-friendly corporate governance systems is growing in the midst of power struggles inside and outside boardrooms and courtrooms – see Chapter 10 on corporate power. The activism of multiple local and global stakeholders, namely institutional investors, creditors, workers, suppliers, citizen-consumers, civil society organizations and governments, appears to be critical in pushing corporate governance systems towards stakeholders' interest, long-term sustainability and the public interest. These active stakeholders, however, need to be further legally, financially and politically empowered in order to foster a lasting stakeholder culture, build a facilitative institutional structure and sustain such a growing convergence towards stakeholder-friendly governance systems.

Suggested readings

- Bebchuk, L. and Tallarita, R. (2022) 'Will Corporations Deliver Value to All Stakeholders?', *Vanderbilt Law Review*, Vol. 75, pp. 1031–91.
- Bessler, W., Drobetz, W. and Holler, J. (2013) 'The Returns to Hedge Fund Activism in Germany', *European Financial Management*, Vol. 21, pp. 106–47.
- Blair, M. and Stout, L. A. (1999) 'A Team Production Theory of Corporate Law', *Virginia Law Review*, Vol. 85, pp. 247–328.
- Jensen, M. C. and Meckling, W. H. (1976) 'Theory of the Firm: Managerial Behavior, Agency Costs and Ownership Structure', *Journal of Financial Economics*, Vol. 3, pp. 305–60.
- Stout, L. A. (2002) 'Bad and Not-so-Bad Arguments for Shareholder Primacy', *Southern California Law Review*, Vol. 75, pp. 1189–210.

Bibliography

Abe, N., Gaston, N. and Kubo, K. (2005) 'Executive Pay in Japan: The Role of Bank-Appointed Monitors and the Main Bank Relationship', *Japan and the World Economy*, Vol. 17, pp. 371–94.

Anderson, S., Kingler, S. and Pizzigati, S. (2013) *Executive Access 2013: Bailed Out, Booted and Busted*, Washington, DC, Institute for Policy Studies.

Asia Nikkei (2016) 'Japan Lags Far Behind US, Europe on CEO Pay', July 13.

Azar, J., Duro, M., Kadach, I. and Ormazabal, G. (2021) 'The Big Three and Corporate Carbon Emissions Around the World', *Journal of Financial Economics*, Vol. 142, No. 2, pp. 674–96.

Basu, S., Hwang, L.-S., Mitsudome, T. and Weintrop, J. (2007) 'Corporate Governance, Top Executive Compensation and Firm Performance in Japan', *Pacific-Basin Finance Journal*, Vol. 15, pp. 56–79.

Bebchuk, L., Kastiel, K. and Tallarita, R. (2022) 'Does Enlightened Shareholder Value Add Value?', *The Business Lawyer*, Vol. 77, forthcoming.

Bebchuk, L. and Tallarita, R. (2022) 'The Perils and Questionable Promise of ESG-Based Compensation', *Harvard Law School Program on Corporate Governance Working Paper, March 1, forthcoming, Journal of Corporation Law*.

Berle, A. (1931) 'Corporate Powers as Powers in Trust', *Harvard Law Review*, Vol. 44, pp. 1049–74.

Berle, A. and Means, G. (1932 [1967]) *The Modern Corporation and Private Property* (revised edition), New York, World Inc.

Bessler, W., Drobetz, W. and Holler, J. (2013) 'The Returns to Hedge Fund Activism in Germany', *European Financial Management*, Vol. 21, pp. 106–47.

Blair, M. and Stout, L.A. (1999) 'A Team Production Theory of Corporate Law', *Virginia Law Review*, Vol. 85, pp. 247–328.

Chizema, A. and Shinozawa, Y. (2012) 'The "Company with Committees": Change or Continuity in Japanese Corporate Governance?', *Journal of Management Studies*, Vol. 49, pp. 77–101.

Clark, R. (1986) *Corporate Law*, Boston, LL Little Brown.

Coates IV, J.C. (1999) 'Measuring the Domain of Mediating Hierarchy: How Contestable are U.S. Public Corporations?', *Journal of Corporation Law*, Vol. 24, pp. 837–67.

Dodd, M. (1932) 'For Whom are Corporate Managers Trustees?', *Harvard Law Review*, Vol. 45, pp. 1145–63.

Easterbrook, F. and Fischel, D. (1991) *The Economic Structure of Corporate Law*, Cambridge, MA, Harvard University Press.

Fairchild, C. (2013) 'Sony CEO Among 40 Execs to Give up Bonuses as Company Struggles', *The Huffington Post*, May 1.

Fauver, L. and Fuerst, M.E. (2006) 'Does Good Corporate Governance Include Employee Representation? Evidence from German Boards', *Journal of Financial Economics*, Vol. 82, pp. 673–710.

Franks, J. and Mayer, C. (2001) 'Ownership and Control of German Corporations', *Review of Financial Studies*, Vol. 14, pp. 943–77.

Gilson, R.J. and Gordon, J.N. (2013) 'The Agency Costs of Agency Capitalism: Activist Investors and the Revaluation of Governance Rights', *Columbia Law Review*, Vol. 113, pp. 863–928.

Gilson, R.J. and Gordon, J.N. (2014) 'Agency Capitalism: Further Implications of Equity Intermediation', *Working Paper No. 239*, European Corporate Governance Institute.

Gilson, R.J. and Milhaupt, C. (2005) 'Choice as Regulatory Reform: The Case of Japanese Corporate Governance', *American Journal of Comparative Law*, Vol. 53, pp. 343–77.

Gold, A.S. (2012) 'Dynamic Fiduciary Duties', *Cardozo Law Review*, Vol. 34, pp. 491–530.

Hall, P. and Soskice, D. (eds) (2001) *Varieties of Capitalism: The Institutional Foundations of Comparative Advantage*, Oxford, Oxford University Press.

Higgins, H. (2004) 'Corporate Governance in Japan: The Role of Banks, Keiretsu and Japanese Traditions', in F.A. Gul and S.I. Tsui (eds), *The Governance of East Asian Corporations: Post Asian Financial Crisis*, New York, Palgrave Macmillan, pp. 95–116.

Hoshi, T. and Kashyap, A. (2010) 'Will the US Bank Recapitalization Succeed? Eight Lessons from Japan', *Journal of Financial Economics*, Vol. 97, pp. 398–417.

Ireland, P. (2005) 'Shareholder Primacy and the Distribution of Wealth', *The Modern Law Review*, Vol. 68, pp. 49–81.

Jackson, G. (2001) 'The Origins of Non-Liberal Capitalism: Germany and Japan in Comparison', in W. Streeck and K. Yamaura (eds), *The Origins of Nonliberal Capitalism*, Ithaca, Cornell University Press.

Jackson, G. (2005) 'Stakeholders Under Pressure: Corporate Governance and Labour Management in Germany and Japan', *Corporate Governance: An International Review*, Vol. 13, pp. 419–28.

Jackson, R. and Milhaupt, C. (2014) 'Corporate Governance and Executive Compensation: Evidence from Japan', *Columbia Business Law Review*, Vol. 1, pp. 111–71.

Jacoby, S.M. (2022) 'Executive Pay and Shareholder Capitalism in Japan and the United States', *Business Review*, Vol. 69, No. 1, pp. 1–18, Meiji University: https://m-repo.lib.meiji.ac.jp/dspace/bitstream/10291/22336/1/keieironshu_69_1_1.pdf (accessed August 2022).

Jensen, M.C. and Meckling, W.H. (1976) 'Theory of the Firm: Managerial Behavior, Agency Costs and Ownership Structure', *Journal of Financial Economics*, Vol. 3, pp. 305–60.

Kawaguchi, D. and Ueno, Y. (2013) 'Declining Long-Term Employment in Japan', *Journal of The Japanese and International Economies*, Vol. 28, pp. 19–36.

Kono, T. (2016) *Strategy and Structure of Japanese Enterprises* (eBook), New York: Routledge.

Kubota, K. (2019) 'Top Bosses in Japan Draw Record Pay but Gap with US Widens', *Nikkei Asia*, August 2.

Lazonick, W. and Mazzucato, M. (2013) 'The Risk-Reward Nexus in the Innovation-Inequality Relationship: Who Takes the Risks? Who Gets the Rewards?', *Industrial and Corporate Change*, Vol. 22, No. 4, pp. 1093–128.

Liedtke, M. (2022) 'Former Theranos Exec Ramesh Balwani Convicted of Fraud', *Los Angeles Times*, July 7.

Macey, J.R. (1989) 'Externalities, Firm Specific Capital Investments and the Legal Treatment of Fundamental Corporate Changes', *Duke Law Journal*, Vol. 38, pp. 173–201.

Macleans (2014) 'Who Earns What: Global CEO-to-Worker Pay Ratios', *Macleans*, September 27, www.macleans.ca/economy/money-economy/global-ceo-to-worker-pay-ratios/ (accessed September 2016).

Marks, S.G. (2000) 'The Separation of Ownership and Control', in B. Bouckaert and G. de Geest (eds), *Encyclopedia of Law and Economics: The Regulation of Contracts*, Volume 3, Cheltenham, Edward Elgar, pp. 692–710.

McCrum, D. (2022) 'Why we Trust Fraudsters', *Financial Times*, June 16.

Millon, D. (2000) 'New Game Plan or Business as Usual? A Critique of the Team Production Model of Corporate Law', *Vanderlit Law Review*, Vol. 86, pp. 1001–44.

Mishel, L., Bernstein J. and Boushery, H. (2003) *The State of Working America, 2002/2003*, New York, Business and Economics.

Morita, S., Ogawa, N., Sato, Y. and Brown, J. (2020) 'CEO pay Landscape in Japan, the U.S. and Europe: 2019 Analysis', *Willis Towers Watson*, December 9.

Nakamura, M. and Rebien, S. (2012) 'Corporate Social Responsibility and Corporate Governance: Japanese Firms and Selective Adaptation', *University of British Columbia Law Review*, Vol. 45, pp. 723–78.

Pan, L. and Zhou, X. (2018) 'CEO Compensation in Japan: Why so Different from the United States?', *Journal of Financial and Quantitative Analysis*, Vol. 53, pp. 2261–92.

Sakawa, H., Moriyama, K. and Watanabel, N. (2012) 'Relations Between Top Executive Compensation Structure and Corporate Governance: Evidence from Japanese Public Disclosed Data', *Corporate Governance: An International Review*, Vol. 20, pp. 593–608.

Sakawa, H. and Watanabel, N. (2013) 'Executive Compensation and Firm Performance in Japan: The Role of Keiretsu Memberships and Bank-Appointed Monitors', *Journal of Modern Accounting and Auditing*, Vol. 9, pp. 1119–30.

Salacuse, J. (2004) 'Corporate Governance in the New Century', *Company Lawyer*, Vol. 25, pp. 69–83.

Salazar, A. and Raggiunti, J. (2016) 'Why Does Executive Greed Prevail in the United States and Canada But Not in Japan? The Pattern of low CEO pay and High Worker Welfare in Japanese Corporations', *The American Journal of Comparative Law*, Vol. 64, pp. 721–44.

Sayer, A. (2015) *Why We Can't Afford the Rich*, Bristol, Policy Press.

Schmidt, R.H. (2004) 'Corporate Governance in Germany: An Economic Perspective', in J.P. Krahnen and R.H. Schmidt (eds), *The German Financial System*, Oxford, Oxford University Press, pp. 387–424.

Stout, L.A. (2002) 'Bad and Not-so-Bad Arguments for Shareholder Primacy', *Southern California Law Review*, Vol. 75, pp. 1189–210.

Tonello, M. and Rabimov, S. (2010) 'The 2010 Institutional Investment Report: Trends in Asset Allocation and Portfolio Composition', 11 November, The Conference Board Research Report, No. R-1468-10-RR, 2010, Available at SSRN: https://ssrn.com/abstract=1707512

Tungler, G. (2000) 'The Anglo-American Board of Directors and the German Supervisory Board: Marionettes in a Puppet Theatre of Corporate Governance or Efficient Controlling Devices', *Bond Law Review*, Vol. 12, pp. 230–71.

Verret, J.W. (2010) 'Treasury Inc.: How the Bailout Reshapes Corporate Theory and Practice', *Yale Journal on Regulation*, Vol. 27, pp. 283–350.

Waitzer, E.J. and Sarro, D. (2012) 'The Public Fiduciary: Emerging Themes in Canadian Fiduciary Law for Pension Trustees', *Canadian Bar Review*, Vol. 91, pp. 163–209.

Waitzer, E.J. and Sarro, D. (2014) 'Fiduciary Society Unleashed: The Road Ahead for the Financial Sector', *Business Lawyer*, Vol. 69, pp. 1081–116.

9 | Corporate responsibility

Kean Birch

Introduction

In 2015 the car maker Volkswagen (VW) admitted that it had been bypassing US air pollution regulations by installing software that tricked regulators during official testing but otherwise did nothing to reduce nitrogen oxide emissions. It's uncommon to catch a business so obviously cheating regulations designed to achieve social and ecological objectives like the reduction of emissions, but that was clearly the case here. As such, it's another example of corporate malfeasance to sit alongside a growing list of issues we highlight in this book and other authors highlight elsewhere (Bakan 2004, 2020). However, we want to stress that the VW case isn't simply an example of deviant organizational wrongdoing; as Baxter (2015) notes, many other car makers – and other businesses – try to 'game' the regulatory system. Instead, then, the VW case raises an important question facing students of business today: What are the non-economic responsibilities of business to society and the environment?

Businesspeople, investors and business scholars increasingly agree that businesses need to take their social and environmental responsibilities seriously and not only because it's the ethical or moral thing to do. Ongoing concerns with corporate social responsibility (CSR) often reflect the pursuit of 'enlightened self-interest', in that businesses act responsibly because it will benefit their bottom line, that is profit (see Carroll and Buchholtz 2015: 40). This notion is evident in the VW case where its actions led to damaging impacts on their share price, consumer and investor confidence, regulatory oversight and so on. In the VW case, for example, the actions of executives and other employees at VW had a major impact on the value of VW shares, largely due to the expectation that the company's actions will result in significant regulatory fines (Nieuwenhuis 2015).

Investors have become increasingly concerned with these sorts of environmental, social and governance issues – now commonly referred to as 'ESG' – and are directly linking their continued willingness to invest in a business with the adoption of ESG strategies and policies (Galbreath 2013; Sherwood and Pollard 2018). For example, in 2020 the global asset management firm Blackrock announced that it would integrate sustainability into its investment decisions, reflecting concerns about the future risks of unsustainable businesses and business sectors (e.g. fossil fuels). Such 'responsible investing' has become a major driver of business decisions and strategies over the last few years, since it determines how much capital they can access and for what ends. For some, moreover, it offers the hope of replacing rampant 'neoliberal' capitalism with a more caring version that will help solve social and environmental issues like inequality and climate change (Bakan 2020).

Although the fallout from the egregious actions of businesses can lead to regulatory and other changes, like the growing concern with ESG in investment decisions, we argue that this doesn't necessarily change the actions and decisions of corporations and businesses (see Chapter 8). Calls for corporate responsibility or responsible investing aren't new; they stretch back well over a century. The growth of CSR and ESG as subjects to study in business schools and elsewhere, the expansion of CSR activities and ESG strategies by businesses, the development of global initiatives to promote CSR (e.g. the UN's Social Compact), and much else besides, hasn't stopped businesses from making socially and environmentally damaging decisions. As such, CSR, ESG and their ilk might not actually make business practices more socially or environmentally responsible. For example, VW boasted of its 'tradition of global CSR engagement' on their website under the heading 'Sustainability and Responsibility',[1] none of which stopped the company from pursuing profit at the expense of the environmental consequences (see Chapter 16).

Key concept: Corporate social responsibility

As a concept, corporate social responsibility (CSR) is not easy to pin down, largely because so many people have different perspectives on what it means and debates about its meaning have shifted and changed over the years, but also because it's often used to refer to quite different things. A broad definition might concern the social responsibility of business to consider their impacts on society, both negative (i.e. harm) and positive (i.e. good). However, a more distinct definition of CSR refers explicitly to the activities of *public corporations* owned by shareholders. In this case, CSR refers more to the need for corporations to consider their impacts on society in relation to their fiduciary obligation to their shareholders (e.g. pursuit of profit). In both cases, though, the responsibility of businesses and corporations can be defined as the requirement to meet their economic or fiduciary obligations, alongside the requirement to obey the laws of the society in which they operate.

Source: Carroll and Buchholtz (2015)

In this chapter, we problematize mainstream perspectives of business responsibility that are based on the idea that profit and responsibility are compatible with one another, even virtuously self-reinforcing. Instead, we unpack the problems with combining social and environmental responsibility and argue that the integration of responsibility – in its many forms – into management training and managerial practices doesn't actually provide a helpful way to address the damaging impacts that business can have on society, on the environment and on our lives. We start with a discussion of mainstream perspectives on the social and environmental responsibility of business, its intellectual history and how it manifests in society today. We then critique this perspective from a number of standpoints, before finishing with a discussion of forms of economic organization that provide better ways to integrate social and environmental concerns into business activity.

Mainstream perspectives on responsibility

Changing attitudes to business. Before asking what social and environmental responsibilities businesses have or should have, it's pertinent to wonder why this is an issue at all. As noted in the Introduction to this book, the relationship between business and society has often been fraught (Sexty 2008). In many countries, public attitudes towards business have changed quite dramatically over the decades stretching back at least to the 1800s – see Table 9.1 for the United States. Moreover, these attitudes have often swung from positive to negative in a short space of time, as evident in the public reactions to the 2007–8 global financial crisis or the popularity of Big Tech firms over the last decade. In our view, it's worth highlighting these changes in attitude to better understand the growing concern with social and environmental responsibility in business practices and decision-making.

Key discussion questions

- How have attitudes to business changed over time?
- How have attitudes to the social and environmental responsibility of business changed over time?
- What are the dominant schools of thought on social and environmental responsibility?
- Are there any problems with these dominant schools of thought?
- How could the question of business responsibility be rethought?
- What are good examples of contemporary business responsibility?

As Table 9.1 shows, public attitudes to business often reflect broader socio-economic context. Primarily, negative attitudes to business are associated with recessions, depressions and crises, while positive attitudes are associated with booms, growth and employment. At the end of the 1800s, for example, there was significant unrest in many countries as a result of the Long Depression starting in 1873 and in the United States in particular because of the increasing

TABLE 9.1 Changing Attitudes to Business through US History

Time period	Attitude	Characteristics
Late 1800s and early 1900s	Negative	'Robber barons' – concentration of businesses in trusts and monopolies.
1920s	Positive	'Roaring twenties' – stock market boom.
1930s	Negative	Great Depression following Wall Street Crash.
1950s and 1960s	Positive	'Golden Age of Capitalism' – full employment, rising wages and mass consumerism.
1970s	Negative	Stagflation – rising unemployment and inflation.
1980s	Positive	Government roll-back of regulations and rising stock markets.
Early 1990s	Negative	Recession and business failures.
Late 1990s	Positive	Dot.com boom and rising stock markets.
Early 2000s	Negative	Dot.com crash in 2000 followed by major corporate scandals (e.g. Enron).
Mid-2000s	Positive	Growing emphasis on corporate social responsibility, 'green' business as well as rising house prices.
Late 2000s	Negative	Global financial crisis of 2007–8 and anger at banks.
2010s	Positive	Rise of digital and social media firms; expectations of their liberatory promise.
2020s	Negative	Market concentration and monopoly under Big Tech firms.

Source: Adapted and expanded from Sexty (2008).

concentration of corporate power in the hands of a few so-called Robber Barons, which included people like John D. Rockefeller who owned Standard Oil. The political theorist Scott Bowman (1996) notes the growing criticism of business corporations by scholars and thinkers of the time, including people like Thorstein Veblen (1899), and the rise of popular social movements against corporate power as well.

As a result of these social critiques and movements, the US government introduced laws like the 1890 Sherman Antitrust Act to stop the formation of business monopolies and the pursuit of anti-competitive practices (Khan 2017; Hubbard 2020). We go into greater detail in our discussion of business regulation in Chapter 18, but for now it's worth stressing that the intention behind such laws, also enacted in other countries, was to break up the power of private business organizations so that they couldn't control markets or exploit consumers. Despite negative attitudes to business during this period, however, it's notable that public attitudes to business shifted quite dramatically in the early 1900s, becoming more positive. For example, during the Roaring Twenties more and more people in the United States invested in corporate shares and benefited from rising share prices, at least up until 29 October 1929 when the Wall Street Crash brought it all tumbling down again (Galbraith 2009 [1955]). More recent public attitudes towards banks and other financial businesses before and after the 2007–8 global financial crisis reflect a similar situation (Birch 2015; van Staveren 2015) as does the rise of numerous commentators criticizing Big Tech firms like Apple, Amazon, Google, Facebook and Microsoft (Teachout 2020; Hubbard 2020).

Intellectual history of corporate social responsibility. While we could write more on the history of public attitudes towards business, that's not our aim in this chapter. Rather, the brief outline earlier is meant to help you better understand the evolution of social and environmental responsibility as a corporate goal and set of practices. According to Kemper and Martin (2010) and Barkan (2013), debates on the social and environmental responsibility of business first emerged in the 1930s at the time when the role of the corporation and corporate management was being hotly debated by American thinkers like Berle and Means (1932) during the Great Depression that followed the Wall Street Crash – see Chapters 7 and 8.

In the US context, business responsibility was associated with the growing influence of managers and executives in society, especially as this related to organizational decision-making (Carroll 1999). Such decisions could have major impacts on communities; for example, these could be negative or positive impacts resulting from the building of new factories and facilities, like growing pollution and employment creation respectively. The influence of managers and executives on society has been defined as *managerial capitalism* or simply *managerialism* by some scholars (Whitley 1999; Locke and Spender 2011) and denotes the role of managers and executives in socio-economic change in contrast to other forms of economic coordination and organization (e.g. the state, the market).

In light of the influence of managerialism, the responsibility of managers became an increasingly important issue in academic debates on the relationship between business and society. Archie Carroll (1999) provides a helpful overview of the evolution of these debates in the latter-half of the twentieth century, focusing specifically on CSR. He splits this evolution into five time periods as follows:

- Modern era begins in the 1950s;
- CSR formalized in the 1960s;
- Definitions of CSR multiply in the 1970s;

- Splintering of CSR concepts in the 1980s;
- Alternative ideas developed in the 1990s.

According to Carroll (1999), when it first emerged in the 1950s CSR was generally conceptualized in terms of the social responsibility of business managers, stressing the power they had over the rest of society. As scholars sought to define CSR more clearly in the 1960s, they argued that socially responsible business practices led to long-term benefits for businesses and that managers need to keep in mind the impact their businesses have on society. These ideas came under serious challenge in 1970 with the publication of a now-famous article by Milton Friedman (1970) in the *New York Times Magazine*. This article, titled 'The Social Responsibility of Business Is to Increase Its Profits', was a direct attack on managerial notions of the social responsibility of business from the perspective of the Chicago School of Economics – sometimes defined as 'neoliberalism' – in which shareholder interests are presented as predominant. Some, like Kemper and Martin (2010), have even argued that academic debates on CSR since then have ended up as one response after another to this argument by Friedman.

Milton Friedman was a professor at the Chicago School of Economics, which was famous for its strongly pro-market position in academic and policy debates. Often characterized as a 'neoliberal' school of thought, the Chicago School of Economics has played and continues to play a major role in the direction of government, law and business (Birch 2015). In the 1970 article and his previous work, Friedman argued that the market provides the best way to coordinate economic activity, which contrasted with dominant perspectives at the time associated with managerialism and Keynesianism. In his *News York Times Magazine* article, Friedman (1970) basically argued that business only has one responsibility, namely the pursuit of profit for shareholders. Friedman argued that the only time a business could pursue social responsibility was when these activities had instrumental and beneficial impact on the business itself (e.g. as a marketing ploy to endear it to customers and increase profits). Other than in such cases, he argued that it's both inaccurate and dangerous to conflate business pursuits and attempts to improve society.

In the 1970s and 1980s, though, debates on CSR proliferated, leading to new concepts and ideas like corporate social responsiveness, corporate social performance, social contract theory and stakeholder theory (Carroll 1999; Kemper and Martin 2010). Some of these ideas are still influential today. Finally, in the 1990s and 2000s a range of new concepts emerged building on ideas of sustainability, sustainable development and sustainable business – see Chapter 16 for more on the roots of these ideas.

Some have observed that the degree and type of emphasis on CSR varies significantly between countries (Matten and Moon 2008). In countries with a relatively weak welfare state, where social goods like health-care and economic security are not provided or guaranteed by the state, one can see more 'explicit' forms of CSR. For example, large US businesses like Exxon or Walmart make efforts to demonstrate their commitment to voluntary actions to curb pollution or monitor their overseas operations. In these liberal-market economies, CSR is called 'explicit' because it acts as a substitute for more institutionalized public provision of social benefits. In such contexts, explicit CSR allows corporations to be less threatening to social cohesion (Kang and Moon 2012). By contrast, CSR tends to be 'implicit' in other countries where the aims of social cohesion are achieved through state regulatory frameworks or strong normative constraints embedded within the business system and often internalized by its participants. One example of implicit CSR is the 'relational' system of corporate governance in Germany where workers' interests gain attention not by separate voluntary actions but by ensuring employee representation into corporate governance bodies (see Chapter 8).

What's interesting is that today we seem to have come back full circle to the early days of CSR. There's an increasing concern with the impact of business on society and the environment, driven, in large part, by growing concerns with climate change (see Chapters 16 and 17). Responsible investing is now an influential driver of business decision-making (IPSP 2018). Responsible investing means taking environmental, social and governance (ESG) issues into account when making an investment decision; so, for example, investors shouldn't invest in businesses with poor environmental records (e.g. high greenhouse gas emitters, significant polluters). ESG is different from CSR, however, in that ESG comes at responsibility from the investment side of business – the 'owners' in Friedman's framing – and reflects investor concerns that they won't be profitable if they invest in companies that face possible regulatory interventions due to the company's socially or environmentally damaging decisions (Sherwood and Pollard 2018; Matos 2020).

Major theories of business responsibility. While the history of CSR and ESG implies that there's been a proliferation of concepts and ideas about what constitutes business responsibility, it's possible to identify a few core theories from which modern CSR theories and practices emerged. Aside from Friedman's pro-market perspective (i.e. that business should only pursue profit), Kemper and Martin (2010) argue that current CSR debates centre on the following theoretical traditions: (1) the three-dimensional model, (2) the social contract model and (3) the stakeholder model.

First, the three-dimensional model originates with the work of Archie Carroll in the late 1970s. Originally, he argued that business has three responsibilities: (1) an economic responsibility to make profit, (2) a legal responsibility to obey the laws of society and (3) an ethical responsibility to avoid harm and do good (Carroll 1979). Later, Carroll added a fourth dimension, a philanthropic responsibility to give back to society and be a good citizen (Carroll and Buchholtz 2015). Carroll emphasized that the economic and legal responsibilities are requirements, while the ethical and philanthropic responsibilities are desirable or expected. Each builds on the other, so ensuring a secure economic foundation for a business is necessary before anything else.

Second, the social contract model of CSR emerged in the 1980s with Thomas Donaldson's (1982) book *Corporations and Morality*. He sought to respond to Friedman's idea that the only responsibility of business is to make profit by stressing that the corporation was both a *moral environment* in itself and a *moral agent*. By this Donaldson meant that, on the one hand, corporations have an internal environment in which ethical questions need to be addressed, including issues like management and employee rights and obligations; on the other hand, as entities corporations have to engage with questions around their impact on other moral actors in society (e.g. customers, government, suppliers, investors). According to Kemper and Martin (2010), these ideas have since influenced notions of corporate citizenship, drawing on the idea of a social contract between business and society.

Finally, the stakeholder model comes from the work of R. Edward Freeman (1984), especially a book called *Strategic Management: A Stakeholder Approach* – see also Chapter 8 on stakeholder models of corporate governance. Freeman argued that all businesses are impacted and in turn impact a range of external social actors (e.g. customers, suppliers, government, workers, investors), who he called *stakeholders* because they all have a stake in the success of the business. As such, this model is based on the notion that businesses, especially corporations, *should* address the impacts of their decisions on more than shareholders or investors; the reason being that many people *are* directly and indirectly impacted by these decisions. For example, employees have to invest in gaining specific skills to work in specific businesses, meaning that if that business simply moves its facilities elsewhere – for cost reasons – then its employees will have wasted their investment of time and energy in gaining skills that might not be transferable to another workplace. The stakeholder approach is based on the observation that the value of a business cannot be reduced to the financial profits it generates, at least not in the long run. In fact, businesses themselves can often financially gain by pursuing better and more constructive relationships to communities, governments, the environment and so on – something that underpins ESG thinking (Sherwood and Pollard 2018).

Examples of corporate social responsibility. Our outline of business responsibility is a brief introduction to a complex topic and one that has evolved considerably over time. Today, CSR, ESG and their close cousin business ethics – see Chapter 19 – are important fields of research and teaching in most business schools. They are also an increasingly important part of business practice in modern businesses and corporations. In fact, most corporations nowadays are keen to present and promote their CSR and ESG credentials as much as they can. We consider two examples here but stress that there are many others.

First, most firms engage in different forms of reporting, organizing and other initiatives in pursuit of CSR and ESG activities. These activities stretch from sectoral and local organizations and groups to global networks, roundtables and the like. For example, there are global networks like the UN's Global Compact, which outlines CSR and ESG principles for businesses seeking to develop 'sustainable business strategies and solutions';[2] national fora like the Devonshire Initiative (Canada), which promotes collaboration between NGOs and mining businesses around social issues and community development;[3] and reporting frameworks like the Global Reporting Initiative, which develops and promotes sustainability reporting by businesses.[4] These three examples are just a tiny selection of groups, organizations, networks and initiatives that promote or support various forms of CSR and ESG activities, best practices, reporting and so on.

Second, philanthrocapitalism refers to the idea that philanthropic giving by wealthy people and businesses can solve our worst social problems, even major global challenges like hunger and food insecurity. The term was coined by Matthew Bishop and Michael Green (2008) in their book originally titled *Philanthrocapitalism: How the Rich Can Save the World*. Perhaps one of the most famous examples is the Bill & Melinda Gates Foundation, which funds a range of projects through grant-giving.[5] Described as a new and increasingly important phenomena, these philanthropic activities have been criticized by many scholars (McGoey 2015, 2021; Bakan 2020; Clarke 2019). Linsey McGoey (2015, 2021), for example, argues that philanthrocapitalism is driven by the idea that social problems can be solved through the dynamism assumed to underpin capitalist business practices. Moreover, as a result of the growing influence of these wealthy philanthropists, their personal preferences and assumptions come to have an increasing influence on what social problems (e.g. which diseases) are deemed important and how they should be tackled. As a result, other social problems (e.g. inequality) end up sidelined or ignored. Others are concerned that philanthrocapitalism ends up undermining the role of the state – that is, democratically elected governments – to determine how best to deal with the abovementioned issues. This raises significant questions about the social good that comes from projects that undermine public participation in social and economic policy (Clarke 2019).

Critical perspectives on business responsibility

While the different theories and forms of CSR and ESG we mentioned earlier may sound like they entail laudable intentions and practices, we critically unpack them in this section to better understand the problematic assumptions underpinning them. To do this, we start this section with a discussion of responsibility as a concept and then turn to specific issues arising from the key theories and ideas we outlined earlier.

What is responsibility? Any discussion of business responsibility is a discussion of ethical questions; that is, what should businesses do? And what should they not do? What are businesses responsible for? And what are they not responsible for? As we mention elsewhere in this book (see Chapter 19) these questions often confuse *descriptive* (or 'positive') issues with *ethical* (or 'normative') ones. For example, if a business is legally required to adhere to certain regulations – like Volkswagen was supposed to – does that mean it's ethically required to adhere to them as well? Answers to such questions are not easy to untangle without some thought.

Starting with the concept of *responsibility*, it's worth considering what this term means and how it relates to ethical decisions; Jonathan Glover (1970) provides a helpful philosophical introduction to responsibility. He argued that responsibility can refer to two quite distinct things. First, it can refer to an obligation or duty to do certain things in the future, which can be both legal and ethical (e.g. not to cheat environmental regulations). Here, responsibility involves intentional action rather than accidental effects, although this doesn't excuse deliberate and wilful negligence. Second, responsibility can mean blame for past actions or undertakings. Here, responsibility can be backward-looking to determine whether something shouldn't have been done when it was. An example would include things like the recent Canadian Truth and Reconciliation Commission that dealt with the horrific impacts of the residential school system on Indigenous peoples.[6]

These differences are important. Thinking about business responsibility necessitates thinking about how business organizations should act now and in the future, *and* how they should have acted in the past. Since legal obligations frequently change, this means that normative (i.e. ethical) concerns might provide stronger direction and, therefore, continuity for the regulation and control of business. Consequently, normative issues are critical to coordinating and managing the relationship between business and society over time. Moreover, it's important to think about intentions when it comes to responsibilities since these establish the goals to which normative decisions are oriented; where these intentions are set by other considerations, such as profit, they limit the actions that business organizations can take. For example, the pursuit of profit means that businesses often seek to externalize their social and environmental responsibilities, so they don't have to pay for them.

Problems with mainstream theories of corporate social responsibility. It's important to consider the various CSR theories we discussed earlier in more depth so we can unpack any problematic assumptions underpinning them. We raise four problematic issues here relating to one or another theory or idea we discussed earlier.

First, it's important to note that Milton Friedman's (1970) arguments were considered radical at the time he wrote them; however, they have since become one of the dominant perspectives to frame business responsibility. This is evidenced by things like the 2014 'shareholder spring' in the UK, which was driven by investors who were worried that the activities of managers and executives would impact shareholder value, that is share prices (Kollewe 2014). There are at least three problems with Friedman's position worth mentioning. First, he conflated 'business' with 'corporation', assuming that the former is the same as the latter, ignoring the fact that they aren't (i.e. corporations have shareholders, businesses need not) and assuming that they both have the same fiduciary obligations (cf. Stout 2012). Second, he accepted that business has a responsibility to conform 'to their basic rules of society, both those embodied in law and those embodied in ethical custom' (Friedman 1970), which rather makes his argument moot. Finally, he conflated social responsibility with socialism by arguing that 'political mechanisms' to achieve those responsibilities are inherently socialist, even though his definition of politics is so broad as to include a range of political systems (Mulligan 1986).

Second, as business activities have globalized through the expansion of international trade and foreign direct investment – as we outline in Chapters 13 and 16 – they have led to an expansion of international regulations, codes, standards and so on (Braithewaite 2005). These rules of the game are often favourable to multinational corporations (MNCs), even when they address concerns about social or environmental responsibilities. One example of this is the UN *Norms on the Responsibilities of Transnational Corporations and Other Business Enterprises with Regard to Human Rights* (2003). According to Barkan (2013), these UN *Norms* treated corporations as the same as nation-states, meaning that the UN largely accepts the extent and spread of corporate power and is merely trying to attach social goals to this power. See Chapters 10 through 13 for more on corporate power. Consequently, Barkan argues that these sorts of international rules merely consolidate the power of MNCs rather than requiring them to meet their specific social and environmental responsibilities. Consequently, the idea of a social contract between business and society misses the point that business can often be the more powerful actor in the relationship, especially if businesses operate globally, and therefore able to dictate the terms of the social contract.

Third, and related to the last point, the globalization of business activities has been accompanied by a growth in international campaigning, social movements, boycotts and lawsuits that are critical of business. While this might seem like it would enable more stakeholders to have a positive impact on business activities as businesses respond to these normative pressures, Shamir (2004) argues that the transnational activities of businesses are impossible to control because there is no comparable transnational government body capable of enforcing legal or ethical constraints. Instead, businesses are subject to a range of private or quasi-private governance entities and standards (e.g. the World Economic Forum's ESG reporting framework), each of which has its own distinct sense of responsibility and issues with accessibility for non-business or non-state actors (e.g. workers and campaigners). Moreover, most of these entities and standards are voluntary – meaning that a business can withdraw at any time with little practical consequence – or are co-opted by business involvement – meaning that they don't challenge business power. Consequently, Shamir argues that something like CSR has ended up as merely an issue of investor and consumer confidence in which branding and image management trump genuine commitment to social and environmental responsibilities (see also Beder 2006; Bakan 2020). This critical concern about the genuineness of CSR has caused some observers to assign the derogatory term 'greenwashing' to many types of CSR initiatives, especially where these initiatives seem to be designed primarily to boost the 'reputational capital' of business firms rather than bring about real change (Elving 2014). It also explains the rise of ESG reporting and responsible investing, which is seen as providing greater oversight of business activities through direct financial impacts, such as the withdrawal of investment, if a business doesn't adhere to its wider responsibilities (Matos 2020).

A final criticism is that business responsibility might not solve the problems engendered by capitalism itself, including poverty, alienation, dehumanization and inequality. The reason for this is that responsibility doesn't challenge the organizational structure of capitalist business – that is, the pursuit of profit for the owners of capital. In contrast, the sociologist Charles Derber (2000) argues that challenging corporate power and capitalist business practices necessitates a wholesale transformation of business organization to make it more democratic and socially responsive. Derber argues that alternative business forms and governance like stakeholder models, employee ownership and workers cooperatives are better structures to achieve social objectives – we come back to these in Chapters 21 and 22. The point of mentioning them here is that they represent ways to embed social or environmental objectives directly in the organization and governance of business rather than relying on external CSR or ESG initiatives, reporting, collaborations and so on.

Empirical example: Investment banks and the global financial crisis

A useful empirical case regarding the problems with mainstream business responsibility is the role and actions of various financial businesses, especially investment banks, leading up to and during the 2007–8 global financial crisis (see Chapter 17). The documentary *Inside Job* (2010, dir. Charles H. Ferguson) and feature film *The Big Short* (2015, dir. Adam McKay) provide insight into these events.[7] At the heart of this example is the question of whether investment banks acted responsibly.

Briefly, in the lead up to the crisis various investment banks – including the now bankrupt Lehman Brothers – constructed a series of financial products (e.g. Collateralized Debt Obligations, or CDOs) that were based on bundling the income from mortgage interest payments from home 'owners'. Part of the bundling involved mixing together income from risky or sub-prime mortgages and less risky mortgages. The ratings agencies then rated these CDOs as safe financial assets, which made them attractive to various investors (e.g. commercial banks, pension funds, mutual funds, insurance funds). As the mortgage market started to turn bad in 2006, some of the investment banks – like Goldman Sachs – began to bet against the CDO market by buying Credit Default Swaps (CDSs) that would pay out if CDOs lost value, which they did (Cohan 2011).

According to then *Rolling Stone* journalist Matt Taibbi (2010), investment banks like Goldman Sachs knew that 'the mortgages it [Goldman Sachs] was selling were for chumps. The real money was in betting against those same mortgages'. Obviously, this raises some serious questions about the responsibility of investment banks to their customers who are buying the financial products they are then betting against. Taibbi describes Goldman Sachs, rather poetically, as 'a great vampire squid wrapped around the face of humanity, relentlessly jamming its blood funnel into anything that smells like money' (2010). In part, Taibbi characterizes Goldman Sachs this way because they were engaged in selling CDOs to investors with the knowledge that other investors were going to 'short' (i.e. bet against) those CDOs (see Cohan 2011: 508–10). In 2010, Goldman Sachs settled a case brought by the Securities and Exchange Commission (SEC) on fraud charges; it agreed to pay a fine of US$550 million but did not admit wrongdoing.[8]

We can look at the activities of these investment banks from a range of perspectives. First, if their only responsibility is profit (e.g. Friedman 1970), then the businesses that survived the crisis fulfilled their social responsibilities. However, this means that the responsibility of business is simply to survive, at whatever cost to society. Second, if the responsibility of the financial businesses was only to adhere to the law – no matter how ineffective it was – and to meet ethical expectations, then it could be argued that they fulfilled their legal obligations. Again, responsibility only becomes an issue after the fact, meaning that it doesn't stop the negative social impacts of business, it only addresses the aftermath. At its heart, business responsibility entails at least two problems: first, it ends up being largely backward-looking and doesn't deal with problems pre-emptively; and, second, there is a contradiction between the benefits it provides to society and to the businesses themselves, the more it benefits the former, the less it benefits the latter.

Conclusion

Our goal in this chapter has been to provide a brief introduction to the issue of corporate responsibility, broadly conceived to include business more generally. We started by outlining the history of public attitudes to business and the intellectual history of mainstream CSR theories. We then provided a brief introduction to a number of key theories and ideas. In the second part of the chapter, we critically unpacked mainstream business responsibility theories and practices, drawing on the example of the global financial crisis to outline the limitations of these approaches. We want to finish by stressing that social and environmental responsibilities are intrinsically tied to the form and logics of business organization and governance; that is, it's not possible to separate out responsibility and treat it as a distinct normative issue from business practice.

Suggested readings

- Carroll, A. (1999) 'Corporate Social Responsibility: Evolution of a Definitional Construct', *Business & Society*, Vol. 38, pp. 268–95.
- Friedman, M. (1970) 'The Social Responsibility of Business is to Increase Its Profits', *The New York Magazine*, 13 September.
- Kemper, A. and Martin, R. (2010) 'After the Fall: The Global Financial Crisis as a Test of Corporate Social Responsibility Theories', *European Management Review*, Vol. 7, pp. 229–39.
- Shamir, R. (2004) 'The De-radicalization of Corporate Social Responsibility', *Critical Sociology*, Vol. 30, pp. 669–89.

Notes

1 Volkswagen website: www.volkswagenag.com/content/vwcorp/content/en/sustainability_and_responsibility/CSR_worldwide.html (accessed May 2016).
2 UN Social Compact website: https://www.unglobalcompact.org/take-action/action/private-sustainability-finance (accessed August 2022).
3 Devonshire Initiative website: http://devonshireinitiative.org/ (accessed May 2016).

4 Global Reporting Initiative website: www.globalreporting.org/Pages/default
.aspx (accessed May 2016).

5 Bill & Melinda Gates Foundation: www.gatesfoundation.org/ (accessed May
2016).

6 Truth and Reconciliation Commission: www.trc.ca/websites/trcinstitution/
index.php?p=3 (accessed May 2016).

7 *Inside Job*: www.sonyclassics.com/insidejob/ and *The Big Short*: www
.thebigshortmovie.com/ (accessed May 2016).

8 *New York Times*: http://dealbook.nytimes.com/2010/07/15/goldman-to-settle-
with-s-e-c-for-550-million/ (accessed May 2016).

Bibliography

Bakan, J. (2004) *The Corporation*, London, Random House.

Bakan, J. (2020) *The New Corporation*, Toronto, Penguin Random House.

Barkan, J. (2013) *Corporate Sovereignty*, Minneapolis, University of Minnesota Press.

Baxter, L.F. (2015) 'VW is Not Alone: How Metrics Gaming is Commonplace in Companies', *The Conversation*, 15 October, https://theconversation .com/vw-is-not-alone-how-metrics -gaming-is-commonplace-in -companies-48393 (accessed May 2016).

Beder, S. (2006) *Suiting Themselves: How Corporations Drive the Global Agenda*, London, Earthscan.

Berle, A. and Means, G. (1932 [1967]) *The Modern Corporation and Private Property*, New York, World Inc.

Birch, K. (2015) *We Have Never Been Neoliberal*, Winchester, Zero Books.

Bishop, M. and Green, M. (2008) *Philanthrocapitalism: How the Rich Can Save the World*, London, Bloomsbury Press.

Bowman, S. (1996) *The Modern Corporation and American Political Thought*, Pennsylvania, Pennsylvania State University Press.

Braithwaite, J. (2005) 'Neoliberalism or Regulatory Capitalism', *ANU: RegNet, Occasional Paper No. 5*.

Carroll, A. (1979) 'A Three-Dimensional Conceptual Model of Corporate Social Performance', *Academy of Management Review*, Vol. 4, pp. 497–505.

Carroll, A. (1999) 'Corporate Social Responsibility: Evolution of a Definitional Construct', *Business & Society*, Vol. 38, pp. 268–95.

Carroll, A. and Buchholtz, A. (2015) *Business and Society* (9th Edition), Stamford, CENGAGE Learning.

Clarke, G. (2019) 'The New Global Governors: Globalization, Civil Society and the Rise of the Rise of the Private Philanthropic Foundation', *Journal of Civil Society*, Vol. 15, No. 3, pp. 197–213.

Cohan, W. (2011) *Money and Power: How Goldman Sachs Came to Rule the World*, New York, Doubleday.

Derber, C. (2000) *Corporation Nation*, New York, St. Martin's Press.

Donaldson, T. (1982) *Corporations and Morality*, Englewood Cliffs, Prentice-Hall.

Elving, W. (2014) 'Communicating Corporate Social Responsibility in a Skeptical World', in D. Türker, H. Toker and C. Altuntas (eds), *Contemporary Issues in Corporate Social Responsibility*, Lanham, Lexington Books, pp. 57–70.

Freeman, R. (1984) *Strategic Management: A Stakeholder Approach*, Boston, Pitman.

Friedman, M. (1970) 'The Social Responsibility of Business is to Increase its Profits', *The New York Magazine*, 13 September, www .colorado.edu/studentgroups/ libertarians/issues/friedman-soc-resp -business.html (accessed May 2016).

Galbraith, J.K. (1955 [2009]) *The Great Crash, 1929*, London, Penguin.

Galbreath, J. (2013) 'ESG in Focus: The Australian Evidence', *Journal of Business Ethics*, Vol. 118, pp. 529–41.

Glover, J. (1970) *Responsibility*, New York, Humanities Press.

Gunningham, N., Kagan, R. and Thornton, D. (2006) 'Social License and Environmental Protection: Why Businesses Go Beyond Compliance', *Law & Social Inquiry*, Vol. 29, pp. 307–41.

Hubbard, S. (2020) *Monopolies Suck*, New York, Simone & Schuster.

Kang, N. and Moon, J. (2012) 'Institutional Complementarity Between Corporate Governance and Corporate Social Responsibility: A Comparative Institutional Analysis of Three Capitalisms', *Socio-Economic Review*, Vol. 7, pp. 105–8.

Kemper, A. and Martin, R. (2010) 'After the Fall: The Global Financial Crisis as a Test of Corporate Social Responsibility Theories', *European Management Review*, Vol. 7, pp. 229–39.

Khan, L. (2017) 'Amazon's Antitrust Paradox', *Yale Law Journal*, Vol. 126, No. 3, pp. 710–805.

Kollewe, J. (2014) 'Shareholder Revolts – Timeline', *The Guardian*, July 17, www.theguardian.com/business/2014 /jul/17/shareholder-revolts-timeline (accessed May 2016).

Locke, R. and Spender, J.-C. (2011) *Confronting Managerialism*, London, Zed Books.

Matos, P. (2020) *ESG and Responsible Institutional Investing Around the World*, New York, CFA Institute Research Foundation.

Matten, D. and Moon, J. (2008) '"Implicit" and "explicit" CSR: A Conceptual Framework for a Comparative Understanding of Corporate Social Responsibility', *Academy of Management Review*, Vol. 33, pp. 404–24.

McGoey, L. (2015) *No Such Thing as a Free Gift: The Gates Foundation and the Price of Philanthropy*, London, Verso.

McGoey, L. (2021) 'Philanthrocapitalism and the Separation of Powers', *Annual Review of Law and Social Science*, Vol. 17, pp. 391–409.

Mulligan, T. (1986) 'A Critique of Milton Friedman's Essay 'The Social Responsibility of Business Is to Increase Its Profits'', *Journal of Business Ethics*, Vol. 5, pp. 265–9.

Nieuwenhuis, P. (2015) 'How Volkswagen Got Caught Cheating Emissions Tests by a Clean Air NGO', *The Conversation*, September 22, https://theconversation .com/how-volkswagen-got-caught -cheating-emissions-tests-by-a-clean -air-ngo-47951 (accessed May 2016).

Sexty, R. (2008) *Canadian Business and Society*, Toronto, McGraw-Hill.

Shamir, R. (2004) 'The De-radicalization of Corporate Social Responsibility', *Critical Sociology*, Vol. 30, pp. 669–89.

Sherwood, M. and Pollard, J. (2018) *Responsible Investing: An Introduction to Environmental, Social, and Governance Investments*, London: Routledge.

Stout, L. (2012) *The Shareholder Value Myth*, San Francisco, Berrett-Koehler.

Taibbi, M. (2010) 'The Great American Bubble Machine', *Rolling Stone*, April 5, www.rollingstone.com/politics/news /the-great-american-bubble-machine -20100405 (accessed May 2016).

Teachout, Z. (2020) *Break 'Em Up*, New York: All Points Books.

Van Staveren, I. (2015) *Economics after the Crisis*, London, Routledge.

Veblen, T. (1899 [1994]) *Theory of the Leisure Class*, New York, Penguin.

Whitley, R. (1999) *Divergent Capitalism*, Oxford, Oxford University Press.

10 | Corporate power

Kean Birch

Introduction

The concern that corporations and private business generally can have too much power has a long history. It stretches back at least to the time of Adam Smith (1723–90), who himself criticized the joint-stock companies (JSC) we discussed in Chapters 3 and 7. The power of JSCs like the English/British East India Company (EIC) led directly to major world events like America's War of Independence starting in 1776. According to Bowman (1996: 5), for example, the United States' 'founding fathers' like Thomas Jefferson objected to the monopoly power held by JSCs because they were 'wary of the antidemocratic tendencies of concentrated power within the business corporation'. Adam Smith held similar views, as did many others at the time. These pre-modern corporations were seen as extensions of royal authority and power, since they were created by grants from the Crown and the grant itself represented the gift of special privileges by the Crown (e.g. monopolies on trade) (Korten 2001; Nace 2003).

Such negative attitudes towards corporations and business have not abated over the centuries, although they have waxed and waned over time. Following the corporate revolution at the end of the nineteenth century (see Chapter 7) and the rise of managerial capitalism during the twentieth century, there was an accommodation, of sorts, between corporations and society – at least in countries like the United States (see Chapter 9). Generally speaking, during the middle of the twentieth century most people in countries like the United States and the United Kingdom considered corporations to be contributing something useful to society through the creation of secure jobs, the provision of cheap products and services and rising living standards (Sennett 2007). Corporate managers were even encouraged to think of themselves as socially responsible and as having a higher calling than simple profit (Khurana 2007). However, this changed in the 1970s and 1980s as greed made a comeback, epitomized by the character Gordon Gecko in the 1987 film *Wall Street* directed by Oliver Stone. These shifting currents eventually gave rise to the more recent chorus of journalists, commentators, academics and activists who criticize corporations and the expansion of *corporate power* (e.g. Monbiot 2000; Bakan 2004, 2020; Birch 2007; Wolin 2008).

Our aim in this chapter is to unpack and examine the concept of corporate power in order to provide it with analytical purchase alongside its wider normative dimension; that is, we want to do more than characterize corporate power as 'bad', we want to be able to identify it and examine how it is exercised in society. We start the chapter by examining mainstream perspectives on corporate power, stretching back to Adam Smith, especially how it relates to the distortion of market efficiency. We then outline several critical takes on corporate power. In order to do this, however, we first discuss the concept of power and how it has been theorized in the social sciences. We then discuss several different aspects of corporate power: for example, its internal, structural and political dimensions. We then use one well-known corporate scandal to illustrate our arguments.

Key discussion questions

- What is power?
- What is corporate power?
- What are the internal and external dimensions of corporate power?
- How is corporate power exercised?
- Why is corporate power a societal problem?
- What are examples of corporate power?

Mainstream perspectives

Markets and efficiency. According to Adam Smith markets are expected to produce the most efficient outcomes for society overall even if we all pursue

154

our own selfish desires (see Chapter 5). Consequently, liberal thinkers since Smith – and especially orthodox economists – have promoted the extension of markets as the best way to secure social progress (Foley 2006; Philippon 2021). However, the corporate revolution we outlined in Chapter 7 problematizes this view since it illustrates the fact that planning within business organizations can be as efficient as markets in the production, distribution and exchange of societal resources (Simon 1991). Consequently, most economies and societies are now dominated by business enterprises, especially large corporations. As Lynn (2010) points out, one key reason for this situation is that no individual business wants to be forced to compete with other businesses, and so they seek to control their market rather than compete in it – this leads to the concentration of control in the hands of a few businesses as they buy up or merge with their competitors, or seek other means to put their competitors out of business.

The impact of business strategies on competition, by reducing it, is seen as a major problem from mainstream perspectives, especially because it leads to market inefficiencies (Keen 2001; Philippon 2021). Writing in the late eighteenth century Adam Smith, for example, argued that because managers of joint-stock companies did not own the JSC, they would be negligent and wasteful in their decision-making – that is, they would be inefficient. This inefficiency would be compounded by the protection afforded to JSCs by their monopoly privileges granted by the Crown. Smith thought that JSCs would not use their resources efficiently in order to compete with other JSCs because they were protected from their competitors by their monopoly privileges. As a result, the *invisible hand* of the market, competition and self-interest would not be able to work their magic and promote the general social good. Today, many academics and others hold similar views about the workings of the invisible hand, especially the view that competition will ensure the efficient functioning of the economy (e.g. Friedman 1962).

Concerns about efficiency are based on continuing fears about the market power that comes from monopolies or oligopolies (Philippon 2021). These represent attempts by business to control whole areas or sectors of the economy – for example, the grocery sector, cellphone sector and so on. As defined by Milton Friedman (1962: 120): 'Monopoly exists when a specific individual or enterprise has sufficient control over a particular product or service to determine significantly the terms on which other individuals shall have access to it.'

What this definition implies is that a monopoly does not mean *only* one individual or one business has control over 100 per cent of a sector, which is a rare if non-existent phenomenon. Instead, a few people or businesses can have enough control to dominate the setting of prices, product conditions, terms of exchange and so on. One example of a monopoly, in these terms, is

Microsoft, which dominates the software sector, especially when it comes to computer operating systems like Windows (Lynn 2010). According to Means (1983), large businesses, and especially corporations, achieved this form of market power in the mid-twentieth century. They were, and still are, able to manage – or 'administer' in Means' terms – prices and other aspects of their activities outside of market influence, meaning that the market has become a less important mechanism in the allocation and distribution of resources.

Balancing corporate power and corporate responsibility. All of this creates a significant conceptual and moral tension in mainstream understandings of the economy, and one that often gets ignored in the media, academia and political debate. The dominance of business, individually and collectively, raises a number of questions about the role, power and legitimacy of these organizations in society – as we discuss in Chapter 9. This is why critics of business often use the term "corporate power" in their discussions of the capacities and actions of business organizations (see later). However, this term does not generally get used in mainstream discussions, preferring instead to focus on 'monopoly' or 'market power' (e.g. Friedman 1962; Philippon 2021), nor is it generally identified as an explanation for the various problems we face (e.g. unemployment, inflation, product quality). Rather, the power of business is assumed to be a problem only when the capacity of an individual firm enables them to dominate or distort efficient markets, or to influence (disproportionately) the political system. Whichever view you take, it is important to understand how business depends on different forms of social legitimacy to function in society.

Key methodological issue: Measuring corporate power

Concepts like corporate power are not only difficult to define; they are also difficult to pin down methodologically. What we mean by this is that corporate power is difficult to measure, both quantitatively and qualitatively. Generally we could differentiate between corporate power in quantitative terms (e.g. influence over number of people) or qualitative terms (e.g. type and form of influence). More specifically, it is possible to identify corporate power in a number of different ways, as we outline in this chapter. A number of people use different indicators to represent this power, including organizational size in terms of value of assets or income; size in terms of market capitalization; social influence in terms of number of employees; social influence in terms of brand recognition; political influence in terms of political lobbying and the 'revolving door' between business and government; market control in terms of monopoly position; and so on. Frequently, corporate power is represented in terms of (1) economic or (2) market power. Economic power reflects the power to control the labour process (e.g. work decisions), strategic decision-making (e.g. through ownership) and allocation of capital (e.g.

lending and investing). Market power reflects the structural power engendered by the concentration of employment, investment, market capitalization, assets and so on in a small number of businesses.

Sources: Carroll (2010); Brennan (2014)

Even though many mainstream thinkers and commentators frequently miss what we think are crucial aspects of the relationship between business and society, they do highlight an important issue. For example, Carroll and Buchholtz (2017) argue that business involves an implicit *social contract* with society. By this they mean that the views and attitudes of the public matter to business because business is dependent for its continuing existence on people working for them, buying from them, selling to them and so forth. Philippon (2021) has argued that the 'failure to nurture free markets is partly responsible for the negative attitude of many citizens towards capitalism' (707). Therefore, if public attitudes to business become so enraged that the public loses faith in the business world, as happened for many people during the recent (and ongoing) global financial crisis, the public – you and us – are likely to withdraw their support and find other ways to organize the allocation and distribution of resources in society – see Chapters 21 and 22 for examples of these alternatives. This helps to explain why there is a growing interest in the idea of corporate social responsibility (see Chapter 9).

We want to finish this section by noting that business has been naturalized as an inherent and normal part of our social fabric, something to be expected in our economies, societies and polities (Bakan 2004, 2020). For example, the prices we pay in stores and the wages we earn can appear to us as nothing more than reflections of our own decisions and choices, rather than those of businesses and their managers. Similarly, the impacts of businesses and their managers are frequently represented as the result of impersonal and inevitable market pressures, forcing businesses to make hard choices about investments, jobs and so on. While we would agree that there are certain *external logics* underpinning business activities – namely, the capitalist drive for profit and growth (see Chapter 1) – we also contend that these logics are very much embedded in the way business is organized (e.g. corporate structure and governance) and in the power of business and corporations to influence the economy as well as society and politics. This is largely ignored in mainstream perspectives, however.

Critical perspectives

The starting point for any critical engagement with the idea and reality of corporate power is to define what we mean by power. While we might want to say simply that 'we know it when we see it', this is an inadequate basis for discussions of contested and contentious topics like corporate power. To start with, we might want to define power as our capability or capacity to make someone else do something we want them to do; especially if it is something they do not want to do (e.g. we force students to write essays for us) – this is often referred to as 'relational' power (Strange 1988). However, this definition needs unpacking. On the one hand, this definition of power necessarily entails other features like jurisdiction and legal or quasi-legal authority; that is, we obey certain people and not others because one set of people can enforce their demands (e.g. police), while others cannot (e.g. a friend). On the other hand, this definition only relates to direct forms of coercion, which misses other forms of power (e.g. ideological influence). Consequently, the next thing we do here is highlight several ways to conceptualize power, before exploring the diversity of corporate power in society.

What is power? Scholars have wrestled with these sorts of questions about power over many years. Here we want to consider Lukes' (1974) conceptualization of power in detail, but refer to others like Michel Foucault, Robert Cox and Susan Strange as important theorists of power. In his book *Power: A Radical View*, Lukes argued that there are three dimensions to or understandings of power. The *first dimension* is the view that power is distributed between diverse groups in society that pursue their own interests and possess different capacities to achieve their goals – this view is often called 'pluralism'. From this perspective power is possessed, visible and intentional. The *second dimension* is the view that power also entails the ability to control societal or institutional agendas so that some people's interests are ignored. Thus power can also involve 'non-decisions' – like the exclusion of certain people from collective decision-making (e.g. government) – although it is still intentional. The *third dimension* is a critique of the other two views; from this perspective, power can also involve the unintentional or unconscious repression of certain people's interests through the establishment of social structures, forms and institutions that embed and reinforce certain systemic and unconscious biases. For example, there is no natural or inherent reason why we work for a wage, but receiving a wage leads us to adopt, unconsciously, certain habits, behaviours and beliefs. In this way power involves the shaping of our identities, personalities and senses of self; moreover, we do not realize that this is happening and come to accept it as normal and even natural.

Others like Foucault (1980), Cox (1987) and Strange (1988) have also theorized power, although in different ways. On the one hand, Foucault (1980), who was an important French philosopher-historian, sought to uncover histories of the entanglement of knowledge and power in social institutions like the prison, hospital and state – although, interestingly, not business. What he sought to illustrate was that knowledge produced power, and vice versa. For example, as modern nation-states emerged just before and during the life of people like Adam Smith, there was a move towards collecting information about national populations (e.g. birth, death and morbidity rates, household sizes), which enabled the state both to understand their populations and to control them. In this way, knowledge is always and necessarily complicit in the exercise of power, although Foucault also thought that should be thought of as productive and not just coercion. On the other hand, Cox (1987) and Strange (1988), who were influential political scientists, sought to define power in 'structural' terms as the power to set the rules of the game; more precisely, it means the power to determine both the rules that govern our relationships (e.g. regulations) and the social frameworks through which we can and do relate to one another (e.g. markets).

In light of this discussion of power and the mainstream perspectives, we think it is important to consider corporate power from a number of different angles, theoretically and empirically. We focus on the internal and external power of corporations in this section.

- *Internal*: who owns, runs and controls corporations is a key question that we need to consider.
- *External*: we also need to look at the forms, agents and sites of corporate power – individually and as an institution (see Chapter 7) – in order to understand their structural and ideological power. While corporations influence society and politics through various means (e.g. lobbying and 'revolving door'), they also shape the political, economic and legal contexts in which they operate, especially and increasingly internationally (see Chapter 14). Corporations and private businesses dominate public debate and influence our behaviour in ways that we might not notice, or that might not be obvious. It is important to understand how they influence our ideas and behaviours without us being consciously aware of it.

Internal corporate power: who controls corporations? The starting point for most discussions of corporate power is the internal structures and dynamics of corporate control; that is, an examination of who runs and controls the actions of business entities themselves. Two important scholars in this area are Edward Herman (1981) and Scott Bowman (1996), and we draw on their work here. This issue of internal control stretches back to the separation of corporate ownership and control following the corporate revolution, which we discuss in Chapters 7 and 8. When it comes to this internal structure, it is important to consider who makes the strategic decisions about what a business does and how those decisions are carried out. Most private businesses are owned and run by the same people, for example, although this is not always the case. Where a private business is not owner-managed, the owner usually has significant control over managerial appointments and therefore influence over managers. Modern corporations, in contrast, have more complex governance arrangements, as we discuss in Chapters 7 and 8. Corporations are not *owned* by anyone *per se*, in that their assets are the property of the corporation itself, although they have shareholders who own shares (also called equity) in the corporation (Stout 2012). As we discuss in Chapter 8, the relationship between shareholders and management is complex and driven by different legal forms of corporate governance.

Generally, however, in Anglo-American countries internal control rests formally with the board of directors (BoD) that sits between shareholders and executive management, and represents shareholder interests – see Figure 10.1 for a simple depiction of the internal structures of control in a corporation. The BoD votes on key decisions, establishes executives' remuneration deals (e.g. pay and bonuses) and provides oversight of executive decisions, including through the formal auditing processes. As Herman (1981) points out, however, whether or not BoD's have formal control over a corporation, internal power still usually rests with the key executive officers like the CEO for several reasons. First, executives generally get to appoint a proportion of BoD members, which means they can stack it with their allies. Second, BoD members generally do not get involved in the day-to-day operations of a corporation, meaning that they often do not know what executives are doing and, therefore, cannot provide adequate oversight. Finally, BoD members and shareholders lack the inside knowledge

FIGURE 10.1 Internal corporate control.

that executives have about the corporation, which means they lack the ability to make informed decisions.

As Bowman (1996) highlights, it is important to appreciate that internal corporate governance structures – that is, how shareholders control the actions of management – have changed quite significantly over time; for example, moving from a more democratic structure (e.g. one vote per shareholder) to a more oligarchic structure (e.g. one vote per share) since the nineteenth century (Ireland 2010). Furthermore, nowadays different shareholders have different levels of control depending on things like: (1) the number of shares they own and (2) the types of shares they own, since some shares have voting rights and others do not. This means that it is not necessarily possible to identify the 'best practice' for internal governance, or the most efficient way to ensure that shareholder interests are met by managers and executives. Moreover, these discussions of internal governance ignore a major element in the discussion of corporate power; namely, the power that managers have over their workers, whether or not there is shareholder oversight. As Ciepley (2013) points out, for example, corporations create their own laws internal to their organizations (e.g. dress code, work practice, wage regime) to which workers are subject with little recourse to external legal jurisdiction, unless those rules contradict national laws (and even then it depends on the jurisdiction in which the corporation operates).

External corporate power: the corporate shaping of society. Corporate power is not just an internal matter, limited to the actions and decisions that happen within a corporation. As people like Charles Derber (1998), Ted Nace (2003) and Joel Bakan (2004, 2020) note, the corporation now dominates many societies, especially countries such as the United States. Focusing on the internal workings of the corporation would miss the power they have to shape and influence their environment – that is, their structural and ideological power (Strange 1988). This power is not new either. Derber (1998) traces the rise of corporate power in the United States back to the corporate revolution; moreover, he argues that the problems associated with corporate power (e.g. concentration of wealth, inequality, excessive political influence) have continued despite the emergence of countervailing forces in the shape of the central government, workers' movements or public citizenry. Today, as at the end of the nineteenth century, corporations are the dominant social institution; they are more powerful, in many ways, than governments, trade unions, professional organizations and even the law. For example, Bakan (2004: 5) claims that 'corporations dictate the decisions of their supposed overseers in government and control domains of society once embedded within the public sphere'.

While it is possible to criticize corporate power in general terms, it is also crucial to be able to understand and consider specific issues when discussing the relationship between society and corporate power. While we want to recognize that there are external controls on the actions of corporations (Herman 1981) in the form of government regulation, markets, societal attitudes, other businesses and so on, these are often as limited in the control they exert as the internal structures we discussed earlier. Consequently, we need to consider the structural and ideological power of business. In detailing this 'external' corporate power, we draw on the work of the Canadian sociologist William Carroll (2009, 2010; Carroll and Sapinski 2018), as well as other critics of corporate power who focus on the increasingly global nature of corporate power (e.g. Sklair 2002; Nace 2003; Beder 2006; Wolin 2008; Brennan 2014).

In his work, Carroll (2010) notes that corporate power has different forms, different agents and different sites. He argues that corporate power takes three forms: *operational, strategic* and *allocative*. Operational power relates to the decision-making of executives who determine the tasks, routines and so on of workers; strategic power relates to the capacity to determine the direction of a corporation, whether through shareholder or management control; and allocative power is about who controls the money corporations depend on for investment. All of these forms of power involve some form of internal and external control – although we are more interested in the latter here – and come to shape society in distinct ways. For example, operational power shapes the decisions of individual people in terms of employment choices (e.g. what jobs we can and cannot get); strategic power shapes the financial returns of different shareholders (e.g. small shareholders may lose out to larger ones who have more control); and allocative power shapes employment opportunities and levels of unemployment (e.g. through lack of investment).

Although the forms of corporate power help us to identify how it shapes society, it is important to identify who exercises this power and where it is centred. Building on earlier research, Carroll (2010) studies corporate elites (e.g. executives, directors, shareholders) and characterizes them as key agents of corporate power. He argues that corporate power has a class dimension to it in that corporate elites hold multiple and inter-locking positions across and within multiple corporations. As a result of these inter-locking relationships, corporate elites come to share the same identities, preferences and ideologies; this means that these elites are more likely to pursue their own class interests rather than the public interest. A number of academics have argued that this elite is increasingly global, representing an important element in what Sklair (2002) calls a *transnational capitalist class*. Importantly, corporate and political elites are increasingly blurred as individual members move from the private to public realm and back again; a number of activists and academics have described this as a 'revolving door' between business and government because it has become so easy to move from one to the other (e.g. Prashad 2002; Rampton and Stauber 2004; Beder 2006).

The power of corporate elites is reinforced as a result of *where* corporate power is exercised outside of the corporation itself. There are many sites of corporate power outside the boardroom, according to Carroll (2009, 2010). These include trade associations (e.g. Chambers of Commerce), policy planning groups (e.g. Trilateral Commission), think tanks (e.g. Fraser Institute, Heritage Foundation) and even government, state agencies and political parties. According to people like Nace (2003) and Beder (2006), these sites of corporate power are increasingly global and contribute to the structural and ideological power of corporations. However, it is important to note that corporate elites change and evolve; they do not stay the same. This is most obvious in the rise of financial corporate elites over the last few decades, especially new financial elites like hedge fund managers, investment bankers and so on. This means that corporate elites often come into conflict with one another and do not always act in concert (Robinson 2010).

A lot of academics have written about the structural power of business and corporations when it comes to the global economy (see Chapter 13). Examples include Robert Cox (1987) and Susan Strange (1988), who both conceptualized structural power as the capacity to shape the global political-economic rules and structures. Closely linked to this structural power is the notion of ideological power, sometimes referred to as hegemony (see Chapter 14). Ideological power, or hegemony, reflects a broader, more social and cultural process of domination; it involves, according to Richard Peet (2007: 12), 'control and the production of consent by non-physically coercive means and institutions'. This form of power is tied to convincing people to accept a particular societal narrative or imaginary – for example, *business is good for society* – as a normal or natural state of affairs. As such, structural and ideological power closely map on to Steve Lukes' (1974) third dimension of power. Increasingly, business and especially multinational corporations are able to shape the rules they have to abide by, the framework in which they engage with each other, and how we understand and value those rules and framework. As Sharon Beder (2006) notes, for example, multinational corporations influence media discourse, regulation and national policymaking through their financing of academic research, their positions on international policy fora (e.g. World Economic Forum), lobbying of national governments, and the revolving door that enables corporate elites to move into and out of government with ease. As this implies, structural and ideological power often go hand in hand.

Empirical example: Corporate scandals – Innovation and fraud from Enron to FTX

Corporate scandals appear in the headlines of the business press on a regular basis and are sometimes so spectacular that they become popular knowledge. While today we might be drawn to explore breakdowns among certain cryptocurrency firms such as FTX, tracing corporate scandals back to the collapse of large and often well-thought-of corporations at the turn of the twenty-first century reveals some interesting patterns. These early century collapses are best exemplified by Enron, an energy trading firm, which went bankrupt in 2001. Similar scandals spread to other corporations or businesses like WorldCom, Global Crossing and Parmalat, which all went into bankruptcy in 2002–3. The reason for their collapse was that these corporations presented misleading financial statements to their shareholders and other investors that hid the fact they had high levels of corporate debt – in some cases (e.g. Enron) the auditors were also implicated in helping these corporations to present false financial statements. Other companies, like Tyco, were also the subject of scandals as their executives were accused of misleading shareholders in other ways.

These scandals can be understood differently from different perspectives. Through a mainstream lens, such as Carroll and Buchholtz (2017), these scandals are presented as a failure of corporate ethics, corporate social responsibility and corporate governance on the part of corporate executives. Simplistically, they can be seen as the consequence of individual greed. For example, we can understand the actions of Enron's Chairman Kenneth Lay and CEO Jeffrey Skilling as the deliberate misleading of shareholders, including their own employees, while these same executives protected their own interests by selling their own shares in Enron when they realized it was in financial trouble. At the same time, they presented a façade to everyone else that showed Enron was still performing strongly; consequently, when it went bankrupt all the other shareholders in Enron lost their investments. The film *Smartest Guys in the Room* (2005) provides a good introduction to what happened with Enron. In 2002, and in response to the Enron and other scandals, the US government introduced a new law called the Sarbanes-Oxley Act (SOX). It was designed to reinforce the interests of shareholders in corporate governance by strengthening financial reporting requirements and accounting standards.

Similar breakdowns in corporate accounting and accountability took place in the financial sector in 2007–8. Firms such as Citibank, Lehman Brothers, AIG and others were speculating with new (and unregulated) financial instruments without properly leveraging their debts (see Chapter 17). Ratings agencies – who are supposed to assess the value and stability of firms – were negligent in their assessment of the safety of these investments which meant that their ultimate devaluation affected institutional investors and companies across many different sectors, sending the stock market into its worst crash since 1929. Unlike the scandals of the early 2000s, this crisis was understood as a systemic breakdown, and large bailouts were provided to many of the very corporate perpetrators of the risky behaviour. While the Dodd-Frank Act

(2010) was passed in order to attempt to discourage financial institutions from engaging in risky behaviour that has the potential to take down the entire financial system, many argue that the largely novel and unregulated world of financial derivatives, hedge funds and private equity thrive on the volatility that still leaves people and firms in other sectors vulnerable to economic collapse (Brown 2012).

Scandals involving medical technology and pharmaceuticals emerging in the late 2010s appear to follow the same pattern of exploiting the lack of investor knowledge about the industry or technology involved in order to engage in fraudulent activity, boost share price, make sales despite risks to the consumer or attract more investment capital. Two particular cases – that of Purdue Pharma and of Theranos – have attracted a lot of attention. In the former the Sackler family was compelled to pay a $4.5 billion settlement for their knowing promotion of the sale of opioids such as OxyContin despite the risk to consumers in the form of severe addiction and overdose. In the case of Theranos, founder and CEO Elizabeth Holmes was found guilty (2022) of defrauding investors with false claims about the revolutionary nature of the company's blood testing technology (Paul 2022). Some industry insiders have argued that measures similar to SOX ought to be applied to medical technology companies in order to protect investors and consumers and to build in legal grounding to hold corporate executives accountable for the activities and technologies of their firms. Robert Pearl, former CEO of the multibillion-dollar health-care organization Kaiser Permanente, has asked:

> If people like Elizabeth Holmes were required to sign audited disclosures – attesting to the accuracy of claims made about their company's medical products or services – one of two outcomes would unfold under this new law. Elizabeth Holmes would already be in jail for willful deception, or she would have never become a household name in first place and Theranos would be just another failed Silicon Valley startup. And if the Sacklers were required to publicly disclose all knowledge of OxyContin's harmful effects or go to prison for their deceit, how different might their actions have been and how many more Americans would still be alive today? (2022)

Indeed, regulators are also starting to ask the same questions of the cryptocurrency industry, especially after the spectacular fall of FTX – a major cryptocurrency exchange that found its way into the American mainstream with celebrity endorsements from people such as comedian Larry David and football star Tom Brady, stadiums under its name, political clout through large political donations to both Democrats and Republicans in the 2022 midterm elections, and significant market dominance with a valuation of $32 billion. In a matter of days FTX collapsed when a significant rival investor sought to pull out his funds, and it was revealed that there had been the unauthorized use of crypto deposits to bolster sister company Alameda Research as it made risky bets in the market and suffered significant losses. Subsequently FTX founder Sam Bankman-Fried, once featured on the cover of Forbes as the world's youngest multibillionaire, was charged with fraud, money laundering and campaign finance violations. *The Washington Post* reports that the Securities and Exchange Commission Chair Gary Gensler 'said in a statement that Bankman-Fried "built a house of cards on a foundation of deception while telling investors that it was one of the safest buildings in crypto"' (Masih and Mark 2022). With no formal board structure in place at FTX, so few people understanding what blockchain technology is or how tokens work on exchanges, and with such little regulatory oversight in the world of cryptocurrency, it is not surprising to find yet another set of spectacular meltdowns, frauds and scandals at the heart of the industry.

From more critical perspectives used to analyse these scandals, the emphasis on individual greed or individual corporate failure – the idea that these corporations or people represent 'bad apples' in an otherwise healthy economic system – ignores their structural and ideological roots. First, if we adopt Carroll's (2010) approach, we might want to ask whether the whole system of financial auditing was compromised by the close relationships between corporate executives sitting on each other's boards. These friendly directors were less likely to provide rigorous oversight than more independent directors. Similarly, the revolving door between Enron and the US government documented by Prashad (2002) and Rampton and Stauber (2004) enabled Enron to lobby for energy deregulation and to avoid strict regulatory monitoring. We can see that this regulatory favouritism was also a factor for financial instruments that led to the 2008 financial crisis, the medical technologies and pharmaceutical products sold by corporations such as Purdue and Theranos, and the crypto companies which trade currencies around the world. Second, if we adopt the perspective of Cox (1987) and Strange (1988), we might question whether corporations like Enron, Citibank, Purdue, Theranos and FTX sought to shape the structural framework in which they operated and did so very successfully for a period of time before their actions caught up with them. Finally, from an ideological power perspective, we might suggest that all of these corporations created a narrative of dynamic and innovative success that others sought to emulate rather than critique, which was reinforced by the adoption of new and experimental forms of accounting, financial trading and investment. However we go about analysing these scandals, it is important to examine the *systemic* relationships rather than just treat them as the consequence of individual actions or decisions. Understanding corporate power requires an understanding of more than the capacity of one or another corporation to change their environment as they wish.

Conclusion

In this chapter we have sought to introduce the notion of corporate power. As we note, it is difficult to clearly define and conceptualize. We presented the mainstream perspective that it can be understood as excessive economic or market power, distorting market prices so that competition no longer works efficiently. However, we also wanted to problematize this approach; in order to do that we discussed different ways to conceptualize power. In discussing corporate power from a more critical perspective, we outlined the internal and external dimensions to corporate power, and especially illustrated the different types of power we need to unpack in order to analyse corporate power. We finished the chapter by using the example of Enron to illustrate how corporate power can explain the corporate scandals that happened at the start of the twenty-first century.

Suggested readings

- Ch. 1, Bowman, S. (1996) *The Modern Corporation and American Political Thought*, Pennsylvania, Pennsylvania State University Press.
- Ch. 1, Carroll, W. (2010) *Corporate Power in a Globalizing World*, Oxford, Oxford University Press.
- Ch. 12, Carroll, A. and Buchholtz, A. (2017) *Business and Society* (10th Edition), Stamford CT, CENGAGE Learning.
- Ch. 1, Herman, E. (1981) *Corporate Control, Corporate Power*, Cambridge, Cambridge University Press.
- Ch. 2, Peet, R. (2007) *Geography of Power*, London, Zed Books.

Bibliography

Bakan, J. (2004) *The Corporation*, London, Random House.

Bakan, J. (2020). *The New Corporation*, Toronto, Allen Lane.

Beder, S. (2006) *Suiting Themselves: How Corporations Drive the Global Agenda*, London, Earthscan.

Birch, K. (2007) 'The Totalitarian Corporation?' *Totalitarian Movements and Political Religions*, Vol. 8, pp. 153–61.

Bowman, S. (1996) *The Modern Corporation and American Political Thought*, Pennsylvania, Pennsylvania State University Press.

Brennan, J. (2014) 'The Business of Power: Canadian Multinationals in the Postwar Era', PhD Thesis, York University.

Brown, T.S. (2012) 'Legal Political Moral Hazard: Does the Dodd-Frank Act End too Big to Fail', *Alabama Civil Rights & Civil Liberties Law Review*, Vol. 1, No. 86, pp. 1–85.

Carroll, A. and Buchholtz, A. (2017) *Business and Society* (10th Edition), Stamford, CENGAGE Learning.

Carroll, W. (2009) 'Transnationalists and National Networkers in the Global Corporate Elite', *Global Networks*, Vol. 9, pp. 289–314.

Carroll, W. (2010) *Corporate Power in a Globalizing World*, Oxford, Oxford University Press.

Carroll, W.K. and Sapinski, J.P. (2018) *Organizing the 1%: How Corporate Power Works*, Winnipeg, Fernwood.

Ciepley, D. (2013) 'Beyond Public and Private: Toward a Political Theory of the Corporation', *American Political Science Review*, Vol. 107, pp. 139–58.

Cox, R. (1987) *Production, Power, and World Order*, New York, Columbia University Press.

Derber, C. (1998) *Corporation Nation*, New York, St. Martin's Griffin.

Foley, D. (2006) *Adam's Fallacy*, Cambridge, MA, Belknap Press.

Foucault, M. (1980) *Power/Knowledge*, New York, Harvester Wheatsheaf.

Friedman, M. (1962) *Capitalism and Freedom*, Chicago, University of Chicago Press.

Herman, E. (1981) *Corporate Control, Corporate Power*, Cambridge, Cambridge University Press.

Ireland, P. (2010) 'Limited Liability, Shareholder Rights and the Problem of Corporate Irresponsibility', *Cambridge Journal of Economics*, Vol. 34, pp. 837–56.

Keen, S. (2001) *Debunking Economics*, London, Zed Books.

Khurana, R. (2007) *From Higher Aims to Hired Hands*, Princeton, Princeton University Press.

Korten, D. (2001) *When Corporations Rule the World*, San Francisco, Berrett-Koehler.

Lukes, S. (1974) *Power: A Radical View*, Basingstoke, Macmillan.

Lynn, B.C. (2010) *Cornered*, Hoboken, John Wiley & Sons.

Masih, M. and Mark, J. (2022) 'What to Know About Sam Bankman-Fried and the FTX Crypto Exchange Collapse', *Washington Post*, 14 December, https:// www.washingtonpost.com/business /2022/12/13/sam-bankman-fried-ftx -collapse-explained/.

Means, G. (1983) 'Corporate Power in the Marketplace', *Journal of Law and Economics*, Vol. 26, pp. 467–85.

Monbiot, G. (2000) *Captive State*, Basingstoke, Macmillan.

Nace, T. (2003) *Gangs of America*, San Francisco, Berrett-Koehler.

Paul, K. (2022) 'Theranos Founder Elizabeth Holmes Sentenced to More Than 11 Years for Defrauding Investors', *The Guardian*, 18 November, https://www.theguardian.com/us -news/2022/nov/18/elizabeth-holmes -theranos-trial-sentencing.

Pearl, R. (2021) 'How To Prevent The Next Elizabeth Holmes Or Sackler Family Scandal', *Forbes*, 27 September, https://www.forbes.com/sites/ robertpearl/2021/09/27/how-to-prevent -the-next-elizabeth-holmes-or-sackler -family-scandal/?sh=6d64d07d13b2.

Peet, R. (2007) *Geography of Power*, London, Zed Books.

Philipon, T. (2021). 'The Case for Free Markets', *Oxford Review of Economic Policy*, Vol. 37, No. 4, pp. 707–19.

Prashad, V. (2002) *Fat Cats and Running Dogs: The Enron Stage of Capitalism*, London, Zed Books.

Rampton, S. and Stauber, J. (2004) *Banana Republicans*, London, Robinson.

Robinson, W. (2010) 'Global Capitalism Theory and the Emergence of Transnational Elites', *UNU-WIDER, Working Paper Number 2010/02*.

Sennett, R. (2007) *The Culture of the New Capitalism*, New Haven, Yale University Press.

Simon, H. (1991) 'Organizations and Markets', *Journal of Economic Perspectives*, Vol. 5, pp. 25–44.

Sklair, L. (2002) *Globalization: Capitalism and Its Alternatives*, Oxford, Oxford University Press.

Smith, A. (1776) *The Wealth of Nations*, www.gutenberg.org/files/3300/3300-h /3300-h.htm (accessed January 2015).

Stout, L. (2012) *The Shareholder Value Myth*, San Francisco, Berrett-Koehler.

Strange, S. (1988) *States and Markets*, London, Continuum.

Wolin, S. (2008) *Democracy Inc.*, Princeton, Princeton University Press.

11 | Corporations and financialization

Audrey Laurin-Lamothe and Richard Wellen

Introduction

The objective of this chapter is to develop an understanding of the current phenomenon of the financialization of firms. Governance strategies, executives' profiles and activities within firms have been greatly impacted by financial imperatives since 1980. Financialization reconfigured those aspects and imposed a new normative institutional framework within firms. Managers were largely independent during the early stages of the modern corporation until the 1980s, when financial actors started to question the corporation's ability to cope with two major problems: the decrease of firms' performance and their ability to expand their activities after two oil price shocks. At the same time, a new kind of shareholder had become predominant: institutional investors. The category of institutional investors comprises different financial organizations, such as asset management companies, pension funds, insurance companies and hedge funds, which together became major shareholders of public firms. This has allowed them to reshape the governance of firms, the structure of their activities and the processes and criteria by which their performance is evaluated. All of these areas are under a new normative framework that seeks to subordinate all firms to the imperatives of financial markets. Firms are increasingly inclined to make profits through financial channels or financial speculation rather than through productive activities (Krippner 2011). This process is called the financialization of firms and it allows companies to maximize profits at lower cost, rapidly and in greater amounts not through traditional trade and commodity production but through financial strategies such as downsizing, subcontracting, merger and acquisitions, securitization and stock repurchases. However, it can have significant negative impacts on, for instance, work conditions and remuneration, as well as decision-making processes inside the firms, especially decisions related to investment and expansion (Fichtner 2020).

This process of financialization can be seen within impacted firms in the following dimensions: governance of the firm, industrial orientation, professional practices (especially accounting and financial engineering), management consulting, executive compensation and inequality among workers and executives. The following sections present each of these dimensions in detail and discuss the political and economic implications linked to financialization in the context of liberal-market economies.

Key discussion questions

- What are institutional investors and what kind of role they have had in the financialization of the firms' process?
- What does 'downsize and distribute' mean?
- What is the financialization of the firm according to Krippner?
- What are the main consequences of the financialization of the firm on the structure and level of inequality?
- What is capital income?

Shareholder value maximization

As discussed in Chapter 8, corporations are a particular institutional and legal form of business characterized by the separation between property (shares owned by shareholders) and control (exercised by managers) (Berle and Means 1932 [1967]). For most of the twentieth century until the 1980s, corporate governance was somewhat friendly to stakeholders' interests in liberal-market economies. It was assumed that there was a common interest in the economic growth of the firm by its key stakeholders, which in turn informs their behaviour. For example, despite the conflictual relations between workers and shareholders, which *a priori* seems irreconcilable, they share a common interest in the profitability of the firm. Workers' share of corporate revenue depends on their bargaining power vis-à-vis the owners of capital, but firms benefit from this since the salary workers receive for their contribution in the production process also allows for the purchase of commodities in the market. This contributes to an understanding that workers' income should rise with growing productivity.

This arrangement, often called the Fordist growth regime (Boyer 2000), changed when a new kind of shareholder emerged: institutional investors. The growing importance of corporations as employers, particularly after the Second World War, created a new form of labour relations, whereby a growing percentage of workers benefited from a pension fund. This new type of pooled financial wealth came as an add-on to the already important private savings traditionally held directly by individuals and rich wealth-holders. The massive capital accumulated by those pension funds, as well as the rapidly growing insurance industry, has been managed by financial intermediaries who invested a large portion of it in the stock market. By 2017 roughly 80 per cent of corporate stock in the United States was held by institutional investors, a significant increase above the 5 per cent share before 1945 and the 20–30 per cent share in the 1980s (Pionline 2017; Fichtner 2020; Blume and Keim 2017). As a result, although these investors are often managing on behalf of others such as pension beneficiaries, these group investors gained a tremendous amount of power over the corporations of which they became important shareholders. Figure 11.1 shows the increase of financial assets owned by Canadian institutional investors from 1990 to 2013.

Shareholder primacy can be defined as the new dominant framework under which all corporate decisions should be made to serve shareholders' interests and maximize shareholder value (see Chapter 8). It is created through the permanent advocacy of shareholders, using their portfolio as leverage, notably by threatening to sell a large proportion of their corporate shares if the managers of the firm fail to maximize returns to shareholders. For example, in the 1970s shareholder value was often pursued by private equity funds which became known as 'corporate raiders' when they bought out firms that would then sell off their least productive parts in order to make them more profitable (Useem 1996). Versions of this strategy still exist today when institutional investors pressure managers to lay off workers and find cheaper sources of supply or use the firm's earnings to buy back the company's shares instead of investing in the future (Davis and Kim 2015). In this context, all the activities within the firm are usually organized according to a short-term vision that aims exclusively to create shareholder value. In order to maintain control and monitor executives' practices, shareholders actively advocate for so-called good governance principles to guide the board of directors. Under the influence of good governance principles, elaborated by the OECD (1999), corporate boards

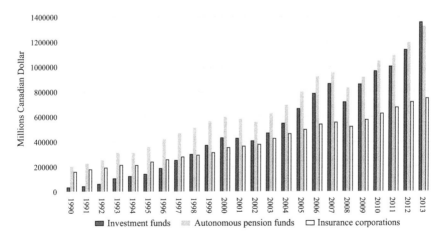

FIGURE 11.1 Financial assets owned by Canadian institutional investors (1990–2013; 2013 current Can$ millions). *Source*: OECD Dataset: Institutional investors' assets.

should be more diversified in terms of gender and cultural composition, but most importantly, the board is supposed to remain independent from family owners and from executives, two groups that might be more interested in the firm's growth rather than its short-term profitability. Although it is possible for family and business partners to maintain control over corporations through special shares with multiple votes, the shareholder value strategy tends to marginalize them from decision-control process and treat them as any other shareholders. The board of directors is supposed to report to serve the interests of shareholders, as the stakeholder group most interested in the efficiency and profitability of the firm.

The emergence of institutional investors reinforced the shift in the general orientation of corporations, which went from an idea of *maximization of revenue* to one of *maximization of shareholder value* (Lazonick and O'Sullivan 2000). The objective of the maximization of revenue can translate into multiple goals, including not only increasing profits and share prices but also compensation and investments. In this perspective, the corporation is seen as an entity where the decision regarding what should be done with the surplus is uncertain and subject to multiple tensions among stakeholders with no clear rules for deciding the best income distribution among actors and activities of the firm (Aglietta and Rebérioux 2005). By contrast, the shareholder primacy perspective is intended to encourage and permit managers to focus on the singular goal of maximizing shareholder value – a clear criterion that can be used to measure managerial performance – when deciding how to allocate the firm's resources (Chapter 8).

Figure 11.2 shows in current Canadian dollars the net operating surplus, corporate income tax paid and dividends paid to shareholders by Canadian corporations, where dividends paid illustrates this shift towards a strategy to maximize shareholder value. Since 1980, the amount of dividends paid is higher than income tax and this gap has grown since 2001. The net operating surplus increased in the same period, but the dividend paid is now practically equal to this surplus. In other words, shareholders successfully secured a greater share of operating surplus despite the 2007–8 financial crisis and have done so at the expense of government tax revenue and real investment within firms.

The financialization of the business model

Industrial expansion considerably decreased during the 1970s because of growing problems of declining profitability in industry (Foster and Magdoff 2009; Lapavitsas 2011). The inability to maintain profitability through the traditional channels in the production sphere by realizing a surplus induced managers to engage more and more in financial activities that could generate profit without having to increase the expenses that the industrial circuit

FIGURE 11.2 Canadian companies' net operating surplus, corporate income tax, and dividends paid (1961 to 2019; 2019 Can$ millions). *Source*: Statistics Canada CANSIM Table 36-10-0116-01 Current and capital accounts – Corporations, Canada, quarterly (x 1,000,000).

generally requires, such as salaries, social benefits and fixed capital (machinery). This resulted in a move towards financial activities at the expense of industrial activities, and the global business strategy shifted from a model of 'retain and reinvest' to one of 'downsize and distribute' (Lazonick and O'Sullivan 2000). Retain and reinvest were the watchwords for corporations until the 1970s and this meant that corporations were likely to retain their employees and income, and to reinvest in fixed capital expansion and employment. By contrast, downsize and distribute are new norms guiding managers: downsize the labour force and peripheral activities, and distribute the returns on equity to shareholders. It is not surprising that from 2000 to 2020, the value of financial assets in Europe, North America and China grew at four times the rate of new investment (Woetzel 2021: vi).

The shift in business model is encapsulated in Krippner's definition of financialization 'as a pattern of accumulation in which profits accrue primarily through financial channels rather than through trade and commodity production, where financial refers to activities relating to the provision (transfer) of liquid capital in expectation of future interest, dividends, or capital gains' (2005: 174–75). A growing proportion of firms' activities are thus related to financial circuits and new or deeper financial channels superimposed on pre-existing industrial channels. In the car industry, for example, profit comes partly from production and sales, which belong to classic industrial channels. What financialization brought is the possibility for car companies to transform direct consumer loans into financial assets through a process of securitization. Securitization refers to the process by which an asset (in this case a loan) is transformed through financial engineering into a security that is sold in the financial market. A loan is a relationship of a concrete individual or corporate borrower to an individual institution like a bank where the risks and opportunities of that loan are between those two parties. By contrast, when a loan is securitized, it becomes more liquid and can be pooled together with similar assets so they can be more efficiently traded and marketed, and the risks can be spread out (Davis and Kim 2015). There is still an industrial circuit, but it is subordinate to a financial circuit that could potentially generate higher profits. The proliferation of company credit card and loans for consumers required financial engineers who are able to transform those loans into derivatives to be sold on financial markets. Securitization allows lenders to generate profits through the interest on loans while removing risk of non-reimbursement. Financial markets and financial actors, especially financial analysts and financial engineers, become more important in the general orientation and dynamics of the capitalist system and have a major impact on the firm's structure.

Another group, financial analysts, provide research about business and investment opportunities and therefore constitute the bridge between the industrial operations of the firm and shareholders. Their job is not only to inform financial markets about the economic performance of the firm but also to influence firm decisions according to the expectations of the financial markets. By doing that, financial analysts contribute to the reinforcement of financialization tendencies and the promotion of the shareholder value framework (Froud et al. 2006). Because they are specialized in a particular sector, financial analysts consider it advantageous when a firm is organized around a core focus. They favour strategies whereby a business concentrates its activities in its main fields – or 'core competencies' – by offshoring, subcontracting or selling other non-essential economic operations (Jung 2016). The industrial diversification that characterizes a conglomerate – a business operating in several markets – is considered to be an obstacle by financial analysts who struggle to determine the asset values of firms with a complex internally differentiated structure and to proceed to a comparison among firms. Corporate financialization therefore leads to an increase in subcontracting, offshoring or closing branches and divisions in order to achieve greater corporate focus. Even managerial activities such as accounting, compensation, taxation, pension fund management and so on can be subcontracted to firms specialized in these services and where workers are paid less. In the past, risk management was previously ensured by the conglomerate structure of the activities, where managers could balance the profits and the loss among different product lines by diversifying the firm's activities across multiple sectors and markets (Fligstein 2005). With the financialization strategy of concentrating on the *core*, the management of risks is left to shareholders when they diversify their portfolio by investing across industries or sectors (Zorn et al. 2005). In fact, the diversification of firm operations is disadvantageous from the point of view of shareholders, because when more firms focus on their core competency the average firm in an investor's portfolio would be expected to be more profitable.

International accounting standards

Accounting is the process by which economic activities are transformed into account categories used for reporting the financial state of business entities. The financial accounting norms used by most of the world, known as International Financial Reporting Standards (IFRS), are determined and disseminated by the International Accounting Standards Board. The United States uses generally accepted accounting principles (GAAP). These accounting standards have changed over time to reflect the development of financialization. The static approach of accounting, largely used for the most part of the twentieth century, aimed to provide economic data of firms in a way aligned with the state's requirements for statistics and fiscal policies. Static accounting takes the 'safe' approach of valuing the firm's assets (machines, intellectual property, etc.) based on what they would be worth if the firm was liquidated and the assets sold. Another conservative accounting approach is called historical cost accounting, which values a firm's assets based on their 'book value' which is what they initially cost to purchase or make, with adjustments for depreciation. However, since the mid-1990s, a far less conservative accounting approach called 'fair value' has become the dominant way to report the firms' activities in a way that is intelligible to – and preferred by – financial markets. Fair value is used by both the IFRS and GAAP standards. With the globalization of investment, shareholders seek standardized ways to compare public corporations all around the world. The fair-value approach is claimed to be better suited for this because it considers the firm as a nexus of transactions and assumes the efficiency of markets in valuing assets (Ramanna 2013). Under this view accounting value can only be truly relevant if it is based on the future profit that the asset is expected to create, since that is how assets like corporate stock are priced in the actual financial market. The fair-value metric is therefore meant to give shareholders a better appreciation of firms in their specific role as buyers and sellers of shares rather than as long-term investors or bank lenders that is predominant in the old static approach.

The growing use of the fair-value accounting approach is intended to reduce the gap between the accounting value of the firm and its stock price, by considering the value of each asset as if it was to be sold on a market in a very short term. This technique is advantageous for financial actors as well as firms that have seen their total stock market value increased. However, some researchers have argued that the constant revaluation of assets and liabilities under the fair-value approach brings greater volatility and instability to markets

(Aglietta and Rebérioux 2005: 127). Other researchers add that the adoption of fair-value accounting reflects the growing influence of financial services professionals in the standard-setting bodies that govern and regulate financial markets rather than a better way of reporting on the operational performance of the firm (Chiapello 2016; Chiapello and Medjad 2009; Allen and Ramanna 2013).

Management consulting firms

Management consulting firms are intertwined with the financialization of firms. Even though they have provided services since the early twentieth century, their market value rose, for instance, from US$4 billion in 1980 to US$90 billion in 1999 (Armbrüster 2010). Consulting firms provide services mainly in the areas of accounting, taxation and management for public entities as well as corporations. For corporations, consulting firms design a strategic branch, restructure the operations, provide compensation plans and conceptualize financial innovations. Especially when they are employed by major corporations across many countries, consulting firms tend to homogenize the structure of the firms and reinforce their global response to financial markets. The rising prominence of these firms like McKinsey & Company is often associated with corporate downsizing that reduces compensation and taxation (Markovits 2020).

Figure 11.3 illustrates the five fields discussed (governance, investment, accounting, strategy and operations) and the new intermediaries who reinforced the financialization process (financial analysts, financial accountants, financial engineers and management consultants).

The financialization of executive compensation

The legitimation of shareholder primacy would not be possible without the growing support that a mainstream approach, often referred to as agency theory, gained during the 1970s. Agency theory postulates that firms should be considered as a nexus of contracts among actors, where there is a fundamental asymmetry between shareholders and managers – what is called an 'agency problem' – that must be corrected by aligning the managers' interests to those of the shareholders (see Chapters 7 and 8). The main justification is that the latter are, of all the stakeholders, the only ones with a strong incentive to increase the economic performance of the firm (Jensen and Meckling 1976). The so-called agency problem, as we saw in Chapter 8, arises from the fact that managers have too many opportunities to be free-riders and that shareholders are likely to be 'rationally apathetic' about overseeing management because they are dispersed. From the shareholders' point of view, managers may not work at their full potential and are not fully committed to generate shareholder

FIGURE 11.3 Synthesis of fields framing the financialization of firms.
Source: Laurin-Lamothe (2019: 66).

value by making innovative or efficiency-enhancing changes because the managers don't own the company's shares themselves. Additionally, managers may be unwilling to take risks and enact significant change since there is a chance it might impact their long-term job tenure or their career and salary progression within the firm. From a governance standpoint, managers are able to get by with less effort since shareholders are diversified across many firms and therefore rarely have time to oversee management of each firm in which they invest. However, notwithstanding their diversification shareholders have a financial interest in seeing that managers in the firms in which they hold shares take the risks to make that firm more profitable. Hence the best way to fix the agency problem is to align the interests of managers with those of shareholders which, as we have seen earlier, would involve assuming shareholders care about one result only, namely the stock price, and tying the compensation and career recognition of managers to that metric (Jung and Dobbin 2012).

For now, we should recall that since the 1970s institutional investors enforced many of the prescriptions of agency theory by encouraging management to make their firms more focused and allow investment analysts to provide better coverage of firms with clear specialties that could be compared with one another (Jung and Dobbin 2012). This would allow financial markets to be more 'efficient'. But this legacy of agency theory has several problems. For example, the threat of takeovers by institutional investors such as private equity funds and hedge funds tends to encourage firms and their management to be very focused on short-term stock price gains. For firms that have been bought or taken over there is an especially great need to increase the share price since this gives leverage for the private equity fund to pay off the debts used to purchase the company. The share price is often increased by taking actions that work against the longer-term interests of employees and other stakeholders (Fichtner 2020). One of the main ways firms keep their stock price high is by using stock buybacks which boosts the share price by diverting funds away from employees and investments in future innovations and putting those funds into the pockets of shareholders. For Lazonick (2011) share buybacks are an extreme form of financialization whereby firms rely on governments and society to finance education, infrastructure and other public goods central to industry's success and profitability while returning less of the profits to society by cutting jobs and investment and diminishing public resources. When a firm suffers from this excessive short-termism it is the state, communities and employees who are negatively impacted more than shareholders since the latter can bear the risk of individual investment failures due to the diversification of their portfolios.

Despite the criticisms mentioned (increasingly well known among practitioners and scholars), agency theory has had an enormous impact on how boards of directors – under the pressure of institutional investors – have changed the rules regarding executive compensation. In order to align the interests of managers with that of shareholders, managers now receive a larger part of their total compensation in stock options and shares. Stock options are units that the executive will convert into shares usually when the stock price of the company is higher, whereas shares are simply the company's shares.

Figure 11.4 shows that financial compensation (shares and stock options) accounted for 51 per cent of the average compensation of the top 100 CEOs in Canada in 2001, while this proportion rose to 60 per cent in 2015. Adjusted for inflation, the total average of compensation has more than doubled, from $4.4 million in 2001 to $9.6 million in 2015.

From active to passive asset management: A new era of financialization?

As we have seen earlier, institutional investors have driven the process of financialization and the shareholder primacy approach that has been reinforced by it. In recent years people have turned their attention to the growing role of asset management companies themselves and the critical role they are playing

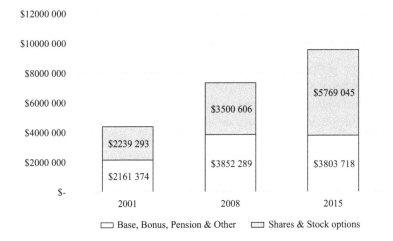

Base, Bonus, Pension & Other   Shares & Stock options

FIGURE 11.4 Average Top 100 CEO's compensation by category in Canada (2001, 2008 and 2015; 2015 Can$). *Source:* TSX Composite Compensation & Performance Report.

in the transformation of financialized capitalism (Fichtner 2020; Braun 2020). Institutional investors – like pension funds or insurance companies – may perform their own asset management themselves by investing the pooled savings of other people, like future retirees and investing in financial markets. However, in the 1980s many pension funds began to pay a fee to hire external asset management companies to do this work, and this was the start of an era which Braun (2020) calls 'asset manager capitalism'. Initially almost all asset managers 'actively' managed their portfolios by selecting stocks using research and assumptions about how to boost returns. Active asset managers make money by proving to their institutional or individual clients that they can 'beat the benchmark' in the asset markets in which they invest. The assumption that institutional shareholders will be 'active managers' is a key foundation of agency theory since these active managers can try to influence company boards to make the firm more efficient, profitable or competitive. Many institutional shareholders are large enough that the threat of 'exit' – and acting as an 'impatient investor' – can translate into the kind of shareholder power that agency theory believes is necessary to make financial markets efficient (Braun 2021).

Over the last two decades a more 'passive' model of asset management has increasingly come to the fore. The key to successful investment is often achieving sufficient diversification among types of industry sectors and geographical areas. Diversification can be done 'passively' rather than paying active managers to locate and bet selectively on potential 'winners' in the market. Passive asset management involves tracking a financial market 'index' and assembling portfolios of financial assets like stocks and bonds in a 'representative' basket that reflects the broader market as a whole or some sector within it. In recent years, the asset management industry has been very successful in selling low-cost index-tracking mutual funds and exchange traded funds (ETFs) that simply replicate the performance of popular indexes like the S&P 500. From 2011 to 2021 the passive share of managed assets has doubled (Wigglesworth 2022). Passive asset management fees can be very low since building passive or index-tracking portfolios is essentially an automated 'rules-based' process involving little research or engagement with individual firms. Passive asset management also benefits from economies of scale since the portfolios can be managed for many clients in a standardized package. From a social point of view this has made low-cost portfolio diversification broadly accessible, largely to pension funds and wealthy families, but increasingly to many ordinary savers who can buy mass marketed index ETFs using smartphone apps supplied by online brokers.

As a result of all these developments, the 'Big Three' leading asset management firms – Blackrock, Vanguard and State Street – have grown enormously; between them it is estimated that they have pooled enough investor savings to own up to 22 per cent of the average large firms' shares in the US economy (Levitz 2022). Some argue that this new form of financialization – and concentration of stock ownership – has exposed the limits of the efficient financial market assumption at the heart of agency theory. That's because these firms are passive shareholders with little incentive to be engaged actively in influencing the performance of individual firms or to pressure any given firm in their portfolio to compete hard against their rivals. Moreover, since they are index trackers these portfolio managers cannot sell their shares in a company if they are disappointed with management. This impossibility of 'exit' in theory should undermine the 'impatient capital' orientation favoured by agency theory (Fichtner and Heemskerk 2020; Braun 2021). Although they are often the largest single shareholder of a firm, a passive asset manager does not have an interest in the success of any one firm but rather in all of the firms in the indexed market or sector taken as a whole. The fees earned by passive managers are determined as a percentage of the current aggregate market value of all the assets they manage for their clients (Levitz 2022). Hence, they do not get paid to demonstrate their stock-picking skills but to expand their client base and see increases to the aggregate market value of all asset holdings they manage for clients.

The larger socio-political and economic impact of the rise of the Big Three asset management firms has been the subject of debate. As we have seen, these firms cannot threaten to sell their shares in a specific company without violating their mandate to track the entire market index. Nevertheless, in countries like the United States they have more shareholder 'voice' (voting power) than any other financial agents in the economy (Braun 2021). Some researchers argue that because a few big financial firms with locked-in ownership of the broad corporate sector have become so influential this creates a pattern 'universal ownership', which has the potential to be a socially beneficial model of financialization (Hawley and Williams 2007). That's because they are invested so broadly that they are exposed to systemic risks and therefore have a long-term interest in pursuing the well-being of communities, workers and possibly even the transition to climate-friendly business strategies and investments (Fichtner and Heemskerk 2020). For example, an active asset manager may be very tolerant of firms in their portfolio that create negative externalities such as a high level of carbon emissions that contribute to the climate crisis if it allows those firms to be more profitable. By contrast, passive 'universal owners' care most of all about the aggregate effect of all business behaviour in their portfolio and therefore are more likely to want to reduce climate-related risks which impact the broader economy. To take another example, passive asset managers might be against strategies for cutting jobs or wage cuts in an industry if they lead to the loss of spending power in the economy as a whole which reduces earnings for other firms.

In reality, this promise of socially responsible finance associated with the rise of diversified universal owners has not materialized (Tallarita 2023). While some of the leading asset management firms like Blackrock have spoken out against stock buybacks and have publicly advocated for changes to address the climate crisis, their actual record of corporate governance influence in these areas remains weak (Braun 2021; Fichtner and Heemskerk 2020). Braun (2022) points out that the rise of universal owners has not turned out well for workers as their economic fortunes have declined relative to wealth-holders in the decades since passive asset management has expanded. While the unequal distribution of income may have some negative society-wide economic effects, corporate policies that lower wages and increase profits provide offsetting benefits to asset management firms since they increase asset prices and therefore asset management fees (Braun 2020). Even pension funds, which ultimately represent the interests of workers as beneficiaries, have not been able to create a system of 'pension fund capitalism' that could steer financialization in a more worker-friendly direction (Bryan and Rafferty 2017; Braun 2022).

Consequences of the financialization of the firms on the structure and level of inequality

Given our discussion earlier, it's not surprising that increasing financialization remains associated with growing inequality. Figure 11.5 shows the tremendous gap between the average Top 100 CEO's compensation in Canada in 2015 and the average earnings of Canadians working full time at minimum wage and the average yearly wage and salary earned by Canadians.

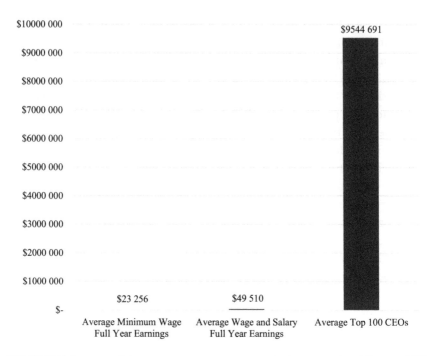

FIGURE 11.5 Average minimum wage, average wage and salary earned and Top 100 CEO compensation in Canada (2015; Can$). *Source*: Mackenzie (2017), see also: Massie and Macdonald (2021).

Along with other capital income (rent, return on capital, royalties, interest, inherited wealth), shares and stock options have been a key factor in the growing inequality gap in Canada (Osberg 2018). Table 11.1 shows that the market income adjusted for inflation of the top 1 per cent in Canada rose from a median of $216,444 in 1982 to $320,700 in 2017, while the bottom 99 per cent experienced a decrease in their real median market income for the same period. In other words, the median market income of the 1 per cent was 770 per cent higher than the rest of Canadians in 1982, and this ratio increased to 1,192 per cent in 2017. However, market income inequality is smaller than capital income inequality. As shown in Table 11.1, in 1982, the top 1 per cent earned 3,300 per cent more in terms of capital income than the bottom 99 per cent, and this ratio reached 7,571 per cent in 2017. Finally, while the majority of Canadian households still remain dependent on wages and salaries, wealthy households tend to secure a good share of their income from a variety of capital income sources, which became more important as a share of the total. Capital income accounted for 14.2 per cent of the total income of the top 1 per cent tax filers in Canada in 2017, compared to 3.6 per cent in 1982. The proportion of capital gains for the bottom 99 per cent also rose, but only from 0.9 per cent to 2.5 per cent for the same period.

TABLE 11.1 Tax Filers' Sources of Income for the Top 1 Per Cent Income Group and the Bottom 99 Per Cent Income Group (1982 and 2017; 2017 Can$)

	Source of income (median)*	Top 1 per cent income group		Bottom 99 per cent income group		Proportion between Top 1% and Bottom 99%
1982	Market income	$ 216,444	96.4%	$ 28,115	99,1%	770%
	Capital gains	$ 7,999	3.6%	$ 242	0.9%	3300%
2017	Market income	$ 320,700	85.8%	$ 26,900	97,5%	1192%
	Capital gains	$ 53,000	14.2%	$ 700	2.5%	7571%

* Constant Canadian dollars 2017 = 100.

Source: Statistics Canada CANSIM Table: 11-10-0055-01: High-income tax filers in Canada.

Similar patterns can be observed in the United States. From 1992 to 2022, the share of the total wealth held by the top 1 per cent went from 25 per cent to 32 per cent, and their share of stock market wealth grew from 42.9 per cent to 53.7 per cent. At the same time, the bottom 50 per cent in the country saw their share of total wealth decreased from 4.23 per cent to 2.78 per cent, and from 4.1 per cent to 3.2 per cent for the specific share of the stock market (Federal Reserve 2022)

Conclusion

In this chapter we explored the way financialization and the pressure from institutional investors and asset managers have reshaped the structure of the firm and reorganized its priorities. When top managers were compensated for industrial expansion, job creation, innovation and sales during the post–Second World War era, employees could advocate for a bigger piece of the pie. Executive managers are now co-opted by financial markets because they receive an incentive linked to stock price performance, which has little to do with industrial development or the contribution of their firm to the overall economy and society. Moreover, financialization has brought a new social contradiction whereby workers' savings in pension funds are managed by institutional investors that advocate for a higher return on equity, which paradoxically undermines the ability of the firm to invest in its labour force, at the same time that it increases costs for the state as well as communities impacted by its economic activities.

Suggested readings

- Fichtner, J. (2020). 'The Rise of Institutional Investors', in P. Mader, D. Mertens and N. van der Zwan (eds), *International Handbook of Financialization*, Routledge, pp.265–75.

- Lapavitsas, C. (2011) 'Theorizing Financialisation', *Work, Employment and Society* Vol. 25, pp. 611–26.
- Lazonick, W and O'Sullivan, M. (2000) 'Maximizing Shareholder Value: A New Ideology for Corporate Governance', *Economy and Society*, Vol. 29, pp. 13–35.
- Ch. 3, Osberg, L. (2018) *The Age of Increasing Inequality. The Astonishing Rise of Canada's 1%*, Toronto, Lormier.
- Van der Zwan, N. (2014) 'Making Sense of Financialization', *Socio-Economic Review,* Vol. 12, pp. 99–129.

Bibliography

Aglietta, M. and Rebérioux, A. (2005) *Corporate Governance Adrift: A Critique of Shareholder Value*, Cheltenham; Northampton, MA, Edward Elgar Publishing.

Allen, A. and Ramanna, K. (2013) 'Towards an Understanding of the Role of Standard Setters in Standard Setting', *Journal of Accounting and Economics*, Vol. 55, No. 1, pp. 66–90.

Armbrüster, T. (2010) *The Economics and Sociology of Management Consulting*, Cambridge, Cambridge University Press.

Berle, A. and Means, G. (1932 [1967]) *The Modern Corporation and Private Property*, New York, World Inc.

Blume, M.E. and Keim, D.B. (2017) 'The Changing Nature of Institutional Stock Investing', *Critical Finance Review*, Vol. 6, pp. 1–41.

Boyer, R. (2000) 'Is a Finance-Led Growth Regime a Viable Alternative to Fordism? A Preliminary Analysis', *Economy and Society*, Vol. 29, pp. 111–45.

Braun, B. (2020) 'Asset Manager Capitalism as a Corporate Governance Regime', in J.S. Hacker, A. Hertel-Fernandez, P. Pierson, and K. Thelen (eds.), *American Political Economy: Politics, Markets and Power*. Cambridge University Press, pp. 170–294, https://doi.org/10.31235/osf.io/v6gue.

Braun, B. (2021) 'Exit, Control, and Politics: Structural Power and Corporate Governance under Asset Manager Capitalism', *Politics and Society*, Vol. 50, No. 4, pp. 630–54.

Braun, B. (2022) 'Fueling Financialization: The Economic Consequences of Funded Pensions', *New Labor Forum*, Vol. 31, No. 1, pp. 70–9, https://doi.org/10.1177/10957960211062218.

Bryan, D. and Rafferty, M. (2017) 'Financialization', In D.M. Brennan, D. Kristjanson-Gural, C. Mulder, and E.K. Olsen (eds.), *Routledge Handbook of Marxian Economics*, Routledge, pp. 255–65.

Byrd, J., Parrino, R. and Pritsch, G. (1998) 'Stockholder-Manager Conflicts and F irm Value', *Financial Analysts Journal*, Vol. 54, pp. 14–30.

Chiapello, E. (2016) 'How IFRS Contribute to the Financialization of Capitalism', in D. Bensadon and N. Praquin (eds), *IFRS in a Global World*, Cham, Springer, pp. 71–84.

Chiapello, E. and Medjad, K. (2009) 'An Unprecedented Privatisation of Mandatory Standard-Setting: The Case of European Accounting Policy', *Critical Perspectives on Accounting*, Vol. 20, pp. 448–68.

Davis, G.F. and Kim, S. (2015) 'Financialization of the Economy', *Annual Review of Sociology*, Vol. 41, pp. 203–21.

Federal Reserve. (2022) *Distribution of Household Wealth in the U.S. since 1989*, Distributional Financial Accounts, https://www.federalreserve.gov/releases/z1/dataviz/dfa/index.html.

Fichtner, J. (2020) 'The Rise of Institutional Investors', in P. Mader, D. Mertens, and N. van der Zwan (eds), *International Handbook of Financialization*, London, Routledge, pp. 265–75.

Fichtner, J. and Heemskerk, E.M. (2020) 'The New Permanent Universal Owners: Index Funds, Patient Capital, and the Distinction between Feeble and Forceful Stewardship', *Economy and Society*, Vol. 49, No. 4, pp. 493–515.

Fligstein, N. (2005) 'The End of (Shareholder Value) Ideology?' *Research in the Sociology of Organizations*, Vol. 17, pp. 223–8.

Foster, J.B. and Magdoff, F. (2009) *The Great Financial Crisis: Causes and Consequences*, New York, Monthly Review Press.

Froud, J., Johal, S., Leaver, A. and Williams, K. (2006) *Financialization and Strategy: Narrative and Numbers*, London, Routledge.

Hawley, J. and Williams, A. (2007) 'Universal Owners: Challenges and Opportunities', *Corporate Governance: An International Review*, Vol. 15, No. 3, pp. 415–20.

Jensen, M. and Meckling, W. (1976) 'Theory of the Firm: Managerial Behavior, Agency Costs and Ownership Structure', *Journal of Financial Economics*, Vol. 3, pp. 305–60.

Jung, J. (2016) 'Through the Contested Terrain: Implementation of Downsizing Announcements by Large US Firms, 1984 to 2005', *American Sociological Review*, Vol. 81, pp. 347–73.

Jung, J. and Dobbin, F. (2012) 'Finance and Institutional Investors', in Karin Knorr Cetina and Alex Preda (eds.), *The Oxford Handbook of the Sociology of Finance*, Oxford, Oxford University Press, pp. 52–74.

Krippner, G.R. (2005) 'The Financialization of the American Economy', *Socio-Economic Review*, Vol. 3, pp. 173–208.

Krippner, G.R. (2011) *Capitalizing on Crisis: The Political Origins of the Rise of Finance*, Cambridge, MA, Harvard University Press.

Lapavitsas, C. (2011) 'Theorizing Financialisation', *Work, Employment and Society*, Vol. 25, pp. 611–26.

Laurin-Lamothe, A. (2019) *Financiarisation et élite économique au Québec*, Québec, Presses de l'Université Laval.

Lazonick, W. and O'Sullivan, M. (2000) 'Maximizing Shareholder Value: A New Ideology for Corporate Governance', *Economy and Society*, Vol. 29, pp. 13–35.

Lazonick, W. (2011) 'From Innovation to Financialization: How Shareholder Value Ideology Is Destroying the US Economy', in M.H. Wolfson and G.A. Epstein (eds), *Handbook of the Political Economy of Financial Crises*, Oxford, Oxford University Press, pp. 52–74.

Levitz, E. (2022) 'Modern Capitalism Is Weirder Than You Think. It Also No Longer Works as Advertised', *New York Magazine*, 15 March, https://nymag.com/intelligencer/2022/03/how-asset-managers-have-upended-how-modern-capitalism-works.html.

Mackenzie, H. (2017) 'Throwing Money at the Problem. 10 Years of Executive Compensation', Canadian Centre for Policy Alternatives, Ottawa, report.

Markovits, D. (2020) 'How McKinsey Destroyed the Middle Class,' *The Atlantic*, 3 February, https://www.theatlantic.com/ideas/archive/2020/02/how-mckinsey-destroyed-middle-class/605878/.

Massie, A. and Macdonald, D. (2021) 'Boundless Bonuses. Skyrocketing Canadian Executive Pay During the 2020 Pandemic', Canadian Centre for Policy Alternatives, Ottawa, report.

OECD. (1999) *OECD Principles of Corporate Governance*, https://www.oecd.org/officialdocuments/publicdisplaydocumentpdf/?cote=C/MIN(99)6&docLanguage=En.

Osberg, L. (2018) *The Age of Increasing Inequality. The Astonishing Rise of Canada's 1%*, Toronto, Lormier.

PIonline. (2017) '80% of Equity Market Cap Held by Institutions', *Pensions & Investments*, 25 April, https://www.pionline.com/article/20170425/INTERACTIVE/170429926/80-of-equity-market-cap-held-by-institutions.

Ramanna, K. (2013) 'Why "fair value" is the rule. Harvard Bus. Rev.(March)'.

Tallarita, R. (2023) 'The Limits of Portfolio Primacy', *Vanderbilt Law Review*, Vol. 76, forthcoming.

Useem, M. (1996) *Investor Capitalism: How Money Managers are Changing the Face of Corporate America*, New York, Basic Books.

Wigglesworth, R. (2022) 'How Passive Are Markets Actually? More Than You Think. Much More', *Financial Times*, 4 September, https://www.ft.com/content/73a6527d-cd59-498e-9923-af5143cbb952.

Woetzel, J., Mischke, J., Madgavkar, A., Windhagen, E., Smit, S., Birshan, M., Kemeny, S. and Anderson, R.J. (2021) 'The Rise and Rise of the Global Balance Sheet. How Productively are We Using Our Wealth?', *McKinsey Global Institute*, report.

Zorn, D., Dobbin, F., Dierkes, J. and Kwok, M. (2005) 'Managing Investors: How Financial Markets Reshaped the American Firm', in K.K. Cetina and A. Preda (eds), *The Sociology of Financial Markets*, New York, Oxford University Press, pp. 269–90.

12 | Corporations and market power in the twenty-first century

John Simoulidis and Kean Birch

Introduction

Unprecedented health and safety measures were imposed by governments all over the world after March 2020 in response to the Covid-19 pandemic. Governments, university researchers and private pharmaceutical companies raced to develop and test vaccines. For example, the US government announced a programme called Operation Warp Speed that made US$10 billion available to researchers, while the Canadian government has, at the time of writing, granted $414 million in total to almost one thousand Covid-19 related research projects. Over 100 vaccines have been developed or are currently in the trial phase. Companies like Pfizer, a major vaccine producer, have benefited from government support both directly through advance purchase agreements (US$1.95 billion from the US government alone) and indirectly through their partnership with BioNTech, which received US$445 billion from the German government (Storeng and Puyvallée 2020).

Pfizer earned US$9.6 billion (CAN$12.5 billion) in profits in 2020, even before the vaccine reached wide distribution. According to one estimate, Pfizer may have earned close to US$1 billion (CAN$1.35 billion) on the sale of its Covid vaccine in 2020 alone (Robins and Goodman 2021). Organizations like Oxfam have decried Pfizer's pricing strategy as a form of corporate profiteering, citing a study which argued that prices are at least five times the cost of production (Oxfam 2021). Yet the company itself believes that vaccines should cost more. In 2001 Frank D'Amelio, Pfizer's CFO, said that the estimated US$19.50 per dose countries were currently paying was 'not a normal price like we typically get for a vaccine – $150, $175 per dose. So, pandemic pricing.' (Sagonowsky 2021). Some may think that so-called surplus profits should go to businesses which innovate first as a legitimate reward for innovation, even in the midst of a global health crisis. Others disagree, arguing that innovation is impossible without government and civil society.

The idea that business represents the dynamic and innovative impulse within society while government stifles this with their regulatory interference is a very powerful one. However, the heterodox economist Mariana Mazzucato (2013) argues that the state has always played an entrepreneurial role in society, making innovation happen by assuming risk and financing capital-intensive investments in infrastructure and research, from railways in the nineteenth century to pharmaceuticals today. If we include the basic research undertaken by generations of academics working at publicly funded universities and research institutes among the conditions that made vaccines like Pfizer's possible, then the exclusivity rights granted to corporations under intellectual property rights regimes may be questionable. If the so-called value created through innovations is a collective process involving private businesses, the state and civil society, we can question the role of corporate power in determining how that value is distributed. Global organizations like the WHO, UN and others have expressed concern that, under pandemic conditions, global public goods such as health and knowledge ought to have been given priority over the intellectual property rights of business to their vaccine formulas (Peacock 2022).

Case study

TRIPs and Covid-19

The Agreement on Trade Related Intellectual Property Rights (TRIPs) was adopted after the Uruguay Round in 1990 by contracting states to the General Agreement on Tariffs and Trade and is now administered through the World Trade Organization, which was also established during this round of multilateral negotiations. This agreement embedded intellectual property (IP) rights into an international trading system for the first time. It was controversial from the start and led to demands from developing countries to a new ministerial gathering of WTO members to ensure access to essential medicines, most notably anti-retroviral drugs to fight AIDS. This resulted in the Doha Declaration on the TRIPs Agreement and Public Health in 2001, which was intended to grant greater flexibility for developing countries to circumvent patent rights. Today, the assertion of IP rights by global pharmaceutical corporations has been identified as an obstacle to poor countries accessing Covid-19 vaccines. The Trade Justice Fund, an international non-profit education and advocacy organization focused on promoting worker's rights, climate protection and trade justice, has criticized a deal struck in June 2022 at the World Trade Organization (WTO) on patents for Covid-19 vaccines in developing countries. They issued a declaration signed by over 300 civil society organizations that urged governments to 'Circumvent the WTO's pharmaceutical monopoly rules when possible and outright defy those rules when needed' (CCPA 2022).

Businesses have a lot of power to determine how the value created by these cumulative processes is distributed. Whether or not businesses have too much power, where that power is exercised, and what ought to be done about this, is the subject of many current debates. While mainstream economists tend to limit their focus to narrowly economic dimensions of market power and legal issues around intellectual property rights, critical approaches to corporate power look at the broader impacts corporate power has on our economic, political, legal, media and scientific systems. Importantly, corporate power is not limited to the economic sphere. Businesses can use their power to influence markets (monopoly pricing) and regulations, particularly through global free-trade agreements protecting intellectual property rights (see Box 1 on TRIPs). But they also wield enormous power that critics claim poses a threat to our societies. In this chapter, we will compare mainstream and critical perspectives on explaining the resurgence of corporate power in the twenty-first century, what social issues excessive concentrations of corporate power fundamentally raises, and what ought to be done about this.

Key discussion questions

- How have attitudes towards business changed over time?
- In what ways are the dominant corporations today different than in the past?
- How does corporate power affect economic inequality, labour and environmental issues?
- How does corporate power affect democracy and human rights?
- How does corporate power influence how we think about corporations themselves?

Corporate power in the twenty-first century: Mainstream perspectives

Growing Fears about Market Power. In Chapter 10 we introduced a general conception of corporate power relating to two dimensions of corporate governance. Internally, corporate power relates to the control over business firms, typically by owners and managers who control short-term investment decisions, marketing strategy, long-term planning and so on. Externally, corporate power pertains to issues of business influence in society, for example the capacity to shape regulation, public opinion and politics. Even mainstream economists are increasingly concerned about corporate power – particularly in the form of monopolies and oligopolies – because of the distorting effects they have on markets (Philippon 2019, 2021).

Mainstream economists refer to monopolies as a kind of 'market failure'. By charging prices that are higher than what theoretically could be obtained under conditions of perfect competition, markets are distorted as investment and production in non-monopolistic sectors are negatively impacted, thus hindering innovation and employment throughout the economy. In this view, when concentration of ownership in an industry reduces competition, it undermines market efficiency and all the benefits supposedly associated with it.

Advocates of free markets say that policies – commonly referred to as antitrust policies – need to be developed to make businesses behave as if conditions of competition did exist in order to ensure that businesses cannot use their market power to distort the functioning of the market mechanism (see Crouch 2011).

Mainstream economists still subscribe to Adam Smith's defence of market efficiency and his view of perfect competition but have extended their analysis of corporate power to their ability to influence the institutional framework within which they operate. Like Smith, mainstream economists argue that concentrations of capital lead to monopolistic strategies that crowd out potential competitors leading to higher prices. This not only redistributes income from households to corporations but also has a negative effect on market efficiency. Economists like Philippon (2019) focus on the role played by lobbying to create monopoly-friendly regulatory regimes. He argues that the ability of businesses to influence regulations through campaign financing ultimately 'distort free markets: across time, states, and industries, corporate lobbying and campaign finance contributions lead to barriers to entry and regulations that protect large incumbents, weaker antitrust enforcement, and weaker growth of small and medium-sized firms' (9). Appearing at the 'intersection' of politics and economics, lobbying that succeeds in effecting a small regulatory change might be worth millions of dollars to a business and entail a significant loss of tax revenues or consumer surplus, leading to an apparent 'loss of faith' in capitalism in the United States and elsewhere (Philippon 2021).

Monopoly as a reward for innovation. Defenders of corporate size and concentration today often invoke arguments that can be traced back to Joseph Schumpeter's (1943 [2003]) classical defence of monopoly. He argues that short-term monopoly provides the incentive for businesses to innovate, thereby renewing capitalism through regular bouts of 'creative destruction'. Capitalism is subject to periodic change, as innovations destroy the old economic structures and create new ones. A good example is the near total decline of DVD videos brought about by the dominance of video streaming services. Here, temporary or cyclical monopoly underpins long-term economic growth as it stimulates innovation, which would not happen under conditions of perfect competition as Smith modelled it.

Drawing on the work of Schumpeter and Chandler, the mainstream and influential management theorist David Teece (2013) argues that businesses with 'dynamic capabilities' are best positioned to 'profit from innovation', therefore, antitrust policies like breaking up monopolies or limiting their power (see Chapter 18) must not undermine their capacity to innovate (pp. 221–4 and 622–5; see also Petit and Teece 2021). Other mainstream thinkers argue that frameworks used to analyse corporate power in the twentieth century are not well suited to the twenty-first century. One of the most disruptive new asset classes today is 'data'. Mass data collection by Big Tech firms and the creation of data enclaves provides these firms with an almost insurmountable market position, largely because the scale of their data collection overwhelms the capacity of startups to compete on a level playing field, leaving them dependent on accessing Big Tech's data enclaves.

It can be argued that material commodities, like energy, minerals and consumer goods, are still fundamentally important to corporate profits, along with the ability to make financial profits by financing consumer credit (e.g. purchases of appliances, cars and the plentiful fruits of consumer society). However, the enclosure of 'knowledge' as well as access to data collected digitally in the form of software, digital platforms and even vaccines has grown considerably. While Alphabet (the parent company of Google) produces a variety of products, including cellphones (the Pixel), it generates most of its revenues from advertising which is not surprising given its near absolute dominance as the world's leading search engine (don't believe us? Just Google it!).

Rethinking corporate power today: Critical perspectives

The Rise of Big Tech. Table 12.1 shows that the top five US companies in the twentieth century (including IBM) usually produced material things like steel, computers and cars, in contrast to the 'tech' companies that dominate the list in the twenty-first century. Today, with Apple's iPhone a partial exception, tech companies make money licensing software and access to digital platforms. The biggest US firms of the early-to-mid-twentieth century were in steel (Bethlehem Steel, Carnegie Company) manufacturing (General Motors and General Electric), oil (Standard Oil and ExxonMobil), computers (IBM) and investment banks (Goldman Sachs). By 2017, so-called Big Tech firms dominate the top five. These Big Tech firms are US-based firms associated with the platform economy (Srnicek 2016; Zuboff 2019; Birch and Bronson 2022), and include Meta/Facebook, Alphabet/Google, Amazon, Microsoft and Apple. There are other 'Big Tech' firms around the world like Naspers (South Africa), Alibaba and TikTok (China), Naver (South Korea) and Flipkart (based in India but incorporated in Singapore).

A key difference between the corporate giants of the twentieth and twenty-first centuries are the 'products' and 'assets' of these industries. Traditional industrial production was usually defined by manufacturing goods in factories, while digital platform-based businesses are defined by the interactions between users and the data firms collect about our viewing habits, browser histories, social networks, buying habits and so on. Big Tech firms gain a major advantage from collecting this data, since their size means they can keep collecting masses of data and limit the capacity of competitors to grow to anywhere near their size

TABLE 12.1 Top Five US Companies (1917, 1967, 2017)

1917					1967					2017			
Rank	Company	Industry	Assets (US$M)		Rank	Company	Industry	Market Cap (US$M)		Rank	Company	Industry	Market Cap (US$M)
1	US Steel	Steel	$2,500		1	International Business Machines	Tech	$35.20		1	Apple	Tech	$768.20
2	American Telephone & Telegraph (AT&T)	Telecom	$762		2	AT&T	Telecom	$27.30		2	Alphabet	Tech	$604.70
3	Standard Oil	Oil & Gas	$574		3	Eastman Kodak	Film	$24.10		3	Microsoft	Tech	$600.00
4	Bethlehem Steel	Steel	$382		4	General Motors	Autos	$23.40		4	Amazon	Tech	$474.50
5	Armour & Co.	Food	$314		5	Standard Oil	Oil & Gas	$14.50		5	Berkshire Hathaway	Conglomerate	$431.90

Source: *Adapted from Jeff Kauflin, 'America's Top 50 Companies 1917–2017', *Forbes*. 27 September 2017. https://www.forbes.com/sites/jeffkauflin/2017/09/19/americas-top-50-companies-1917-2017/?sh=425bf6a41629

(Zuboff 2019; Birch et al. 2021). One advantage of 'bigness' in the digital age comes from network effects, which means that the more users a digital service attracts the more valuable it becomes to future users as it collects more useful data and learns more about what potential users might want (Bedre-Defolie and Nitsche 2020). Even if a startup thought it could compete, investors would not fund it because the likelihood of it growing to a competitive size are small. Economists and others have likened this to the establishment of a 'kill zone' around these Big Tech firms (Birch and Bronson 2022).

What the shift from the control of market prices to the control of platforms entails is that conventional antitrust policies that focus on things like price fixing do not address the basis of the new corporate power. New policies are needed to address the forms of market power associated with the platform economy. In the European Union, for example, the Digital Markets Act and Digital Services Act (both passed in 2022) give consumers the right to uninstall software on devices and greater control over the use of their data. Google has been the target of several antitrust investigations in the European Union for anti-competitive behaviour, most recently for illegally promoting its own shopping services over its competitors in search results, having lost an appeal in 2021 over a fine of €2.4 billion (Satariano 2021). In 2021, the Biden administration in the United States appointed the Big Tech critic and antitrust scholar Lina Khan as chairperson of the Federal Trade Commission as the legal cases brought against Facebook and Google by the previous administration continued (Khan 2017). Countries like Canada, however, are lagging behind as the policy debate there has been underpinned by analytical and political assumptions from orthodox economics and law that focus exclusively on economic efficiency rather than the larger social consequences of new types of firms wielding so much power over our lives (Quaid 2022) (see Chapter 5). As we discuss further in Chapter 23, some researchers argue that platform businesses which operate as key infrastructures should be regulated as public utilities with significant public control.

The social and political consequences of corporate power

Economic inequality, labour unions and the environment. It's ironic that two of the key economic issues raised by corporate power in the twenty-first century also inaugurated the twentieth century, while environmental issues gained global attention with the publication of *Our Common Future* (commonly known as the Bruntland Report) in 1987. By prioritizing shareholder interests over all other interests and by externalizing costs wherever they can, corporations have become powerful drivers of inequality within and between states. The heterodox economist Jordan Brennan (2017) views corporations as 'non-statist political institutions' which, by concentrating power, depress GDP and increase economic inequality. He argues that corporate concentration is strongly and inversely related to GDP growth and income equality. Thomas Piketty's research shows that we have returned to levels of income inequality that haven't been seen since before the Great Depression, and this is a concern for those who value security and stability: 'When the rate of return on capital exceeds the rate of growth of output and income . . . capitalism automatically generates arbitrary and unsustainable inequalities that radically undermine the meritocratic values on which democratic societies are based' (Piketty 2014: 1).

One way to get a bird's eye view of the development of corporate power is by distinguishing different historical eras in the development of corporate capitalism on the basis of the distinctively dominant forms of capitalist activity and capital-labour relations. We can look at this history through the lens of the types of goods that shaped these eras (steel in the late nineteenth and early twentieth centuries, the automobile in the mid-twentieth century and computers since the 1980s), energy (coal, oil/gas and electricity) and infrastructure needs (railroad, roads and digital networks). Throughout each of these eras, we can also imagine the types of distributive relationships that prevailed between owners and workers.

For example, despite the economic boom that steel made possible, workers faced many obstacles in forming unions, from political repression to physical violence. Brecher (2014) looks at how labour organized to counter corporate power in the United States in the late nineteenth and early twentieth centuries. He examines the history of efforts by companies like Carnegie Steel to use private companies like Pinkerton, to break the power of the Amalgamated Association, which was affiliated with the American Federation of Labor, in response to the waves of strikes that hit the steel industry in the late nineteenth century and culminating in the Seattle general strike of 1919. After the Second World War, the Taft-Hartley Act (1947) was passed in response to another wave of strikes in 1945–6. The act prohibited certain kinds of union actions (like secondary boycotts and wildcat and solidarity strikes) as the anti-communist sentiment of the emerging Cold War spread into the legal sphere. In return, unions were recognized as the sole legal bargaining agent of their members and the right to legal strikes became enshrined in law. It defined the regulatory context of labour-management relations in the United States and is credited with establishing what is referred to as a 'capital-labor accord', a relative peace between employers and workers in the United States that formed the basis of the postwar boom from the 1950s to the early 1970s. During this time, the United States' United Auto Workers were able to negotiate contracts for their members which guaranteed them a growing slice of the economic pie as US GDP growth surged thanks to 'Fordism' (Harvey 1992).

This history of labour struggles is relevant to contemporary debates around the position of labour within the so-called platform economy. It invokes the spectre of the capital-labour struggles of the past in the efforts to unionize Uber drivers, Amazon workers and Starbucks baristas today. For example, the Taft-Hartley Act permitted employers to deliver anti-union messages to their employees. While current laws prohibit this type of action, Amazon was accused of using these techniques with very chilling effect during the unionization drive at their Chester facility in 2016. They were accused of surveilling workers and threatening reprisals for those supporting the unionization effort (Streitfeld 2021). Amazon workers in Alabama also narrowly rejected unionization in a March 2022 vote, where Amazon faced the same criticisms. Since then, the United States' Retail, Wholesale and Department Store Union has filed twenty-one objections to the National Labor Relations board (*The Economist* 2022).

Other concerns here include the emergence of new forms of exploitation of workers, especially gendered and racialized workers, by digital platforms (van Doorn 2017). The rise of the gig economy (see Chapter 23), for example, has been facilitated by the active exploitation of 'gig' workers selling their services or products through digital platforms like Uber, DoorDash, TaskRabbit and others (Srniceck 2016). While these platforms are framed as liberating workers by enabling them to plan their work around their other interests or responsibilities, the platform businesses that depend upon gig workers have fought long-running campaigns to ensure that gig workers are not defined or treated as their employees with the attached rights to employment benefits like sick or disability leave, paternity, health benefits and so on that this would entail. For example, platform companies like Uber and Lyft spent enormous sums in 2020 to convince Californian voters to pass Proposition 5, which limited employment regulation coverage and ensured that gig workers remained defined as independent contractors instead of employees. Rather than demonstrating their innovativeness, these strategic actions by tech firms illustrate the extent to which twenty-first-century capitalism is often underpinned by tech firms simply inserting themselves as intermediaries in existing political-economic relations or even degrading employment or other regulations to make a profit (Sadowski 2020).

Finally, perhaps the defining issue of corporate power in the twenty-first century is the need to address climate change and environmental degradation (see Chapter 16). As ecological economists remind us, the economic life of every society takes place within an ecosystem and the health of this ecosystem will determine the prospects for our survival on this planet. Joel Bakan (2020) critically examines the new corporate social responsibility movement in which corporations themselves are expected to take the leading role in addressing the climate crisis (see Chapters 9 and 16). Members of this movement have proclaimed their commitment to social purpose and the common good. For example, corporations like Walmart, Coca Cola and Proctor and Gamble have pledged to be 100 per cent carbon neutral in the near future. Critics like Bakan have dismissed this as corporate greenwashing to avoid the more effective and (potentially) democratic tools of government regulation (see Chapter 9). The 2015 Paris Agreement is an international treaty signed by 196 countries designed to address climate change that took effect in 2016. It promises to work towards limiting global average temperature rises to under 2° C compared to pre-industrial levels, yet without any effective global enforcement mechanisms. In the meantime, demand for fossil fuels continues to rise. Extractive industries are boosting production targets and making massive investments in megaprojects. ExxonMobil, for example, expects by 2025 to increase oil and gas production by 25 percent over 2017 (Bakan 2020).

Democracy, human rights and the public interest. Neoclassical economists view globalization as a natural economic and technological process that no one consciously controls, and which businesses, like the rest of us, simply respond to (see Chapter 17). Such a techno-economic process needs an 'international financial architecture', like the one provided by the IMF, World Bank and WTO (see Chapter 13). Free-trade doctrine provides the core ideological justification of the power corporations acquire as a result of successfully responding to this process (for a critique, see Bowman 1996). Defenders of globalization like Jadgdish Bhagwati (2004) argue that corporations do not generate a 'race to the bottom' when it comes to labour and environmental regulations and, in his view, economic growth will lead to increased demands for 'democracy' which will eventually translate into effective political feedback promoting positive environmental change. This is part of the so-called Washington Consensus (see Chapter 14), which refers to the widely shared view among these organizations, banks, policymakers and government officials that free trade, deregulation, privatization, fiscal restraint and strong private property regulations help poorer countries develop and catch up with richer ones. While some mainstream thinkers acknowledge that business has too much power in this system, they are often more concerned about how this power undermines support for free markets, which, in this view, is treated as a public good (Philippon 2021).

Critics argue that the current phase of globalization has been driven by 'several hundred global corporations and banks' and the result has been 'a concentration of economic and political power that is increasingly unaccountable to governments, people or the planet and that undermines democracy, equity and the environment' (Cavanagh et al. 2006: 32). Critics highlight numerous problematic consequences of this concentration of power, including cultural homogenization; dependent development;

concentration and centralization of capital; decline in the scope/quality of public goods; climate change and rampant environmental degradation; and, finally, a shift in the global 'balance of power' from national governments to business (Carroll and Sapinski 2018). Business has secured a wider sphere of freedom while states have lost sovereignty, a point which we explore further in Chapter 14. If we understand sovereignty as the ability to act in the public interest and determine how to use what is called the 'new commons', today that sovereignty is gradually being ceded to business as they claim control over things as wide-ranging as genetic material, public services and even our personal data in addition to land and resources of the 'old commons'. As noted earlier, much of this control depends on the rise of strong intellectual property rights protections, enabling business to claim ownership of once public or collectively controlled resources and assets. Certain countries, like the United States, the EU and Japan, benefit from this arrangement, while many countries in the Global South do not (UNCTAD 2018).

Is there anything wrong with prioritizing intellectual property rights over global access to vaccines? On the one hand, we can look to the market power of monopolistic pharmaceutical companies to explain how they earned unprecedented profits from producing vaccines during the pandemic. Mainstream thinkers like Teece (2013) have developed a 'profiting from innovation' (PFI) framework which aims to provide an explanatory framework as well as a normative justification for these profits. His theory focuses on several factors: appropriability, industry evolution, complementary assets and system integration. Fundamentally, the amount of profit a corporation can make on an innovation has to do with a variety of factors and not just the robustness of intellectual property regimes. Corporations seek to profit from innovation by developing technologies that integrate with one another (e.g. iPhones, iPads and MacBooks) and by developing ways to effectively deter piracy and control access to fee-paying services (e.g. Microsoft 365). In this case, for example, Pfizer could be said to have made its profits in large part due to how the pandemic shaped the 'appropriability regime': it was able to negotiate favourable contracts with governments and hospitals while also avoiding incursions to its intellectual property by generic pharmaceutical firms

In the previous example, many have argued that individual security – protection from the Covid-19 virus – should take priority over private profits (Krishtel and Malpani 2021). This raises questions on how we might develop an understanding of the influence corporate power has over human rights more broadly. To say that individuals have human rights implies that institutions should be designed to ensure that they have secure access to these rights. Birchall (2021: 43) argues that corporate power over human rights can be defined by the production of 'effects that shape the capacities of individuals to enjoy their human rights'. This corporate power is exercised over individuals, material conditions, institutions and collective knowledge. Regulatory arbitrage, which refers to the practice of business 'shopping around' for favourable regulatory environments, encourages countries to weaken their labour and environmental protections in order to attract such investment, hence undermining access to these rights.

Occupy Wall Street activist (see Chapter 17) and cryptocurrency expert Micah White points out that the corporation is 'capitalism's main vehicle for telling, and bringing to fruition, its overarching story' (quoted in Bakan 2020: 178). Capitalism needs individuals to think of themselves as self-interested and competitive by nature and to believe their happiness consists of enjoying the ever-expanding fruits of consumer society. At the same time, Bakan (2020) emphasizes the role of the 'new corporation' and CEO activism in convincing the public that they can 'do well by doing good', embracing a social purpose that aligns with their profit-driven self-interest as the way to solve our problems (see Chapter 9). This 'new corporation' promises to serve the interests not only of shareholders but of workers, communities and the environment too, but critics have pointed out that over the past twenty years inequality has widened, publicly funded services have declined, social divisions have intensified, and environmental degradation has accelerated (Bakan 2020). To take one example, after George Floyd's murder, Amazon promised to stand in solidarity with Black communities against systemic racism and injustice, yet it has consistently intimidated workers seeking to unionize a workforce whose lowest paid members are predominantly Black and Latino and where the majority are women. In the face of these developments, it is hard to support the claim that corporations can adequately substitute for empowered communities and democratic institutions (like a well-functioning government) to achieve the public good and social inclusion.

What can be done about corporate power?

Given all of these dimensions of corporate power, what can be done? If they have too much power, how can we set effective limits? Should we break up large corporations? While antitrust advocates might argue in favour of doing so in some cases (e.g. Khan 2017), other economists argue that this would be either impractical or undesirable. Instead, policymakers should focus on how value is co-created and how to ensure that this is shared by all stakeholders: 'Governments can and should be shaping markets to ensure that collectively created value serves collective ends' (Mazzucato et al. 2022). In this view, policy changes can lead to a more equitable and socially useful distribution of co-created value.

Should more be done to make corporations pay taxes? Free-market advocates like Phillipon (2019) acknowledge that Big Tech firms often pay little tax and this is not very different from other multinational corporations who can take advantage of cross-border accounting methods that allow them to record profits in the jurisdiction with the lowest taxes (commonly referred to as 'tax arbitrage'). Corporate lobbying for lower taxes, tax breaks and state aid is also considered inefficient since they often consist of loopholes tacked on to the legislation. Yet Phillipon (2019) distinguishes this from the broad-based tax cuts to marginal rates that economists advocate for as part of national policy. However, trillions of dollars of profits within the global economy are effectively removed from the pool of potential tax revenues by virtue of being de-nationalized, while at the same time calls are made for governments to encourage privatization and reduce the social state. In response, some have argued that governments can do more to address economic inequality through a progressive global tax on capital to properly fund the welfare state (Piketty 2014), or a guaranteed annual basic income (Glyn 2006).

At the national level, states need to rethink and redesign competition policies and laws and other regulatory frameworks. To get at the heart of the issue of corporate power today, policymakers need to hear from more diverse voices and perspectives that show how Big Tech and digital markets can, and do, impact our societies in very negative ways such as by increasing polarizing discourse and privatizing social infrastructure under the control of unaccountable corporations (see Chapter 23). We cannot separate the economic causes of market power from their social consequences without ceding our capacity to do something about these potentially egregious effects. If we want to address contemporary forms of corporate power then we need to consider the wider societal, political and economic implications of Big Tech and the concentration of markets.

Conclusion

While we devote an entire chapter later in this book to the topic of alternatives to corporate capitalism (see Chapter 21), we can conclude this one by outlining a few more radical proposals for challenging corporate power. First, we can support alternatives to corporate power by promoting the social and solidarity economy, which aims at a more egalitarian, inclusive and environmentally sustainable social and economic space (Williams 2014; see Chapter 22). Second, we can challenge corporate power by joining local, national and international civil society movements that directly oppose it. For example, there is a Global Campaign spearheaded in 2012 by the Transnational Institute (led by globalization researcher Susan Strange) to dismantle corporate power and corporate impunity with respect to environmental and human rights abuses that are hidden within multinational corporations' global supply chains (https://www.tni.org/en/page/about-global-campaign-dismantle-corporate-power-and-stop-impunity). Finally, we can look at other models of property relations to imagine how innovation might work to serve the public interest in a post-corporate world. To conclude this chapter with how we started – on the development of Covid-19 vaccines – there is the example of Cuba, a tiny community island of 11 million people that is subject to harsh US sanctions, which developed not one but five homegrown vaccines in their state-run biotechnology centres (Beaubien 2022). Not only has it produced enough to immunize over 85 per cent of its own population, but it is producing enough to export to countries that would otherwise struggle for access to vaccines.

Suggested readings

- Carrol, W.K. and Sapinski, J. (2018) *Organizing the 1%: How Corporate Power Works,* Winnipeg, Fernwood.
- Mazzucato, M. (2013) *The Entrepreneurial State: Debunking Public vs. Private Sector Myths,* London, Anthem Press.
- Philippon, T. (2019) *The Great Reversal: How America Gave Up on Free Markets,* Cambridge, Belknap Press.

References

Bakan, J. (2020) *The New Corporation,* Toronto, Allen Lane.

Beaubien, J. (2022) 'A Small Island Nation has Cooked Up Not 1, Not 2 but 5 COVID Vaccines. It's Cuba!', *NPR,* 1 February, https://www.npr.org/sections/goatsandsoda/2022/02/01/1056952488/a-small-island-nation-has-cooked-up-not-1-not-2-but-5-covid-vaccines-its-cuba (accessed 21 August 2022).

Bedre-Defolie, Ö. and Nitsche, R. (2020) 'When Do Markets Tip? An Overview and Some Insights for Policy', *Journal of European Competition Law and Practice,* Vol. 11, No. 10, pp. 610–22, https://doi.org/10.1093/jeclap/lpaa084.

Berle, A.A. (1955) *The Twentieth Century Capitalist Revolution,* London, Macmillan.

Bettig, R.V. (1996) 'Critical Perspectives on the History and Philosophy of Copyright', in R.V. Bettig, *Copyrighting Culture: The Political Economy of Intellectual Property,* Boulder, CO, Westview Press, pp. 9–32.

Bhagwati, J. (2004) *In Defense of Globalization,* Oxford, Oxford University Press.

Birch, K. and Bronson, K. (2022) 'Big Tech', *Science as Culture,* Vol. 31, pp. 1–14.

Birch, K., Cochrane, D.T. and Ward, C. (2021) 'Data as Asset? The Measurement, Governance, and Valuation of Digital Personal Data by Big Tech', *Big Data & Society,* Vol. 8, pp. 1–15.

Birchall, D. (2021) 'Corporate Power over Human Rights: An Analytical Framework', *Business and Human Rights Journal,* Vol. 6, No. 1, pp. 42–66.

Bowman, S. (1996) *The Modern Corporation and American Political Thought,* Pennsylvania, Pennsylvania State University Press.

Brecher, J. (2014) *Strike!* (2nd Edition), Oakland, PM Press.

Brennan, J. (2017) 'The Twenty-first Century Capitalist Revolution: How the Governance of Large Firms Shapes Prosperity and Inequality', in Tae-Hee Jo, Lynne Chester, and Carlo D'Ippoliti (eds.), *The Routledge Handbook of Heterodox Economics*, New York, Routledge, pp. 471–87.

Carrol, W.K. and Sapinski, J.P. (2018) *Organizing the 1%: How Corporate Power Works*, Winnipeg, Fernwood.

Cavanagh, J., Mander, J. and Broad, R. (2006) *Alternatives to Economic Globalization: A Better World Is Possible; a Report of the International Forum on Globalization*, San Francisco, CA, Berrett-Koehler.

CCPA. (2022) 'The TRIPs COVID-19 Waiver', https://policyalternatives.ca/newsroom/updates/trips-covid-19-waiver.

Chandler, A. (1977) *The Visible Hand*, Harvard, Belknap Press.

Chandler, A. (1990) *Scale and Scope*, Harvard, Belknap Press.

Cox, R. (1987) *Production, Power, and World Order*, New York, Columbia University Press.

Crouch, C. (2011) *The Strange Non-death Neoliberalism*, Cambridge, Polity.

Davis, G.F. (2016) *The Vanishing American Corporation: Navigating the Hazards of a New Economy*, Oakland, CA, Berrett-Koehler Publishers.

Economist. (2022) 'What Happens When Amazon Comes to Town', 26 March.

Glasbeek, H. (2017) *Class Privilege, How Law Shelters Shareholders and Coddles Capitalism*, Toronto, Between the Lines.

Glyn, A. (2006) *Capitalism Unleashed: Finance, Globalization and Welfare*, Oxford, Oxford University Press.

Harvey, D. (1992) *The Condition of Postmodernity*, Oxford, Blackwell.

Khan, L. (2017) 'Amazon's Antitrust Paradox', *Yale Law Journal*, Vol. 126, pp. 710–805.

Krishtel, P. and Malpani, R. (2021) 'Suspend Intellectual Property Rights for Covid-19 Vaccines', *BMJ*, Vol. 373, pp. 20–1.

Mazzucato, M. (2013) *The Entrepreneurial State: Debunking Public vs. Private Sector Myths*, London, Anthem Press.

Mazzucato, M., Enstminger, J. and Kattel, R. (2022) 'Reshaping Platform-Driven Digital Markets', in M. Moore and D. Tambini (eds), *Regulating Big Tech: Policy Responses to Digital Dominance*, Oxford, Oxford University Press.

Mikler, J. (2018) *The Political Power of Global Corporations*, Cambridge; Medford, MA, Polity Press.

Nace, T. (2003) *Gangs of America*, San Francisco, Berrett-Koehler.

OXFAM. (2021) 'Vaccine Monopolies Make Cost of Vaccinating the World Against COVID At Least 5 Times More Expensive Than It Could Be', https://www.oxfam.org/en/press-releases/vaccine-monopolies-make-cost-vaccinating-world-against-covid-least-5-times-more.

Peacock, S.J. (2022) 'Vaccine Nationalism Will Persist: Global Public Goods Need Effective Engagement of Global Citizens', *Globalization and Health*, Vol. 18, No. 14, pp. 1–11

Petit, N. and Teece, D.J. (2021) 'Big Tech, Big Data, And Competition Policy: Favoring Dynamic Over Static Competition', *SSRN Electronic Journal* (January), pp. 1–31.

Philippon, T. (2019) *The Great Reversal: How America Gave Up on Free Markets*, Cambridge, Belknap Press.

Philippon, T. (2021) 'The Case for Free Markets', *Oxford Review of Economic Policy*, Vol. 37, No. 4, pp. 707–19.

Piketty, T. (2014) *Capital in the Twenty First Century*, Cambridge, MA, Harvard University Press.

Quaid, J. (2022) 'Clashing Visions of Competition Policy in the Digital Era', *Policy Options*, March 2.

Rahman, K.S. (2018) 'The New Utilities: Private Power, Social Infrastructure, and the Revival of the Public Utility Concept', *Cardozo Law Review*, Vol. 39, pp. 1621–89.

Robbins, R. and Goodman, P.S. (2021) 'Pfizer Reaps Hundreds of Millions in Profits from Covid Vaccine', *New York Times*, 4 May.

Sadowski, J. (2020) 'The Internet of Landlords: Digital Platforms and the New Mechanisms of Rentier Capitalism', *Antipode*, Vol. 52, pp. 562–80.

Sagonowsky, E. (2021) 'Pfizer Eyes Higher Prices for COVID-19 Vaccine after the Pandemic Wanes: Exec, Analyst', *Fierce Pharma*, 23 February, https://www.fiercepharma.com/pharma/pfizer-eyes-higher-covid-19-vaccine-prices-after-pandemic-exec-analyst (accessed 21 July 2022).

Satariano, A. (2021) 'Google Loses Appeal of $2.8 billion Fine in E.U. Antitrust Case', *The New York Times*, 10 November, https://www.nytimes.com/2021/11/10/business/google-eu-appeal-antitrust.html (accessed 2 August 2022).

Schumpeter, J.A. (2003) *Capitalism, Socialism, Democracy*, New York, Routledge.

Srnicek, N. (2016) *Platform Capitalism*, Cambridge, Polity.

Storeng, K.T. and de Bengy Puyvallée, A. (2020) 'Why does Pfizer Deny the Public Investment in its Covid-19 Vaccine?', https://www.internationalhealthpolicies.org/featured-article/why-does-pfizer-deny-the-public-investment-in-its-covid-19-vaccine/.

Strange, S. (1988) *States and Markets*. London, Continuum.

Streitfeld, D. (2021) 'How Amazon Crushes Unions', *The New York Times*, 16 March (updated 21 October) (accessed 17 August 2022).

Teece, D. (1981) 'The Multinational Enterprise: Market Failure and Market Power Considerations', *MIT Sloan Management Review*, Spring, pp. 3–17.

Teece, D. (2013) 'Profiting from Innovation', in Eric H. Kessler (ed.), *Encyclopedia of Management Theory*, Vol. 1. Thousand Oaks, Sage Publications, pp. 622–5.

UNCTAD. (2018) *Trade and Development Report*, Geneva, United Nations Conference on Trade and Development.

Van Doorn, N. (2017) 'Platform Labor: On the Gendered and Racialized Exploitation of Low-Income Service Work in the 'On-Demand' Economy', *Information, Communication & Society*, Vol. 20, pp. 898–914.

Williams, M. (2014) 'The Solidarity Economy and Social Transformation', in V. Satgar (ed.), *The Solidarity Economy Alternative*, Durban, University of KwaZulu-Natal Press, pp. 37–63.

Zuboff, S. (2019) *The Age of Surveillance Capitalism*, New York, Public Affairs.

13 | Global economy and varieties of capitalism

Kean Birch and Richard Wellen

Introduction

The world is getting smaller: not in physical terms – Earth remains the same size – but rather in terms of distance and time. This shrinking of the world has been called 'time-space compression' by the geographer David Harvey (1989), who links this shrinking of the world to the rise and spread of capitalism (see Chapter 3). We need to emphasize, however, that the world is getting smaller for *some* people, and not for everyone. What we mean by this is that some people – notably many of those living in the Global North – are now able to communicate across thousands of miles almost instantaneously using telephones, email, Facebook, Skype, Zoom and other technologies. Moreover, the same people are now able to travel thousands of miles in a few hours by jet airplane, whereas only a hundred years ago it would have taken days if not weeks to travel the same distance by ship and train. It's important to remember, though, that for the vast majority of the world's population the world remains as large and difficult to traverse as ever.

Key concept: Time-space compression

This term refers to the expansion of economic markets (space) and the increase in travel and communication speed (time) of goods, raw materials and money as they can be acquired from further afield and yet transported in a shorter period of time. This largely benefits large, multinational corporations which have operations or facilities in a number of countries around the world.

Source: Harvey (1989)

This shrinking of distance and time is often presented as a process of *globalization* (Strange 1998; Brenner 2004; Dicken 2011). If we focus on the economy alone, as we do in this chapter, this process of globalization can be defined as the functional integration of different economic activities across territorial boundaries. As we outline later in this chapter, however, there's an enormous amount of debate about what globalization is, what its impacts are and whether it's actually happening or not. Despite this ongoing debate, however, there's general agreement that the last few decades have been witness to the growing interdependence of countries, peoples, cultures, economies and so on around the world. For example, what happens in China has a very real impact on what happens in Canada – and vice versa. Evidence of these impacts is visible in the aftermath of the 2007–8 global financial crisis (GFC) when collapsing house prices, sub-prime mortgages and financial derivatives in the United States led to the so-called 2009 Great Recession around the world (Varoufakis 2013). In more recent years global pandemics, geopolitical tensions and populist resentment about workers displaced by increased trade have raised questions about the future extent of globalization and cross-national economic integration (Levinson 2020). We discuss these global crises in detail in Chapter 17.

Globalization is such an important process because it has been promoted by numerous governments, international financial institutions (IFIs) and multinational corporations or enterprises as a means of economic development (Peet 2007). These social actors frequently present globalization, or one particular form of *financial* globalization, as inevitable and irreversible, meaning that all countries need to restructure their economies to adapt to emerging global imperatives (Clark 1999), no matter their current situation or the impacts of this restructuring on their populations. Growing disquiet with this view of globalization emerged in the 1990s and continues today (see Chapters 9 and 21). Globalization has very real and frequently negative impacts on people in many different countries, including lost jobs through global outsourcing of work to countries with lower labour costs; financial volatility through free capital mobility as investors seek the highest returns on their investments; poverty and inequality as governments reduce their social welfare spending to accommodate the demands of IFIs, MNCs and other governments; and so on.

Definition: International financial institutions

IFIs are large non-governmental and non-business organizations that provide the framework for global governance and regulation. Examples include World Bank, International Monetary Fund (IMF) and World Trade Organization (WTO), all of which have their origins in the Bretton Woods System that was developed after the Second World War and which is discussed further in Chapter 14. Since the 1970s they have been criticized for promoting a particular form of globalization that narrowly sees 'free' trade and 'free' markets as the key foundations of economic development.

Key organization: Multinational corporations and multinational enterprises

An increasing number of businesses straddle the world in their activities. These businesses are commonly referred to as multinational corporations (MNC) or multinational enterprises (MNE). Both MNCs and MNEs are large businesses with operations, facilities and subsidiaries in a number of different countries, all of which are functionally integrated in the organization of production, trade or investment. As (public) corporations, MNCs are different from MNEs because they are owned by shareholders, even though their operations may be located in very different countries from the country where they are listed on a stock exchange. Because of their size, several countries have developed specific rules about how MNCs and MNEs should operate globally (e.g. rules against bribery), as has the United Nations with its Global Compact, which is defined later. MNCs and MNEs are particularly associated with the so-called 'globalization' of the world economy.

In this chapter we go over the evidence of globalization as well as the mainstream and critical perspectives of it. We start by discussing the mainstream perspectives on the integration of the global economy, before briefly analysing the global economy as it stands today. We then turn to the critical perspectives, especially drawing on literature in economic geography, international political economy and sociology. We then discuss the case of the so-called BRICS and the transformation of their fortunes over the last decade or so to illustrate how mainstream perspectives ignore several important factors in explaining why some countries prosper while others do not in the global economy.

Key discussion questions

- Is there a global economy?
- What is globalization?
- In what ways has the world globalized? In what ways has it not?
- Who benefits from globalization? What are the problems with globalization?
- How powerful are multinational corporations?
- Is there one form of capitalism?

Mainstream perspectives

Hyper-globalists and their dreams of development. A number of people, including journalists, academics, politicians and international policymakers, have promoted the idea that *financial* globalization is good for everyone, no matter what country they live in and no matter the level of economic development in that country (Clark 1999). The idea that globalization is great is not restricted to a particular end of the political spectrum – left or right – but stretches from one end to the other. It's perhaps best exemplified in the academic literature by the Japanese management thinker Kenichi Ohmae (1990) in his book *Borderless World* and the American former secretary of Labor Robert Reich (1992) in *The Work of Nations*. Both authors, coming from different perspectives, arrived at similar conclusions in the early 1990s: namely, national economies face unprecedented pressure from global markets to change and adapt to new business networks, practices and demands. Furthermore, both agreed that these pressures cannot be avoided and, moreover, should not be avoided. Their perspective has been described as 'hyper-globalist' in light of their positive support for globalization (Held et al. 1999).

Ohmae and Reich define globalization as a process in which the expansion of global financial markets and global businesses (e.g. MNCs) has eroded the national organization of capitalism. As such, their theories imply an 'end of geography' as they argue that the national characteristics of each country no longer drive the success of businesses or national economies. Moreover, their conception of globalization places a particular emphasis on the benefits of reducing national government intervention in the economy (MacKinnon and Cumbers 2007). From this orthodox perspective, two things follow. First, globalization is meant to create a win-win situation in which countries around the world all benefit from the (expected) growth in trade and investment that free-trade and capital mobility are expected to generate. According to another well-known exponent of this view, the journalist Thomas Friedman (2005), the world is now flat because there are no longer barriers to businesses integrating the design, production and retail of products and services across different national borders – and everyone benefits from their participation in this globalized world. Second, national governments must adopt business-friendly policies in order to benefit from globalization; anything less will simply result in stagnation and economic ruin. In an earlier book, *The Lexus and the Olive Tree*, Friedman (1999) argued that every country and their people needed to fit themselves into this 'golden straightjacket' to reap the benefits of globalization.

Key methodological issue: Identifying world regions

There are different ways to describe different parts of the world. During the Cold War commentators and academics differentiated between First World (modern capitalist democracies), Second World (socialist states) and Third World (peripheral countries). However, since the end of the Cold War this terminology has become obsolete and was viewed as disparaging anyway (i.e. 'Third World' implying bottom of the pack). Since then people have used terms like 'developed' and 'developing' countries to differentiate between modern capitalist countries and peripheral countries, but this terminology can also be criticized for its underlying assumptions (e.g. developing countries want to and should become 'developed' like Western Europe and North America – see Chapter 3). People increasingly use the terms 'Global North' and 'Global South' to represent differences between core capitalist economies like the United States and peripheral capitalist economies. It's important to note that these terms are fluid (i.e. a country can move from one category to another) and that they are not strictly geographical (e.g. Australia is in the Global North, yet also in the southern hemisphere).

This approach relates to the controversial measures promoted by the Washington Consensus – discussed further in the next chapter – whereby countries in the Global North have pressured countries in the Global South to adopt supposedly 'globalization friendly' policies such as low public spending, low inflation, low trade and investment barriers, low-wage protection, limited regulation of business, limited social welfare, limited taxation and limited government involvement in the economy (van Waeyenberge 2010). These policies, however, have been criticized for promoting global wealth inequalities and for prioritizing the interests of global business over the livelihoods of workers and citizens around the world (Stiglitz 2002).

Homogeneous global economy? One starting point in an attempt to characterize the global economy is to identify the world's major economies, their relationships to one another and other countries and regions in the world, and how this has changed over time. This will help ground the various theoretical debates about globalization. It might be surprising to note that up until the late nineteenth century, the world's biggest economies were China and India. Western Europe and North America only became the world's dominant economic blocs after that period, especially from 1900 when the United States became the world's largest economy (Dicken 2011: 15). The United States is still the largest economy in the world today, but China is re-emerging as the second-largest economy after nearly a century – this will be discussed in more detail later. According to data from the World Bank, presented in Table 13.1, the largest economies in the world by gross domestic product (GDP) in 2020 are mostly from the Global North, but also include a number of rising powers like China and India. The list of largest economies has changed over time, being somewhat different in 2000 and especially since 1980 and 1960, although the United States remains on top throughout. What this data cannot show, however, is *how* globalized the world's economy is, or how globalization has happened; for that we have to turn to other indicators.

TABLE 13.1 Top Ten Countries by GDP in Current Prices (US$)

1961	1980	2000	2020
United States	United States	United States	United States
United Kingdom	Japan	Japan	China
France	Germany	Germany	Japan
Japan	France	United Kingdom	Germany
China	United Kingdom	France	United Kingdom
Italy	Italy	China	India
Canada	Canada	Italy	France
India	Brazil	Canada	Italy
Australia	Spain	Mexico	Canada
Sweden	Mexico	Brazil	South Korea

Source: http://data.worldbank.org/indicator/NY.GDP.MKTP.CD (accessed June 2022).

Key methodological issue: Gross domestic product

GDP refers to the total spending on goods and services in an economy plus any sales taxes and minus any subsidies. Using GDP is a very common way to calculate differences between economies, but it's important to note that it has been criticized and that it does not reflect a country's level of well-being or development (see Chapter 6). GDP is often calculated in different ways, including current prices to take account of inflation over time and make calculations comparable over time; nominal prices that do not take inflation into account; and purchasing power parities to take account of differences in spending power between countries since the cost of one thing in one country is not the same in another.

Source: World Bank

It's important to note that globalization is a contradictory process. On the one hand, production by businesses has become more fragmented across many countries as their supply chains have become more global; on the other hand, countries have become more integrated as trade and investment barriers have been removed through international treaties. These two trends are, obviously, related to one another, but to understand how integrated different countries are around the world it's useful to look at certain indicators like trade flows and foreign investment.

Definition: Foreign investment

Businesses in different countries do not simply trade with one another; they also make investments in other countries. These investments take two main forms: portfolio investment and foreign direct investment (FDI). Portfolio investment involves the purchasing of stocks and bonds in another country, while FDI involves the creation of subsidiaries or purchase of companies in a foreign country. The key difference between portfolio investment and FDI is the level of control that the investment provides, with the former representing an 'indirect' form of control while the latter is 'direct'.

According to Dicken (2011), the following major trends are important for understanding the global economy.[1] First, the world's economy has become increasingly interconnected since the 1960s, creating a *global* economy as more and more countries trade with one another. Between 1970 and 2008 trade between countries (as a % of GDP) rose rapidly and consistently from 25 per cent to 61 per cent (World Bank 2022). Second, while trade has increased significantly, foreign direct investment (FDI) has increased even more (Dicken 2011: 21), especially after 1985. Third, this increase in FDI is important because FDI represents direct means for controlling resources and assets by MNCs outside their home countries. Fourth, because of increasing FDI between one-third and a half of all trade is now intra-firm trade, involving businesses producing, assembling and retailing products in very different parts of the world (20). This necessitates an enormous amount of shipping and transportation between countries. Fifth, world trade and foreign investment flows predominantly happen between the global *triad* of world regions – Western Europe, North America and Asia – although this is gradually changing (19). It's important, therefore, to recognize that certain world regions are more *globalized* than others.

Finally, although the global economy has become more interconnected since 1980, with rising levels of exports and FDI, it has also become increasingly volatile with significant rises and falls in levels of exports and FDI across years (Dicken 2011: 17, 21). Overall, when looking at these trends it's evident that only a few countries dominate the global economy. For example, just fifteen countries represent 75 per cent of world manufacturing output, 80 per cent of world agricultural output and 80 per cent of outward FDI stock (25). In more recent times some of the key indicators of globalization such as FDI and global trade have begun to peak or have seen some declines, a point which we return to later when examining claims that the pace of globalization may be moderating or slowing. For example, annual FDI flows declined as a percentage of GDP from 4.2 per cent in 2000 to 1.9 per cent in 2021 (OECD 2022). In the ten years between 2010 and 2020 trade as a percentage of global GDP actually declined from 60 per cent to 52 per cent (World Bank 2022).

In light of the information presented earlier, it's necessary to maintain a sceptical perspective about globalization as a stable and inevitable process *and* as a policy prescription for promoting economic development around the world

(Stiglitz 2002; Chang 2008). However, what it also illustrates is that businesses now play a significant role in the organization, coordination and governance of the global economy.

Critical perspectives

Questioning globalization. Globalization is a difficult concept both to define analytically and to identify empirically. Many critics of globalization take issue with at least three claims about globalization in these debates:

- *conceptual claims* that globalization is the best theory to explain the transformation of our economies over the last few decades;
- *empirical claims* that globalization has led to the end of geography or the creation of a 'borderless' world through the erosion of the nation-state and national sovereignty; and
- *normative claims* that globalization is an inevitable and irreversible process we can do nothing about and which benefits everyone equally.

First, many critics of globalization point out that capitalism is a world-wide system (see Chapter 3) and that, therefore, globalization is not new – we have been here before. For example, a number of critics have suggested that there are at least two ages of globalization (McGrew 2011). These are outlined in Table 13.2.

Second, critics have empirically questioned the idea that globalization has led to the erosion of the nation-state and national sovereignty as countries have converged on one economic system – namely, (neo-)liberal capitalism. There have been numerous claims that national governments, for example, have lost their capacity to create and enforce laws and regulations in their own territories as international organizations (e.g. IMF, World Bank and WTO) have accumulated more power to govern the global economy (e.g. set rules on international trade). Moreover, there have been numerous claims that national governments are no longer as influential or important as global forces have led to the restructuring of national economies. These claims have been criticized for being wrong or too simplistic (Weiss 1998; Clark 1999; Brenner 2004; Hay 2011).

Definition: The nation-state

The state can be defined as an array of institutions, public and semi-public, that have sovereignty (i.e. legal authority) over a particular territory (i.e. geographical area). The state comprises institutions like the government, the civil service, the legal system, the police, the education system and so on.

TABLE 13.2 Two Ages of Globalization

Characteristics	First age of globalization	Second age of globalization
Time period	1820–1914	1950–present
Main countries	European colonial powers (e.g. UK, France etc.)	The United States (plus Japan and China)
Dominant world power	British Empire	The United States
Trade flows	Raw materials from colonial periphery to core imperial homeland; manufactured goods from core to periphery. British system of free trade.	Raw materials and products from Global South to Global North; knowledge and services from Global North to Global South. Gradual international elimination of trade barriers.
Investment flows	Portfolio investment in colonies by businesses. British system of free trade.	Foreign direct investment by multinational corporations. Gradual elimination of capital controls.
International governance	Gold standard enforced by British Empire.	Bretton Woods System (until 1971) and then US$ dominance enforced by the United States.

Sources: Hirst and Thompson (1999); McGrew (2011).

The state has not withered away, nor has every country converged on one ideal model of the state. Colin Hay (2011: 325–6) argues, for example, that the state is still an important social actor and government spending represents a significant proportion of national GDP in most developed countries, ranging from 35 per cent in the United States to 54 per cent in Sweden in 2005. Since then, the role of the state became even more obvious as many countries bailed out their national banks after the 2008 global financial crisis – without this support, there was a chance that national economies would have totally collapsed (Varoufakis 2013). Hence, it's important to note that while there's no doubt the current era of globalization is shaped by the global activities of businesses, especially by MNCs and their strategic decisions in regard to production, trade and investment (Dicken 2011), this global dominance of business is supported *and* enforced by national governments, especially those in the Global North like the United States and the UK (Helleiner 1994; Weiss 1998). Attempts to create international institutions for governance of the global economy, such as the WTO, have been criticized for working in the interest of countries and businesses with the greatest global power (see Chapter 14).

Third, critics have especially questioned the idea that globalization is either an unalloyed good – benefiting all and sundry around the world – or an inevitable and irreversible process we can do nothing about. A number of important thinkers like Anthony Giddens (1990) and Manuel Castells (1996) have argued for the need for a more nuanced analysis of global change; while they might agree that globalization is happening, they do not assume that it's wholly new or necessarily has positive impacts (Peet 2007, 2009). In fact, since the financial crisis of 2008 there have been signs that the long second phase of globalization may have peaked, which may be a reminder of a similar deglobalizing period between the two world wars, including the Great Depression of the 1930s (Bergeijik 2019). This partial reversal has caused some observers to consider whether we are entering a new stage of globalization, which some prominent media outlets have labelled 'slowbalisation' (Bakas 2015; Economist 2019; Hierskaia et al. 2020).

To some extent slowbalization is an economic consequence of the fact that workers making products for export in newly industrializing countries now have more income to buy products formerly made for export (Hierskaia et al. 2020). But slowbalization is also partially the result of the collision of economic and political issues expressed through public dissatisfaction with some of the impacts of global economic activity. For example, the manufacturing success of countries in Asia and elsewhere has created a populist backlash among some workers in the Global North who expect their political leaders to 'reshore' manufacturing jobs lost to countries like India, China and Vietnam. Some economists like Branko Milanovic (2018) have shown how economic globalization has, on average, reduced inequality between countries but that this has come at the expense of increasing inequality within countries. The consequence has been calls for increasing protectionism and economic nationalism in the United States and some European countries, which is associated with the election of populist world leaders. The rise of Donald Trump and his 'Make America Great Again' campaign in 2016 was partly an attempt to defend American workers from global immigrants and supposedly unfair trade competition with China. Similar populist movements and parties in the EU appear to reflect the same pattern (Bergeijik 2019).

Other developments have also contributed to a renewed questioning of the economic justification for globalization. For example, the Covid-19 pandemic has led to trade disruptions which have exposed the 'brittleness' of global supply chain networks (see Chapter 17). This brittleness has developed over time as the drive to lower costs has led certain countries or regions in those networks to specialize in particular area of production, leaving many countries unable to cope when there are disruptions in flows of trade or investment. In this context critics argue that unchecked trade and financial globalization has over-emphasized cost-efficiency in structuring global economic integration. While such a system may be profitable and advantageous in the short term, it fails to encourage investments in sustainable and resilient national and international economic resources and relationships (Stiglitz 2022).

In 2022 anti-globalization and deglobalization trends were reinforced by the Russian invasion of Ukraine, which prompted a broad coalition of countries and major corporations to cut economic ties with Russia. This is part of a larger pattern where some states – and even corporations – try to reduce overreliance on trade and investment flows involving countries that are seen as unacceptable global partners due to their poor human rights records. The trend towards 'regionalization' of trade was highlighted as East Asian and Pacific countries initiated a regional economic partnership and there was a new initiative in Africa to develop the 'African Continental Free Trade Area' (UNCTAD 2022). Meanwhile, in early 2022 the United States officially announced that it would more closely link trade and economic relationships to national security concerns. US government officials coined the term 'friend-shoring' to describe the preference for developing more 'resilient' supply chains selectively focused on politically Allied countries and trade partners with acceptable human rights records and which share similar labour and environmental standards (Rajan 2022).

Increased efforts to address climate change may also reinforce some aspects of deglobalization as well. While policies to address climate change require ambitious global policy collaboration, they also demand that the emissions from the global supply chain be reduced considerably. From an economic point of view decarbonization would almost certainly require some reduction in transportation and shipping. In addition, 'green economy' policies encouraging investments in the transition to renewable energy industries often give 'buy local' preferences to domestically made climate-friendly products. This allows political leaders to show they have a plan to replace the jobs that inevitably would be lost in carbon-intensive industries (Hanna et al. 2020).

Finally, some features of digital technology may also shorten or reduce reliance on global supply chains. This is somewhat counterintuitive since many technological improvements in transport and telecommunications have promoted increased globalization and integration across borders. That's because the 'transaction costs' (see Chapter 7) of coordinating fragmented production are lower with rapid transport, digital networking and data transfer. Yet other new technologies like artificial intelligence and robotics may lead to less fragmented production. For example, robots used in manufacturing can replace workers. This can make it more profitable for some businesses to 'reshore' production since there would be less need to use as much cheap labour in far-flung regions (Levinson 2020). As artificial intelligence becomes increasingly embedded within machines each of these machines can perform more tasks, a process called additive manufacturing, which allows what used to be sequentially separate stages of production to be combined. There's a growing debate about whether this will lead to a 'reshoring' of production as there's less need to have large inventories of components shipped from different locations (Johns 2022).

It's too early to tell whether the trends reviewed earlier point to a new period of decline in globalization or simply a reconfiguration. What they do demonstrate is that globalization is complex, has many dimensions – economic, political, technological and cultural – and is hard to understand using a uniform model. For example, even if critics are right that 'hyperglobalization' is problematic, it does not necessarily mean that increased protectionism and nationalistic competition among countries should be embraced as the alternatives. With all of these criticisms and shifting currents of globalization in mind, it's evident that the global economy is not homogeneous or converging on one, best economic system; nor can it do so, conceptually, empirically or normatively. Rather, and as we illustrate next, the global economy and globalization are better understood as an interconnected and interdependent system of diverse, often national-centred, *capitalisms* – in the plural – which have their own distinct qualities and flaws.

Varieties of capitalism in a global economy. The theory and reality of globalization are often very different from one another, as the previous discussion should illustrate. This opens two rather important questions: *How* has globalization impacted different countries and *why* has it had different impacts? We think these two questions help us to understand the variety and diversity inherent in capitalism that often gets obscured in debates about globalization and the expected convergence of national economies to a free-market ideal – often called 'neoliberalism'. In answering these questions, we can identify at least two different senses in which capitalism is varied and diverse: first, capitalism may go through different stages at different points in time (i.e. temporal diversity); and second, capitalism may be different in different places (i.e. geographical variety).

Key concept: Neoliberalism

Neoliberalism is a contested term used to refer to a range of things, including policy practices, economic system, political project and epistemic community. For ease, we use it here to refer to a political-economic system based on the idea that (free) market interactions – that is, those with no or limited state or social intervention – are the most efficient way to organize the economy *and* to coordinate all social institutions. This does not mean, however, that the state plays no role in the economy; quite the opposite. The state's role is to create new markets, maintain the rule of law (especially when it comes to competition) and ensure social stability through penal policies. As such, neoliberalism does not simply imply 'deregulation' of the economy, but rather its 'reregulation' as new rules are instituted.

Source: Birch (2015)

First, the idea that capitalism has changed over time is best exemplified in the notion that there was a shift from Keynesianism to neoliberalism in the early 1980s. While not everyone characterizes this shift as the emergence of neoliberalism, most scholars agree that there was a significant change following the 1970s. One important thinker in this regard is Bob Jessop (2002) who argues that the transformation of capitalism has been accompanied by the transformation of the state – in fact, the economy and state necessarily change together as the former is *regulated* – by which he means stabilized – by the latter. Jessop (2002) identifies several differences between what he calls the Keynesian National Welfare State (KNWS) and Schumpeterian Competition State (SCS). The former emerged after the Second World War and was based on a national-centred form of capitalism supported by different social welfare systems. After the KNWS broke down during the 1970s, it was replaced by the SCS in which the state supported global capital mobility and global competition through policies like wage restraint, low taxation, employment flexibility and so on, all designed to attract international investment. While these are distinct forms of capitalism, it's notable that both stress the role of the state in buttressing the activities of business, rather than the erosion of the state altogether.

Second, there's a large body of literature discussing the 'varieties of capitalism' around the world, drawing on the work of Peter Hall and David Soskice (2001) and others like Bruno Amable (2003). In their work, Hall and Soskice (2001) argue that different countries sit on a spectrum from liberal-market economies (LME) to coordinated market economies (CME). Anglo-Celtic economies, like the United States, the UK, Canada and Ireland, are often contrasted with social democratic or coordinated economies in Scandinavia, Northern Europe and Japan (Amable 2003). Hall and Soskice (2001) examine the firm- or business-level characteristics of different countries in order to understand what differentiates the performance of different economies. For example, they look at industrial relations between management and workers, education and training systems, corporate governance – as discussed in Chapter 8 – and inter-business interaction (e.g. competitive or collaborative). What they argue is that LMEs are less regulated, less egalitarian, more competitive, more legalistic, lower taxed and more flexible than CMEs. In making these claims, academics like Hall and Soskice provide an important counter to the claims of hyper-globalists about the inevitable, irreversible and homogenizing forces of globalization. What is clear from the literature on the varieties of capitalism is quite the reverse in fact; many national economies have a strong, institutional heritage which is not simply wiped away by a global steamroller forcing every country to adopt one set of global market rules. Moreover, different countries, especially those in the Global North, have adopted very different policies in light of globalization, helping to alleviate the worst effects of global change.

Empirical example: The 'BRICS' countries

It's useful to look at a specific example in order to illustrate the notion that there are varieties of capitalism and not a homogeneous global economy. While the global economy is still dominated by a small number of countries it's evident that things are changing. In particular, over the last few decades the Global South has become a more important site of economic development, trade and investment. According to data presented by Dicken (2011: 25; 2015: 25), for example, 'developing countries' grew from around 18 per cent of world GDP, 19 per cent of world exports and 21 per cent of world FDI in 1990 to around 35 per cent, 32 per cent and 35 per cent respectively by 2012. It's important, once again, to note that the growth in these three indicators reflects the emergence of a few countries, mainly in the Global South, as global players rather than all countries. In particular, Brazil, Russia, India, China and South Africa – the so-called BRICS – have witnessed significant growth in GDP, exports, FDI and production; in 2020 they represented 24.4 per cent of world GDP (World Bank 2022). While the BRICS are increasingly important, they are not all the same. The economies of Brazil and Russia are based on commodity exports, especially agriculture (Brazil) and oil and gas (Russia), while China is a major product exporter and commodity importer, and India is a major services exporter.

The BRICS can be distinguished from one another on the basis of differences in their economic system; they are also diverse forms of capitalism (Hall and Soskice 2001; Amable 2003). On the one hand, China is an authoritarian political system in which one party controls the state, while India is the largest democracy in the world. Although these political differences are important, it's also necessary to understand the political-economic characteristics of each country. What is interesting in light of (neoliberal) arguments about the need to adapt to globalization is that China and India, for example, did not adopt the policies promoted by the Washington Consensus, and yet they achieved significantly higher growth rates than those that did (Peet 2007). One example of the differences is the Chinese state's continuing control over its own currency – it's not free floating – and over new companies set up in China – they maintain a controlling share in them. Whether these growth rates are also a result of China's and India's sizes is beside the point; they show that each and every country is different and should not be forced to adopt one set of (very prescriptive) policies. Development comes in many forms, it would seem.

Not only do the BRICS represent diverse forms of capitalism, their relationship to the rest of the world is not always as simplistic as sometimes presented in the globalization narrative. China is an interesting example in this regard. While we might think that China is now the workshop of the world, since most of the products we buy (e.g. apparel and electronics) seem to have 'Made in China' stamped on them, this hides a complex set of international trade and investment relationships. China has positioned itself at a particular point in the global value chain as outlined by Dicken (2011) and Thun (2011).

Key methodological issue: Global value chains

There are various ways to study the global economy. One way is to conceptualize the process of production, distribution and retail as a 'value chain' in which different social actors capture value from the creation of a product or commodity as it moves between different locations around the world. For example, an iPhone may be sold in the United States or Canada, but its component parts were produced and assembled elsewhere (e.g. China, Taiwan, South Korea), while the raw materials used to make those parts come from somewhere else entirely (e.g. Democratic Republic of the Congo, Indonesia). Moreover, at each stage of the value chain, workers and owners capture different levels of value depending on their relative power to one another. What this approach does is help researchers explore the social, political and economic dynamics behind the production, distribution and retail of goods and services, rather than assume that this is a neutral process from which everyone benefits.

Source: Thun (2011)

As an economy, China has grown at astonishing rates since the early 1990s and has become the second-largest economy in the world. It's the world's largest manufacturer, 75 per cent larger than the United States (Richter 2020) (the largest merchandise exporter) and second-largest importer (IMF Data 2020). It's notable that, contrary to popular impressions, China is a major importer of raw materials *and* manufactured goods; it's not simply an exporter. We can explain this by noting that China is tied into a series of intra-Asian trade relationships through multinational business networks in which component or intermediate parts are produced in a variety of Asian countries (e.g. Thailand, Malaysia, Indonesia) – and elsewhere – before being shipped to China for assembly and then final export to overseas markets like North America and Western Europe (Dicken 2011: 33). The Chinese economy, in this sense, is built on the back of foreign business investment in Chinese factories that seeks to exploit low-cost Chinese labour (Thun 2011: 361).

Conclusion

In this chapter we sought to do a number of things. First, we have provided an outline of ongoing debates about the importance of globalization on our economies and societies, especially as this relates to how this era of globalization might be distinct and different from past eras how we might have to be cautious about seeing it as subject to counter-movements. Second, we have discussed how globalization has been used to make particular claims about what is development, what is happening to the nation-state and what governments should do to restructure their societies. Third, we challenged these claims by outlining how globalization is a contested concept and process, and how we have to be careful when making normative claims about it. Fourth, we showed how it's more useful to represent the global economy as an interconnected and interdependent system of national *capitalisms* – a plural amalgam of diverse and varied economies, each with their own institutional heritage and state.

Suggested readings

- Ch. 1, Chang, H.-J. (2008) *Bad Samaritans*, London, Bloomsbury.
- Ch. 2, Dicken, P. (2015) *Global Shift* (7th Edition), New York, Guildford.
- Hay, C. (2011) 'Globalization's Impact on States', in J. Ravenhill (ed.), *Global Political Economy* (3rd Edition), Oxford, Oxford University Press, pp. 312–44.
- Ch. 2, Hirst, P. and Thompson, G. (1999) *Globalization in Question* (2nd Edition), Cambridge, Polity Press.
- Ch. 2, Peet, R. (2009) *Unholy Trinity* (2nd Edition), London, Zed Books.

Note

1 Note here that we have added data from the World Bank (2022) in order to supplement Dicken's analysis.

Bibliography

Amable, B. (2003) *The Diversity of Modern Capitalism*, Oxford, Oxford University Press.

Bakas, A. (2015) *Capitalism and Slowbalization – The Market the State and the Crowd in the 21st Century*, Amsterdam, Dexter.

Bergeijk, P. (2019) *Deglobalization 2.0: Trade and Openness During the Great Depression and the Great Recession*, Cheltenham, Edward Elgar.

Birch, K. (2015) 'Neoliberalism: The Whys and Wherefores . . . and Future Directions', *Sociology Compass*, Vol. 9, pp. 571–84.

Brenner, N. (2004) *New State Spaces*, Oxford, Oxford University Press.

Castells, M. (1996) *The Rise of the Network Society*, Oxford, Blackwell.

Chang, H.-J. (2008) *Bad Samaritans*, London, Bloomsbury.

Clark, I. (1999) *Globalization and International Relations Theory*, Oxford, Oxford University Press.

Dicken, P. (2011) *Global Shift* (6th Edition), New York, Guildford.

Dicken, P. (2015) *Global Shift* (7th Edition), New York, Guildford.

The Economist. (2019) 'Globalization has Faltered: It is Now Being Reshaped', *The Economist*, 24 January, https://www.economist.com/briefing/2019/01/24/globalisation-has-faltered.

Friedman, T. (1999) *The Lexus and the Olive Tree*, New York, Farrar, Straus & Giroux.

Friedman, T. (2005) *The World Is Flat*, New York, Farrar, Straus & Giroux.

Giddens, A. (1990) *The Consequences of Modernity*, Cambridge, Polity.

Griffin, K. (2003) 'Economic Globalization and Institutions of Global Governance', *Development and Change*, Vol. 34, pp. 789–807.

Hall, P. and Soskice, D. (eds) (2001) *Varieties of Capitalism: The Institutional Foundations of Comparative Advantage*, Oxford, Oxford University Press.

Hanna, R., et al. (2020) 'After COVID-19, Green Investment Must Deliver Jobs to Get Traction', *Nature*, Vol. 582, No. 7811, pp. 178–80.

Harvey, D. (1989) *The Condition of Postmodernity*, Cambridge, Blackwell.

Hay, C. (2011) 'Globalization's Impact on States', in J. Ravenhill (ed.), *Global Political Economy* (3rd Edition), Oxford, Oxford University Press, pp. 312–44.

Held, D., Goldblatt, D. and Perratton, J. (1999) *Global Transformations*, Cambridge, Polity Press.

Helleiner, E. (1994) *States and the Reemergence of Global Finance*, Ithaca, Cornell University Press.

Hierskaia, J., Staamegna, C., Kononenko, V., Navarra, C. and Zumer, K. (2020) *Slowing Down or Changing Track: Understanding the Dynamics of 'Slowbalisation'*, Brussels, European Parliamentary Research Service.

Hirst, P. and Thompson, G. (1999) *Globalization in Question* (2nd Edition), Cambridge, Polity Press.

IMF Data. (2022) *Access to Macroenconomic and Financial Data*, http://data.imf.org.

Jessop, B. (2002) *The Future of the Capitalist State*, Cambridge, Polity Press.

Johns, J. (2022) 'Transforming Manufacturing? An Additive Manufacturing Research Agenda', in J. Bryson, C. Billing, W. Graves, and G. Yeung (eds), *A Research Agenda for Manufacturing Industries in the Global Economy*, Cheltanham, Elgar, pp. 49–65.

Levinson, M. (2020) *Outside the Box: How Globalization Changed from Moving Stuff to Spreading Ideas*, Princeton, Princeton University Press.

MacKinnon, D. and Cumbers, A. (2007) *An Introduction to Economic Geography*, Harlow, Pearson.

McGrew, A. (2011) 'The Logics of Economic Globalization', in J. Ravenhill (ed.), *Global Political Economy* (3rd Edition), Oxford, Oxford University Press, pp. 275–311.

Milanovic, B. (2018) *Global Inequality: A New Approach for the Age of Globalization*, Cambridge, MA, The Belknap Press of Harvard University.

OECD. (2022) *FDI in Figures*, April 2002, https://www.oecd.org/investment/investment-policy/FDI-in-Figures-April-2022.pdf.

Ohmae, K. (1990) *The Borderless World*, London, Collins.

Peet, R. (2007) *Geography of Power*, London, Zed Books.

Peet, R. (2009) *Unholy Trinity* (2nd edition), London, Zed Books.

Rajan, R. (2022) 'Just Say No To "Friend Shoring"', *Project Syndicate*, 3 June, https://www.project-syndicate.org/commentary/friend-shoring-higher

-costs-and-more-conflict-without
-resilience-by-raghuram-rajan
-2022-06.

Reich, R. (1992) *The Work of Nations*, New York, Vintage Books.

Richter, F. (2020) 'These Are the Top 10 Manufacturing Countries in the World', *World Economic Forum: Global Agenda*, February 2020, https://www.weforum.org/agenda/2020/02/countries-manufacturing-trade-exports-economics/.

Stiglitz, J. (2002) *Globalization and Its Discontents*, London, W.W. Norton & Company.

Stiglitz, J. (2022) 'Getting Deglobalization Right', *Project Syndicate*, 31 May, https://www.project-syndicate.org/commentary/deglobalization-and-its-discontents-by-joseph-e-stiglitz-2022-05.

Strange, S. (1998) *Mad Money*, Manchester, University of Manchester Press.

Thun, E. (2011) 'The Globalization of Production', in J. Ravenhill (ed.), *Global Political Economy* (3rd Edition), Oxford, Oxford University Press, pp. 345–69.

UNCTAD. (2022) *UNCTAD Global Trade Update*, February 2022, https://unctad.org/system/files/official-document/ditcinf2022d1_en.pdf.

Van Waeyenberge, E. (2010) 'Tightening the Web: The World Bank and Enforced Policy Reform', in K. Birch and V. Mykhnenko (eds), *The Rise and Fall of Neoliberalism*, London, Zed Books, pp. 94–111.

Varoufakis, Y. (2013) *The Global Minotaur* (2nd Edition), London, Zed Books.

Weiss, L. (1998) *The Myth of the Powerless State*, Cambridge, Polity Press.

World Bank. (2022) 'National Accounts Data', https://data.worldbank.org/indicator/NY.GDP.MKTP.CD.

14 | Global governance

Kean Birch and Richard Wellen

Introduction

In the previous chapter we stressed on the need to adopt a nuanced perspective when trying to understand the global economy, taking into account the varied and uneven economic geography of globalization processes as well as changes in the degree of global trade and investment flows (Dicken 2015). The same could be said about global governance. Our views about governance of the global or transnational economy have been shaped by the experience of the post–Second World War institutions that assumed that truly *global* agreements and arrangements could be obtained. Developments in recent years have illustrated how the national interests of many countries come into conflict with one another during times of economic dislocation, transformation and geopolitical tension. For example, the World Trade Organization (WTO) has been mired in negotiations over agricultural subsidies since 2000 where countries in the Global South have objected to the export of subsidized agricultural products from the Global North (Rodrik 2019a). As we saw in Chapter 12 similar tensions have arisen around the WTO's emphasis on placing intellectual property protection at the core of global trade governance, which clearly works to the advantage of countries where the companies at the forefront of technological innovation have their headquarters.

These kinds of strains have prompted some countries to pursue bilateral or regional multilateral governance agreements where a consensus that avoids the 'one size fits all' golden straightjacket (Friedman 1999) might be reached. In fact, since 1990 the number of regional trade agreements has increased from 50 to 354, demonstrating the complexity and challenges of the system of global governance (Smillie 2018; World Trade Organization 2022).

Mainstream theories of global governance assume that globalization itself can be collectively managed by agreements among nation-states in global policymaking through international institutions like the United Nations (UN), European Union (EU), WTO and so on (Griffin 2003). What this implies is that globalization can benefit everyone if it's managed in the right way. Drawing on the work of Weiss (2013) and May (2015), we define this sort of *global governance* as the systematic and collective attempt to organize and coordinate global activities in the pursuit of common global goals, which would be beyond the capacity of any individual country to undertake.

Yet global governance is particularly complex since national governments are defined by their territorially specified scope of authority. When they participate in intergovernmental organizations or trade agreements their scope of political authority is inherently limited by the interests and potential rivalry of other nation-states. By contrast transnational businesses, while they may compete globally, are 'multiscalar' since they span across global production networks (Kobrin 2017). The world's economies are increasingly interdependent which means that business entities are fragmented across the global value chain and are therefore harder to control politically. In this context MNCs may benefit from coordination across local, national or global levels in ways that may not benefit nation-states. Indeed, part of the recent backlash against globalization and economic integration stems from the fact that the global success of a corporation headquartered in one country may create more investment and jobs in other countries.

In what follows we consider how the operations and objectives of contemporary institutions of global governance have become controversial in the face of the tensions sketched earlier. We also discuss what that might mean for a world in which globalization itself is being transformed, destabilized and challenged.

Definition: Governance

Often compared with the concept of 'government' – which refers to the formal political system and formal authority – the term 'governance' is used to conceptualize the coordination of the political-economic system across an array of social actors and institutions (e.g. government, business and civil society). Increasingly, governance is associated with the growing role and importance of private actors in political-economic decision-making, especially at the global scale.

Key discussion questions

- What is global governance?
- Why does global governance matter?
- What institutions are involved in global (economic) governance?
- How is the current system of global governance implicated in the development of problematic national policies?
- How does business help to make global governance rules?

Backgrounder on intergovernmental arrangements and the transnational order

In order to understand global governance, it's important to have a basic grasp of international relations between countries and their origins (Clark 2000). As a starting point, it's helpful to consider where national sovereignty comes from. By this we mean the power of a nation-state to pursue certain policies, enact specific laws, regulate particular activities and so on. A quite simple question helps illustrate this point: Why can't one country enact laws or regulations (e.g. labour or product standards) in another country? If asked this question, most political scientists would point to the emergence of national sovereignty from the seventeenth century onwards as the explanation. In particular, they would probably highlight the 1648 *Treaty of Westphalia* as the key historical event in the development of modern state sovereignty. The treaty was the culmination of the Thirty Years' War, which had ravaged Europe as the result of religious divisions and conflict between Catholic and Protestant Christianity.

In the wake of Westphalia, the modern nation-state, defined as geographically specific territories (e.g. England, France and Spain), came to be seen as the focus of constitutional claims about nation-state sovereignty (Bobbitt 2002). This meant that only a state underpinned by a territorial designation could enact or introduce laws in that territory, which meant that nation-states increasingly had to find ways to coordinate their activities with one another in order to facilitate things like international trade. Today, this is especially the case as the result of the increasing technological, social, political and economic connectivity between countries around the world, and the increasing need to solve global problems like climate change (see Chapter 16).

Contemporary global governance. The form that global governance takes today largely emerges from a meeting held by the Allied nations in 1944 at Bretton Woods, New Hampshire. This came to be known as the Bretton Woods Conference and set the stage for post–Second World War capitalism in countries like the United States, the UK and Japan, as well in Western Europe and other parts of the world. It led directly to the establishment of three core global governance agreements or organizations: the World Bank, the International Monetary Fund (IMF) and the General Agreement on Tariffs and Trade (GATT), which turned into the WTO. These institutions as well as the fixed currency system underpinning them are called the Bretton Woods System (BWS), which lasted until 1971 in its original form. This BWS represents a cornerstone in what John Ruggie (1982) has called the 'embedded liberal' order that dominated the post–Second World War era, up until the 1970s at least.

The BWS was based on the growing dominance of the United States in the world capitalist economy at the end of the Second World War, reflected in its emergence as one of the post–Second World War superpowers alongside the USSR (see Chapter 10). At the time, the United States was the only major capitalist economy not severely damaged by the war, and it took on a major role in the global governance of the world's capitalist economies (Eichengreen 1996, 2006). The BWS was designed as a way to coordinate trade and investment activities between nation-states by controlling the flow of capital (i.e. money) between countries and promoting international trade by reducing tariffs. Capital controls were meant to reduce the economic volatility caused by the free movement of capital investment between countries, while tariff reductions were meant to increase trade between countries. The BWS incorporated a range of international organizations or agreements, which we discuss later, but was also based on a fixed exchange system dominated by the US dollar. In many ways, it was an attempt to return to the 'gold standard', although it was largely controlled by the United States (Eichengreen 1996).

Key global institution: 'Gold standard'

The gold standard involves a government fixing the value of its currency in gold and redeeming its currency notes in gold on demand. This means that a person could exchange a certain number of dollar notes for their equivalent in gold at a bank. One advantage of such a system is that a country's money supply cannot outgrow its reserves of gold, something perceived to curtail inflation associated with excessive government spending.

A return to a form of gold standard underpinned the BWS established at the end of the Second World War. It worked through the fixing of the rate of exchange between a country's currency and the US dollar, while the dollar value was fixed to a certain value of gold (US$35 per ounce). The system curtailed currency speculation because there were exchange controls that limited access to foreign currency.

The United States came off this modern 'gold standard' in 1971 when President Nixon sought to release government spending from the constraint of the need to retain significant gold reserves and because of the trade deficits – which, under the BWS, had to be backed by gold – that the United States had accumulated with its trading partners. A system of fixed (but periodically adjustable) exchange rates gave way to a system, still in existence today, of floating exchange rates, whereby the value of a currency fluctuates in accordance with the demand for and supply of that currency. The system of floating rates also paved the way for financial globalization, whereby foreign currencies can be acquired without limit on currency markets.

Source: Eichengreen and Flandreau (1997)

There are a number of other international arrangements and organizations that constitute a part of global governance. Generally speaking, organizations like the United Nations (UN) represent one element in this global governance, but in this chapter we want to focus on the organizations charged with a primarily *economic* role: for example, organizations like the World Bank, IMF and WTO – more details of these organizations are contained in Table 14.1. It is important to acknowledge, though, that these supposedly *economic* organizations are as much political entities as they are economic; by this we mean that they influence the political process globally and reflect the political influence of powerful states and powerful interests within states.

There is quite a range of international agreements and organizations tasked with a role in coordinating international economic activity, whether this is the promotion of international economic development or the stabilization of the global financial system. In Table 14.1 we highlight some of the most significant ones and of these the World Bank, IMF and WTO are probably the most well known. Here we briefly outline their roles and activities:

- *World Bank*: the World Bank started as an organization to help reconstruct Western Europe after the Second World War, but its primary role nowadays is to provide development loans and guarantees for loans, as well as to support development through its advisory arm. Loans, guarantees and advice are designed to support countries in the restructuring of their economies in order to make them more pro-market and more internationally competitive. More recently, the World Bank has supported a range of poverty-focused policies, such as the Millennium Development Goals (Peet 2009; van Waeyenberge 2010).
- *IMF*: the IMF's mandate was to regulate currency exchange and enable members to resolve balance of payments problems (i.e. where imports exceed exports) through short-term loans. Over time, the IMF sought to add conditions to its loans as a way to push countries into adopting certain types of structural reforms to change their economies, with the aim that this would make them more internationally competitive and end any balance of payments problems (Peet 2009).
- *WTO*: a more recent organization, the WTO has its origins in the GATT. It is meant to operate as a way to reduce trade tariffs and thereby encourage international (free) trade. It also establishes a set of basic ground rules for things like intellectual property rights (IPRs) and other forms of property protection – see Chapter 12 for more.

These organizations not only construct global governance but also have their own internal governance structures which can work to the advantage of certain nations and interest groups. As an example of how important this internal governance structure is, it is helpful to compare the IMF and WTO:

- *IMF*: membership consists of 190 (of the nearly 200) nation-states of the world. Upon becoming a member, each nation pays a quota, and the number

TABLE 14.1 Global Governance Agreements and Organizations

Name	Location	Founded	Role	Changes over time
Bank for International Settlements	Basel, Switzerland	1930	Owned by central banks and set up to enable coordination of central banking around the world.	Established Basel Accords (Nos. I, II and III) as regulatory frameworks for global banking (1988, 2004, 2019).
World Bank	Washington, DC	1944	Group of organizations set up to fund reconstruction of Europe after the Second World War.	Mandate shifted to other countries after reconstruction of Europe.
International Monetary Fund	Washington, DC	1944	Organization set up to lend money to countries to cover short-term balance of payments problems.	Shift in role from 'neutral' lender to active lender from 1970s; started requiring economic restructuring in exchange for loans (e.g. Structural Adjustment Programme).
General Agreement on Tariffs and Trade	Geneva, Switzerland	1947	Agreement to reduce taxes on trade (i.e. tariffs) and other 'barriers to trade'.	Converted into WTO in 1994
International Organization for Standardization	Geneva, Switzerland	1947	Organization set up to promote spread of standards through coordination of national standards organizations.	Not applicable.
World Trade Organization	Geneva, Switzerland	1995	Organization set up to regulate international trade.	Stuck in 2001 'Doha Round' of negotiations over agricultural subsidies.

Sources: Helleiner (1994); Peet (2007, 2009).

of votes a country has is proportionate to its quota. The main determinant of a country's quota is its GDP, while total population plays no part establishing a country's quota. Hence, between them, the wealthy G7 countries (United States, the UK, France, Germany, Italy, Japan and Canada) hold over 41.2 per cent of the votes, with the United States being the largest vote-holder (16.5 per cent of the total votes of the IMF). These countries represent only 10.2 per cent of global population, but their high vote total is based on their collective wealth and the high quota that they contribute. In total the BRICS countries (Brazil, Russia, India, China and South Africa) comprise 42.2 per cent of the world's population yet hold only 6.1 per cent of the votes in the IMF (IMF 2022).

- *WTO*: membership consists of 164 nation-states, each of which has one vote irrespective of its population, GDP, geographical location, and so on. Furthermore, most decisions are made on the basis of consensus, so each country has, in theory, veto power over each policy proposal (Eagleton-Pierce 2013; Footer 2006). Usually, however, representatives of richer countries and a few select countries of the Global South set the WTO's agenda in so-called 'green room meetings' at which a 'take-it-or-leave-it' agenda is determined with representatives from countries in the Global South most often being marginalized (Hoekman and Mavroidis 2016).

Global governance and global development. The main reason that these global organizations and agreements are so significant is because they directly impact the economic development policies that countries pursue around the world. Organizations like the World Bank, IMF and WTO have been distinguished by their support for and promotion of a particular form of economic development, which has been called the 'Washington Consensus' (Williamson 1990, 1993). The economist John Williamson (1993: 1334) came up with the term as a way to refer to 'the common core of wisdom' which was 'embraced by all serious economists' in the United States administration (e.g. Treasury, Federal Reserve Board), international financial institutions (e.g. World Bank, IMF) and various US-based or international think tanks and policy groups.

The term 'Washington Consensus' is used to define a range of commonly accepted economic policy reforms designed to support (free) trade and unrestricted capital mobility (i.e. foreign direct investment, FDI) from the 1980s onwards, especially in the Global South. Described as a 'golden straightjacket' by the likes of Thomas Friedman (1999), the Washington Consensus includes policy reforms such as tight fiscal discipline (i.e. public spending cuts); phase-out of subsidies for domestic producers; tax cuts; financial and trade liberalization; privatization; deregulation; strengthened property rights; and so on (Williamson 1993). In this sense, then, the Washington Consensus prescription for successful economic development is liberal, open and democratic institutions, especially ones that support and reinforce the (free) market.

The Washington Consensus described by Williamson involved the embrace of a neoliberal model that displaced the earlier period of embedded liberalism which spanned from the end of the Second World War in 1945 until the early 1980s (Hopewell 2016). During the heyday of embedded liberalism institutions like the IMF favoured free markets, but their loan and financing programmes did not try to aggressively interfere with the domestic policy space in countries benefiting from these programmes. This was largely due to the geopolitical rivalry between the United States and the Soviet bloc, which forced Western-led governance institutions to be more accommodating to maintain Western influence and credibility in the Global South (Babb and Kentikelenis 2021). The demise of the Soviet bloc and the end of the Cold War in the late 1980s gave the Western-controlled global governance institutions a freer hand to pursue the neoliberal Washington Consensus approach as the primary model of economic development (Beeson 2007). During the high point of neoliberal reform in the 1980s and 1990s the IMF became known for intervening to resolve debt crises by demanding harsh conditions like cuts to public sector wages and other social protections (Griffiths 2014).

The Global South has been most impacted by the implementation of rules and governance based on the Washington Consensus. As the World Bank and IMF re-oriented their mandates, they became more focused on lending to countries in the Global South – frequently defined as *developing* or *less-developed* economies (see Chapter 3). These international financial institutions (IFIs) have pursued an approach to development based on market principles in which conditions are attached to loans that are meant to alleviate economic crises or help countries integrate into the global economy. These conditions are commonly referred to as structural adjustment programmes (SAPs) and are meant to force countries to restructure their economies so they can better withstand global competition (Chang 2008). In his book *Unholy Trinity*, Peet (2009) describes the IFIs as global debt collectors who, through the introduction of SAPs in the Global South, ensure that capital investment is returned to businesses or governments in the Global North (also Harvey 2003). Citizens in the Global South end up paying for this debt through reductions in government spending (e.g. health care, education and social welfare). The WTO developed trade dispute mechanisms that could sanction countries not only for erecting discriminatory tariffs but also for subsidizing their industries, using loose intellectual property rules and limiting foreign investment, all policies which are disproportionately used by countries in the Global South as a form of economic protectionism. Institutions like the IMF and the World

Bank increasingly promoted privatization, deregulation and domestic austerity measures that countries needed to receive economic rescue packages and development financing.

Global hegemony of the United States. Critics have maintained that the Washington Consensus approach imposed by the IFIs is not simply a neutral set of technical rules of the (capitalist) game; rather, it is how the game is played and won by a limited number of countries, especially the United States, based in the Global North (Chang 2008). According to Richard Peet (2007) these hallmark policies of the Washington Consensus represented a powerful policy regime combining the political power of IFIs and US state agencies with the economic power of capitalist business (e.g. banks) and the ideological power of (neoclassical) economic ideas developed in elite universities and think tanks. Although the increased economic and political clout of countries like China has made the world more multi-polar the role of the United States as a hegemonic global power continues to shape global governance institutions. By dint of its economic, political and even cultural power, the United States has often been able to override or ignore global organizations and agreements, as evidenced by its record of pulling out of major climate change agreements like the Paris Accord and demanding the renegotiation of regional trade agreements such as NAFTA (North American Free Trade Agreement).

This takes us back to Chapter 3 where we discussed capitalism as a 'world system' in which one country usually plays a hegemonic role, dominating the world's economy and, hence, dominating international decisions and activities. Giovanni Arrighi (1994 [2010]) has reviewed how the rise of successive hegemonic powers has been evident in the cycles of capitalist expansion and development. For example, Arrighi outlined the hegemony of the Italian city-states of Genoa and Venice (*c.* 1300–1600), then the Netherlands (*c.* 1600–1750), then the UK (*c.* 1750–1900), before the emergence of the United States as the global hegemon in the early-to-mid-twentieth century. Each period of hegemony lasted for over 100 years, during which time the dominant country was the centre of international production, trade and finance. This was in the European context initially, and then globally as these countries conquered and colonized other parts of the world (see Chapter 3). Arrighi argued that the United States dominated the world economy through the expansion of American multinational corporations and the BWS of global governance after the Second World War.

Respected economist and ex-finance minister of Greece Yanis Varoufakis (2011) has described the United States as a 'Global Minotaur' in his book by the same name. By this he means that the United States remade the global order after the Second World War in order to ensure its military and economic hegemony, using the BWS and global governance organizations and agreements. Although the dominant US role was seen as stabilizing early on in the BWS, Varoufakis argues that the United States sought to bind capitalist economies to US power through this global system. As it evolved, however, US dominance ensured that it could run a huge trade deficit *and* huge government budget deficit simultaneously; basically, it was 'based upon a constant flow of tribute from the periphery to the imperial centre' (2011: 23). While this plan ensured US hegemony, it had implications for global stability in that many other countries and businesses became dependent on the US economy. For example, China and Germany depend on the United States as an export market, and many businesses, especially oil companies, recycle their profits through investments in US stocks and bonds.

The problem with this era of US hegemony is that it has proven to be inherently unstable. According to critics such as Joseph Stiglitz (2003) the Washington Consensus imposes a 'one size fits all' model of development which is inadequate for balancing global integration on the one hand and respect for the unique national interests of countries on the other hand. Moreover, the model of US global economic hegemony became heavily dependent on systems of private wealth and consumption, without necessarily boosting the public and social resources upon which much of the economic well-being of workers and communities depend. This inherently unbalanced view of an exclusively market-driven model of economic growth contributed to the financial crisis of 2008 (see Chapters 11 and 17). As Varoufakis pointed out, the crisis could only be resolved by government bailouts to the financial institutions that caused the crisis itself (Chapter 17). In the meantime, rising inequality has led to populist resentment within countries. As a result, even leaders of Western countries that have the WC model have begun to question free trade and the models of economic integration that require the outsourcing of jobs and so on.

In addition to these changes, since the early 2000s there has been a shift away from a US-centric model of global economic governance to a multi-polar world where BRICS countries, and particularly China, are increasingly shaping such arrangements (Beeson 2007). China and the United States are economically interdependent, but they are also competing to shape the international economy and the future of globalization, including engaging in trade wars with each other. While China has benefited greatly from globalization and free trade through its export success, its model of industrial development has been more explicitly state led. Moreover, since 2013, China has been pursuing its 'Belt and Road' initiative which consists of development grants and loans in Africa and Asia to establish infrastructure and energy and transport systems to support trade and development in those regions through a connection to Chinese industries (Smith 2021). To take another example, the Asian Infrastructure and Investment Bank (AIIB) was initiated by China in 2013 in order to provide an alternative to Western-dominated multilateral development banks like the World Bank. Many countries in the Global South are now starting to have more choice about where to seek development financing and have therefore begun to expect more freedom from the preferred policies of the Western-dominated IFIs (Babb and Kentikelenis 2021). Due to the declining legitimacy of the Washington Consensus, the IMF has acknowledged the need for more flexibility in its conditionality polices (i.e. SAPs) and questioned the acceptability of policies such as capital controls (Grabel 2011).

Although proponents of the Washington Consensus claim that markets should drive innovation and industrial development decisions within and between countries, in practice countries like the United States have always selectively abandoned free-market approaches in order to protect their key strategic national interests and leading business firms (Chang 2008). For example, in 2022 US president Biden signed into law a bill called the 'Chips and Science Act' which provides billions in subsidies and tax credits for major semiconductor manufacturers to invest in new plants and research in the United States rather than overseas. This is widely seen as part of a trend towards economic nationalism that runs counter to the free-market approach promoted by the dominant postwar global governance institutions but is seen as necessary for enlisting corporations in the competition between countries (Knight 2022). The bill not only seeks to match a massive state subsidy programme by China to assert leadership in one of the world's most strategically important industries, it also disqualifies semiconductor firms from receiving US subsidies if they build semiconductor plants in China (Wang and DeBonis 2022). Notably, the passage of the 'Chips' bill was promoted by unprecedented lobbying efforts by the leading firms of the US Semiconductor industry (Birnbaum 2022; Bloomberg). This suggests that the cyclical policy shift towards state-led economic nationalism may involve different policies but is just as much driven by business interests and lobbying as the previously dominant pattern of free-market globalism.

Critical perspectives on global governance

Based on the foregoing we can argue that critical perspectives on global governance need to address the fact that existing and dominant global governance organizations and agreements are not open, not democratic and not even (economically) liberal (Acemoglu and Robinson 2013). This runs counter to the more mainstream approach that assumes that global institutions are neutral technocratic means for countries to cooperate on collective problems beyond the policy sphere they govern as sovereign national entities.

Globalization researchers nevertheless agree that global governance arrangements need to be reformed by placing less emphasis on ensuring that markets allocate capital and goods efficiently, and more emphasis on addressing collective global problems, aiming to avoid forms of asymmetric globalization in which certain countries and people benefit from globalization while others do not (Griffin 2003; Rodrik 2019). In order to deliver improved global governance, Griffin argues that global organizations and agreements need to become *more* democratic with representative democracy scaled up from the national to the global scale (i.e. individual people from all countries voting for representatives at global institutions like the UN, IMF, WTO etc.).

Private rules, private rule. In our current context, it is imperative to think about who gets to set global rules, how they get to set them and what this means for everyone else. As May (2015) points out, the state-centric view of global governance misses the role played by business in creating the international standards, rules, regulations and so on that configure the global economy. As we have already discussed in this book, the global economy has become more fragmented and more integrated at the same time (see Chapter 13). Supply chains are increasingly stretched across more and more national borders, fragmenting production in different geographical places; at the same time, though, MNCs and MNEs are increasingly integrating these fragmented supply chains in their operations (Dicken 2015). This has led to a complex array of business and corporate relationships between core companies (e.g. Apple) and their suppliers (e.g. FoxConn), across several national jurisdictions. It's important to understand that these supply chains are coordinated and governed by private social actors like MNCs and MNEs, rather than only or primarily through state regulations. As many researchers have noted, this creates a kind of regulatory gap since a globalized business can only be regulated by national states in an awkward and incomplete way. Global businesses pursued through globally networked affiliates and subsidiaries possess a kind of economic unity but they are divided into separate legal entities in each country (Ruggie; Scherer et al. 2009). This weakens the ability of nation-states to participate in the regulation of business since they can't do it alone; they need to morally persuade other states to adopt certain policies, or they need to work within global or multilateral governance organizations. The latter solution can be problematic, since multilateral organizations are inherently limited due to a lack of central authority at the global level and the different interests or policy objectives of the different states involved.

As a result, globalized business relationships are governed by *private* global rules created and enforced by business through things like contract law, standard-setting, arbitration agreements and so on (May 2015). For example, corporate social responsibility (CSR), which we discussed in Chapter 9, represents a form of private regulation in that it is often created, regulated, monitored, enforced and audited by private or quasi-private organizations (e.g. NGOs) in coordination with business, rather than by the state. This means that private organizations increasingly sit at the centre of global governance, which has implications for how international environmental, labour and social regulations and standards are created and enforced. Some CSR researchers argue that in an age where firms are expected to be good global corporate citizens there is hope that the privatization of global governance can help to address global political issues in a constructive way that compensates for the limited capacity of states in global economic regulation (Scherer and Plazzo 2007). On the other hand, critics have argued that the idea of corporations operating as global citizens or as political agents leads to a 'corporatization of the public sphere' (Rhodes and Fleming 2020: 944), which would actually undermine democracy by limiting both transparency and accountability in decision-making processes.

It is important to emphasize the role of business in creating new forms of private regulation and private rules because many critical commentators, journalists, politicians and academics claim that globalization, especially in the 'neoliberal' form promoted by the Washington Consensus, has led to a significant erosion of regulations (e.g. Bakan 2004; Klein 2007; Varoufakis 2011). This deregulation argument, however, may be too simplistic if it ignores the rise of private regulation (Tusikov 2016). This is important for a number of reasons: first, it means that citizens have less control over the regulation of business because these *private* rules no longer fall within the purview of the *public* state and democratic decision-making; and second, business and private interests increasingly influence our conception of *good* global governance, more than states or their citizens. The privatization of global governance has been illustrated by the rising influence of organizations such as the World Economic Forum (WEF), an NGO with a membership dominated by global business leaders and CEOs. In 2019 the UN invited the WEF into a strategic partnership to work collaboratively on promoting the UN sustainability goals that led 280 civil society groups to argue that this privileged access of a private sector lobbying group would amount to a 'corporate capture' of global governance (Monsalve 2021; Gleckman 2019).

As these arguments and examples suggest, then, although global governance is intended to function as a transnational public sphere, it has increasingly become a set of private rules to assert private control over resources, people and decisions. It is largely a form of corporate- or business-led governance, rather than government or democratic governance. We could argue, as both Barkan (2013) and Veldman (2013) do, that business, especially large corporations and businesses, should be understood in the same way as the state; they set rules, they govern lives, they negotiate international agreements and so on.

Conclusion

In this chapter we have sought to examine global governance and explore different ways to understand the coordination of the global economy. We outlined the postwar mainstream model of global governance, especially as it is embodied in global governance organizations and agreements like the World Bank, IMF and WTO. In so doing, we highlighted how this form of global governance, often characterized as the Washington Consensus, promoted a particular form of economic development which has now been called into question both by critics and by the recent rise of economic nationalism. In turning to the critical perspectives of global governance, we highlighted the need to understand global governance as both a state-led *and* business-led process. In particular, we emphasized the importance of understanding the increasing importance of private rules and corporate influence in global governance.

Suggested readings

- Brühl, T. and Hofferberth, M. (2013) 'Global Companies as Social Actors: Constructing Private Business in Global Governance', in J. Mikler (ed.) *The Handbook of Global Companies*, Chichester, Wiley-Blackwell, pp. 351–70.
- Ciepley, D. (2013) 'Beyond Public and Private: Toward a Political Theory of the Corporation', *American Political Science Review*, Vol. 107, pp. 139–58.
- Griffin, K. (2003) 'Economic Globalization and the Institutions of Global Governance', *Development and Change*, Vol. 34, pp. 789–807.
- May, C. (2015) 'Who's in Charge? Corporations as Institutions of Global Governance', *Palgrave Communications*, Vol. 1, pp. 1–10.
- Ch. 4, Peet, R. (2007) *Geography of Power: The Making of Global Economic Policy*, London, Zed Books.

Bibliography

Acemoglu, D. and Robinson, J. (2013) *Why Nations Fail*, New York, Crown Business.

Arrighi, G. (1994 [2010]) *The Long Twentieth Century*, London, Verso.

Babb, S. and Kentikelenis, A. (2021) 'Markets Everywhere: The Washington Consensus and the Sociology of Global Institutional Change', *Annual Review of Sociology*, Vol. 47, pp. 521–41, https://doi.org/10.1146/annurev-soc-090220-025543.

Bakan, J. (2004) *The Corporation*, London, Random House.

Barkan, J. (2013) *Corporate Sovereignty*, Minneapolis, University of Minnesota Press.

Barnett, M. and Finnemore, M. (2004) *Rules for the World: International Organizations in Global Politics*, Ithaca, Cornell University Press.

Beeson, M. (2007) *Regionalism and Globalization in East Asia: Politics, Security and Economic Development*, New York, Palgrave.

Birnbaum, E. (2022, July 20) 'Intel Spends Record Sum on Lobbying Amid Global

Chip Shortage', *BNN Bloomberg*, https://www.bnnbloomberg.ca/intel -spends-record-sum-on-lobbying-amid -global-chip-shortage-1.1794832.

Bobbitt, P. (2002) *The Shield of Achilles: War, Peace, and the Course of History*, New York, Alfred A. Knopf.

Braithwaite, J. (2005) 'Neoliberalism or Regulatory Capitalism', ANU: RegNet, Occasional Paper No. 5.

Brühl, T. and Hofferberth, M. (2013) 'Global Companies as Social Actors: Constructing Private Business in Global Governance', in J. Mikler (ed.), *The Handbook of Global Companies*, Chichester, Wiley-Blackwell, pp. 351–70.

Carroll, A. and Buchholtz, A. (2015) *Business and Society* (9th Edition), Stamford, CT, CENGAGE Learning.

Chang, H.-J. (2008) *Bad Samaritans*, London, Bloomsbury.

Ciepley, D. (2004) 'Authority in the Firm (and the Attempts to Theorize it Away)', *Critical Review: A Journal of Politics and Society*, Vol. 16, pp. 81–115.

Ciepley, D. (2013) 'Beyond Public and Private: Toward a Political Theory of the Corporation', *American Political Science Review*, Vol. 107, pp. 139–58.

Clark, I. (2000) *Globalization and International Relations Theory*, Oxford, Oxford University Press.

de Soto, H. (2000) *The Mystery of Capital: Why Capitalism Triumphs in the West and Fails Everywhere Else*, New York, Basic Books.

Dicken, P. (2015) *Global Shift*, New York, Guildford.

Eagleton-Pierce, M. (2013) *Symbolic Power in the World Trade Organization*, Oxford, Oxford University Press.

Eichengreen, B. (1996) *Globalizing Capital*, Princeton, Princeton University Press.

Eichengreen, B. (2006) *Global Imbalances and the Lessons of Bretton Woods*, Cambridge, MA, The MIT Press.

Eichengreen, B. and Flandreau, M. (eds) (1997) *The Gold Standard in Theory and History* (2nd Edition), London, Routledge.

Footer, M. (2006) *An Institutional and Normative Analysis of the World Trade Organization*, Leiden, Martinus Nijhoff.

Friedman, T. (1999) *The Lexus and the Olive Tree*, New York, Farrar, Straus & Giroux.

Gleckman, H. (2019, 2 July) 'How the United Nations is Quietly Being Turned into a Public-Private Partnership', OpenDemocracy, https://www.opendemocracy.net/en /oureconomy/how-united-nations -quietly-being-turned-public-private -partnership/.

Grabel, I. (2011) 'Not Your Grandfather's IMF: Global Crisis, "Productive Incoherence" and Developmental Policy Space', *Cambridge Journal of Economics*, Vol. 35, No. 5, pp. 805–30, https://doi.org/10.1093/cje/ber012.

Griffin, K. (2003) 'Economic Globalization and the Institutions of Global Governance', *Development and Change*, Vol. 34, pp. 789–807.

Griffiths, J. (2014) *The State of Finance for Developing Countries, 2014*, https:// assets.nationbuilder.com/eurodad /pages/1053/attachments/original /1601475698/The_State_of_Finance _for_Developing_Countries.pdf?.

Hall, P. and Soskice, D. (eds) (2001) *Varieties of Capitalism: The Institutional Foundations of Comparative Advantage*, Oxford, Oxford University Press.

Harvey, D. (2003) *The New Imperialism*, Oxford, Oxford University Press.

Helleiner, E. (1994) *States and the Reemergence of Global Finance*, Ithaca, Cornell University Press.

Hertz, N. (2002) *The Silent Takeover: Global Capitalism and the Death of Democracy*, New York, The Free Press.

Hoekman, B. and Mavroidis, P. (2016) *World Trade Organization: Law, Economics, and Politics* (2nd Edition), London, Routledge.

Hopewell, K. (2016) *No TitleBreaking the WTO: How Emerging Powers Disrupted the Neoliberal Project*, Stanford, Stanford University Press.

Ietto-Gillies, G. (2014) 'The Theory of the Transnational Corporation at 50+', *Economic Thought*, Vol. 3, pp. 38–57.

IMF. (2022) *IMF Members' Quotas and Voting POwer, and IMF Board of Governors*, https://www.imf.org/en/About/executive-board/members-quotas and https://worldpopulationreview.com/countries.

Klein, N. (2007) *The Shock Doctrine*, Toronto, Knopf Canada.

Knight, W. (2022, July 28) 'The US Throws $52 Billion at Chips—But Needs to Spend It Wisely', *Wired*, https://www.wired.com/story/chips-act-52-billion-semiconductor-production/.

Kobrin, S.J. (2017) 'Bricks and Mortar in a Borderless World: Globalization, the Backlash, and the Multinational Enterprise', *Global Strategy Journal*, Vol. 7, No. 2, pp. 159–71, https://doi.org/10.1002/gsj.1158.

Mason, R. (2016) 'David Cameron Calls for Political Courage to Seal TTIP Deal', *The Guardian*, 4 May, www.theguardian.com/business/2016/may/04/david-cameron-political-courage-ttip-trade-deal (accessed May 2016).

May, C. (2015) 'Who's in Charge? Corporations as Institutions of Global Governance', *Palgrave Communications*, Vol. 1, pp. 1–10.

Monsalve, S. (2021, September 20) 'The Corporate Capture of the UN Food Summit', *Project Syndicate*, https://www.project-syndicate.org/commentary/un-food-systems-summit-corporate-capture-by-sofia-monsalve-2021-09.

Peet, R. (2007) *Geography of Power: The Making of Global Economic Policy*, London, Zed Books.

Peet, R. (2009) *Unholy Trinity: The IMF, World Bank and WTO*, London, Zed Books.

Polanyi, K. (1944 [2001]) *The Great Transformation*, Boston, Beacon Press.

Rhodes, C. and Fleming, P. (2020) 'Forget Political Corporate Social Responsibility', *Organization*, Vol. 27, No. 6, pp. 943–51, https://doi.org/10.1177/1350508420928526.

Rodrik, D. (2019a) 'Putting Global Governance in Its Place', *World Bank Research Observer*, Vol. 35, No. 1, pp. 1–18, https://doi.org/10.1093/wbro/lkz008.

Rodrik, D. (2019b) 'Straight Talk on Trade', *Straight Talk on Trade*, https://doi.org/10.2307/j.ctvc779z4.

Ruggie, J. (1982) 'International Regimes, Transactions, and Change: Embedded Liberalism in the Postwar Economic Order', *International Organization*, Vol. 36, pp. 379–415.

Ruggie, J.G. (2018) 'Multinationals as Global Institution: Power, Authority and Relative Autonomy', *Regulation and Governance*, Vol. 12, No. 3, pp. 317–33, https://doi.org/10.1111/rego.12154.

Scherer, A.G. and Palazzo, G. (2007) 'Toward a Political Conception of Corporate Responsibility: Business and Society Seen from a Habermasian Perspective', *Academy of Management Review*, Vol. 32, No. 4, pp. 1096–120.

Scherer, A.G., Palazzo, G. and Matten, D. (2009) 'Introduction to the Special Issue: Globalization as a Challenge for Business Responsibilities', *Business Ethics Quarterly*, Vol. 19, No. 3, pp. 327–47.

Smillie, D. (2018) *Regional Trade Agreements*, https://www.worldbank.org/en/topic/regional-integration/brief/regional-trade-agreements.

Smith, C. (2021) 'From Washington Consensus to Beijing Consensus: The Chinese Belt and Road Initiative as an

Alternative Model of Development', *LSE International Development Review*, Vol. 2, No. 1, pp. 1–8.

Stiglitz, Joseph E. (2003) *Globalization and its Discontents*, New York, W.W. Norton.

Tusikov, N. (2016) *Chokepoints: Global Private Regulation on the Internet*, University of California Press.

Van Waeyenberge, E. (2010) 'Tightening the Web: The World Bank and Enforced Policy Reform', in K. Birch and V. Mykhnenko (eds), *The Rise and Fall of Neoliberalism*, London, Zed Books, pp. 94–111.

Varoufakis, Y. (2011) *The Global Minotaur: America, the True Origins of the Financial Crisis and the Future of the World Economy*, London, Zed Books.

Veldman, J. (2013) 'Politics of the Corporation', *British Journal of Management*, Vol. 24, pp. S18–S30.

Vogel, S. (1996) *Freer Markets, More Rules*, Ithaca, Cornell University Press.

Wang, A. and DeBonis, M. (2022) 'Senate Passes Bipartisan Bill to Subsidize U.S.-Made Semiconductor Chips', *The Washington Post*, 27 July, https://www.washingtonpost.com/politics/2022/07/27/senate-chips-funding-bill-pass/.

Weiss, T. (2013) *Global Governance: Why? What? Whither?*, Cambridge, Polity Press.

Whitley, R. (1999) *Divergent Capitalism*, Oxford, Oxford University Press.

Williamson, J. (1990) 'What Washington Means by Policy Reform', in J. Williamson (ed.), *Latin American Adjustment*, Washington, DC, Institute for International Economics.

Williamson, J. (1993) 'Democracy and the 'Washington Consensus'', *Critical Perspectives on International Development*, Vol. 5, pp. 56–77.

World Trade Organization. (2022) *Regional Trade Agreements*, https://www.wto.org/english/tratop_e/region_e/region_e.htm

15 | Global migration and immigrant-led business

Salewa Olawoye

Introduction

We have seen throughout this book the way in which the world's economies, cultures and populations have become increasingly interconnected. Indeed, the world has become a global village with a growing connection among people, businesses and governments. Historically, trade has been an important motive for migration. During pre-colonial and colonial periods, people moved, either voluntarily or involuntarily, from their locations of birth for economic reasons (see Chapter 3). Nowadays, migration often occurs among people in search of greener pastures (World Bank 2018). These greener pastures can be economic, academic and/or family related. Whatever reasons people have, the number of people migrating around the world has increased through the years. The 2022 United Nations World Migration Report has the number of global immigrants – defined here as first-generation immigrants – at about 281 million (McAuliffe, Lee and Abel 2021). This means that every one in thirty people around the world is an immigrant and for this one in thirty people, they have to find ways to integrate into economic, social and cultural systems that they have never been a part of before.

Because there are so many people migrating annually, the issue of immigrant integration is very important. The integration process for immigrants into their new home-away-from-home varies per immigrant and per country. Some countries have structures in place that make the integration process relatively easy for immigrants while other countries do not. A lot of immigrants who relocate for economic reasons are faced with decisions such as what career paths to take or what business to start or continue. This requires both an understanding of the economic norms in the country to which they have relocated and engagement in processes of integration. If the immigrant decides to take the business route, they must find the balance between entrepreneurial institutions and social structures in their home country and those in the host country (Griffin-EL and Olabisi 2018). With the goal of surviving, and even thriving in the host country, immigrant entrepreneurs are often required to adjust their expectations, business practices and ideologies to the social structure of the host country over time.

In this chapter we will explore the issue of global migration in general, along with the motivating factors that influence people to migrate in the first place. We then address processes of integration for immigrants to their host countries and theories on immigrant-led business. We conclude with a state-specific focus on the issues surrounding immigrant-led businesses in Canada, a country with very high levels of immigration and immigrant-led business. These issues include access to finance and adaptation to the local business structures.

Global migration: Motivation and integration

Global migration is defined as the movement of people across state borders to other countries either voluntarily or involuntarily. Voluntarily, a person moves for family (re)unification, the search for a better quality of life, academic reasons and/or economic reasons. Involuntary global migration occurs when people are forced out of their home countries due to slavery, conflicts, human trafficking, climate change, insecurity, political repression or natural disaster. The reasons for migration are often complex. For example, using the example of Korean immigrants to the United States, Light and Bonacich (1998) show how the US political, military and economic involvement in South Korea in the 1950s led to important dislocations in the South Korean political economy, which in turn induced some classes of people to migrate out of the country despite the alliance between the two states. Beyond geopolitical reasons such as those listed earlier, global migration has been influenced by factors such as inequality and advances in transportation and technology.

Inequality as motivation for migration. A major source of global migration can be attributed to the growing inequality in income and security levels between the Global North and Global South (Castles 2013). This inequality has historically arisen from issues such as imperial conquests, trade and colonialism. Conquests and colonialism were largely driven by economic factors (see Chapter 3). They impact both the societies conquered and the societies doing the conquering (Acemoglu and Robinson 2017). Not only were the natural and human resources of the colonies plundered, the colonies were made ready markets dependent on the colonial masters for finished products. During most colonial periods, there was a switch from traditional and subsistence farming (see Chapter 1) to the extraction of raw materials, which further increased the inequalities as the final goods and services imported by the colony tend to cost far more than the raw materials being exported. The inequality being created meant that those at a disadvantage would be more prone to move to advantaged areas. Also, colonialism and conquests can be likened to an uninvited guest that shows up and constantly talks about how much better their house is and the things that are missing in the host's house. This uninvited guest goes ahead to destroy things in the host's house. Eventually, the host would want to experience the 'greatness' that has been implied or expressed by the uninvited guests. As a result, the global migration that was once mostly a move from the Europe to other parts of the world has become a move from the rest of the world to Europe and other prosperous countries in the Global North.

Another major cause of inequality-led global migration is neoliberalism (see Chapters 1, 9, 16 and 17). This free-market capitalist ideology features, among other things, deregulation of industry in order to promote the free-market, privatization of state-owned properties, reduction in government spending, reduction of taxes for businesses and wealthy individuals. These measures have led to a growing inequality of wages and profits, and in society as a whole (Kotz 2009). The free-market ideology has garnered global support (see Chapters 13 and 14). It has emphasized cross-border movements and financialization that has increased profits faster than wages, thus leading to more household inequality (Bandelj, Shorette, and Sowers 2011). Because neoliberal-induced inequality has occurred both within countries and among countries, it has contributed to the increasing rate of cross-border migration. In a lot of countries, the neoliberal commitment of market economies to individual rights has in many cases aided migration (Natter 2018). Rather than a communal system geared towards a collective interest, the individualism of neoliberalism has advocated for the individual above all. If that means moving across the globe to maximize individual interest, the system has created a working environment to aid the move.

Advances in transportation and technology as drivers of migration. Technology has been a contributory force in the increase in migration primarily because of advances in transportation and communication. Migrants no longer rely upon ships or arduous overland routes to move across borders and have access to air transport. Communication has gone from paper mail to electronic mail that gets to the end of the world in seconds. Teleconferencing and applications designed for easy video calls allow loved ones to see each other even from continents apart. This has made decisions in migration easier. The technology of the world has grown from having to wait weeks on a ship in order to migrate to another country to making the same trip in hours. This has made cross-border family reunification easier as well as general migration. Similar advancement in technology has also occurred in the area of communication. While snail mail was the order of the day in the 1980s and earlier, text messages, email, social media communication tools have made communication quicker, cheaper and more efficient. This enhanced connectivity alleviates the emotional burdens such as home sickness associated with moving to a new country and may allow more opportunities for networking upon settlement (McAuliffe and Triandafyllidou 2021).

The advancement in technology has also influenced the financial sector which has in turn aided the migration process. In the world today, there is now a globally interconnected finance systems and more efficient financial systems (Bandelj, Shorette and Sowers 2011). This has made sorting out the financial obligations tied to migration easier. Remittance flows quicker through these channels and even the finances required for various migration fees around the world have become easier. Remittances are the money sent by migrant workers in host countries to individuals in their home countries for different reasons such as personal, small business and philanthropic purposes (Olawoye-Mann 2023). Global migration has become easier with technological growth (McAuliffe and Triandafyllidou 2021).

Overall, global migration has increased through the years and has contributed to society in many ways. The current neoliberal economic system has supported this migration moves and to a large extent encouraged it. With increasing levels of inequality, more people are moving in search of greener pastures, regardless of what greener pastures means to the individual. Migrants contribute to development through remittances, investment in diaspora bonds, entrepreneurship and labour force contributions (McAuliffe 2019). Advancements in technology then help to encourage migration as well as make the migration and adjustment process easier. With an increasing focus on private ownership and the ensuing effects, migration has increased. It is now not uncommon to see even global migration agencies that walk people through the migration process and sometimes offer services that help immigrants settle into their new home. There are now businesses geared towards migration, integration and all it entails. These immigration agencies/consultants register with the host country's ministry of immigration and citizenship, and familiarize themselves with up-to-date immigration laws that aid migration and settling in the host country.

The immigrant entrepreneur and theories of immigrant-led business

Immigrant integration. Migration is more than just a physical move to a new geographical area. It involves and affects every part of a person such as the economic, psychological, financial and cultural dimensions. Often migrants don't sever ties with their home countries and as a result they maintain transnational relationships (Castles 2013). This creates an identity for the immigrant that is a mixture between the cultures of their home and host countries. Useem et al. (1963) refer to immigrants that fall under this cross-cultural identity phenomenon as 'Third Culture Kids'. Also called 'Third Culture Individuals', these are people who are cultural nomads who have lived in places that are not their home country (Pollok and Van Reken 2009). These people have to go through a process of adaptation and integration into their new home country that oftentimes clashes with their home country identities. Yet, as individuals, they have to merge their home country identities with their host country identities to create an identity that helps them integrate better into their new society. Oftentimes, for immigrants to be socially included, education and sports have been used as integration tools into the new society (Carter-Thuillier et al. 2018). Regardless of the educational qualification the individual had before migrating, additional degrees, diplomas and/or certifications are used to integrate into the labour force in the host country. Immigrants may also pursue sporting activities as an inclusionary tool in their host country.

However, immigrants' movements and integration are closely tied to the social, political and economic system of the host country (Light and Bonacich 1998). While we focus on economic integration in this chapter, the social and political angles are equally important in ensuring that the immigrant's quality of life improves in their host country. A lack of social networking can make the entrepreneurial journey more difficult for the immigrant entrepreneur than the non-immigrant business owner (Graham and Pottie-Sherman 2021). So, social integration is equally as important as the economic integration because as we have seen, business is embedded within society (Chapters 1 and 2). The immigrant integrates on many levels, including engaging with social services, places of worship, transportation, housing, employment, education, training and neighbourhoods. These help the immigrant build their local networks and influence their social and civic engagement. Integration involves multiple channels, and economic integration in particular is not linear. While education and sports are routes towards inclusion in the host country, entrepreneurship is another pathway. The immigrant might take a path in entrepreneurship for many reasons. If an immigrant faces issues with transferring their educational credentials from their home country to their new country, it may encourage the immigrant to switch to entrepreneurship which does not bear educational requirements (Lofstrom 2019). Sometimes, the other paths taken in the host country such as education and sports may not work for the immigrant because of language, ability or financial resources, other times, the immigrant may start with the entrepreneurship journey because of the community they settle in or the nature of the individual. For the immigrant, this entrepreneurial journey may be solely tied to the host country, or it may be transnational. In all, the social, political and economic system prevalent in the host country is an important influence on the immigrant entrepreneur.

Theories of immigrant-led business. Different theories exist on why immigrants take the path of entrepreneurship. The two primary theories explored here deal with the social context of the immigrant businessperson. The first focuses on solidarity formed between immigrant groups who face discrimination within a new country, and the second on the desire to become socially embedded within the new country. In both cases, social inclusion and social networks are fundamentally important, which explains the growing interest of researchers in studying the power of home and host networks.

Bonacich (1973) shows how discrimination – be it based on language, ethnicity, race or other factors – and other struggles associated with integration have led to solidarity within immigrant groups. Often this solidarity takes the form of pooling of resources and joining together in economic activities, which has ultimately encouraged immigrant-led businesses (see Chapters 20 and 22). An immigrant's journey towards integration is like a race in life. The immigrant either voluntarily or involuntarily gets moved from one race track to another. On this race track, the immigrant loses familiar social connections from the initial track, then in some cases, they experience different kinds of discrimination. Each instance of discrimination or struggle becomes a hurdle in the new race track. Faced with discrimination caused by issues such as language, accent and racial barriers, it is not uncommon to see immigrants venture into entrepreneurship to survive and overcome barriers to integration. In some places, a preference is given to host country work experience. This adds an extra hurdle to the immigrant's catch-up journey. As a result, some immigrants give up on the quest to get a job and choose a different path instead – that of entrepreneurship.

The concept of social embeddedness (Granovetter 1985) underlies a second theory of immigrant entrepreneurship. Here, immigrants choose the path of entrepreneurship because it is prevalent in the community where they settle in their host country. The social relations they are exposed to in their new communities often favour entrepreneurship. With an increase in migration, immigrants go through an adjustment period that is often accompanied by a deskilling of labour due to non-transference of skills or credentials from the home country to the host country (Bauder 2003). This leads to an increase in poverty that affects other social issues such as housing, health and basic needs. This also leads to cultures of poverty in the home country and the emergence of clusters of immigrants as a collective coping mechanism, creating what are often called 'ethnic enclaves' in the host country (Achidi Ndofor and Priem 2011). The problem of deskilling often leads immigrants to turn to entrepreneurship as a viable economic alternative to their prior occupations. With an increase in entrepreneurship in the immigrant cluster, or enclave, other immigrants become influenced by the social relation of the clusters in which they belong. With shared experiences of difficulties in integration and a familiar cultural background, immigrants tend towards group solidarity. In these groups, trust and loyalty are built so much so that resources are pooled together. These pooled resources make up the key ingredients for immigrant-led businesses (Gomez et al. 2020).

Immigrant entrepreneurship: The power of a home-host network. In many countries of the Global North, such as Canada, the United States and the United Kingdom, entrepreneurship is more prevalent among immigrants than among native-born citizens (Fairlie et al. 2010, and Lofstrom 2019). Kerr and Kerr (2017) suggest some possible reasons why immigrants are drawn to entrepreneurship. The first possible reason is that the self-selection process of migration favours individuals with a great affinity to risk and uncertainty. This explains why these immigrants are able to make the decision to leave their familiar home country for the uncertainty of a host country. This affinity to risk becomes beneficial in venturing into entrepreneurship and surviving the rigours it comes with. The second possible reason is that immigrants experience different forms of social exclusion, such as language and assimilation barriers, and these lead to immigrants earning lower wages in the job market. These limiting factors influence immigrants' decisions to venture into entrepreneurship. The third possible reason given by Kerr and Kerr (2016) is the support from some immigrant groups provides a safe space for the risk-taking that is involved in business. In a lot of multicultural societies, it is not uncommon to see certain business fields being dominated by specific nationalities and or ethnic groups. This provides communal *economies of scale* for the business venture. The immigrant entrepreneurs in this situation get a cost advantage from producing and cooperating with people who they are familiar with, and are often able to negotiate for cheaper goods and services within their ethnic community.

These networks and resources within immigrant communities can be combined with networks from the host country in the immigrant's entrepreneurial journey. We have seen how the entrepreneurial journey can begin once the immigrant has moved to a new host country. But this journey can also begin before migration occurs, in which case the journey is transnational in nature. A transnational entrepreneurial journey often occurs because of the ties to business in the home country. The business and social networks the immigrants maintain with their home country make it easier to conduct bilateral and international trade than businesses of entrepreneurs from the host country (Rauch and Trindade 2002). Not only would the immigrant entrepreneurs benefit from the business and social contacts that help make the bilateral trade easier, their knowledge of their home country's culture, language and business practices aid the business. The networks for a lot of immigrants act as a catalyst for business (Rauch and Trindade 1999). These networks and linkages with their home country give the immigrant a natural propensity to internationalize their business practices and encourage more growth in business (Wang and Liu 2015). The business, social and cultural knowledge and contacts that the immigrants bring into the host country merge with the business, social and cultural knowledge and contacts the immigrants gain from the host country through integration. Together, they aid the immigrant in their transnational business. Thus, the immigrant entrepreneur gets a home country advantage in business over the non-immigrant entrepreneur.

With these advantages, entrepreneurship positively influences labour market integration in both low-skilled and high-skilled sectors. It also strengthens and helps immigrant communities in economic, social and cultural terms. Many would argue that the influences of labour market integration and stronger immigrant communities benefit the host country and the world at large. For example, the technology and engineering sectors of Silicon Valley have benefited from the contributions of immigrant entrepreneurs (Fairlie and Lofstrom 2015). As a result, these important economic contributions cannot be neglected. This has also meant that immigrant-led businesses are becoming increasingly popular in the Global North. As a result, a lot of these host countries have development policies specifically geared towards immigrant entrepreneurs such as entrepreneurship training, mentoring, help in raising startup capital, counselling and legal advice for immigrants (Desiderio 2014; OECD/European Commission 2021).

Immigrant-led business in focus: The Canadian experience.

The need to encourage global migration due to depleting work forces in much of the Global North has become a matter of global discussion over the course of the last fifty years. With an increasing rate of global migration, the size of the work force in Global North countries has been growing. In Canada, about 13.4 million workers are set to leave the labour force within the next two decades because of retirement, while the replacement population within Canada is not commensurate to the number of people retiring (McArthur-Gupta 2019). This has led Canada to embark on different programmes that encourage immigration through various paths that emphasize economic, family and humanitarian grounds. The programmes which encourage this immigration are numerous and include the federal 'Express Entry' point system used to attract skilled labour; 'provincial nomination' used by specific provinces to attract labour; the business immigration path such as the 'Start-Up Visa' Program, student visas and work visas; the refugee immigration path for immigrants seeking asylum; and the family immigration path for immediate family members of Canadian citizens and Permanent Residents. Once the immigrants get into Canada, they begin a process of integration into both Canadian society and the Canadian economy.

Like most countries dependent upon migration to sustain population growth, Canada has experienced a saturation of immigrants in her major cities and this has led to subsequent integration struggles in these areas. As a response, Canada has embarked on programmes targeted towards a more equitable distribution of immigrants to encourage immigration to smaller provinces and cities in Canada, thus encouraging an equitable spread of the new members of the labour force and aid in the economic integration of immigrants into cities with a relatively small labour supply (El-Assal 2019).

Canada, like many of the countries receiving large numbers of immigrants, has been faced with the integration of immigrants into their new home-away-from-home. As we saw earlier, there are many limitations to immigration into Canada such as the cultural regulation of labour in Canada that requires a re-education and re-certification in some fields such as law, medicine and architecture, in order to get employed in those fields within Canada (Bauder 2003). These barriers to economic integration led to a racialization of poverty (Galabuzi 2006). Some immigrants come into Canada and realize that they have limited chances in getting a professional career that is consistent with the status from their home countries. After a season of unsuccessfully applying for jobs consistent with their education and/or experience, some immigrants get frustrated and move in the path of entrepreneurship (Rahman 2018). As a result, a major source of integration for immigrants has been through entrepreneurship. In Canada, there are many policies in place to encourage entrepreneurship at the federal, provincial and local levels. The Start-up Visa Program introduced in Canada in 2017 was created to target immigrant entrepreneurs especially innovative ones that could potentially compete on a global level. Also, some universities, including Dalhousie University and Toronto Metropolitan University, have been made hubs for immigrant entrepreneurs.

With a World Bank ranking of 22 out of 190 countries in the area of doing a business, Canada's policies of low business taxes and favourable business conditions have made entrepreneurship attractive for immigrants. The added advantage of maintaining links with their home country and friendships with fellow immigrants has aided immigrants in their entrepreneurial path in Canada.

Integration through entrepreneurship is particularly important in Canada because many small business entrepreneurs are getting to the retirement stage (El-Assal and Taylor 2019). Just like the general labour force, the population within Canada is not enough to fill the void that will be left from this retirement. With a large inflow of immigrants who have the advantage of owning a network and an understanding of business that can be beneficial to Canada, immigrant-led businesses have become increasingly important. Overall, immigrant-led business has become increasingly popular in Canada with a reported 40 per cent of recent immigrants going into entrepreneurship compared to 20 per cent for Canadian-born entrepreneurs (Statistics Canada 2017 data).

Case study: The experience of immigrant entrepreneurs in British Columbia, Canada

'Keep Trying': A tale of two immigrant entrepreneurs in Penticton, BC

The following stories are derived from the reports on immigrant entrepreneurs by South-Okanagan-Similkameen Local Immigration Partnership (SOSLIP) in collaboration with Castanet and South Okanagan Immigrant and Community Services (SOICS). The goal is to highlight entrepreneurship and encourage immigrant-led businesses in the area.

'We wanted a business that our daughter could carry on and enjoy. The printing house made a perfect sense,' shares Raul Fernandez. Raul came to Canada with his then fiancée who is now his wife, Diana Molina. As an entrepreneur from Mexico, they struggled to run a successful business in Quebec because of the language barrier so they moved to Edmonton, Alberta. During the pandemic, a fellow immigrant friend had invited them to Penticton, a relatively small city in British Columbia. They loved the natural environment and moved, transferring their drafting and design company 'Flatiles Design' to Penticton. Flatiles Design is a home business that started out in the basement and grew successful enough to provide services to many schools.

Raul and Diana hope to overcome the issue of economic integration and wealth transfer by setting up this company in order to pass it on to their daughter in the future. In speaking about immigrant-led businesses, Raul advises newcomers to persevere. In his words, 'Keep trying. It's worth it. Set your goals and break them into smaller, short-term goals. This way you can achieve them one by one, and not be overwhelmed'.

Shalindra K. C. migrated with his wife Laxmi to Canada from Dubai, where they had lived for eight years. He is originally from Nepal. He had worked in retail in Dubai and came into Canada through an immigration consultant who promised him a retail job that would help him secure his permanent residency. He landed in Vancouver in April 2013 and discovered that the promises by the immigration consultant were false.

After two months of joblessness, he moved to a less populated city Yellowknife, in the Northwest Territories, to train for four months, then to Surrey, BC, for a two-month training. After a period of struggling to integrate into the society, Shalindra now works as a 7/11 store manager while at the same time owning his own financial business, a franchise of the Experior Financial Group. Here, Shalindra offers a range of financial services, which include life, disability, critical illness and travel insurances, health and dental coverage, as well as various kinds of saving plans and investments. His goal for business is generational wealth transfer. In his words, 'It is also about building your legacy. Whatever money and business I have, I can transfer to my next generation – my son.'

In his interview, Shalindra advises newcomers to learn how various systems work before moving to Canada. He also stressed the need for an immigrant community. According to him, 'Don't think that you will come to Canada and do a certain job. Do your research – find out what kind of education and skills you need for this job. You might need a licence for your profession. Research about the financial situation – taxes and other costs. Learn about the health and education systems. These services are not completely free. Most importantly, create a circle of friends and join community groups, such as South Okanagan Immigrant and Community Services. They helped us a lot. I got my Food Safe, first aid and Serving It Right certificates there. I also attended the Toastmasters program that helped me with my public speaking skills. My wife learned English there. We met many people and developed friendships.'

Source: Castanet.net

Access to finance for immigrant entrepreneurs in Canada. Access to finance is a very important part of the entrepreneurship journey for new and growing businesses. It is usually one of the biggest constraints for the new entrepreneur and a determinant in the success of the business. There are two main types of financing: formal and informal. Formally, securing financing for entrepreneurship is done in several ways, such as self-funding, angel financing, loans from a financial institution, securing venture capital, private funds from private equity firms, and from external investors in the form of Initial Public Offerings (IPOs) (Owers and Sergi 2019). Informal financing is done through savings, friends and family. In many cases, new businesses face difficulties in obtaining formal finance, which affects their level of commercialization. Obtaining credit from financial institutions may sometimes prove difficult for small business owners that do not meet the requirement of obtaining loans (see Chapters 20 and 22). This is even more difficult for new immigrants who have had to transplant themselves in a new country. The new immigrants' insufficient credit history tends to make obtaining external finance more difficult. They may also have insufficient collateral needed for the loans. As a result, the already difficult process of access to external credit for entrepreneurs is even more challenging for immigrant entrepreneurs.

A major source of capital for the immigrant in business is personal savings. With personal savings as a major contributory source for the immigrant going into business, other sources include loans from financial institutions and family and friends. Immigrants largely depend on their personal savings from work and from their liquidized assets of pre-migration in order to raise capital for their businesses. Another related source of capital for immigrant-led businesses, even in Canada, is through indigenous methods of saving within informal solidarity networks (Stoesz et al. 2016).

In a recent study of Nigerian immigrant entrepreneurs in Canada, yet another source of capital for businesses was highlighted. The social banking system is called *Ajo,* and is used to raise capital for businesses that range from restaurant businesses to car dealership (Olawoye-Mann 2023). This *Ajo* system of social banking is a rotating savings and credit association (see Chapters 20 and 22). Among immigrant entrepreneurs, it has proven to be an effective savings strategy for raising a pool of capital for immigrant-led business. This is a cheaper option for the new immigrant that has not built sufficient credit and would not have access to loans from a bank. If they were to manage to get a loan from a financial institution, the interest rates would be quite high because the lender does not have sufficient credit information on the immigrant and increases the rate to offset the perceived risk. Unfortunately, in the expansion of the immigrant-led business, if more financing is sought, immigrants often turn to costly debt financing when personal and family bailouts are not available (Ostrovsky et al. 2019).

Since entrepreneurship is important to economic growth within most economies, the difficulty in accessing finance for entrepreneurship has become an important issue for policymakers around the world (Kerr and Nanda 2011). It has not only been left to individuals and financial institutions. The Canadian government has played a vital role in supplying finance for entrepreneurship. Various government grants, subsidies and loans are available for entrepreneurs, including immigrant entrepreneurs. However, research shows that immigrant entrepreneurs are still less likely to turn to government financing than Canadian-born entrepreneurs (Ostrovsky et al. 2019), so further work on outreach may be required in future policymaking endeavours.

Conclusion

Immigration has become so widespread through the years and issues relating to it have been up for debate in the academic and policy world. With an interconnected world, people are constantly moving from their home country to another country in search of greener pastures. However, these movements are not always seamless and an adjustment period is usually required. This adjustment may include immediate entrepreneurship or entrepreneurship after an unsuccessful stint in the job market. Regardless of the beginning of the immigrant's journey into entrepreneurship, this chapter highlights some of the issues the immigrant faces with integration and entrepreneurship in the host country. The immigrant experience is non-linear so a proper understanding of the social, economic and political structure of the host country goes a long way in helping the immigrant entrepreneur survive and thrive in their host country. The immigrant's host country and home country network also help the immigrant entrepreneur. Overall, with the increasing rate of global migration, it has become important to study the experiences of immigrants in settling in the host country. In understanding the immigrants' experiences in integrating into the host country, immigrant entrepreneurship is a vital part of the discussion as the hurdles in the path of the immigrant entrepreneur require a strong network and a proper understanding of the social, economic and political structure prevalent in not just their home country but also in their host country.

Suggested readings

- Ch. 5, Haltiwanger, J., Hurst, E., Miranda, J. and Schoar, A. (eds). (2017). *Measuring Entrepreneurial Businesses: Current Knowledge and Challenges*, Chicago, The University of Chicago Press.
- Chs 1, 2, 7 and 8, Borjas, G. J. (2014). *Immigration Economics*, Cambridge, MA: Harvard University Press.

References

Acemoglu, D. and Robinson, J.A. (2017) 'The Economic Impact of Colonialism', in S. Michalopoulous and E. Papaioannou (ed.), *The Long Economic and Political Shadow of History Volume I. A Global View*, pp. 81, Centre for Economic Policy Research.

Achidi Ndofor, H. and Priem, R.L. (2011) 'Immigrant Entrepreneurs, the Ethnic Enclave Strategy, and Venture Performance', *Journal of Management,* Vol. 37, No. 3, pp. 790–818, https://doi .org/10.1177/0149206309345020.

Bauder, H. (2003) '"Brain Abuse", or the Devaluation of Immigrant Labour in Canada', *Antipode*, Vol. 35, No. 4, pp. 699–717.

Bandelj, N., Shorette, K. and Sowers, E. (2011) 'Work and Neoliberal Globalization: A Polanyian Synthesis', *Sociology Compass*, Vol. 5, No. 9, pp. 807–23.

Bonacich, E. (1973) 'A Theory of Middleman Minorities', *American Sociological Review*, Vol. 38, pp. 583–94, http://dx.doi.org/10.2307/2094409.

Carter-Thuillier, B., López-Pastor, V., Gallardo-Fuentes, F. and Carter-Beltran, J. (2018) 'Immigration and Social Inclusion: Possibilities from School and Sports', *Immigration and Development*, pp. 57–74.

Castles, S. (2013) 'The Forces Driving Global Migration', *Journal of Intercultural Studies*, Vol. 34, No. 2, pp. 122–40.

Desiderio, M.V. (2014) *Policies to Support Immigrant Entrepreneurship*, Washington, DC, Migration Policy Institute.

El-Assal, K. (2019) 'Immigration beyond the GTA: Toward an Ontario Immigration Strategy', Conference Board of Canada, www .conferenceboard.ca/e-library/abstract .aspx?did=10342.

El-Assal, K. and Taylor, S.R. (2019) *Turning the Corner: Improving Canadian Business Immigration*, Ottawa, Conference Board of Canada, www. conferenceboard. ca/e-Library/abstract .aspx.

Fairlie, R.W. and Lofstrom, M. (2015) 'Immigration and Entrepreneurship', in B. Chiswick and P. Miller (ed.), *Handbook of the Economics of International Migration*, No. 1, North-Holland, pp. 877–911.

Fairlie, R.W., Zissimopoulos, J. and Krashinsky, H. (2010) 'The International Asian Business Success Story? A Comparison of Chinese, Indian and Other Asian Businesses in the United States, Canada and United Kingdom', in *International Differences in Entrepreneurship*, University of Chicago Press, pp. 179–208.

Galabuzi, G.-E. (2006) *Canada's Economic Apartheid: The Social Exclusion of Racialized Groups in the New Century*, Toronto, Canadian Scholars Press Inc.

Gomez, C., Perera, B.Y., Wesinger, J.Y. and Tobey, D.H. (2020) 'Immigrant Entrepreneurs and Community Social Capital: An Exploration of Motivations and Agency', *Journal of Small Business and Enterprise Development*, Vol. 27, No. 4, pp. 579–605.

Graham, N. and Pottie-Sherman, Y. (2021) 'The Experiences of Immigrant Entrepreneurs in a Medium-Sized Canadian City: The Case of St. John's, Newfoundland and Labrador, Canada', *The Canadian Geographer/Le Géographe canadien*, Vol. 65, No. 2, pp. 184–96.

Granovetter, M. (1985) 'Economic action and social structure: The problem of embeddedness', American journal of sociology, Vol. 91, No. 3, pp. 481–510.

Griffin-EL, E.W. and Olabisi, J. (2018) 'Breaking Boundaries: Exploring the Process of Intersective Market Activity of Immigrant Entrepreneurship in the Context of High Economic Inequality', *Journal of Management Studies*, Vol. 55, No. 3, pp. 457–85.

Kerr, S.P. and Kerr, W.R. (2017) 'Immigrant Entrepreneurship', in J. Haltiwanger, E. Hurst, J. Miranda, and A. Schoar (eds.), *Measuring Entrepreneurial Businesses: Current Knowledge and Challenges*, Chicago, IL, University of Chicago Press, pp. 187–249.

Kerr, W.R. and Nanda, R. (2011) 'Financing Constraints and Entrepreneurship', in *Handbook of Research on Innovation and Entrepreneurship*, Cheltenham, Elgar, pp. 88–103.

Kotz, D.M. (2009) 'The Financial and Economic Crisis of 2008: A Systemic Crisis of Neoliberal Capitalism', *Review of Radical Political Economics*, Vol. 41, No. 3, pp. 305–17.

Light, I. and Bonacich, E. (1988) *Immigrant Entrepreneurs: Koreans in Los Angeles 1965–1982*, Berkeley and Los Angeles, University of California Press.

Lofstrom, M.W. (2019) *Immigrants and Entrepreneurship*, Germany, IZA World of Labor.

McArthur-Gupta, A., El-Assal, K. and Bajwa, A. (2019) 'Can't Go It Alone: Immigration is Key to Canada's Growth Strategy', in *Conference Board of Canada*, Ottawa, ON.

McAuliffe, M., Abel, G. Oucho, L., and Sawyer, A. (2022 '7) International Migration as a Stepladder of Opportunity: What do the Global Data Actually Show?', *World Migration Report*, 2022(1), e00028.

McAuliffe, M., Kitimbo, A. and Khadria, B. (2019, November) 'Reflecting on Migrants' Contributions in an Era of Increasing Disruption and Disinformation', in *International Metropolis/Pathways to Prosperity Conference*, Toronto, ON.

McAuliffe, M., Triandafyllidou, A. (2022) 'Migration Research and Analysis: Recent United Nations Contributions', *World Migration Report*, 2022(1), e00025.

Natter, K. (2018) 'Rethinking Immigration Policy Theory beyond "Western Liberal Democracies"', *Comparative Migration Studies*, Vol. 6, No. 4, pp. 1–21.

OECD/European Commission. (2021) *The Missing Entrepreneurs 2021: Policies for Inclusive Entrepreneurship and Self-Employment*, Paris, OECD Publishing.

Olawoye-Mann, S. (2023a) 'Remittances', in L.P. Rochon and S. Rossi (eds.), *The Encyclopedia of Post-Keynesian Economics*, Edward Elgar, pp. 357–8.

Olawoye-Mann, S. (2023b) 'Beyond Coping: The Use of Ajo Culture among Nigerian Immigrants in Countering Racial Capitalism in North America', in C. Hossein, S. Wright-Austin, and K. Edmonds (eds.), *Beyond Racial Capitalism: Co-operatives in African Diaspora*, Oxford University Press.

Ostrovsky, Y., Picot, G. and Leung, D. (2019) 'The Financing of Immigrant-Owned Firms in Canada', *Small Business Economics*, Vol. 52, No. 1, pp. 303–17.

Owers, J.E. and Sergi, B.S. (2019) *The evolution of financing entrepreneurship. In Entrepreneurship and Development in the 21st Century*, Emerald Publishing Limited.

Picot, G., and Rollin, A.M. (2019) *Immigrant entrepreneurs as job creators: the case of Canadian private incorporated companies* (No. 2019011e). Statistics Canada, Analytical Studies Branch.

Pollock, D.C. and Van Reken, R.E. (2009) *Third Culture Kids: Growing Up Among Worlds* (3rd Edition), Boston, Nicholas Brealey.

Rahman, M.M. (2018) 'Development of Bangladeshi Immigrant Entrepreneurship in Canada', *Asian and Pacific Migration Journal*, Vol. 27, No. 4, pp. 404–30.

Rauch, J.E. (1999) 'Networks versus Markets in International Trade', *Journal of International Economics*, Vol. 48, No. 1, pp. 7–35.

Rauch, J.E. and Trindade, V. (2002) 'Ethnic Chinese Networks in International Trade', *Review of Economics and Statistics*, Vol. 84, No. 1, pp. 116–30.

Stoesz, D., Gutau, I. and Rodreiguez, R. (2016) 'Susu: Capitalizing Development from the Bottom Up', *Journal of Sociology & Social Welfare*, Vol. 43, No. 3, p. 121.

Useem, J., Useem, R. and Donoghue, J. (1963) 'Men in the Middle of the Third Culture: The Roles of American and Non-Western People in Cross-cultural Administration', *Human Organization*, Vol. 22, No. 3, pp. 169–79.

Wang, Q. and Liu, C. Y. (2015) 'Transnational activities of immigrant-owned firms and their performances in the USA', *Small Business Economics*, Vol. 44, pp. 345–59.

World Bank. (2018) *Moving for Prosperity: Global Migration and Labor Markets*, Washington, DC, The World Bank.

16 | Global environmental change

Kean Birch

Introduction

We often have a very romantic notion of nature, associating it with images of forests, mountains, streams and the wildlife that inhabit these places. Our understanding of nature is not only romantic, however, it also involves a series of assumptions about what it means to be 'natural' and – as importantly – what it means to be 'unnatural'. For example, forests are natural, but plastic is not; moose are natural, but cars are not; and humans are natural, but also not at the same time. The reason we have such a complex relationship with nature and the environment is because nature itself – and what it means to be natural – is constituted by a diverse set of human practices and knowledges ranging from the findings of scientific research through cultural representations of nature in film and other media to the organization of business within capitalism. This has led a number of scholars to argue that, in a very real sense, our imaginations and our socio-economic practices actively shape nature and the natural world, not only in our minds but also in reality (e.g. Smith 1984 [2008]; Whatmore 2002; Moore 2015). Thus, they argue that humans are both products of nature and the producers of nature.

This impact of humans on the environment – which we define, for simplicity's sake, as the world's biosphere – has been well documented over the last few decades, but awareness of our human imprint on the world and the implications this has for our livelihoods and survival has a much longer history. In fact, it's possible to identify environmental movements as far back as the nineteenth century, when various peoples and groups sought to highlight the damaging impacts of industrialization on society. Examples include the romantic poets like William Wordsworth, Lord Byron and Percy Bysshe Shelley at the end of the eighteenth century and start of the nineteenth century; the Sierra Club established in 1892 in the United States; and the Garden City movement that sprang up at the start of the twentieth century in countries like the UK. The modern environmental movement, though, emerged in the 1960s and 1970s as a response to a range of environmental issues and crises like chemical pollution, oil spills, anti-whaling campaigns, toxic waste, biodiversity loss and animal extinctions (Millington and Pickerill 2005). One particular driving force was concerns about the 'limits to growth' – the title of an influential report in 1972 – and the impact of continuous economic growth on the natural world.

More recently, these varied concerns have transformed into a focus on how human actions have had far-reaching and intergenerational environmental impacts, leading many thinkers to start calling our current era the Anthropocene – or, 'age of humans' (Castree 2014; Haraway 2015; Bonneuil and Fressoz 2017). The Anthropocene is especially characterized by the impacts of human activity on the world's climate. As a result of these impacts, one of the key global challenges facing us today is how to mitigate (i.e. stop) and adapt to (i.e. live with) anthropogenic climate change, especially the significant shifts in global and local temperatures (e.g. warmer winters, colder summers), increasingly violent weather events (e.g. hurricanes, floods, storms, forest fires), melting ice caps and permafrost and so on. How we deal with climate change and its impacts is shaped by the assumptions we have about the environment: this is not only in terms of romanticized visions of a pristine, untouched nature, but also in terms of how nature is treated by governments and businesses as both a private resource and a common dumping ground for pollution and waste. In this chapter, we emphasize that capitalism in particular has created the environmental problems with us today and, yet, remains the primary solution considered by world leaders. It's important, in light of this contradiction, to consider what other perspectives we might bring to bear to resolve these issues.

> **Definition: Anthropogenic climate change**
>
> According to the UN Environmental Programme, anthropogenic climate change results from the release of greenhouse gas (GHG) emissions, especially carbon dioxide (CO_2), from human activity like the burning of fossil fuels (e.g. coal, oil, natural gas). Climate change is caused by the emission of GHGs *and* their concentration in the atmosphere. By 2021, the world passed 414 parts per million (ppm) of CO_2 in the atmosphere. According to the Intergovernmental Panel on Climate Change (IPCC), global temperatures have already increased by 1.1 degrees Celsius since the late 1800s and will rise an estimated 3 degrees Centigrade by 2100 if current GHGs emissions continue.

We cover several issues in this chapter relating to global environmental change. First, we look at mainstream perspectives on the environment, pollution, limits to economic growth and concepts of sustainable development. We also outline the main ways that capitalist businesses seek to resolve environmental problems. Second, we present a critical approach to understanding the environment called *political ecology*, which incorporates notions of environmental justice and political-economic change to challenge prevailing and dominant business solutions. Third, we outline climate change as an empirical example of a global environmental crisis, one which has become a seemingly intractable political and policy problem.

Key discussion questions

- What is nature? What is natural?
- How does business cause and seek to solve environmental problems?
- What are the other solutions to these environmental problems?
- Why is climate change a seemingly intractable problem?

Mainstream perspectives

What is the environment? What are its limits? The natural environment can be defined technically as the world's biosphere, its biomes and its diverse and varied ecosystems. The biosphere comprises three interconnected parts: the atmosphere, which is the air cover around the Earth; the hydrosphere, which is the surface-level (e.g. oceans) and below surface waters (e.g. aquifers); and the lithosphere, which is the upper levels of the Earth's crust and includes the soil, plants and animals. Within the lithosphere there are a number of different biomes; these are the plants and animals that inhabit distinct areas of the Earth's surface (e.g. desert, grassland, rainforest). Within the biomes there are smaller ecosystems of interacting, self-regulating animal and plant populations adapted to specific local climates, topographies and so on (Robbins et al. 2010). As we've mentioned already, this technical definition obscures the human shaping of the environment through economic actions and decisions leading to pollution, waste production, biodiversity loss, climate change and so on. According to Barry Commoner (1971), there are four laws of ecology that humans cannot escape, no matter what they do to the environment.

Key thinker: Barry Commoner and the 'four laws of ecology'

Barry Commoner was an influential US biologist who came up with four laws of ecology that define the limits of human actions on the environment. First, the biosphere (i.e. world) is a system in which 'everything is connected to everything else'; second, if everything is linked then 'everything must go somewhere', which means waste does not simply disappear; third, 'nature knows best', so any attempts to change the environment simply leads to unforeseen problems; and finally, 'there is no such thing as a free lunch' since the use of natural resources will turn them into useless waste by-products.

Source: Commoner (1971)

Mainstream approaches to the environment are often dominated by the assumption that the natural world exists for humans to exploit and use as we see fit and with little regard for the consequences. John Bellamy Foster (2002) argues that this assumption is particularly strong in Western cultures (e.g. North America, Western Europe) and stretches back several centuries.

The reason that environmental change causes such concern in mainstream circles is because the Earth's resources are seen as scarce – because they are finite – while human population is seen as growing considerably in a very short period of time, in geological timescales at least. For example, a hundred years ago the world's population was below 2 billion people, and yet there now are over 7 billion people on the planet, all of whom need resources to survive (e.g. food, housing, water, tools, energy). Concerns with population growth go back hundreds of years.

In the early nineteenth century an Anglican priest from Britain called Thomas Malthus argued that countries like Britain simply could not sustain the massive rise in population that followed industrialization; in his view, the world was overpopulated and this would lead to famines, poverty, disease and wars as humans fought over the finite resources (Robbins et al. 2010). While Malthus' views have been disproved by subsequent events, such as the huge growth in the world's population, it still holds a strong popular and political appeal for its simplicity – that is, environmental problems result from too many people chasing too few resources and producing increasing levels of pollution and waste. This appeal is still evident in the revival of environmentalism and its global spread since the 1960s and 1970s.

More recent environmental awareness and campaigns have led to growing international concern with global environmental change. The global environment has become a major focus of international policy debate and intervention over the last few decades (see Table 16.1), especially around the issue of climate change (see example). It's important to note, however, that international action is not always successful.

A major driver behind these international efforts are longstanding fears about the limits of the natural world. For example, in 1972 the Club of Rome, a global think tank, produced an influential report called *Limits to Growth* in which they set out the physical limits of continuing economic growth. The report's conclusions were that 'resource scarcities would push prices up and slow down the possibilities for future growth' and that 'the resource base itself would collapse' (Jackson 2009: 7). Similar concerns motivated the establishment of the World Commission on Environment and Development by the UN in 1983. This Commission produced a report called *Our Common Future* in 1987 – more commonly known as the *Brundtland Report* – in which they set out to define 'sustainable development' in an attempt to make capitalism and environmental sustainability compatible with one another. And, finally, these concerns have inspired a range of thinkers to promote a more radical notion of 'degrowth' as an alternative to unbridled capitalism; this degrowth

TABLE 16.1 Timeline of Major Global Environmental Events and Agreements

Date	Events and agreements
1968	UNESCO Biosphere Conference
1972	UN Conference on the Human Environment *Limits to Growth* report published by Club of Rome
1980	IUCN launches World Conservation Strategy
1987	*Our Common Future* report (aka *Brundtland Report*) published by World Commission on Environment and Development
1992	Rio Summit on Environment and Development UN Framework Convention for Climate Change (UNFCCC) created
1997	Kyoto Protocols established
2000	UN launches Millennium Development Goals
2002	World Summit on Sustainable Development
2009	Copenhagen UNFCCC Conference of the Parties (COP)
2011	Canada withdraws from the Kyoto Protocols
2015	UN Sustainable Development Goals established
2021	Paris UNFCCC COP
2022	Glasgow UNFCCC COP (postponed from 2020 due to Covid) IPCC Sixth Assessment Report Released

Source: Adapted and updated from Millington and Pickerill (2005: 156)

movement has become increasingly important in recent years (see Kallis 2018). Here, degrowth does not mean economic stagnation or contraction but, rather, an attempt to find new ways to allocate and share the world's resources more equitably (see also Chapter 24).

Key methodological issue: Defining 'sustainable development'

Sustainable development is a contested term introduced by the *Brundtland Report* in 1987. It's a concept that seeks to combine the notion of (environmental) sustainability – that is, the idea that human actions should not negatively impact the environment – with economic growth under capitalist relations. It was defined as: 'development which meets the needs of the present without compromising the ability of future generations to meet their needs'. It has been criticized as too vague and compromised by its association with business and capitalism. It's, therefore, very difficult to identify and discuss sustainable development, especially from different conceptual perspectives.

Source: Millington and Pickerill (2005: 158)

Solving environmental problems with capitalism. Now, it's notable that the Anthropocene is not simply about the general impact of humans on nature (and vice versa), especially where this assumes these impacts result from overpopulation. It's about the specific impact of capitalism on nature and what this means for the environment (Smith 1984 [2008]). Some people prefer the term 'Capitalocene' to highlight the specific role of capitalism in environmental degradation (see Moore 2016). A good way to illustrate this impact is through the concept of 'the commons' (Ostrom 1990) – see Chapters 1 and 18 for more discussion of the commons. We can define nature and the environment as part of the commons; this means it's something held in common by all peoples, since no-one created it, and it has certain characteristics that 'make it difficult to fully enclose and partition, making it possible for non-owners to enjoy resource benefits and owners to sustain costs from the actions of others' (Robbins et al. 2010: 52). Capitalism entails certain logics, processes and practices that erode the commons, meaning that our common environmental heritage faces particular pressures to adjust to capitalist imperatives. For example, since anyone can use the commons (e.g. graze common land) without cost, this means that some people can exploit the commons (e.g. over-graze common land) without anyone else being able to stop them. This leads to something Garrett Hardin (1968) called 'the tragedy of the commons' (Chapter 6). Hardin argued that it's in the interest of each person to use as much of the common resource as they can for their own benefit, leading ultimately to the destruction of that common resource as everyone over-uses the resource.

These ideas, that there are limits to growth and numerous tragedies of the commons, have provided theoretical and normative support for the claim that capitalist markets and business are best able to provide solutions to various environmental problems (Moore 2015). Despite some *mea culpas* about the problems caused by markets – see the book *Value(s)* by the ex-governor of the Bank of England Mark Carney (2021) – neoclassical economists still argue that markets can *and* should be used to resolve environmental problems because they're the most efficient way to price and value the cost of environmental deterioration, degradation and destruction (Dasgupta 2021). This has been described as 'market environmentalism' by a number of scholars (see Bailey 2007). The starting point for solving environmental problems with markets and business is understanding why there are environmental problems in the first place. For neoclassical economists and their ilk, this requires an understanding of *externalities* as examples of market failure – see the *Dasgupta Report* produced by the UK's Treasury as an important recent example of this perspective (Dasgupta 2021). Closely related to the tragedy of the commons, an externality is the effect of economic activity on everyone not directly involved in that activity – an example is the pollution or waste from factories. Neoclassical economists argue that environmental problems are simply externalities that can and should be incorporated into capitalist relations through a range of market and business solutions we outline later.

Definition: Externalities

An externality is the negative or positive impact of an economic activity that affects someone who is not directly involved in or benefiting from the economic activity. The classic example of an externality is pollution from a factory since everyone living near the factory suffers from the pollution but may not benefit from the factory or its production of goods.

Definition: Market failure

The notion of market failure is very specific to how neoclassical economics defines economic activity. It does not mean, despite first impressions, that a market has failed; rather, it means that a market has not been instituted, or has not spontaneously emerged.

This form of environmentalism involves promoting three main market and business solutions to environmental problems, all of which are based on neoclassical economic assumptions (Leonard 2010). These include privatization, commodification and marketization. We critique these three solutions in the next section, but for now we simply define them as the following:

- *Privatization*: this process involves turning the environment and natural resources into private property through changes to the law and regulations. The rationale behind this process is the assumption that only private owners (e.g. business) have an incentive to protect their property because it's valuable to them.
- *Commodification*: this process involves creating commodities out of the environment for sale or new technologies to improve resource efficiencies. The rationale here is the assumption that profit motivates everyone and that the market will efficiently determine how much everyone values the environment through their purchasing choices, and this will drive innovations to solve environmental problems.
- *Marketization*: this process involves the creation of new markets to achieve environmental goals (e.g. reducing greenhouse gas emissions). It's based on the assumption that markets are the most efficient mechanism to achieve these goals because markets promote new ideas and products through competitive pressures.

What these three processes illustrate is that the emphasis on the market and business as the determinants of the price of natural resources ignores the environmental costs of the human activities required to extract and process these resources – for example pollution, biodiversity loss, deforestation and so on (Robbins et al. 2010). Further, while climate change is creating an increasing array of problems for our lives, it has been very difficult to coordinate collective action across diverse social and political groups who often have differing perceptions of its importance and impacts. Some degree of collective action is being stimulated through the actions and decisions of certain financial institutions (e.g. banks, insurance companies) that are coming around to the view that climate change will impact their bottom line by destroying the financial assets borrowers use as collateral (e.g. fossil fuel reserves, housing). For more on this, see the case study on the Taskforce on Climate-Related Financial Disclosures. A number of scholars argue, quite forcefully, that this sort of market-based approach to solving climate change and its effects is unlikely, however, to succeed without a significant shift in the way we manage environmental resources (Webber et al. 2022). Further, relying on the financial bottom line to motivate climate action is neither democratic nor dependable as global markets fluctuate in the wake of wars and other crises (see Chapter 17). As Elinor Ostrom (1990) argued, we don't have to rely on markets or business since there are actually many different ways to govern our environments and environmental resources, including through cooperatives, community organizations and trade unions (see Chapters 6 and 22).

Case study

Taskforce on Climate-Related Financial Disclosures

In 2015, the Taskforce on Climate-Related Financial Disclosures (TCFD) was established by the Financial Stability Board (FSB), chaired by the then-governor of the Bank of England, Mark Carney. The FSB is an international financial institution set up to coordinate the work of central banks and standards agencies in developing international regulations and oversight of the financial sector after the global financial crisis.

The TCFD itself has been developing a range of disclosure metrics, standards and mechanisms that can be used by businesses, investors and governments to assess the risk of climate change to business and investment activities. Financial disclosures are a key part of this process since they are meant to reveal to investors exactly how exposed a business is to climate change impacts. For example, insurance companies would have to reveal the financial impacts of flooding on their business, where this might be increasing significantly over time as major flood events become more common.

The TCFD has released a series of recommendations since 2015. As noted, these are meant to be used by businesses to determine when they need to disclose climate risks to their investors, which are then meant to motivate investors to push businesses to change their activities. Recommendations are meant to be adoptable by a range of businesses, included in financial reports, focus on future financial impacts and outline risks and opportunities of transitioning to a low-carbon future.

The aim of the TCFD is to harness financial reporting metrics, procedures, processes and, ultimately, logics to drive businesses to change their practices to become more sustainable and less environmentally destructive. Whether this financialized approach (see Chapter 11) will succeed is a hotly debated topic right now.

Source: https://www.fsb-tcfd.org/

Critical perspectives

Environmental justice and political ecology. Like most scholarly debates, we can approach global environmental change from several different and distinct theoretical standpoints. For example, it's possible to conceptualize something like sustainable development on a continuum from *weak* sustainability to *strong* sustainability (Hopwood et al. 2005), where the former reflects a more business- and technology-centred view of the world and the latter a more egalitarian- and ecological-centred one. Where people sit on the continuum reflects not only their attitude to nature and the use of natural resources, but it also reflects their attitude to issues of social justice, equality, redistribution and forms of social action (see Table 16.2). For example, who benefit from the extraction of natural resources and suffer from the resulting waste from production processes are ecological and socio-economic issues, not one or the other. They reflect an important

TABLE 16.2 Two Views of Sustainability

Characteristics	Weak sustainability	Strong sustainability
Capitalism	Can solve environmental problems through markets	Causes environmental and socio-economic inequality and injustice
Technology	Provides solutions to problems	Cause of problems as much as solution
Nature	Nature as resources for human use (scarcity)	Inherent value in nature and ecological systems
Social justice	Largely irrelevant	Entwined with environmental problems
Social action	Market-based, individual consumer choice	Collective, democratic decision-making
Examples	Green capitalism (e.g. 'green' goods)	Deep ecology

Source: Adapted from Hopwood et al. (2005)

distinction between environmental problems that involve the *over-use* of natural resources and those that involve the over-burdening of ecological systems, or *sinks*, with waste outputs (Dicken 2011). Over-use by one group of people deprives others of access to that resource, while over-burdening the environment with pollution and waste always entails decisions about where those negative outputs go and which groups will be most impacted. Understanding these human-environment interactions is critical for understanding environmental justice and injustice.

Our aim here is to outline and illustrate one alternative approach that is critical of neoclassical economics and the solutions business and economists propose to solve environmental problems – as outlined in the previous section. The approach we discuss is called *political ecology* and it seeks to combine insights from political economy – see the Introduction – with 'an understanding that nature and society are produced *together* in a political economy that includes humans and non-humans' (Robbins et al. 2010: 6). What this means is that to understand the environment involves understanding (1) human socio-economic relations, systems, processes, practices, knowledge claims and so forth – especially those related to business – *and* (2) ecological processes, systems, forces and so on. The main strength of the political ecology approach is that it enables us to analyse the relationship between global environmental change and socio-economic change, especially where this raises normative questions about who *is* and who *should be* most affected by environmental problems and who is and who should contribute most to their resolution. Political ecology, therefore, provides a powerful tool to critique the claims of neoclassical economists when it comes to finding solutions to environmental problems, as we illustrate later.

Rethinking environmental problems. At the end of the previous section we identified three ways that the markets and business seek to resolve environmental problems. From a political ecology perspective, these solutions are deeply problematic for the following reasons:

- *Privatization*: this implies that there can and should be no commons, and that environmental protection depends upon turning *all* of nature into private property.
- *Commodification*: this depends on finding techno-fixes to turn nature into commodities (e.g. how do we commodify a beautiful landscape?) or to improve resource efficiencies; the latter is subject to something called Jevons' Paradox.
- *Marketization*: the creation of markets leads to the fragmentation of responses to environmental problems since it's left to individual businesses and consumers to drive change.

Definition: Techno-fix

This is another common assumption. Namely, that humans will solve all environmental problems through the development of new technologies. It's problematic because it promotes the idea that we don't have to change our behaviour or actions as there will always be a technological solution to any problems we create if we wait long enough. In that sense, it promotes the continued expansion of resource usage.

Definition: Jevon's paradox

This describes the fact that increasing the relative efficient use of resources leads to an increase in the absolute use of that resource since it becomes cheaper to use the resource. For example, increasing the oil efficiency of cars means that more cars can be built because they use less petroleum, thereby leading to an overall increase in the consumption of oil.

First, transforming the environmental commons into private property involves changing laws and regulations in a country and/or globally; we want to emphasize that it's not an automatic or spontaneous process that magically happens when capitalist markets are unleashed. Even though our socio-natural environments are products of human action, we don't create the biosphere, which is a shared common good; consequently, it can be considered an example of what Karl Polanyi calls a *fictitious commodity* – see Chapters 1 and 2. This is an important point because the transfer of an environmental common good provides a private individual or business with access to a 'cheap' input into their production or consumption process: this could be cheap labour, cheap resources or cheap energy (Moore 2015; Patel and Moore 2017). They're considered cheap because the individual or business doesn't have to pay for the social (or other) costs of degrading or destroying the environment. Two things are important to note here:

- Privatization is legitimated by a range of theories and claims, including Garrett Hardin's notion of the tragedy of the commons mentioned earlier; and
- Nature has to be *turned into* a resource since resources are social categories, not natural ones: as Bridge (2009) argues, resources are 'a primary social category through which we organize our relationships with the non-human world'.

From a political ecology perspective, then, this means that we have to examine how the state turns nature into a resource and property, how it assigns

TABLE 16.3 Classifying Resources

Non-renewable/stock			Renewable/flow	
Consumed in use	Recoverable	Recyclable	Critical zone	Non-critical zone
Oil	All minerals	Metallic minerals	Fish	Solar energy
Natural gas			Forests	Tides, waves, wind
Coal			Soil	
			Water in aquifers	Water
				Air

Source: Adapted from Bradshaw (2008)

or sells that resource and how different resources entail different processes of privatization because of their different biophysical characteristics (see Table 16.3). Taken to the extreme, privatization implies the total conversion of nature into private property, which raises serious concerns about the potential for it to inflate conflicts over resource use between countries and between social groups.

Second, mainstream approaches to environmental problems have gradually incorporated a wider range of factors in their models since the 1970s, moving away from a simple focus on population growth and resource use. For example, in the 1970s the ecologist Paul R. Ehrlich and others came up with something called the IPAT formula (Jackson 2009). This formula seeks to explain environmental problems as the outcome of three interacting elements:

I (environmental impacts) = P (population) × A (affluence, or consumption) × T (technology)

The IPAT formula avoids the assumption that population drives environmental problems and highlights the role of consumption and technology – or what can be defined as the commodification or assetization of nature (Castree 2003; Birch and Muniesa 2020). It's important to incorporate these consumption and technology variables because different countries consume different amounts of resources and create different technologies. From a political ecology perspective, consumption levels and technology can simply reinforce environmental problems and environmental injustice. On the one hand, the commodification of nature produces new types of goods and services; for example, it might be possible to turn certain environmental elements (e.g. landscapes) into commodities for sale. However, this then limits access to the environment since consumption depends on a consumer's ability to pay. On the other hand, commodification might produce new technologies that improve resource efficiencies, or a techno-fix: for example, new electric vehicles. However, these efficiencies often entail Jevons' Paradox, which results from improvements in relative resource usage leading to increases in absolute resource usage so that more resources end up being used overall (Robbins et al. 2010). For example, leading critics of market environmentalism point out that a more sustainable transportation system might be better achieved by investing in public transit infrastructure than by preserving the current emphasis on personal vehicle usage (Buller 2022). What these two issues illustrate is that commodification does not resolve environmental problems, it merely shifts them around or reinforces the original problem; for example, commodifying nature may mean certain groups end up losing their access to nature and natural resources (Castree 2003), while new technologies may end up increasing the overall use of natural resources (Leonard 2010).

Finally, the mainstream emphasis on market and business solutions to environmental problems – or 'market environmentalism' (Bailey 2007) – results in a number of problematic consequences. After the 2007-8 global financial crisis, policymakers around the world proposed a Green New Deal to get us out of recession and address global environmental problems at the same time; an example of this policy proposal was the UNEP's Green New Deal (Jackson 2009). The underlying aim was to transition to a more sustainable version of capitalism, based on the assumption that replacing fossil fuels with renewable energy would solve environmental problems like climate change. While there is some potential in this proposal, it was never implemented.

Why it wasn't pursued illustrates the problems with market environmentalism more generally. It's based on the assumption that the market will automatically and spontaneously promote new products and services *if* the cost of environmental problems is incorporated into existing prices of products and services. There are several criticisms we can make of this approach if we take a political ecology perspective. First, market environmentalism is based on a tension between individual, atomistic decision-making (e.g. consumer choice) and collective, coordinated action (e.g. enforcing environmental costs). Second, there is a lack of political agency as any collective action tends to be arrogated to international institutions (e.g. UN and WTO) making 'technical' decisions about whether something meets certain criteria, rather than democratic deliberation among national electorates. Finally, the response to environmental problems is left in the hands of individual consumers and businesses as they make decisions about what to spend their money on. This reinforces existing inequalities in access to and use of resources and environmental benefits, since wealthier consumers can demand and receive better environmental conditions than poorer consumers. What these criticisms should show is that environmental problems are deeply bound up with human socio-economic institutions, practices and knowledge claims – we cannot separate one from another. Trying to reduce all actions to economic calculations misses the complexity of nature–society relationships.

Empirical example: Climate change as an intractable global challenge?

Climate change is a useful example for illustrating the complexity in nature–society relations we've been stressing in this chapter. We focus on anthropogenic climate change because it's probably the biggest environmental problem facing the world today and has significant near-future implications. We can only provide a brief outline of climate change, and its causes and effects, here; we suggest reading Robbins et al. (2010: Ch. 9) for a more detailed discussion. Put simply, anthropogenic climate change is caused by the release of greenhouse gases (GHGs), especially carbon dioxide (CO_2), into the atmosphere as a result of burning fossil fuels (e.g. oil, natural gas, coal). The release of CO_2 into the atmosphere is not a problem *per se*, since this constitutes part of the carbon cycle; what is a problem is the rising CO_2 content of the atmosphere that has built up as humans have burned more and more carbon – it's now at over 410 parts per million (ppm). This means that it's important to understand both GHG emissions and the GHG content in the atmosphere when discussing climate change because the GHG buildup in the atmosphere contributes to the greenhouse effect which regulates global temperatures.

The buildup of CO_2 (and other GHGs) from human activity has led to an increase in global temperatures of around 1.1 degrees Celsius since 1880 and will lead to global temperatures rising between 1 and 4 degrees by 2100 (Robbins et al. 2010). While this does not sound dramatic, the rise obscures the fact that some parts of the world will experience far more significant shifts in temperature than others, resulting in major changes in the environment. For example, predicted effects include drought, floods, declining sea ice and glaciers, sea level rises, among others. This is why at the 2015 Paris UN Climate Change Conference countries around the world agreed to limit global temperature rises to below 1.5 degrees Celsius. However, limiting temperature rise to below 1.5 degrees means that the world can only release a certain amount of CO_2 into the atmosphere before 2050, which we're currently way off target in meeting. What's more, there are major economic constraints on achieving this goal because to limit our CO_2 emission we need to stop burning fossil fuel reserves. So, rather than resource scarcities, our real problem is too many fossil fuel resources and too much economic and financial reliance on those resources. For example, if the world agrees to limit the burning of those fossil resources, then that would wipe out the wealth of fossil fuel businesses, governments reliant on fossil fuel incomes and individuals whose pensions and savings are invested in those fossil fuel companies. According to McKibben (2012) it would mean wiping out US$20 trillion of wealth, which 'makes the housing bubble look small by comparison'.

It might seem sensible, in light of the potential catastrophe looming large in our near future, that governments, businesses and people around the world agree on ways to mitigate (i.e. stop) and adapt to climate change. This has not happened, nor is it likely to happen in the near future. Why this has not happened is an interesting, if depressing, example of how partisan government, business and personal interests and ideologies can scupper collective attempts to find solutions for global problems. There is a growing literature on how conservative think tanks, politicians and business people, as well as certain businesses, have financed a campaign of climate change denial (e.g. McCright and Dunlap 2010; Oreskes and Conway 2010). This campaign against climate change has been very successful at convincing people that climate change is not happening, is not a big deal or is simply an environmentalist conspiracy to bring down capitalism (Klein 2014). It's, therefore, not surprising that governments around the world have found it difficult to agree on a plan of action, especially as the main polluter – the United States – is witness to the most vociferous climate denial. Instead, we are left with more versions of market environmentalism, such as carbon trading. However, there are numerous problems with carbon trading, which Lohmann (2010) outlines in his work. In particular, Lohmann argues that it's, once again, another example of governments simply giving away resources to businesses, and then letting the market decide the value of carbon emissions – it does not, therefore, necessarily lead to a significant (if any) reduction in the emission of GHGs. Moreover, Lohmann highlights the global disparities and inequalities that result from carbon trading, especially in terms of the Global North simply buying more carbon credits, thereby stunting socio-economic development in the Global South.

Key methodological issue: Climate change denial and misinformation – who to trust in climate debates.

There is an unequivocal scientific consensus that climate change is happening and that it's caused by human activity, including the burning of fossil fuels. This consensus is demonstrated by the work of the Intergovernmental Panel on Climate Change (IPCC), which is a global body set up by the UN and World Meteorological Organization in 1988. The IPCC collects and collates all the scientific research in the world and produces regular 'Assessment Reports' to help guide policymaking; the last one was released in 2022.

Despite this global scientific consensus, however, many people, politicians, policymakers and so on either reject the idea that anthropogenic climate change is happening or believe that there is no need to reduce our dependence on fossil fuels. The factors behind these denials and misinformation are important to recognize. One reason is that there has been a concerted and coordinated effort to deny or downplay climate change pursued by right-wing and free-market think tanks funded by conservative businesspeople and businesses. In his book *The New Climate War* (2021) leading climate scientist Michael Mann shows how the earlier trend of denying climate change explicitly has given way to efforts to obstruct viable solutions to the climate crisis if those solutions threaten vested interests like those of the fossil fuel industry. Moreover, social media provides a fertile breeding ground for information campaigns portraying climate change as a hoax.

What all this means is that when researching climate change, it's important to examine who finances the literature you are reading, especially when it's not written by academics. There are several websites that help in this regard, including Climate Action Against Disinformation (https:/caad.info/).

Source: Oreskes and Conway (2010)

Conclusion

In this chapter we sought to raise several issues to do with global environmental change. First, we discussed the environment and how environmental problems are framed in neoclassical economics and then resolved in capitalism. We presented three key processes used to solve environmental problems: privatization, commodification and marketization. Second, we sought to question this mainstream perspective by introducing the concept of environmental justice and political ecology as an approach to understanding the interaction between humans and the environment. We then criticized the three mainstream solutions to environmental problems by highlighting several tensions, inconsistencies or problematic normative assumptions. Finally, we finished the chapter by examining climate change as a specific environmental problem which persists despite the need for an urgent response and despite several years of awareness of it as a problem, and numerous global conferences, treaties and so on. We suggested that climate change is unlikely to be resolved precisely because it's being addressed through market-based measures like carbon trading.

Suggested readings

- Ch. 5, Jackson, T. (2009) *Prosperity without Growth*, London, Earthscan.
- McKibben, B. (2012) 'Global Warming's Terrifying New Math', *Rolling Stone*, 19July.www.rollingstone.com/politics/news/global-warmings-terrifying-new-math-20120719 (accessed September 2016).
- Ch. 4, Robbins, P., Hintz, J. and Moore, S. (2010) *Environment and Society*, Oxford, Wiley-Blackwell.

Bibliography

Bailey, I. (2007) 'Market Environmentalism, New Environmental Policy Instruments, and Climate Policy in the United Kingdom and Germany', *Annals of the Association of American Geographers*, Vol. 97, pp. 530–50.

Bellamy Foster, J. (2002) *Ecology against Capitalism*, New York, Monthly Review Press.

Birch, K. and Muniesa, F. (eds) (2020) *Assetization*, Cambridge MA, MIT Press.

Bonneuil, C. and Fressoz, J.-B. (2017) *The Shock of the Anthropocene*, London, Verso.

Bradshaw, M. (2008) 'Resources and Development', in P. Daniels, M. Bradshaw, D. Shaw and J. Sidaway (eds), *An Introduction to Human Geography*, Harlow, Pearson, pp. 105–34.

Bridge, G. (2009) 'Material Worlds: Nature Resources, Resource Geography and the Material Economy', *Geography Compass*, Vol. 3, pp. 1217–44.

Buller, A. (2022) *The Value of a Whale*, Manchester, Manchester University Press.

Carney, M. (2021) *Value(s)*, London, Penguin Random House.

Castree, N. (2003) 'Commodifying What Nature?', *Progress in Human Geography*, Vol. 27, pp. 273–97.

Castree, N. (2014) 'The Anthropocene and Geography I: The Back Story', *Geography Compass*, Vol. 8, pp. 436–49.

Commoner, B. (1971) *The Closing Circle*, New York, Knopf.

Dasgupta, P. (2021) *The Economics of Biodiversity: The Dasgupta Review*, London, HM Treasury.

Dicken, P. (2011) *Global Shift* (6th Edition), New York, Guildford.

Haraway, D. (2015) 'Anthropocene, Capitalocene, Plantationocene, Chthulucene: Making Kin', *Environmental Humanities*, Vol. 6, pp. 159–65.

Hardin, G. (1968) 'The Tragedy of the Commons', *Science*, Vol. 162, pp. 1243–8.

Hopwood, B., Mellor, M. and O'Brien, G. (2005) 'Sustainable Development: Managing Different Approaches', *Sustainable Development*, Vol. 13, pp. 38–52.

Jackson, T. (2009) *Prosperity without Growth*, London, Earthscan.

Kallis, G. (2018) *Degrowth*, Newcastle-upon-Tyne, Agenda.

Klein, N. (2014) *This Changes Everything: Capitalism vs. the Climate*, Toronto, Simon & Schuster.

Leonard, A. (2010) *The Story of Stuff*, London, Constable.

Lohmann, L. (2010) 'Neoliberalism and the Calculable World: The Rise of Carbon Trading', in K. Birch and V. Mykhnenko (eds.), *The Rise and Fall of Neoliberalism*, London, Zed Books, pp. 77–93.

Mann, M. (2021) *The New Climate War*, New York, PublicAffairs.

McCright, A. and Dunlap, R. (2010) 'Anti-reflexivity: The American Conservative Movement's Success in Undermining Climate Science and Policy', *Theory, Culture, and Society*, Vol. 27, pp. 100–33.

McKibben, B. (2012) 'Global Warming's Terrifying New Math', *Rolling Stone*, 19 July, www.rollingstone.com/politics/news/global-warmings-terrifying-new-math-20120719 (accessed September 2016).

Millington, A. and Pickerell, J. (2005) 'Environment and Environmentalism', in P. Daniels, M. Bradshaw, D. Shaw and J. Sidaway (eds.), *An Introduction to Human Geography* (2nd Edition), Harlow, Pearson, pp. 145–67.

Moore, J.W. (2015) *Capitalism in the Web of Life*, London, Verso.

Moore, J.W. (ed.) (2016) *Anthropocene or Capitalocene?*, Oakland, CA, PM Press.

Oreskes, N. and Conway, E. (2010) *Merchants of Doubt*, New York, Bloomsbury Press.

Ostrom, E. (1990) *Governing the Commons*, Cambridge, Cambridge University Press.

Patel, R. and Moore, J.W. (2017) *A History of the World in Seven Cheap Things*, Oakland CA, University of California Press.

Robbins, P., Hintz, J. and Moore, S. (2010) *Environment and Society*, Oxford, Wiley-Blackwell.

Smith, N. (1984 [2008]) *Uneven Development*, Athens, GA, University of Georgia Press.

Webber, S., Nelson, S., Millington, N., Bryant, G. and Bigger, P. (2022) 'Financing Reparative Climate Infrastructures: Capital Switching, Repair, and Decommodification', *Antipode*, Vol. 54, pp. 934–58.

Whatmore, S. (2002) *Hybrid Geographies: Natures Cultures Spaces*, London, Sage.

17 | Global disorders and crises

Sonya Marie Scott

Introduction

If you regularly watch the news or follow your Twitter feed, it might seem as if the world is in a constant state of crisis. In the past few years, we've witnessed the threat of climate change, a global pandemic, financial meltdowns, supply chain delays, rising inflation, housing shortages, increasing inequality, war, volatile energy prices, food insecurity and more. But 'crises' aren't new to the capitalist system – in fact they date back to its very origins. Thinkers such as Karl Marx (Chapters 2 and 6) argued in the nineteenth century that crisis is inherent to capitalism because of the contradictions within the system itself. Marx thought that the promise of freedom and wealth on the one hand combined with the reality of exploitation and inequality on the other hand would eventually lead to a revolutionary movement of workers across the globe who would overthrow the system, and many influential thinkers of the late nineteenth and early twentieth centuries agreed with this assessment (Luxemburg 1899 [1973], Lukacs 1923 [1972], Gramsci 1948 [2003]). This revolutionary theory has not been limited to European thinkers, however, and many both in the Global South and on the margins of the Global North also believed that the injustices of capitalism and colonial violence (see Chapter 3) would lead to transformative social and economic change at a systemic level (Fanon 1961 [2004], Rodney 1972 [1981], Robinson 1983 [2000]).

With the benefit of 175 years of hindsight from Marx and Engels' famous *Communist Manifesto*, we can see that capitalism has been both adaptive and resilient, able to resist large-scale revolutionary movements and popular uprisings in part because of how effectively capital and political power are consolidated globally (see Chapters 10, 12 and 13) and how strong large corporations have become (see Chapter 12). Indeed, the capitalist mode of production sometimes even seems to *thrive* from the crises that mark its history, making up a process that some have termed *disaster capitalism* (Klein 2007).

In this chapter we'll take a look at the crises that are a part of our contemporary economic reality and explore the responses that different groups have to these very real material challenges. After first giving a synopsis of four contemporary global crises – the crisis of neoliberalism, the global food crisis, the global financial crisis and the global Covid-19 pandemic – this chapter first examines mainstream responses to disorder and crises. These include the somewhat counterintuitive free-market solutions to markets problems and the introduction of regulation that attempts to correct perceived causes of crises, or mitigate the harms that they inflict. Finally, we turn to popular and critical responses to crises, including the growth of protest movements and the rise of alternative forms of economic thinking.

A brief history of crises

When we talk about the crises of capitalism, or disorders within the capitalist system, we run the risk of focusing solely on the epicentres of capital and finance – historically located first in London and then in New York (see Chapters 7 and 11) – thus presenting a skewed picture of the global economy and the diverse peoples who live within it (see Chapters 3, 15 and 20). For this reason, we will here consider crises that have borne a global impact and elicited global responses. Since the turn of the twenty-first century there have been a myriad of global crises which have shaped the relationship between business and society. These include the alter-globalization movement of the early 2000s, to the global food crisis of 2006–8, to the global financial crisis of 2008, the global pandemic (2020–) and the ongoing climate crisis. Each of these events falls outside of usual economic expectations and can radically alter the nature of employment, consumption patterns, supply chains, corporate behaviour, among many other components of economic life affecting every country and community around the globe. We'll now give a brief outline of each.

The crisis of global neoliberalism and the alter-globalization movement. The late 1990s and early 2000s saw the policy effects of *neoliberalism* come to a head, both in the Global North and Global South (Chapters 13, 15 and 22). The erosion of social spending by governments and their active promotion of free markets as the solution to social ills (see Chapter 13) had begun to correspond with increasing rates of inequality and poverty, even in countries which previously had well-established and secure middle classes in the Global North. Coupled with a rise in global economic treaties designed to facilitate the movement of capital (see Chapter 13), entrench private intellectual property rights over medicine and technology (see Chapter 23), and economic discourse that had established the neoliberal order as 'common sense', many protest movements and attempts at *globalization from below* (the globalization of people instead of the globalization of capital) began to emerge. While this 'crisis' might be best described as a growing awareness of a systemic disorder – that is, the ailment of global neoliberal capitalism – it's important to us here because it paved the way for a series of international broad-based protest movements in the late 1990s and early 2000s that were foundational to later movements. These movements grappled with the inequalities of global finance, the War on Terror and the 2003 US invasion of Iraq, the fallout of the 2008 global financial crisis and 2020–1 anti-racism movements in the United States and around the world.

The 2006–8 global food crisis. In the mid-2000s, while the housing market was booming in the United States and other parts of the Global North, and anti-globalization sentiment had been quelled in part by increasing restrictions on protest brought on by the War on Terror in the United States and further laws relating to security, a global food crisis was beginning to take hold in the Global South. The global food crisis does not have an exact start and end date. Instead, what unfolded was a rise in global commodity prices (i.e. the prices at which basic food supplies – such as rice, corn or wheat – were traded on the global market) and subsequent food shortages in many nations of the Global South and for the economically vulnerable in the Global North. These effects lasted longer and were more profound in some regions, thus some will define the global food crisis as lasting even longer than listed earlier. Nicola Colbran (2012) points out that during 2006–8 the global number of malnourished and food insecure people increased by 75 million, leading to unrest in more than forty countries as food import costs for the world's least developed countries increased by 78 per cent.

This series of events reveals the way in which changes in the Global North – such as commodity prices which fluctuate wildly because of financial speculation (Chapter 11), policies that favour production by the most powerful producers (Agarwal et al. 2021), and the concentration of corporate control over food production (Murphy 2008) – can have profound effects on realities in the Global South. It also reveals the way interconnected global supply chains can lead to economic marginalization even when – under the assumptions of mainstream economics – they are expected to create efficiencies resulting from greater trade.

Key concept: Food sovereignty

We all need food to survive, but many people in this world are food insecure – that is, lacking in the basic foods to make up a nutritious diet, or lacking food altogether. In order to measure, assess and promote a solution to this gross inequity, scholars have begun to move beyond the question of food security – which does not necessarily account for where the food comes from, how it's produced, or the politics of its exchange – and have instead focused on what is termed *food sovereignty*.

The term 'food sovereignty' was first coined by *La Via Campesina*, a global agricultural peasant movement which seeks to find alternatives to the neoliberal production and distribution of food. Their work has formally made its way to the international stage by way of the 1996 World Food Summit, and many of their ideas have been adopted within international organizations such as the Food and Agriculture Organization (FAO) which is the United Nations agency that monitors the state of global food production and consumption. *La Via Campesina* has identified many key points necessary in order to ensure food sovereignty. These include (1) prioritizing local agricultural production and access to land; (2) promoting both small-scale producers' and consumers' right to decide what to produce and how it should be produced; (3) advocating for the right of nations to prevent the 'dumping' of cheap food by foreign producers as this undercuts the ability of local producers to compete; (4) enabling the capacity for price controls on food items; (5) committing to democratic control over food policy and (6) recognizing the rights of farmers, especially women farmers who are often overlooked yet are essential to food production.

Source: https://viacampesina.org/en/food-sovereignty/, Desmarais (2007).

The global financial crisis (2007–8). The global financial crisis (GFC) has been discussed already in many chapters of this book (see Chapters 9–13, 18 and 19) because of the profound impact it had not only on financial markets, businesses, workers and communities the world over, but also because it became a fundamental point of reckoning for governments, economists and even the discipline of economics itself (see Chapter 6).

Here we give a summary in order to put these events into context. The years 2007–8 saw a dramatic collapse in the centre of finance – that is, on Wall Street – precisely where an economic crisis was not supposed to happen and where stability and growth had long been assumed to be inherent to the system. The GFC was first evident through the sub-prime mortgage collapse in the United States. Sub-prime mortgages – mortgages given to people who would not have qualified for mortgages with the conditions of more standard lending institutions – began to go into default in 2007, and all of those who had invested in these mortgages as a form of speculation (i.e. had bought the debt as an investment) were now incurring losses. The speculative housing price bubble that had developed since the early 2000s burst in short order as those who had secured easy financing at unsustainably low interest rates and credit requirements were no longer able to hold on to their homes. People who had sought mortgages or loans leveraged by rising house prices now found themselves in massive debt or in bankruptcy as the value of housing fell dramatically. Further, those in the financial sector who had insured these debts were now liable for huge payouts coming due, and for this reason we saw the bankruptcy of insurance giant AIG in the fall of 2008. The fallout from this crisis was dramatic. Stock prices fell across the board in a manner not seen since the crash of 1929 that preceded the Great Depression. Effects were felt across the world, and economies, especially in the Global North, entered into a period termed the Great Recession (Piketty 2014), which was characterized by higher rates of unemployment and a stagnating economic recovery.

The global Covid-19 pandemic. We have already seen some of the effects of both the global Covid-19 pandemic and climate change discussed in Chapters 12 and 16. Most of us already understand what these crises entail. We'll look at climate change insofar as it relates to business and society in the Conclusion of this book. Here, however, we'll turn to the pandemic, which represented the largest global shutdown of economic activity in modern history. Industries which had previous been thriving such as air travel, tourism and hospitality were shuttered around the globe in a matter of weeks. Many lost their jobs or were laid off without means of income support. Health-care systems were pushed to the brink, and millions of people worldwide died of the disease. Many still suffer from the effects of long Covid, and the greater long-term consequences of the disease on the human population are unknown. From a business point of view, many cracks in the economic system became apparent during this new reality, including the vulnerability of the poorest nations with respect to the power to purchase vaccines, ventilators, lifesaving antivirals and more (Bhutto 2021). This vaccine inequality is part of what is a long-established pattern of global inequality between regions (Chapter 3) that stems from centuries of colonial and imperial relations. We've also seen how certain pharmaceutical corporations such as Pfizer can benefit from the advantages of intellectual property rights (see Chapters 12 and 18) in order to reap record profits during this dramatic global crisis.

During the pandemic there were disproportionate effects along age, class, gender and racial lines. This has happened for various systemic reasons. Care workers and front-line health-care workers are disproportionately women in almost every region of the world (Addati et al. 2018). Those who belong to the working class, featuring a disproportionate amount of racialized women (Chapter 6), do the vast majority of the labour required for 'essential services' (Pirtle 2020). This includes labour in grocery stores and pharmacies, labour along all the points in the global supply chain, migrant agricultural labour and a disproportionate amount of social reproductive labour in the home (Dunaway 2014; Chang 2016; Selwyn 2019). The effects of class can be seen in the fact that those who were able to work safely from home and avoid the daily risks of contagion were able to have the commodities that they needed delivered to their doors through Amazon packages or online grocery services, all by the efforts of the precarious yet essential workers from all over the globe. Finally, the generational dynamics of the pandemic means that the elderly, in both the Global North and Global South, are disproportionately likely to die from disease (O'Driscoll et al. 2021), a fact that has been exacerbated in the pandemic in settings that employ privately owned long-term care homes for the elderly, or in countries with overburdened health-care systems.

Mainstream responses to disorder and crises

We now turn to some of the mainstream responses to these crises, that is, responses coming from those in positions of power be it politically or economically. While there are different strategies and schools of thought, what mainstream responses have in common is the idea of repairing or rebuilding the global capitalist system without fundamentally changing its dynamics. We'll examine two primary categories of mainstream responses: (1) market solutions to market problems and (2) new regulatory frameworks and bailouts.

Market solutions to market problems. As we discussed earlier, neoliberalism is an economic approach that stipulates that markets are the best way to solve most economic problems. This approach tends to involve privatization of public resources, reduction of government spending, the deregulation of industry, the encouragement of foreign investment and the promotion of free trade between nations and blocs of nations (Ross 2010). All of this 'free-market' activity requires the active participation of governments and often involves special favours or rules that help large-scale enterprise like multinational corporations. Neoliberalism was also flagged as the source of a profound anti-globalization or alter-globalization sentiment in the late 1990s and early 2000s. In light of all of this, you might find it surprising to see that the market solution has continued to be proposed and adopted by many governments as a response to subsequent crises. Here we'll examine that market response in relation to the global financial crisis and the Covid-19 pandemic.

Global financial crisis. Regulation might be the first thing that comes to mind when we consider responses to the global financial crisis, but in fact there were pro-business responses as well, intended to keep both firms and financial markets running without much government intervention. Indeed, the idea with market solutions is that there is nothing inherently wrong with financial markets and increased levels of speculative activity (see Chapter 11), yet corporations and financial institutions do need to better assess the risk of these complex forms of value-generation. In much corporate governance literature after the GFC we see a call for increased 'risk management' in large firms – which entails 'risk assessment,' that is, technical conclusions about the ratio between debt and assets, the types of financial investments firms from different sectors should make, and the overall volatility (or instability) of the market. Risk management also includes a corporate governance component (Kirkpatrick 2009), where the assessment made by economists and other risk assessors in the firm is implemented by the board or by directors (see Chapter 8 for more on corporate decision-making structures) in order to ensure the continued functioning and profitability of the business. Some even suggested that firms create the new role of chief risk officer (CRO) in certain types of firms so that the 'risk appetite' of any particular firm – presumably based on shareholder interests or the interests of other stakeholder groups – is reflected in the decisions at the highest levels of the firm (Karanja and Rosso 2017). Ultimately the goal with all of these risk management solutions is not to limit the scope of activities possible on financial markets or the types of decisions that firms or investors can make, but rather for firms to better navigate the volatility and risks inherent to these largely unregulated financial markets.

Global Covid-19 pandemic. To many the economic reality experienced during the first two years of the pandemic would feel like anything but the active promotion of the 'free market'. Yet the call from business leaders and corporations around the world – especially those in industries which were badly affected by the shutdown of tourism and hospitality – was to 'reopen the economy' – so that business activity would not be sacrificed to public health priorities. Like many of these purportedly market-based solutions, the results of this strategy tended to favour the large corporation and other large business entities. In much of the Global North the economy has been 'stimulated' in such a way as to create, what Grace Blakeley (2020) calls, a 'state capitalist monopoly'. Ironically, this stimulation of economic activity has involved bailouts and public subsidies:

> The present combination of state-provided liquidity and full-on bailouts mirrors the extraordinary interventions undertaken by states in the Global North to save their finance sectors in 2008 – only this time, the money is being directed towards the entire corporate sector. [. . .] States and central banks are now being forced to engage in the active planning of their entire economies under the imperial coordination of the Federal Reserve. Except that the planning that is taking place is neither democratic nor rational. (Blakeley: 31)

Such a response to the pandemic has only led to the further concentration of Big Tech and platform firms (Fernandez et al. 2020), increased the wealth of the corresponding billionaires in heretofore unimaginable ways (Beer 2021), boosted the profits of already dominant corporations even outside of the tech industry (MacMillan, Whorisky and O'Connell 2020) and made the post-pandemic future a dangerous time for those on the front lines of serious economic recession (see Chapters 12 and 23). The conditions necessary for genuine free-market competition (see Chapter 5) – the hallmark of free-market ideology – are even further out of reach for small businesses as corporate concentration and monopoly power grows (see also Chapter 12).

Key theory: Disaster capitalism and the shock doctrine

In her book *The Shock Doctrine: The Rise of Disaster Capitalism* (2007), Canadian journalist Naomi Klein explains that events such as US War on Terror, Hurricane Katrina and even military coups often serve a destabilizing and distracting function. The shock doctrine is adopted by those who wish to participate in this opportunism, and we see the business opportunities in the military industrial complex, including mercenaries and corporations dedicated to operating in war zones, disaster relief companies that specialize in rebuilding post-natural disasters, among others. Klein explains that 'believers in the shock doctrine are convinced that only a rupture – a flood, a war, a terrorist attack – can generate the kind of vast, clean, canvases they crave. It is in these malleable moments, when we are psychologically unmoored and physically uprooted, that these artists of the real plunge in their hands and begin their work of remaking the world' (26).

In response to the Covid-19 pandemic, Klein once again explained how the shock doctrine would be used to promote a lucrative 'disaster capitalism' while the vast majority of citizens were preoccupied with daily survival and all the drastic changes that came about through lockdowns, mass hospitalizations and shifts in the social order: 'The "shock doctrine" is the political strategy of using large-scale crises to push through policies that systematically deepen inequality, enrich elites, and undercut everyone else. In moments of crisis, people tend to focus on the daily emergencies of surviving that crisis, whatever it is, and tend to put too much trust in those in power. We take our eyes off the ball a little bit in moments of crisis' (Solis 2020).

Sources: Klein 2007, Solis 2020

New regulatory frameworks and bailouts. Despite the fact that all of the crises that we have discussed so far are global in nature, regulation that emerges in response to each of these crises tends to be either national or regional (e.g. via blocs like the European Union) in nature. While this may help stabilize industries that are disproportionately powerful in certain countries or regions (i.e. finance), it poses challenges with respect to truly global problems such as food supply, climate change (see Chapter 24) and global pandemics.

Global food crisis. Given the profound effect of food insecurity around the world, one might expect a unified global response promoting and supporting food sovereignty strategies. Unfortunately, here too responses tend to follow the pattern of national and regional policymaking. Further, it is primarily countries in the Global South that have made an effort to implement regulatory policies because of the disproportionate impact that the crisis has had on their populations. These policy responses have entailed what Bryan (2014) terms a 'cacophony', implying that we see radically different strategies across regions and countries. Agarwal et al. (2021) report that 'Of the 81 developing countries surveyed by FAO to assess their responses to the crisis, 43 reduced import taxes, and 25 (mostly in Asia) either banned exports or increased taxes on them. Forty-five developing countries implemented measures to provide relief or partial relief from high prices to consumers' (159).

Given the variety of responses out there, it's useful to organize them into three general categories: (1) increasing food production; (2) reducing or stabilizing food prices, and (3) protecting vulnerable groups (Bryan: 52). Increasing domestic food production can involve a variety of things such as investment in infrastructure and food storage facilities, subsidies for producers and high levels of export tax on foods destined to leave the country. Reducing or stabilizing food prices can take the form of government control on the maximum cost of certain food items, either as a commodity (mass production) or at the consumer (retail) level. Finally, the protection of vulnerable groups can involve things such as income support or subsidies, food programmes and other government aid. Of course, governments in the Global South often lack options due to either a lack of state resources or the policies of international institutions such as the World Bank and the International Monetary Fund which may have placed conditionalities on their ability to control prices, impose export taxes, restrict cheap imports that undermine national production capacity or nationalize private industry (see Chapters 3 and 14).

Global financial crisis. The issue of regulating the banking sector reemerged in the wake of the GFC, not long after much of the financial industry had been deregulated under the neoliberal Financial Services Modernization Act (1999) in the United States under President Clinton. The renewed interest in regulation means that government is called upon to manage risks that the market itself cannot. For example, financial regulators in most countries with developed stock markets have the power to investigate and limit the practice of 'insider trading' so that people with privileged information cannot engage in unfair manipulation of markets. Assurance against such manipulation is necessary to ensure that there is sufficient trust in the financial system, which in turn can create a more efficient flow of investment and cheaper access to capital. Other regulations are meant to discourage excessive risk-taking, going well beyond the internal and voluntary corporate risk management strategies that we saw earlier.

Many of the world's largest investment banks like Goldman Sachs, JP Morgan and Citibank were themselves exposed to these so-called 'toxic' investments, but those institutions were not ordinary victims. Rather, they were bailed out by governments after they were deemed 'too big to fail' (Stiglitz 2010). In fact, the extreme risk-taking behaviour that caused the crisis was almost certainly made possible in the first place by the fact that these banks knew that government knew they could not afford to let them fail. This is called a 'moral hazard'. Brown (2012) explains that 'moral hazard describes a situation where an institution does not take the full consequences and responsibilities of its actions, and therefore has a tendency to act less carefully than it otherwise would, leaving another party to hold some responsibility for the consequences of those actions – a perversion of insurance theory' (6). To this day it is not clear that regulators have been able to curb the incentives for socially dangerous private risk-taking on the part of the financial industry (Stiglitz 2010), despite the 2010 enactment of the Dodd-Frank Act which was designed to help reduce the concentration and size of financial institutions in the United States, and limit the risk of the most powerful firms. Serious revisions to this Act took place under President Trump (2016–20), including the watering down of the Volker Rule which aimed to limit the involvement of large banks with hedge funds and risky derivative markets (Ghosh and Lee 2022).

Global Covid-19 pandemic. Because the global pandemic was a public health crisis first and foremost, most regulation that applies involves government decisions – at national, regional and local levels – about how to restrict movement, regulate the type of businesses that were allowed to open and at what capacity, require vaccination and proof thereof for both work and leisure activities, determine whether masking is required, who has access to emergency health facilities and more. Responses varied radically from region to region, and many would argue that the nature of these responses is deeply connected to social and economic attitudes about the relationship between the individual and society (Bradd and Scott 2021), and the level of social solidarity that pre-dated the pandemic (Tomasini 2021). The mainstream response of 'reopening the economy' didn't lead to any significant economic regulation or regulatory innovation, but rather to emergency state funding to facilitate the survival of business, and to a lesser extent workers, with things such as social subsidies, income supports and large bailouts. Of course, these responses varied across the world depending on the resources of each state and the attitude towards the pandemic itself. In the next section we describe some of the bailout measures employed in the United States during the pandemic, as this is a particularly striking example of income redistribution upwards in times of crisis.

Case study

TARP and CARES: Bailouts for business

The global financial crisis saw financial institutions across the United States either falling into insolvency (i.e. becoming unable to pay their debts) or in serious risk of

---

becoming insolvent. This had a dramatic effect on the stock market where the share values of major corporations across the board plummeted in a fashion not seen since 'Black Tuesday' – 29 October 1929, the crash which preceded the Great Depression of the 1930s. Not only financial institutions but also major auto manufacturers and other typically 'blue chip' corporations were in dire positions because of high levels of corporate debt and reliance upon share value as collateral. As a result, the US government put forth a dramatic proposal: issue a major injection of public money in order to save these private businesses, which were 'too big to fail'. Just after the financial crisis took hold in the fall of 2008 the US Congress approved the TARP (or Targeted Asset Relief Program) with an original budget of US$700 billion at its disposal. As of 2022 the Congressional Budget Office reported that $444 billion had been disbursed (2022). The monies for this relief programme didn't go to the aid of everyday people who had lost their homes, jobs and financial security due to the crisis, but rather to the largest of corporations like major automotive firms and some financial firms like Citigroup which issued the types of toxic securities that were at the core of the market plunge. Many critics noted that there were few conditions placed on these bailouts, unlike loans to developing nations in the Global South that almost always bear conditions and imply a loss of economic sovereignty (see Chapter 3). As a result, many CEOs continued receiving bonuses even after employees had been laid off and investors had lost significant amounts of capital (Walsh 2012). Critics continue to argue that these types of programmes promote a significant moral hazard because risky behaviour that caused massive socio-economic problems was ultimately rewarded (Brown 2012).

Unlike the 2008 bailouts, the Covid-19 pandemic cannot be attributed to the risky behaviour of financial institutions and the deregulation that preceded it. But like the global financial crisis the early days of the pandemic in March 2020 saw a dramatic drop across most stock markets and a radical slow- or shutdown to business across the world. As a result, the United States once again issued a major bailout package aimed at targeted relief for those who were suffering most during the pandemic. The CARES Act (Coronavirus Aid, Relief and Economic Security Act) offered US$2.2 trillion in aid to individual households, municipalities, small businesses and large corporations. The result of this bailout was actually one of the most dramatic shifts in wealth in a single piece of legislation, once again aiming the aid upwards in a strategy reminiscent of 'too big to fail' and the 'trickle down economics' of the 1980s in the Global North. In the years subsequent to this legislation reports have shown how the money was distributed, once again favouring large companies that had a better ability to weather the pandemic, while individuals and vulnerable communities were given a one-time payment of $1,200 per adult and $500 per child. For example, companies backed by private equity funds (a significant source of investment) received $5 billion in relief (Morgenson 2021), and others which were largely unaffected by the pandemic nonetheless claimed significant tax cuts: 'The bill included $651bn in business tax breaks that often went to companies unaffected by the pandemic and others that laid off workers. Cheesecake Factory, for example, furloughed 41,000 people, and said it will claim a tax break worth $50 million' (Whoriskey et al. 2021).

Critical responses to disorder and crises

Public protests and popular movements are by far the most prominent forms of critical reaction to crises. Often these are the spaces in which people who do not have recourse to official institutions such as government and the courts can express not only dissent but new ideas about how to cooperate and how to begin thinking differently about economics. For more on these alternatives, see Chapters 21 and 22. Here we will discuss popular movements in response to the crisis of neoliberal globalization and to the global financial crisis.

Anti- and alter-globalization movements. In the Global North this anti-globalization sentiment came to head in a variety of key moments of protest such as the 'Battle of Seattle' in 1999, anti-FTAA (Free Trade Area of the Americas) protests in Quebec City and Genoa, Italy, in 2001. In these protests labour unions, environmental groups and activists concerned with the fate of the Global South mounted massive public demonstrations against trade agreements, international trade organizations and governmental conferences such as the G7, G8 and now G20. Each saw tens of thousands of people on the streets, and the discourse of globalization and neoliberal trade reform was directly challenged in public discourse. What was clear by the 2003 anti-Iraq War protests that were surging around the world is that the effects of several decades of neoliberal policy (Chapter 13, 15 and 16) were prompting large-scale global responses challenging the very core principles of the global capitalist order (see also Chapters 20, 21 and 22). This brought new awareness to the public eye and encouraged groups that were previously not accustomed to cooperating – such as labour and environmental organizations – to come together and create new mandates. Some of the fruit of this type of cooperation can be seen today in initiatives to combat both climate change and precarious employment such as the Green New Deal in the United States (see Chapter 16).

In the Global South the effects of neoliberal reforms had been disastrous because of increasing levels of debt, vulnerability to multinational corporations through open international markets and the erosion of state sovereignty as a result of the introduction of free-trade and export processing zones as well as conditionalities attached to loans (Chapter 13). The *alter-globalization movement* sought to establish the international capacity for democracy from the grassroots level – focusing on solidarity between regular people in different regions rather than on the top-down approach that had prevailed on the global market. Perhaps one of the most famous examples of alter-globalization theory and action during this time came from the Zapatistas of the Chiapas region of Mexico (Marcos and Ponce de Leon 2001; Rovira 2019). The alter-globalization movement advanced many of the causes espoused by *The Via Campesina* (discussed earlier) such as political autonomy, control over education, land

and economic decision-making at the local level, combined with cooperation with other people, not corporations, at the global level.

Global financial crisis. As a result of the global financial crisis, several popular movements against inequality have arisen. This includes the Occupy Wall Street movement, which started in New York in 2011 following the financial meltdown and the resulting increase in rates of unemployment, loss of middle-class savings and cuts to government spending on social services (van Gelder 2011). It was during this period that the term 'the 1%' emerged to describe the class of financial capitalists who benefited from financial volatility and speculation. While Occupy itself eventually ended, it nonetheless left its mark on popular understandings of wealth inequality and the deregulated world of derivative finance (see Chapter 11).

In Europe we saw anti-austerity movements, committed to pushing back against the measures that governments imposed to pay for the fallout of financial meltdowns, and for increasing levels of debt in countries that didn't have the economic resilience of the financial core. These protest movements were especially prominent in Spain and Greece (Carretero Miramar and Bradd 2019). Both of these countries suffered massive economic turmoil and the imposition of harsh cutbacks in government spending and social welfare (termed 'austerity measures'). These movements have raised a public voice against many of the practical results of mainstream economics (Chapter 5). They point to the irony of intensifying the practices of neoliberalism, which uses mainstream principles as its justification, to alleviate the very problems caused by neoliberal policies (Flassbeck and Lapavitsas 2015). We should note, however, that the market solution is not what has been prescribed for everyone within the economy. As former Greek finance minister Yanis Varoufakis has argued, these crises have been treated with socialism for the rich (i.e. the state rescue of corporations and propping up of financial values) and market-centered austerity measures for everyone else (Varoufakis 2022). South Korean economist Ha-Joon Chang argues that these apparently contradictory tendencies are not new and have in fact been endemic to the neoliberal project (Chang 2007).

While the global pandemic did not bear the same degree of protest and dissent – in part because of the medical nature of the crisis that required isolation, social distancing and other measures that discouraged large gatherings – we nonetheless witnessed large-scale anti-racism protests throughout the United States in the summer of 2020 under the banner of 'Black Lives Matter', and a reckoning with the contradictions of racialized capitalism that had started to become ever clearer during the pandemic. With intensification of economic troubles and inflation following the pandemic and new stresses on the global supply of food, it remains to be seen which types of popular mobilization will emerge in the coming years and decades.

Conclusion

Economic crises often draw attention to the state of economic thought and public policy. After all, when things go very wrong, we often question whether our beliefs and assumptions are accurate. In the case of all the crises we have discussed in this chapter, much attention has focused on the nature of the distribution of wealth in society. After a long process of neoliberal reforms and financial deregulation, where entire industries and forms of investment were left to a free and self-making marketplace, many started to question the role of the neoclassical economists who promoted deregulation, low corporate taxation, tax shelters for the ultra-rich and governments who bailed out risky and reckless industries with public monies. Many also started to see the correlation between these practices and the growing gap in the distribution of wealth worldwide (Piketty 2014). In this chapter we have explored four significant crises of the twenty-first century, looking at the ways in which both mainstream and critical voices have responded. While these responses are deeply divergent, what is nonetheless clear is that so long as our economic system continues to face regular shocks and adjustments, the space for debate, reform and even revolution remains open to the many communities of the world.

Suggested readings

- Section 2 ('Beneath the Mask'), Marcos (2001). *Our Word Is Our Weapon: Selected Writings*, New York, Seven Stories Press.
- Ch. 15, Klein (2007) *The Shock Doctrine: The Rise of Disaster Capitalism*, Toronto, Random House.
- Ch. 5, Mirowski, P. (2014) *Never Let a Serious Crisis Go to Waste*, New York, Verso.
- Ch. 2, Blakeley, G. (2020) *The Corona Crash*, New York, Verso.

Bibliography

Addati, L., et al. (2018) *Care Work and Care Jobs for the Future of Decent Work*, International Labour Organization (ILO) Report, 28 June, https://www.ilo.org/wcmsp5/groups/public/---dgreports/---dcomm/---publ/documents/publication/wcms_633135.pdf .

Agarwal, M., et al. (2021) '2007–2012 Food Price Spikes and Crisis – A Decade and a Half Later', in Agarwal et al. (eds.), *Food for All*, Oxford, Oxford University Press, pp. 139–95.

Beer, T. (2021) 'Report: American Billionaires Have Added More than $1 Trillion In Wealth During Pandemic', *Forbes*, 26 January.

Bhutto, F. (2021) 'The World's Richest Countries are Hoarding Vaccines. This is Morally Indefensible', *The Guardian*,

17 March, www.theguardian.com/
commentisfree/2021/mar/17/rich
-countries-hoarding-vaccines-us-eu
-africa.

Blakeley, G. (2020) *The Corona Crash*, New
York, Verso.

Bradd, C. and Scott, S.M. (2021)
'Foreword: Language and Crisis in the
Time of the Pandemic', in Sonya Marie
Scott (ed.), *Languages of Economic
Crises*, New York, Routledge, pp. ix–xv.

Brown, T.S. (2012) 'Legal Political Moral
Hazard: Does the Dodd-Frank Act End
too Big to Fail', *Alabama Civil Rights &
Civil Liberties Law Review*, Vol. 1, No.
86, pp. 1–85.

Bryan, S. (2014) 'A Caucophony of Policy
Responses: Evidence from Fourteen
Countries during the 2007–8 Food
Price Crisis', in Pinstrup-Andersen
(ed.), *Food Price Policy in an Era of
Market Instability: A Political Economy
Analysis*, Oxford, Oxford University
Press, pp. 51–75.

Carretero Miramar, J.L. and Bradd, C.
(2019) 'Confronting Spain's Crises:
From the Language of the Plazas
to the Rise of Podemos', *Journal of
Cultural Economy*, Vol. 12, No. 5, pp.
423–40.

Chang, G. (2016) *Disposable Domestics:
Immigrant Women Workers in the Global
Economy*, Chicago, Haymarket.

Chang, H.-J. (2007) *Bad Samaritans:
The Myth of Free Trade and the Secret
History of Capitalism*, New York,
Bloomsbury.

Colbran, N. (2012) 'The Financialisation
of Agricultural Commodity Futures
Trading: The 2006–08 Global Food
Crisis', in Rayfuse and Weisfelt
(eds.), *The Challenge of Food Security:
International Policy and Regulatory
Frameworks*, Cheltenham, Edward
Elgar, pp. 168–89.

Desmarais, A. (2007) *La Via Campesina:
Globalization and the Power of Peasants*,
Winnipeg, Fernwood.

Dunaway, W. (ed.) (2014) *Gendered
Commodity Chains: Seeing Women's
Work and Households in Global
Production*, Stanford, Stanford
University Press.

Fanon, F. (2004) *The Wretched of the Earth*,
New York, Grove Press.

Fernandez, R., et al. (2020) *Engineering
Digital Monopolies: The Financialisation
of Big Tech*, Amsterdam, SOMO
(Center for Research on Multinational
Corporations).

Flassbeck, H. and Lapavitsas, C. (2015)
*Against the Troika: Crisis and Austerity
in the Eurozone*, New York, Verso.

Ghosh, K. and Lee, Y. (2022) 'Reflections
on the Volcker Rule: Innovations in
the Financial Services Industry and
Fixing Too Big to Succeed', *Challenge*,
Vol. 65, No. 1–2, pp. 1–10.

Gramsci, A. (2003) *Selections from the
Prison Notebooks of Antonio Gramsci*,
London, Lawrence & Wishart.

Karanja, E. and Rosso, M.A. (2017)
'The Chief Risk Officer: A Study of
Roles and Responsibilities', *Risk
Management*, Vol. 19, No. 2, pp.
103–30.

Kirkpatrick, G. (2009) 'The Corporate
Governance Lessons from the
Financial Crisis', *Financial Market
Trends*, OECD, Vol. 96, pp. 52–81.

Klein, N. (2007) *The Shock Doctrine: The
Rise of Disaster Capitalism*, New York,
Verso.

Lukacs, G. (1972) *History and Class
Consciousness: Studies in Marxist
Dialectics*, Cambridge, MIT Press.

Luxemburg, R. (1973) *Reform or
Revolution*, New York, Pathfinder
Press.

MacMillan, D., Whorisky, P., and
O'Connell, J. (2020) 'America's Biggest
Companies are Flourishing During the
Pandemic and Putting Thousands of
People Out of Work', *The Washington
Post*, 16 December, https://www
.washingtonpost.com/graphics/2020

/business/50-biggest-companies
-coronavirus-layoffs/.

Marcos, S. and Ponce de Leon, J. (2001) *Our Word is Our Weapon: Selected Writings*, New York, Seven Stories Press.

Morgensen, G. (2021) 'Companies Backed by Private Equity Firms Got $5 billion Out of $2 trillion in Federal Covid Relief', *NBC News*, 15 September, https://www.nbcnews.com/business /corporations/companies-backed -private-equity-firms-got-5-billion-out -2-n1279058.

Murphy, S. (2008) 'Globalization and Corporate Concentration in the Food and Agriculture Sector', *Development (Society for International Development)*, Vol. 51, No. 4, pp. 527–33.

O'Driscoll, M., et al. (2021) 'Age-specific Mortality and Immunity Patterns of SARS-CoV-2', *Nature*, Vol. 590, pp. 140–5.

Piketty, T. (2014) *Capital in the Twenty First Century*, Cambridge MA, Harvard University Press.

Pirtle, W. (2020) 'Racial Capitalism: A Fundamental Cause of Novel Coronavirus (COVID-19) Pandemic Inequalities in the United States', *Health Education and Behavior*, Vol. 47, No. 4, pp. 504–8.

Robinson, C.J. (2000) *Black Marxism: The Making of the Black Radical Tradition*, Chapel Hill, NC, University of North Carolina Press.

Rodney, W. (1981) *How Europe Underdeveloped Africa*, Washington, Howard University Press.

Ross, T. (2010) 'Recent Canadian Policy Towards Industry: Competition Policy, Industrial Policy and National Champions', in Abel M. Mateus and Teresa Moreira (eds.), *Competition Law and Economics: Advances in Competition Law Enforcement in the EU and North America*, Cheltenham, Edward Elgar Publishing, pp. 332–60.

Rovira, G. (2019) 'Alter-Globalization', in Kaltmeier (ed.), *The Routledge Handbook to the History and Society of the Americas*, Routledge, pp. 222–7.

Selwyn, B. (2019) 'Poverty Chains and Global Capitalism', *Competition & Change*, Vol. 23, No. 1, pp. 71–97.

Solis, M. (2020) 'Coronavirus is the Perfect Disaster for Disaster Capitalism', *Vice*, 13 March, https://www.vice .com/en/article/5dmqyk/naomi-klein -interview-on-coronavirus-and-disaster -capitalism-shock-doctrine.

Stiglitz, J. (2010) *Freefall: America, Free Markets, and the Sinking of the World Economy*, New York, W.W. Norton & Co.

Tomasini, F. (2021) 'Solidarity in the Time of COVID-19?,' *Cambridge Quarterly of Healthcare Ethics*, Vol. 30, No. 2, pp. 234–47.

van Gelder, S. (ed.) (2011) *This Changes Everything: Occupy Wall Street and the 99% Movement*, San Francisco, Barrett-Koehler.

Varoufakis, Y. (2022) 'Inflation as a Political Power Play Game Gone Wrong', *Project Syndicate*, 22 June, https://www.project-syndicate.org /commentary/inflation-is-result-of -empowered-financial-markets-by -yanis-varoufakis-2022-06.

Walsh, M.W. (2012) 'Audit of TARP Faults U.S. Over Executive Pay,' *New York Times*, 24 January, https://www .nytimes.com/2012/01/24/business/ audit-of-tarp-faults-us-over-executive -pay.html.

Whorisky, P., et al. (2021) "Doomed to Fail': Why a $4 trillion Bailout Couldn't Revive the American Economy', *The Washington Post*, 5 October, https://www .washingtonpost.com/graphics /2020/business/coronavirus-bailout -spending/.

18 | Business, regulation and policy

Richard Wellen and Alberto Salazar

Introduction

There are few more important and controversial topics for public policy than the regulation of business. At a general level, we can say that regulation is the set of rules, norms and enforcement (or sanctioning) mechanisms that are used by the state – or other authorities – to control and steer socially important activities such as business. Regulation itself is not always performed by the state, but the most common use of the term tends to refer to state regulation of the activities of business and, of course, other institutions such as schools, professional associations, prisons and so on. Politicians and policymakers are responsible for creating business regulatory systems and establishing the agencies that supervise, monitor and sanction businesses. Nevertheless, regulators themselves are typically quasi-independent, non-elected administrators who work in specialized public agencies delegated to perform regulation.

In the broadest sense business regulation is part of a complex set of political, legal and organizational norms and sanctions that are designed to pursue the public interest, or, in other words, align business practices with social priorities. As we shall see later, business regulation that is seen through a 'public interest' lens is meant to correct 'market failures' or social harm not sufficiently contained by the forces of the market.

In Chapter 10 we saw how corporate power can impact social institutions and the economy in problematic ways, not just by undermining efficiency but also by concentrating power and creating relationships of inequality among social groups. In this chapter we will see how regulation has emerged as a means for societies to address many of these problems. The success of regulation has been questioned by many, and since the late 1970s there has been a deregulatory backlash against the perceived excesses of 'big government'. Part of this is due to the observed capture of regulators and the supposed tendency of government to stifle innovation and business competitiveness (Ogus 2004). This has led to the dismantling of many forms of industry protection and the deregulation of telecommunications and other industries. More recently, increasing inequality, financial crises, Big Tech monopolies and the climate crisis have led to a revival of policy interest in regulation, both within states and at the international level.

After discussing the contending theories of regulation, we turn to surveying the various forms of regulation such as mandates, restrictions, standard-setting and information requirements. Finally, we address important cases of business regulation and policymaking, including new approaches like 'nudging' and pressures on regulations and policy resulting from processes like innovation and globalization.

Key discussion questions

- What is regulation?
- Is regulation best understood in terms of its public interest? Or is it better to understand regulation in terms of government failure?
- What are market failure and government failure?
- What types of regulation exist?
- How have recent social, technical and economic changes impacted on regulation?

Mainstream theories of regulation

It has been commonplace to see regulation as synonymous with government intervention in the market. Of course, regulation is not the only policy instrument that governments use to control and influence economic and business activities and institutions. Government can also enact the policies in conjunction with – or as alternatives to – regulation, or as indirect forms of regulation (Stiglitz and Sappington 1987). These include:

- *Inducements*: imposing taxes or levies on businesses and individuals to discourage certain activities, or the subsidizing of selected activities (such as clean technologies) to encourage them.
- *Compensation*: redistributing wealth and income through government assistance or insurance (like employment insurance).
- *Direct service provision*: government often provides services and products which would otherwise not be provided by private business or in a socially desirable way by private sector business firms.

While we cannot ignore these other forms of government intervention, since they are close cousins to regulation or function as indirect regulations, in this chapter, however, we focus on theories of government regulation. In particular, we examine two key mainstream theories that emphasize the 'public interest' and 'government failure' aspects of regulation.

Public interest theory. The classic economic argument in favour of government regulation of the economy is based on the idea of market failure. According to the standard economic model, the market is the most efficient and welfare-promoting way of coordinating our economic activity (Smith 1977). Yet this model is an idealization. It assumes that the costs and benefits of anything we produce or consume ultimately get reflected in its price in a competitive market. Broadly speaking, Stiglitz (2010a) argues that the market's efficiency – and its ability to serve the public interest – is premised on three assumptions that are often not met:

- that there will be a competitive market;
- that people will have adequate information about what they are buying in that market; and
- that the costs are all absorbed (and benefits enjoyed) by the people participating in the market exchange.

When these conditions are not met then it's said that markets 'fail' and government regulation or intervention may be needed to correct those market failures. In other words, the *invisible hand* of the market does not always lead to the best result for society, and government regulation may be necessary to ensure that the public interest can be served (Leight 2010; Stiglitz 2010a).

To see the role of regulation according to the 'public interest' theory, we need to look more closely at the causes of market failure that this theory tries to address. These include negative externalities (unaccounted for costs), imperfect information and limits to competition. We spell out each of these in turn.

First, negative externalities are costs associated with economic transactions which one of the parties can shift on to another person or group without paying for them. Negative externalities are literally the 'unpriced costs' of a market activity or transaction. Most economists agree that negative externalities undermine the efficiency of markets that neoclassical economic theory prizes so highly (Bakan 2004). When there are negative externalities at least some of the costs of producing or consuming a product are not reflected in the price. Water pollution is a good example of a negative externality because making a product that pollutes the water supply imposes an unpriced cost on those who like or depend upon clean water. Business firms that pollute or exhaust the clean water of streams, lakes and rivers are getting these resources for free, as are those who dump waste without paying to clean it up (see Chapter 16 for more on this). In fact, they are really receiving a subsidy from society because in the end society is bearing the cost of making the product (Stiglitz 2010a).

There are many ways governments have addressed externalities. One way is to tax the industry that is causing the social harm so that the producers – and consumers – internalize the cost of the externality. Many conventional economists are drawn to this approach because it assumes that prices in the market can be adjusted or tweaked to reflect the true cost of harm-causing behaviour. This is often called the 'polluter pays' principle; cigarette or gasoline taxes are good examples of this as they give people a price-based incentive not to consume a harmful product as we saw in the discussion of "market environmentalism" discussed in chapter 16. Or government can simply prohibit or limit the harm-causing behaviour by setting safety or pollution standards for an industry, as we see in the case of many product categories such as children's toys or electrical products. In either case, public interest theorists say these government interventions are more welfare-promoting than if we were to rely on the invisible hand of the market alone to direct our economic activities (Pigou 1938).

Second, mainstream economic models assume that markets will be efficient because people will have all the information needed to know the value of what they are buying (see Chapters 5 and 6). The problem is the market is not a good mechanism to ensure that people are informed or have the 'right' information to make good choices – that is, people may have 'imperfect information'. Many products are technically complex and so it's hard for consumers to acquire information; and even if the information is available at an affordable price, it's costly in terms of time and effort to acquire. Perhaps more importantly, information about products in the market is a public good, which means if one person produces it, many other people can acquire it as well without paying for it (Stiglitz and Sappington 1987). Because information is subject to this 'free-riding' behaviour, people who might otherwise produce it lack an incentive to do so. Instead, producers will primarily provide information that is designed to convince consumers to buy products (e.g. advertising) rather than inform them of the full range of costs, benefits and alternatives. This is another market failure and many government regulations try to address it by prohibiting false advertising or requiring certain kinds of information be provided to consumers which would not be voluntarily provided by businesses. For example, most countries will only allow the sale of pharmaceutical drugs upon submission of a prescription notice from a physician, and a number of countries restrict advertising of prescription drugs, cigarettes and so on. Major government agencies such as the USA Food and Drug Administration (FDA) supervise these kinds of regulations. Imperfect information is also addressed by many other forms of reporting requirements as well as ongoing government inspection or certification activities (Baldwin et al. 2012).

Third, another type of market failure involves 'limits to competition' (Stiglitz 2010a). By the end of the nineteenth century, large businesses – often public corporations – came to dominate many markets, sometimes due to economies of scale and the efficiencies caused by mass production and vertical integration. For example, at the end of the nineteenth century, US Steel, Standard Oil and other corporations in transportation and communication industries had become large enough to control their markets and effectively undermine competition (Furner 2010). Industrial concentration was sometimes seen as undermining democracy by giving business too much power to shape society or undermine the interests of workers and at other times critics were more concerned with the economic costs of losing the efficiency of competitive markets and incentives to innovate.

One response to this was the set of policies that grew out of the so-called *Progressive Movement* in US politics, which began in the 1890s and lasted more than two decades (Nace 2003). Some governments began to listen to social reformers who observed that many business firms had become monopolies or groups of firms formed cartels and trusts which allowed several firms to collude and fix prices. These were all instances of market failure which called forth so-called 'antitrust' legislation such as the US Sherman Act of 1890 which provided tools for government to restore competition by forcing the breakup of monopolistic companies or to tightly control or regulate industries where there was a concentration of power in a few firms (Ogus 2004). In many cases even economic reformers and progressives acknowledged that some business enterprises were large because it was more efficient for them to be so. They labelled such cases 'natural monopolies' that emerged in some industries such as radio broadcast and argued that firms in those industries should be closely regulated (Baumol 1977; Furner 2010). As we saw in Chapter 12 some influential economists like Joseph Schumpeter were able to argue that the rise of dominant firms may be linked to innovation, an argument that is now sometimes used by mainstream economists to defend today's Big Tech giants like (Amazon and Alphabet/Google) from aggressive antitrust enforcement. Other antitrust scholars take an opposing view echoing earlier reformers by seeing the rise of Big Tech firms as marking a second 'Gilded Age' posing new threats to democracy (Wu 2018).

Theory of government failure. Public interest theory tends to focus on the benefits of controlling or reducing the social costs of business through government regulation. Yet the rise of the interventionist state during the twentieth century has always been controversial, especially among conservative supporters of business. By the 1970s many policymakers and academics in countries like the United States and the UK were looking for explanations for the economic turbulence caused by rising energy prices, competition from low-wage countries and so on (Furner 2010). This emboldened many supporters of the free market who opposed extensive regulation to criticize the interventionist regulatory state. For example, George Stigler (1971), a professor at the University of Chicago and a well-known *public choice theorist*, helped to solidify these ideas by developing a model of 'government failure' in opposition to concerns about market failure expressed by public interest theorists.

Following other public choice theorists like Mancur Olson (1965), Stigler posited a built-in tendency of democratic systems in capitalist societies to promote the interests of organized groups over less organized groups. These theorists observed that regulatory systems are steered by politicians who are motivated by the desire to be elected and re-elected to office. These politicians have a great incentive to favour the interests of established businesses which provide jobs in their communities, donate money to their campaigns and compete against rival firms from other communities or countries. Realizing that every regulatory system creates winners and losers, politicians are likely to be as opportunistic as anyone else in such a situation. From this perspective, if aligning themselves with influential corporations will help them, politicians will choose the regulations that help those corporations, even if it comes at the expense of the public interest in the long run or the emergence of new firms using new technologies.

This also creates a phenomenon Ogus (2004) and others call 'regulatory capture' in which regulators fall under the influence of the industry they are supposed to control, inspect and monitor. Indeed, some studies during this period showed that there was a 'revolving door' between industry and government where many regulators in government agencies actually ended up taking jobs in the industry they regulated (Mitnick 1980).

The general point is that phenomena like regulatory capture may mean that the 'political market' is even less efficient than the economic market. Democratic politics is structured to favour those economic actors who have the loudest voices rather than those who might make the economy work better. The political market is also dysfunctional because members of the general public are not good at organizing to pursue policies that will really achieve the public interest. Public choice theorists say this is because anyone who wants to be engaged or become very informed about a specific public issue must make a very large investment with a small expected individual payoff. As a result, citizens tend to become 'rationally ignorant' (Downs 1957); that is, ordinary citizens do not have a big enough stake in any one issue related to business regulation to justify the enormous effort required to seriously rival professional lobbyists hired by business. Conversely, businesses which can gain by concentrating their government lobbying efforts on one or two problems that matter a great deal to them have a great advantage. Ordinary citizens stand to gain more from general policies which bring better jobs or have more say in the workplace, yet governments tend to focus on areas where there's opportunity for capture by special interests, which typically reinforces the business bias of government. This is why some leading critics of capitalism often oppose the regulatory state as much as those trying to free business from the intervention of government (Novak 2014).

Widespread cynicism towards the public interest mandate of government reached its heyday with the rise of the governments of Margaret Thatcher (UK) and Ronald Reagan (United States) during the 1980s. These political leaders promoted the ideas of individual responsibility and the economic superiority of the market. The deregulation movement of the 1970s owed much to the influential analysis of the causes of government failure and its argument that government interference typically has a worse outcome than letting the market operate freely. Academics like Ronald Coase (1960) influenced the deregulatory movement by arguing that disputes about the impact of economic activities are not about the public interest, or about bad businesses harming innocent bystanders, but rather ultimately about disputes among private parties who want different goals. After all, a price can be put on any behaviour, so we could (and should) set up a kind of market that would let people decide how much they want to pay to pollute or let people who might be affected by the pollution negotiate a price that could be paid by those who have an interest in making a mess. Coase assumed that such a market-oriented approach would often allow people to find a way of resolving problems better than government. In particular, it would avoid having government engage in paternalistic, top-down regulation of economic activity and instead encourage bargaining between the private parties that are potentially affected by each other's behaviour.

Assessing the two leading theories. On the one hand, public interest theory does need to be tempered by realism. Bruce Yandle (2011) argues that the most convincing theory of regulation is one that includes elements of both the public interest and private interest theories. He points out that regulation is often the product of interest alignment between promoters of public interest regulations and the businesses that are regulated. The process of regulation may start with pressure groups trying to influence government about addressing some negative externality. The government will then actively consider regulations in response to these demands. While some businesses may oppose the prospect of any regulatory initiative, other firms may see some kinds of new regulations as a market opportunity. This is especially true if those businesses have some kind of technological head start or other advantage that puts them in the best position to compete in the market once a specific set of regulations are in place. For this reason, not all businesses want to suppress regulation, and they may in fact be allies with the pressure groups that want to bring changes to the industry. For example, Yandle says this might explain why General Motors lobbied government to bring in stricter fuel standards at a time when it was further along than other American car manufacturers in shifting production to smaller, more fuel-efficient cars.

On the other hand, the problem with the public choice theory of government failure is its categorical distrust of both government and constructive democratic approaches to public issues. It starts from the fictional assumption that all participants in the political process inherently prioritize their economic self-interest above all else and that citizens are inherently under-informed or easily manipulated 'consumers' in the political 'marketplace'. This is clearly problematic as we see today the number of civic groups and other participants who involve themselves in public interest campaigns and are motivated by the power of ideas and even social justice. One would have to adopt a very narrow model of human action and rationality to say that people – including politicians – are incapable of coming together to deliberate effectively about what policies would best contribute to the public good (Furner 2010).

Forms of regulation and their challenges

Having surveyed mainstream debates around regulation, we want to review different forms of regulation as they relate to specific areas of economic life and industries where state regulation typically applies. In this section we cover (1) restrictions on business, (2) mandates, licensing and standard-setting and (3) disclosure rules.

Restrictions. Restrictions on businesses stipulate what kinds of activities that business firms and their agents cannot perform or limits they cannot exceed. This is perhaps the most well-known and controversial form of government regulation. Antitrust laws, for example, prohibit certain activities on the part of business that might limit competition in the market. A recent well-known case brought by the US Department of Justice and global regulators led to a 2015 guilty plea by some of the world's largest banks (e.g. JP Morgan Chase, Royal Bank of Scotland, Citigroup) for the serious offence of fixing foreign exchange prices. The case resulted in fines of over $5.7 billion (Henning 2015). Earlier accounting scandals in 2001 involving Enron and WorldCom corporations – discussed in Chapter 6 – prompted the US government to pass a package of regulatory laws known as the 2002 Sarbanes-Oxley Act (Soederberg 2008). The Act criminalized the perpetration of certain types of financial irregularities and also set up new conflict of interest guidelines applying to financial auditing firms with the hope of reducing incentives to exaggerate corporate earnings – or conceal corporate losses – from outsiders.

Some people see restrictive regulations and bans as unwarranted interference with private business decision-making. Business leaders often warn that regulations could create 'red tape' and expensive compliance procedures that would create inefficiencies and stifle innovation and thus offset their intended benefits. Economists who dislike restrictive regulations often cite their 'paternalistic' character, which means that they rely on using government as a 'nanny state' (Le Grand and New 2015) and treating workers or consumers as children unable to learn how to look after their own safety or become informed about risks (Joskow 2011). Even critics of business are sometimes sceptical of regulations, saying they are often selectively enforced or too lax for fear of harming industry. These critics also say that regulations only tend to scratch the surface of corporate behaviour without having any real impact on the structural factors such as power relations that cause concentrations of wealth and various forms of harm and risk for consumers, workers and communities (Glasbeek 2002). Indeed, businesses are often characterized as 'one step ahead' of regulators since politics and technical complexity make it hard for regulations to be fully comprehensive or systematic and to account for all possible externalities. Mazzucato and Ryan-Collins (2022) argue that regulation and government policy are too often focused on 'correcting' market failures, which wrongly assume that markets themselves can be perfected. In their view government policy should be more about 'creating public value' (11) than correcting the market.

Mandates, licensing and standard-setting. In many cases, governments may want to ensure that a specific public goal is achieved by businesses operating in a particular industry by positively mandating actions or requiring a certain level and type of service provision or safety feature. For example, in some countries banks must provide certain services that are deemed to be important to the public, such as access to loans for poorer communities or, as in the case of Ireland and the UK, free access to all ATMs. Telecommunications companies may be required to provide certain services as well. In many countries phone companies must provide universal landline telephone services to all communities at a standard rate even though in remote or sparsely populated regions many such services are so expensive that they would never be provided if end users had to pay the full cost.

In many industrial sectors, businesses not only are overseen by specialized agencies but also must be licensed by those agencies. This is the case in areas like media broadcasting, taxi services and legalized cannabis production. In Canada, for example, the Canadian Radio and Television Corporation (CRTC) requires cable TV providers as well as TV networks to provide a certain minimum amount of Canadian content in order to 'level the playing field' against the flood of US content that has the advantage of being imported from one of the world's largest markets (Edwardson 2008).

Critics of these kinds of policies often point to the fact that government cannot legislate for good or safe or beneficial behaviour. Others say that by licensing an industry or mandating certain standards of provision the government is stifling competition and innovation in ways that are actually harmful to the public interest. For example, the CRTC in Canada has long been criticized for assuming that its Canadian content rules can actually encourage viewers or listeners to watch Canadian content (Hunter et al. 2010).

Disclosure. On the surface, one of the best ways of regulating is to require businesses to provide information and transparency of the potentially harmful business activity or product. A good example is food labelling (Howells 2005). If consumers are made aware of the excessive sugar content of a breakfast cereal, then the consumer of the product has the power to avoid the potentially harmful consequences. This solution avoids paternalism and leaves it in the hands of each individual to determine which consequences they want to avoid. No product is perfectly safe, and each person assigns a different weight to different values such as safety, enjoyment and so on. Hence, rather than restricting or banning products, perhaps it's more effective for government to simply require producers to provide full information for consumers.

Mainstream economists tend to prefer disclosure over other forms of regulation because it simply builds upon and restores the power of consumer choice at the foundation of the competitive market. Nevertheless, we know that information by itself is not the same as providing for social needs and providing alternatives for people who lack resources to attain them (Howells 2005). Governments around the world require cigarette marketers to inform people they might suffer illnesses from smoking. Yet there's strong evidence that even when warnings exist, certain groups of people maintain a high rate of smoking. In fact, there's a higher prevalence of smoking among people from lower socio-economic groups, which suggests that the problem is not one of good information but rather deeper structural issues such as lack of access to the social supports conducive to healthy behaviour (Hiscock et al. 2012).

Different approaches to regulation and policymaking

Theories of regulation, of whatever type, influence politicians and policymakers by providing legitimation and justification for new policies or approaches to new societal issues (see Case Study on banking regulation). In this section we want to address an example of each of these things. First, we examine the emerging policy approach based on theories of 'nudging' people's behaviour; and second, we examine the policy approaches to innovation and globalization (see Chapter 13).

Libertarian paternalism and nudging policy. There's an emerging and popular policy approach called 'libertarian paternalism', which seeks to influence and regulate people's behaviour by drawing on insights from behavioural economics. It has proved particularly popular in the UK and the United States (Salazar 2012). The basis of this approach is that individuals have cognitive biases which lead them to act in irrational ways, defined as against their own self-interest (see Chapter 5). It departs from other rational choice theories since it does not assume that consumers and other market participants act rationally to maximize their self-interest. Rather, it's based on the theory that we need policy interventions – what Thaler and Sunstein (2008) call 'choice architecture' – to enable people to overcome their cognitive biases and enhance their self-interest. According to Thaler and Sunstein (2008: 6), a 'nudge' includes:

> any aspect of the choice architecture that alters people's behaviour in a predictable way without forbidding any options or significantly changing their economic incentives. To count as a mere nudge, the intervention must be easy and cheap to avoid. Nudges are not mandates. Putting the fruit at eye level counts as a nudge. Banning junk food does not.

Nudging is a policy approach that aims to change 'self-destructive' behaviour into 'self-interested' behaviour without restricting individual freedom *and* without altering the behaviour of individuals who already act in a self-interested manner (Salazar 2012). Consequently, it's meant to preserve freedom of choice and legitimate policymakers and others in their promotion of particular policies (based on notions of self-interested, rational action) (Thaler and Sunstein 2012). An example might be changing where 'healthy' foods (e.g. fruit) appear in a cafeteria or shop, so that they appear before 'unhealthy' foods (e.g. cake). Placing fruits before desserts steers consumers towards healthy food without removing choice.

In policy terms, nudging is appealing over other policy options (e.g. institutional change) because it offers a seemingly simple and low-cost solution that does not require primary legislation. As such, nudging can replace formal regulations, mandates or bans, while imposing no extra cost on citizens (i.e. no extra taxation is needed). Policymakers and politicians might find this attractive because it implies that public health, for example, can be improved without extra spending in terms of both regulatory cost and taxation while avoiding the typical failures of a 'nanny state'.

While it might appear benign, nudging can be highly problematic as a policy solution. Nudging can simply induce short-term cosmetic behavioural changes, predominantly among more savvy and informed – that is, affluent – consumers. It does not address important problems like consumers misperceptions; income inequality; resource access; structural lifestyle decisions; existing knowledge, attitudes and values that hinder long-term behavioural change; the influence of business marketing; and so on. Ignoring these sorts of problems means that nudging policy intervention can raise unrealistic expectations of societal change and welfare, which downplays other important regulatory interventions (e.g. bans) (Salazar 2012).

Policymaking and regulation in a technological, global world. It's important to note that policymaking and regulations are not static; they are, necessarily, dynamic and evolving rules for at least three reasons. First, new innovations and technologies call into question the applicability of old regulations, a point to which we return in greater detail in Chapter 23 when discussing the regulation of digital platforms.

For example, with regard to rides marketed by digital platforms like Uber, the question arises of who should be responsible when safety standards go wrong – the platform service that helps match riders and drivers or the driver that provides the direct service? Likewise, as we review further in Chapter 23, the question of whether digital platform work should be regulated as an employment relationship or as a service provided by a self-employed worker is still largely unsettled in many jurisdictions (Koutsimpogiorgos et al. 2020).

In addition, conventional state-based regulation has been strongly challenged by the globalization of business whereby firms increasingly subcontract production and services across borders (see Chapters 13 and 14). Major multinational corporations (MNCs) like Nike, The Gap and Apple have been accused of 'regulatory arbitrage' because they allegedly globalize their operations to take advantage of relaxed labour, safety and environmental standards in less regulated economies (Vogel 2010). Regulations are meant to make business more accountable to societal needs, and globalization is seen as a process that has meant government regulation is becoming less effective and businesses less accountable. Conversely, MNCs have also pushed for transnational business laws that protect their investments around the world from national regulations. International investment protection agreements proliferated throughout the 1990s and 2000s and often limit governments' abilities to introduce policies that respond to the needs and demands of their citizens. Pursuant to such agreements, MNCs have sued host governments for perceived interferences with their investments, and these hearings are held before non-state arbitral tribunals that are often criticized for being ideological, biased, costly and uncertain as they lack an appeal process (Grant 2015). These lawsuits against regulating governments have resulted in the state having to pay extremely expensive compensations to foreign investors and to restrain itself from further regulating the economy. One of the most controversial examples of such investment protection agreements is the Energy Charter Treaty, signed by fifty-three countries, which has allowed energy firms to sue signatory governments for enacting policies to reduce carbon emissions (Nelsen 2022).

In response, many theorists of business and society have heralded the prospects of non-state or civic regulation (Bakan 2004), whereby NGOs, students, labour activists and others hold corporations accountable through non-state actions, organizations and campaigns. Such initiatives involve persuading business to adopt voluntary codes and standards, or promoting consumer markets for products with eco-labels and fair-trade certification (see Chapter 16). Clearly, civic regulation may be effective in establishing market and reputational rewards for socially beneficial business practices and also helps to legitimize and professionalize business practices that are more socially aware. Yet civic regulation has also been criticized as opening opportunities for insincere 'greenwashing', allowing corporations to selectively adopt a few new policies or practices to brand themselves as socially responsible without embracing more meaningful changes (Bakan 2020; Cherry and Sneirson 2010). There's a robust debate about whether civic regulation should be considered an important complement to government regulation, filling in some of the gaps and shortcomings of the latter, especially in a more complex world of globalized production and networked activists and socially aware consumers in the public sphere (Mayer and Gereffi 2010).

Comparing regulatory approaches among countries. Although we have made a number of generalizations about major regulatory trends it's important to recognize that different countries often take different approaches to regulation. David Vogel (2012) has pointed out that before 1990 the United States imposed much stricter regulations than European countries did in addressing product safety and environmental risk. After 1990 that pattern reversed itself as European countries became more assertive than the United States in monitoring safety, restricting food ingredients and proactively addressing climate change. A major reason for this change has been the pressure from those countries with stronger regulations to harmonize regulations with other member states within the European Union (EU). Vogel (2012), for example, points to the fact that EU regulators have restricted genetically modified organisms (GMO) in the food industry, while very few restrictions exist in the United States. He explains this by showing that US policymakers over the years have become more insulated from 'public pressures' as the burden of proof has shifted on to those proposing restrictions and regulations. By contrast, in the EU there has been a strong interest in legitimizing European integration, and this has led to a demand for EU institutions and regulators to become more precautionary and to demonstrate their responsiveness to strongly voiced public pressures (Vogel 2012: 278). This shows that different systems of political and economic governance can lead to very different regulatory approaches, even in societies facing otherwise similar types of social harms from business practices.

Case study

Regulating digital gatekeepers: Why is Europe more aggressive than the United States?

The contrast between EU and US models of regulation has been demonstrated by the different approaches for addressing the market power of Big Tech digital platform companies. As explained in Chapters 12 and 23, these companies have so much access to consumer

---

data, and so much control over access to digital services, that they can take unfair advantage of their dominant positions in the market. In 2022 the EU passed the Digital Markets Act (DMA), which designated major platforms like Amazon and Alphabet/Google as possessing 'gatekeeping' power over key digital infrastructures that users and consumers have come to depend upon (European Commission 2022). Under this law platforms classified as 'gatekeepers' would be subject to special rules requiring dominant digital services – like Google's online search engine (which controls 90 per cent of the market) – to treat consumers and competitors more fairly. This would mean, for example, that Google would not be allowed to give a preferential ranking to its own services – like YouTube videos – in its search results. To take another example, firms like Apple would have to allow third-party, independent app stores to be installed by users on Apple's smartphone and tablets.

The DMA allows European regulators to be more proactive rather than reactive in responding to dominant technology companies. Until now, when these companies used their dominant position in the market unfairly the enforcement agencies responsible for overseeing market competition had to launch separate investigations and lawsuits that could take years to conclude. Sanctions, punitive fines or regulations that were typically imposed under such investigations were imposed in an *ex post* manner, often after many years, rather than in the *ex ante* (beforehand) approach of the DMA.

It is notable that in late 2022 the US Congress was also considering enacting similar proactive, *ex ante* public governance rules for gatekeeper platforms but these proposals were suddenly removed from antitrust reform legislation passed at the end of that year. Observers noted that Big Tech firms like Amazon, Meta/Facebook and Alphabet/Google spent many millions of dollars lobbying and launching advertising campaigns against these bills. Some of the ads even suggested that regulating Big Tech firms would deprive consumers of the services to which they have become so attached (McKinnon and Day 2022). Researchers like Thomas Phillipon (2019) claim that greater spending on lobbying and political campaign contributions in the United States has led to weaker antitrust enforcement against industry leaders, less competitive markets and greater corporate concentration as compared to Europe. Others attribute the more aggressive approach of European regulators to the 'geopolitical' fact that they are looking to create a more even playing field for European companies in a world where the leading digital businesses are based in the United States and China (Larsen 2022).

Conclusion

Business regulation is often intended as a way of protecting the interests of society from potentially harmful business activity or overly powerful corporations. Yet as we have seen, it's perhaps too simplistic to see regulation as simply a limitation imposed on business activity. Rather, regulations are political-legal instruments that fundamentally shape business opportunities and activities, and even help explain how business structures and practices have evolved and adapted to political-legal instruments. Our discussion of the forms of business regulation and the debates and controversies about them drives home one of the key points of this book, namely that business must be understood as an institution that involves a dynamic interplay of economic, social and political factors (see Chapter 1).

Suggested readings

- Lecture 16, Atkinson, R. H. and Stiglitz, J. (1980) *Lectures on Public Economics*, New York, McGraw Hill.
- Part I, Baldwin, R., Cave, M. and Lodge, M. (2012) *Understanding Regulation: Theory, Strategies and Practice*, Oxford, Oxford University Press.
- Chs 6 and 7, Le Grand, J. and New, B. (2015) *Government Regulation: Nanny State or Helpful Friend?*, Princeton, NJ, Princeton University Press.

Bibliography

Alba, D. (2015) 'In California, Uber Loses Another Round in Driver Debate', *Wired*, 10 September, www.wired.com /2015/09/california-uber-loses-another -round-driver-debate/ (accessed 26 October 2015).

Bakan, J. (2004) *The Corporation*, London, Random House.

Bakan, J. (2020) *The New Corporation: How 'Good' Corporations are Bad for Democracy*, New York, Penguin Books.

Baldwin, R., Cave, M. and Lodge, M. (2012) *Understanding Regulation: Theory, Strategies and Practice*, Oxford, Oxford University Press.

Baumol, W. (1977) 'On the Proper Cost Tests for Natural Monopoly in a Multi-Product Industry', *American Economic Review*, Vol. 67, pp. 809–22.

Brynjolfsson, E. and McAfee, A. (2014) *The Second Machine Age*, New York, W.W. Norton.

Cherry, M. and Sneirson, J. (2010) 'Beyond Profit: Rethinking Corporate Social Responsibility and Greenwashing after BP Oil Disaster', *Tulane Law Review*, Vol. 85, pp. 983–1038.

Coase, R.H. (1960) 'The Problem of Social Cost', *The Journal of Law and Economics*, Vol. 3, pp. 1–44.

Downs, A. (1957) *An Economic Theory of Democracy*, New York, Harper.

Edwardson, R. (2008) *Canadian Content: Culture and the Quest for Nationhood*, Toronto, University of Toronto Press.

European Commission. (2022, 31 October) 'Digital Markets Act : Rules for Digital Gatekeepers to Ensure Open Markets Enter into Force', *European Commission Press Release*.

Furner, M.O. (2010) 'From "State Interference" to the "Return of the Market": The Rhetoric of Economic Regulation from the Old Gilded Age to the New', in E. Balleisen and D. Moss (eds), *Government and Markets: Toward a New Theory of Regulation*, New York, Cambridge University Press, pp. 92–142.

Glasbeek, H. (2002) *Wealth by Stealth*, Toronto, Between the Lines.

Grant, K. (2015) 'The ICSID under Siege: UNASUR and the Rise of a Hybrid Regime for International Investment Arbitration', Osgoode Legal Studies Research Paper Series, Paper 108.

Henning, P. (2015) 'Guilty Pleas and Heavy Fines Seem to be Cost of Business for Wall St.', *The New York Times*, 10 March, www.nytimes.com /2015/05/21/business/dealbook/guilty -pleas-and-heavy-fines-seem-to-be -cost-of-business-for-wall-st.html?_r=0 (accessed September 2016).

Hiscock, R., Bauld, L., Amos, A. and Platt, S. (2012) 'Smoking and Socioeconomic Status in England: The Rise of the Never Smoker and the Disadvantaged Smoker', *Journal of Public Health*, Vol. 34, pp. 390–96.

Howells, G. (2005) 'The Potential and Limits of Consumer Empowerment by Information', *Journal of Law and Society*, Vol. 32, pp. 349–70.

Hunter, L., Iacobucci, E. and Trebilcock, M. (2010) *Scrambled Signals: Canadian Content Policies in a World of Technological Abundance*, Toronto, C.D. Howe Institute, www.cdhowe.org/sites/default/files/attachments/research_papers/mixed/commentary_301.pdf (accessed September 2016).

Joskow, P. (2011) 'Market Imperfections versus Regulatory Imperfections', *CESifo DICE Report*, pp. 3–7.

Koutsimpogiorgos, N., van Slageren, J., Herrmann, A.M. and Frenken, K. (2020) 'Conceptualizing the Gig Economy and Its Regulatory Problems', *Policy and Internet*, Vol. 12, No. 4, pp. 525–45.

Larsen, B.C. (2022, 8 December) 'The Geopolitics of AI and the Rise of Digital Sovereignty', *Brookings Report: The Economics and Regulation of Artificial Intelligence and Emerging Technologies*.

Leight, J. (2010) 'Public Choice: A Critical Reassessment', in E. Balleisen and D. Moss (eds), *Government and Markets: Toward a New Theory of Regulation*, New York, Cambridge University Press, pp. 213–55.

Mansell, R. (2014) 'Global Media and Communication Policy: Turbulence and Reform', in Giuliana Capaldo (ed.), *Global Community: Yearbook of International Law and Jurisprudence 2013*, Oxford, Oxford University Press, pp. 3–26.

Mayer, F. and Gereffi, G. (2010) 'Regulation and Economic Globalization: Prospects and Limits of Private Governance', *Business and Politics*, Vol. 12, No. 3.

Mazzucato, M. and Ryan-Collins, J. (2022) 'Putting Value Creation Back into "Public Value": From Market-fixing to Market-Shaping', *Journal of Economic Policy Reform*, Vol. 25, No. 4, pp. 1–16.

McKinnon, J.D. and Day, C. (2022) 'Tech Companies Make Final Push to Head Off Tougher Regulation', *Wall Street Journal*, https://www.wsj.com/articles/tech-companies-make-final-push-to-head-off-tougher-regulation-11671401283.

Mitnick, B. (1980) *The Political Economy of Regulation: Creating, Designing and Removing Regulatory Forms*, New York, Columbia University Press.

Morgenson, G. and Rosner, J. (2011) *Reckless Endangerment*, New York, Henry Holt and Co.

Nace, T. (2003) *Gangs of America*, San Francisco, Berrett-Koehler.

Neslen, A. (2022, 14 November) 'Revealed: Secret Courts that Allow Energy Firms to Sue for billions Accused of "Bias" as Governments Exit', *The Guardian*, https://www.theguardian.com/business/2022/nov/14/revealed-secret-courts-that-allow-energy-firms-to-sue-for-billions-accused-of-bias-as-governments-exit.

Novak, W. (2014) 'A Revisionist History of Regulatory Capture Theory', in D. Carpenter and D. Moss (eds), *Preventing Regulatory Capture: Special Interest Influence and How to Limit it*, New York, Cambridge University Press, pp. 25–48.

Ogus, A. (2004) 'Whither the Economic Theory of Regulation? What Economic Theory of Regulation?', in J. Jordana and D. Levi-Faur (eds), *The Politics of Regulation: Institutions and Regulatory Reforms for the Age of Governance*, Cheltenham, Edward Elgar, pp. 31–44.

Olson, M. (1965) *The Logic of Collective Action: Public Goods and the Theory of Groups*, Cambridge, MA, Harvard University Press.

Philippon, T. (2019) *The Great Reversal: How America Gave up on Free Markets*, Cambridge, MA, Harvard University Press.

Pigou, A. (1938) *The Economics of Welfare* (4th Edition), London, Macmillan.

Rifkin, J. (2014) *The Zero Marginal Cost Society: The Internet of Things, the Collaborative Commons and the Eclipse of Capitalism*, New York, Palgrave Macmillan.

Salazar, A. (2012) 'Libertarian Paternalism and the Dangers of Nudging Consumers', *King's Law Journal*, Vol. 23, pp. 51–67.

Smith, A. (1977) *An Inquiry into the Nature and Causes of the Wealth of Nations*, Chicago, University of Chicago Press.

Soederberg, S. (2008) 'Deconstructing the Official Treatment for 'Enronitis': The Sarbanes-Oxley Act and the Neoliberal Governance of Corporate America', *Critical Sociology*, Vol. 34, pp. 657–80.

Stigler, G. (1971) 'The Theory of Economic Regulation', *Bell Journal of Economics and Management Science*, Vol. 3, pp. 3–18.

Stiglitz, J. (2010a) 'Government Failure vs. Market Failure: Principles of Regulation', in E. Balleisen and D. Moss (eds), *Government and Markets: Toward a New Theory of Regulation*, New York, Cambridge University Press, pp. 13–51.

Stiglitz, J. (2010b) *Free Fall: America, Free Markets and the Sinking of the World Economy*, New York, W.W. Norton.

Stiglitz, J. and Sappington, D. (1987) 'Information and Regulation', in E. Bailey (ed.), *Public Regulation*, London, MIT Press, pp. 3–43.

Thaler, R.H. and Sunstein, C. (2008) *Nudge: Improving Decisions about Health, Wealth and Happiness*, New Haven, Yale University Press.

Thaler, R.H. and Sunstein, C. (2012) 'Behavioral Economics, Public Policy, and Paternalism: Libertarian Paternalism', in S. Holland (ed.), *Arguing about Bioethics*, London, Routledge, pp. 386–91.

Vogel, D. (2010) 'Private Regulation of Global Corporate Conduct', *Business and Society*, Vol. 49, pp. 68–87.

Vogel, D. (2012) *The Politics of Precaution: Regulating Health, Safety and Environmental Risks in Europe and the United States*, Princeton, Princeton University Press.

Wu, T. (2018) *The Curse of Bigness: Antitrust in the New Gilded Age*, New York, Columbia Global Reports.

Yandle, B. (2011) 'Bootleggers and Baptists in the Theory of Regulation', in D. Levi-Faur (ed.), *Handbook on the Politics of Regulation*, Cheltenham, Edward Elgar, pp. 25–33.

19 | Ethics and business

Mark Peacock, Richard Wellen and Kean Birch

Introduction

Much of this book is concerned with *positive* issues, that is, with matters of fact which tell you how the world is. To express how the world is, we use *positive* or *descriptive* statements, for example, *in 2016, the world's richest twenty-six people owned as much wealth as the poorest 50 per cent of the world's population.* Whether this statement is true or false can be ascertained by comparing the content of the statements with the way the world is. For instance, we can test this statement by identifying the twenty wealthiest people and comparing their wealth with that of the poorest 50 per cent (about 4 billion people). If the former sum exceeds the latter, the statement is true – we have confirmed it; the statement is a *fact*, as Oxfam established (Elliott 2019). When we compare a positive statement with the way the world is, we are undertaking *empirical* investigation, that is, we are examining the world. This often involves measurement, as in the previous example.

In contrast to positive or descriptive statements, other statements are *normative* or *evaluative*, for example, *the national debts of Sub-Saharan African countries owed to foreign creditors ought to be cancelled.*

Normative statements often have words like 'should', 'fair', 'unfair', 'ought', 'good' and 'bad' in them; these words are evaluative. Normative statements don't tell you how the world is but how it ought to be, or what we should do to change the world or whether something about the world is good or bad. Such statements are often referred to as *ethical*. *Ethics* is a branch of practical philosophy which is important to the study of business and society.

Philosophers have spent centuries analysing the relationship between positive and normative statements. The Scottish Enlightenment philosopher David Hume (1711–76) observed that writers often switch from positive statements to normative ones without justification. This gives rise to what philosophers call the 'is-ought problem,' which concerns whether one may infer a normative ('ought') statement from a positive ('is') statement. For example, if you look back at the positive statement mentioned earlier, you might think that it automatically leads to the normative statement: *the global distribution of wealth is unfair.* But in itself, the positive statement does not tell us whether wealth distribution is unfair. If one isn't careful in distinguishing positive from normative statements, one might be accused of committing the 'naturalistic fallacy', that is, deriving an 'ought' from an 'is' statement without attempting to justify this derivation.

In this chapter we're not arguing that one may never infer a normative from a positive statement. In Chapter 9, we met a candidate for such an inference with Milton Friedman's (1970) perspective on the responsibility of corporate executives. Friedman claims that executives usually have one responsibility – to make as much profit as possible. This is a positive statement which tells us what the responsibility of executives is. Does it follow from this that business executives *ought to maximize* the corporation's profit? If so, we have derived an 'ought' from an 'is' statement. Those philosophers who think this inference is permissible note that if someone has a responsibility to do *x*, it follows that she ought to do *x* – that is what having a responsibility means. For example, if a corporate executive signs a contract in which they promise to maximize the profits of the corporation, they ought, by virtue of signing this contract, to maximize profits to the best of their abilities (Searle 1964). Although there are cases in which 'ought' seems to derive from 'is', very often normative statements don't follow from positive statements. One approach to this problem is to acknowledge that normative statements are based on values, and to state these values explicitly if someone makes a normative claim. Later in this chapter, we look at some of the values commonly used as a basis of normative statements. This requires that we delve into the realm of ethics and how it applies to the study of business and society.

The distinction between positive and normative statements is important in policymaking. Government policies are usually based on a mixture of positive and normative claims. Consider a policymaker who observes data on economic inequality which shows that inequality has increased sharply since the year 2000. The policymaker might ascertain that if one increases taxes on inheritance, inequality will decrease. This is a positive statement which identifies a relationship between inheritance tax and inequality. But this statement does not automatically lead to the normative policy recommendation that the government should try to reduce inequality by taxing inheritance; before we recommend raising taxes on inheritances, we need to state why reducing inequality is desirable and whether raising taxes on inheritance is the best policy to reduce inequality. Might increasing tax on yearly incomes over $1 million be a better way to reach this end? Policy proposals are based on both positive and normative analysis, and it is important to be aware which aspects of policy analysis belong in which category.

Key discussion questions

- What is the difference between positive and normative statements?
- What are some problems of business ethics?

- Explain some differences between utilitarianism and rights-based theories of ethics.
- Can business be ethical?

Ethics in business and society

If business always improved the well-being of everyone in society, we might not need to discuss ethics. Unfortunately, business does not just make some people better off; it also makes some people worse off, and it frequently involves wrongdoing. This is why we must look at business from an ethical perspective. Think of environmental destruction (Chapter 16) or workplace discrimination against racial minorities and LGBTQ people (Chapter 20); most people think these are bad. Many ethical problems of business are hidden from us because firms do not publicize their unethical practices. Consider for example the production of goods and services you consume. Does the chocolate you eat contain cocoa grown using child labour (Mistrati 2010, 2014; Hinch 2018)? Or consider issues of privacy when it comes to smart phones, apps and other digital devices. Sometimes new technologies raise new ethical questions, like the collection and use of our personal data (see Chapter 24).

Ethics is not only of interest to those who study business; it's important to businesses themselves because ethics is related to what some call the 'social licence' to do business (Gunningham et al. 2004; Morrison 2014). This social licence refers to the acceptability of business practices in the eyes of those affected by business (e.g. workers, consumers). Earning the goodwill of people requires that a business go beyond conforming to legal and regulatory requirements imposed by government because businesses face *social* expectations which constrain the way businesses conduct themselves. These expectations are rooted in ethical understandings of what is permissible and what is unacceptable business practice; if businesses fail to conform to these expectations, they face opposition, adverse publicity or consumer boycotts, all of which damage the reputation of business and therefore reduce its profits.

Consider an example. In the aftermath of natural disasters like hurricanes, businesses sometimes increase the prices of goods and services which are desperately needed by those affected but in short supply. Bottled water, hotel rooms and portable electricity generators might be life saving items to people whose houses have collapsed. Electricity generators might go up in price significantly in the aftermath of a hurricane as consumers scramble to obtain one. This phenomenon is known as *price-gouging*. While it's illegal in some US states, in most jurisdictions, it's perfectly legal. But whether legal or not, price-gouging often creates outrage because businesses are making excess profits by exploiting the desperation of consumers who cannot do without the goods and services mentioned (Sandel 2009: 3–10). Businesses which adopt such practices breach a sense of fairness and risk losing the goodwill of those they serve (Kahneman et al. 1986; Roth 2007). This is an example a business losing its social licence. Sometimes a precarious social licence affects a whole sector which the public distrusts. For example, food producers that use genetically modified ingredients are subject to widespread distrust in Europe.

The risk of losing its social licence means that business has to be concerned with ethics. *Business ethics* is the field that deals with these issues (De George 1987; Parker 2002). Its origins can be traced back to the corporate revolution (Chapter 7) and attempts to bind corporations to the social good, especially in countries like the United States. Public fears about big business at the end of the nineteenth century led to calls from business leaders as well as from the public and politicians that the goals of business be aligned with broader social goals like creating jobs and supporting economic growth (Khurana 2007). Business schools, dating from the early twentieth century in the United States, emphasized the importance of the social role of business as social and public institutions in American society. However, this approach didn't last. During the 1970s and 1980s business leaders asserted that business should only be concerned with profit. Business schools ended up adopting this view and teaching that firms should focus on their bottom line, as measured by their financial success, share price and returns to investors.

This new approach has significant ethical implications. Business ethics became an established part of management science with its own scholarly journals, textbooks and specialized academic programmes (Bowie 1986; De George 1987). Business ethics scholars showed how business decision-making has a large impact on society and 'stakeholders' (e.g. workers, consumers, community members). The 1984 Bhopal chemical accident in India and the Exxon Valdez oil spill off the coast of Alaska in 1989 are important examples of these negative impacts of business. It's important to note that when we discuss business ethics, we must be careful to distinguish what we mean by 'business' (Avi-Yonah 2005), since the form of business has changed over time. This is important since business ethics also entails examining how business can be changed in order to produce impacts we want or to reduce impacts we don't want (see Chapters 20, 21 and 22). This involves normative analysis, for it concerns how business ought to be organized.

Understanding business ethics

Here we'll unpack business ethics in two ways. First, we'll consider the 'level' at which we want to understand the ethics of business. Second, we'll consider the way in which ethics is shaped by economic theories of the market.

Level of impact. According to Manuel Velasquez (2012: 15), business ethics can be used to examine different levels of business: (1) systemic, (2) corporate and (3) individual. At the systemic level, business ethics analyses social institutions and structures. Questions arising at this level are broad and include things like: Is capitalism an ethically acceptable mode of production or is it systematically exploitative? Or: Is 'free' trade fair to poor countries? At the corporate level, business ethics examines particular organizations, for example, businesses like Walmart or Gazprom, or international organizations like OPEC or the World Bank. Here, business ethics explores the activities and impacts of the organization, and whether the procedures it follows are fair. At the individual level, business ethics looks at the people involved in business; for example, do managers bribe politicians to gain businesses contracts? Do executives investigate allegations of sexual harassment in the workplace? According to Velasquez, then, business ethics can in principle turn its attention to just about anything related to business – from macroscopic items at the systemic level to the smallest details of a particular firm and the executives who work for them.

Ethics and theories of the market. A second way of understanding business ethics concerns the way in which business ethics situates itself in relation to the market economy and theories thereof. There are two primary positions to be considered here: the 'strong' and the 'pragmatic'. The strong position is propounded by market fundamentalists – or 'neoliberals' (see Chapter 1) – who contend that the market is the best and therefore most ethical way to organize society. Neoliberal thinkers tend to make strong normative claims, even when using the seemingly neutral language of economics (see Chapters 5 and 6). Those associated with the neoclassical school of economists use the concept of *efficiency* to support the market, whereby 'efficiency' is understood in terms of markets optimally satisfying people's preferences (see Chapter 5). This view is often traced back to Adam Smith and his contention that individual self-interest rather than benevolence can promote the common good (Chapter 2). Neoliberals like Friedman (1962) and Friedrich Hayek (1944 [1994]), by contrast, base their normative arguments in favour of the market not on the notion of efficiency but liberty, whereby they argued that free markets ensure the greatest possible freedom to people.

Friedman's view of the relationship between freedom and capitalism feeds into his market-centred approach to business ethics. He famously argued against claims that corporate executives should consider a wide range of social responsibilities when making business decisions. If they were to prioritize 'social responsibility', Friedman argued, they would be in conflict with their primary responsibility, that is, to act as agents of the corporation's owners (shareholders) (see Chapter 9). According to Friedman, business executives are responsible only to the shareholders of the company, which means that they should try to maximize profits so long as they follow the constraints of law and the ethical customs of society. A business executive who promotes other goals, like reducing pollution or promoting economic equality, is acting like a politician rather than fulfilling their duty as a corporate executive. (Friedman 1970: 122).

In contrast to Friedman's 'strong', market-centred position on business ethics, others like Velasquez (2012) take a 'pragmatic' position. This pragmatic position is not driven by a set of first principles (e.g. people are self-interested, markets are optimal allocators of resources, markets promote liberty); instead, Velasquez investigates which specific decisions will solve particular problems. He argues that:

> ethical behavior is the best long-term business strategy for a company – a view that has become increasingly accepted during the last few years. This does not mean that occasions never arise when doing what is ethical will prove costly to a company. . . . Nor does it mean that ethical behavior is always rewarded or that unethical behavior is always punished. . . . To say that ethical behavior is the best long-range business strategy just means that, over the long run and for the most part, ethical behavior can give a company significant competitive advantages over companies that are not ethical. (2012: 7)

Unlike Friedman, Velasquez believes that a wide range of ethical decisions can be advantageous for a business because ethical behaviour promotes the long-term good of the business. As a result, corporate executives can widen their responsibilities to include all sorts of socially beneficial goals without compromising their fiduciary duties to shareholders. Making ethical decisions, according to Velasquez, is not easy, and so executives and other employees in businesses need help in ascertaining what the right decision is. Business ethics informs managers and executives of how to make ethically sensitive decisions on a case-by-case basis. By doing so, a corporation which follows the precepts of business ethics will appear more trustworthy in the eyes of its stakeholders, and this promotes the corporation's goal of maximizing profitability.

Critique of business ethics

As we have seen, the difference between the strong and pragmatic views of business ethics opens a door for a more general critique. Consider how each view would answer the following question: Should a manager or executive take an ethical decision if doing so will reduce profitability? Friedman's answer is clearly 'no', but Velasquez's answer is not so predictable. If ethics and profits conflict, what should corporate executives do? This leads to a crucial question for business ethics: Should managers and executives adopt an ethical management strategy only when it is helpful in attaining profits? If so, when ethical decisions threaten profitability and competitiveness, profits trump ethics. This is what Friedman counsels. If Velasquez wishes to avoid Friedman's position, he should put forward a more robust notion of ethical decision-making as something worthy of pursuing for its own sake, rather than because pursuing it leads to long-term profitability. When ethical decisions and profitability go hand in hand, there's no need to question whether a manager or executive is being ethical for the sake of being ethical or for the sake of ensuring profitability. But if being ethical leads to a competitive disadvantage, should the executive choose profits over ethics or *vice versa*? Velasquez evades this question by arguing that ethical companies have a competitive advantage over unethical companies. Yet it's our argument that any approach to business ethics which does not provide a clear answer is evading a crucial issue. And approaches which say that profits trump ethics are simply not taking a sufficiently critical approach to business.

The view that ethics and profitability go hand in hand has become prevalent among executives and lobbyists. This has led to a shift in business regulation. Regulation is often seen as a task of government and the regulatory agencies which oversee the business world (Chapter 18). Governments create laws and policies for the regulation of business such as minimum wage, environmental protection, health and safety and antitrust laws. Today, governments are still concerned with regulation, but since the 1980s, a new *self-regulation approach* has emerged with regard to business. According to this view, business is best placed to regulate itself. The self-regulation view became popular in the era of neoliberal government like those of Margaret Thatcher in the UK and Ronald Reagan in the United States. It is understandably supported by many business executives and investors, but it is also supported by many business ethics scholars. Few of these scholars deny that businesses have been the cause of many egregious harms and injustices, but they nonetheless claim that businesses have learned from their past and have reformed themselves to become responsible organizations. They have learned, as Velasquez states, that malpractice is bad for long-term performance, and consequently it is in the interest of businesses to conduct their affairs in a socially responsible manner. There is therefore no need, according to proponents of the self-regulation view, for close oversight or strict regulation of business by government.

But how exactly do businesses regulate themselves? A prominent way is through codes of conduct (Bondy et al. 2004). The codes can be firm-specific or industry-wide. They can address many issues, such as workplace discrimination and harassment, standards of consumer service and environmental impact. They are written sometimes by representatives of the business to which the code applies, and though they may be developed in consultation with external stakeholders (e.g. government, consumer groups, NGOs), the influence of industry or business representatives is strong. Although they outline procedures for dealing with breaches of the guidelines, codes of conduct differ from government regulation because they're not legislated by government or imposed by regulatory agencies, meaning that compliance is often voluntary, and breaches are not met with serious sanctions.

Advocating for self-regulation is a central task of what Joel Bakan (2020) calls the 'new' corporation. Contemporary corporations portray themselves as 'new' by claiming that they are concerned with social issues like climate change, workers' rights, employee discrimination and so on. But beyond these claims, 'new' corporations claim they can effectively pursue these goals without government regulation. This type of self-regulation has earned the name 'soft' regulation in contrast to the 'hard' regulation of government. As Bakan (2020: 67) writes: 'The advantages for corporations are obvious. They're free to create their own rules and decide when and how to follow them rather than being bound by the government's mandatory edicts.' But Bakan doubts whether the new corporation's goals can be aligned with broader social goals through self-regulation (2020: 66–78). He lists numerous areas in which government regulation has receded and the catastrophes which have resulted from poor regulation, including the 2008 global financial crisis (see Chapters 17 and 18). If ethics always aligned with corporate profitability, we wouldn't have to worry about regulating firms, for the profit-oriented executive would, in the interest of the firm, adopt ethical business strategies in the knowledge that they are to the advantage of the firm and its shareholders. But the fact that self-regulating firms and industries have been the cause of malpractice, mismanagement and economic misery should make us wary of claims that corporations can be trusted to regulate their own affairs.

A further criticism holds that business ethics is too individualistic; it focuses on managerial decision-making and asks how executives ought to make decisions (Parker 2002: 97). From this point of view Velasquez relies too heavily on the individual rather than the corporate or systemic level to develop his position. A consequence of adopting an individualistic approach to business ethics is that business structures are taken as given, and attention is directed to decision-making within those structures. As we have seen already, one widely held view is that the goal of corporations is to maximize the profits of their owners. If executives become preoccupied with devising means to maximize profits, they can lose sight of the fact that the means proposed might violate ethical standards. Consider the increasingly common practice of random drug testing of employees in the workplace. In some contexts such as professional sports we might find this quite normal, but its extension to other spheres of work raises ethical questions (Christie 2015). Is compulsory drug testing a violation of employees' privacy rights? Are employees who agree to be tested in a position of weak bargaining power, such that they cannot refuse to submit themselves to drug tests because they fear being fired if they do so? If so, insisting that employees undergo drug tests would be a coercive measure. If managers become too absorbed in the task of maximizing profits, they can impose policies on workers which, to an outsider, might seem outrageously unethical. In 2015, for example, Oxfam uncovered allegations that US poultry workers were denied bathroom breaks during their shift, which resulted in the poorly paid workers in this branch either urinating in their pants or wearing diapers at work (Oxfam America 2015). Business ethics scholars are as likely to condemn such practices as anyone else, but the culture of business, as it exists in the corporate world, is one in which decision-makers can lose their ethical bearings in the name of pursuing profit. Business schools, despite placing business ethics in their curriculum, can fail to instil ethical beliefs in their students who are destined to become the future executives of the corporate world. It's important, therefore, to understand how and where people learn ethics and not just what ethical principles might be best suited to particular business activities.

Key ethical issue: How do we learn ethics? The role of the business school

How do people learn ethics? Is the way that ordinary people develop an understanding of ethics different to the way future corporate executives learn ethics in business schools? Business schools have played an important role in training managers and executives and, consequently, they play a key role in shaping the field of business ethics. What influence do business schools have on their students' ethical understanding? Examining business school curricula can help us to understand how and why businesspeople adopt specific ethical practices in their workplaces. The examination reveals something rather worrying: people who receive their education at business schools – and in (neoclassical) economics programmes more generally – tend to believe that everyone is self-interested; acting upon that belief, they behave more selfishly themselves (Ferraro et al. 2005). There are even studies that show that managers and executives with MBAs from business schools are more likely to commit unethical acts than those who are not trained in business schools. Perhaps some of the egregious ethical outrages perpetrated in the pursuit of corporate goals would be less frequent if ethics were taught differently. Consequently, it is important to think about how and where ethics is taught.

Sources: Ferraro et al. (2005); Khurana (2007)

Ethics beyond business

Business ethics is a special kind of ethics applied to business. But business ethics is strongly influenced by ethical principles and theories which have been developed outside the field of business over many centuries by thinkers like Confucius, Aristotle, Thomas Aquinas, Jeremy Bentham, Immanuel Kant, Mary Wollstonecraft and John Stuart Mill. We now consider some of the moral theories in the European tradition that have influenced business ethics and can be used to guide ethical decision-making. It's also worth noting that ideas about how business might be conducted ethically are prevalent in the Global South and by those who practice business in the Social and Solidarity Economy (see Chapters 20, 21 and 22).

Utilitarianism. Jeremy Bentham (1748–1832), the original exponent of utilitarianism, put forward the *principle of utility* according to which we should approve of actions that produce happiness or individual utility and disapprove of actions that produce pain, unhappiness and disutility (see Chapter 5). Bentham's principle contains positive statements which describe the actions of which people approve or disapprove. But Bentham moves from his principle of utility to the normative precept: 'Of an action that conforms to the principle of utility one may always say that it ought to be done' (Bentham 1789 [1879], I.X). This is an example of an author who apparently derives an 'ought' from an 'is' statement.

Utilitarianism holds that people's actions should be judged according to the 'net' pleasure (the pleasure minus the pain) they create; pleasure is the highest good we all seek, and the best action is the one that produces the 'greatest good for the greatest number'. This applies not only to individuals but also to policymakers. Utilitarianism does not tell people in which specific actions pleasure is to be sought; it leaves this up to people themselves. Similarly, governments should take their citizens' preferences as given and ask which laws and policies will maximize utility among citizens. So, if citizens want a high minimum wage or a generously funded public broadcasting company, that is what government should bring about.

We can summarize three characteristics of utilitarianism:

1. Utilitarianism is *value neutral*: it doesn't tell people which preferences they should have or what kinds of values are most important; it takes people's preferences as a given – much like economists typically do, as we discussed in Chapter 5 – and it tries to satisfy the greatest number of them.
2. Utilitarianism is a *consequentialist* ethical approach: utilitarians judge people's actions according to their consequences, and the consequences of actions are assessed in terms of how much utility they produce.
3. Utilitarianism is *impartial*: in assessing which action will bring about the most pleasure for most people, utilitarians treat all people *equally*; it does not say that the pleasures of a special group of people are more important than those of other people.

Point 3 requires elucidation. Most actions bring about pleasure as well as pain; for instance, if I occupy the only available space in a parking lot, I'll be happy but you won't. Imagine that you stop and tell me that you are the CEO of a well-known corporation and you are so important that you should get the parking space instead of me. A utilitarian would object: *who* you are makes no difference to the best outcome; all that matters is which outcome – you getting the parking space or me – maximizes net pleasure; if net pleasure is maximized when I get the parking space, that is a better outcome than you getting the space.

Utilitarianism is very influential in public policy, and it also underlies how economists view markets as mechanisms for allocating goods and services in society. Economists claim to 'prove' that a market equilibrium maximizes welfare (i.e. utility) in society, but there are many, often dubious, assumptions on which this 'proof' relies, and utilitarianism does not necessarily support the market fundamentalist view (Boatright 2003; Velasquez 2012). Indeed, before we can ascertain whether, from a utilitarian perspective, the market is a better way of allocating goods than a different system, or whether the for-profit corporation is better or worse way of organizing business than, for example, cooperative business, a great deal of detailed analysis based on reasonable assumptions is required.

Utilitarianism requires that you take actions to your disadvantage if doing so produces happiness in other people which outweighs your own unhappiness. If, for example, large numbers of people in developing countries are dying from preventable diseases because of a lack of affordable vaccines, then giving away two-thirds of your income to a vaccination programme which can prevent many premature deaths is going to increase net happiness far more than if you spend your income on a new car or luxury holiday (Singer 1972). Some people think utilitarianism is too demanding: Are you doing something bad by not giving most of your income to charity every year? Utilitarians often say 'yes' – acting ethically involves sacrifice, and even if we do not often live up to the demands of utilitarianism, the theory is important in letting us know when our actions fall short of its ethical standards.

Rights theory. The concept of a 'right' is another important basis for ethical theory. Rights are entitlements of individuals and groups regarding their interests, freedoms or choices. There are many types of rights: human rights, natural rights, legal rights, rights created by contracts and so on, though we do not comment on them all here (Dworkin 1984; Raz 1984). If someone has a right, other people have a duty to respect this right, and so we need to consider correlative duties which rights impose on others. For example, if a customer has a right to privacy, businesses have a duty not to collect and share their information with others, at least not without the customer's consent; privacy rights are the basis of policies that limit the surveillance powers of businesses and governments. Other examples include the right to pursue the profession of one's choosing or the right to own property, to which we return later. These rights, like privacy rights, impose a *duty or obligation of non-interference* on other people, including governments and organization like businesses. For instance, if I choose to pursue a career as a dentist, nobody has a right to stop me; in fact, everyone else has a duty not to interfere with my career pursuits. Rights which entail this duty of non-interference by others in your affairs are called *negative* rights; they are 'negative' because these rights impose a duty on others to refrain from interfering with you. Negative rights circumscribe a 'private sphere' for individuals. Within that sphere, an individual has a right, or is free, to act as they choose. The private sphere grants individuals *autonomy* to make choices without intervention or hindrance by others. Some of your fundamental rights are negative: the right to practise the religion of one's choosing or not to practise a religion at all; the right to marry or not to marry at all; the right to vote for a political party of one's choosing.

Negative rights are important in the economic sphere. We have already mentioned the right to pursue the profession of one's choosing, something which is important for the determination of the social division of labour in a capitalist society discussed in Chapter 4. The right to own property privately is also essential to a capitalist society. The English philosopher, John Locke (1632–1704), claimed that humans have a 'natural right' to property based on what we fashion or create through our labour as individuals. More recently, Locke's approach has been used by so-called libertarians, such as Robert Nozick (1974), as a moral argument against government interference with the economic decisions of private individuals and businesses. Libertarians offer a rights-based theory in which property rights are held to be inviolable and therefore protected from interference by others, particularly by government. According to this view, you have a right to do what you like with your property (use it, sell it, give it away, even destroy it), and nobody can force you to do anything with your property against your will. As long as you do not infringe the rights of others, you are free to do with my property what you wish. This includes using your property as capital to set up a business. Libertarianism is therefore strongly aligned with free-market capitalism. According to libertarians, one way in which governments interfere with property is through taxation on income which you earn therefrom (e.g. collecting rent). They believe that government powers should be limited because they advocate a 'minimal state' which provides basic public goods like national defence and a judicial system, but should not redistribute income or wealth from the rich to the poor.

Rights-based ethical theories contrast with utilitarianism in that they are not consequentialist but *deontological* (*'deon'* being the ancient Greek word for *that which obliges*). Recall that utilitarians judge actions by the consequences they bring about; rights-based theorists judge an action by asking whether anyone's rights are violated by actions. If an action doesn't infringe upon anyone's rights, it's permissible, but if it violates somebody's rights, it's forbidden. If certain actions lead to a large increase in utility for many people, utilitarians are likely to support the necessary means for bringing about those actions. But rights-based theories are against compelling people to act in ways which will maximize utility. For instance, on utilitarian grounds it would be better if pharmaceutical companies produced more effective medicines which cure or prevent diseases like cholera, dysentery and malaria instead of developing technologies for erectile dysfunction, breast implants or hair loss. But theories which take property rights seriously would object because the owners of pharmaceutical companies have a right to use their property as they wish, not according to whether their company produces medicines which save the most lives.

Rights-based theories not only defend people's rights from potential violation on utilitarian grounds; sometimes rights themselves conflict. To adapt a well-known case, if a bakery refuses to make a cake for my same-sex wedding celebration because the bakery's owner objects to gay rights, it seems like a straightforward case of discrimination which infringes my right as a consumer to receive service from a business independent of my sexual orientation. But if the baker's refusal is based on their religious conviction that gay marriage is wrong, it becomes a matter of conflicting rights, because, against my right not to suffer discrimination, the baker asserts their right to religious freedom. If they were compelled to provide the wedding cake, the right of the bakery's owners to practise the religion of their choice without impediment would be infringed. Whose rights should be given priority? Such cases are usually decided by courts, and you can find examples in the Masterpiece Bakery case (*Masterpiece Cakeshop v. Colorado Civil Rights Commission* 2018) in the United States and Ashers Bakery (*Lee v. Ashers Bakery Company Ltd. and others* 2018) in Northern Ireland.

We've seen that many rights theorists, libertarians included, focus predominantly on negative rights. Other rights are called *positive* rights. These ensure that a person has the ability to do what is inscribed in the right. One recognizes a positive right in the duties they impose on others: if the constitution of a country grants a right to clean drinking water, ensuring that its citizens enjoy this right is not simply a matter of not interfering with citizens' autonomy; rather, if a citizen lacks access to drinking water, somebody has a duty to provide it. This 'somebody' is often the government (Fabre 2000).

In modern liberal constitutions and charters of rights, negative rights outnumber positive rights. Examples of positive rights include the right to employment, a decent standard of living, a universal basic income, paid holiday from work and affordable housing. If societies fail to grant such positive rights, citizens who lack a decent standard of living are left vulnerable, and negative rights do not provide relief; for all that they provide protection from interference, negative rights for a poor person might mean little else than a right to starve unless government grants rights to food, housing and the other constituents of a decent standard of living (Fabre 2000).

Conclusion

This chapter has explained the distinction between positive and normative statements, both of which are essential components in the study of business and society and in the field of policymaking. We have also offered an account of business ethics and critiques of the limits of mainstream business ethics as it is taught in business schools. Business ethics, we argued, often takes an insufficiently critical view of business practice and the social structures within which business operates. In the final part of the chapter, we have introduced two ethical theories – utilitarianism and rights-based theories – which are widely used as a basis in normative discussions of business and society.

Bibliography

Avi-Yonah, R. (2005) 'The Cyclical Transformations of the Corporate Form: A Historical Perspective on Corporate Social Responsibility', *Delaware Journal of Corporate Law*, Vol. 30, pp. 767–818.

Bakan, J. (2020) *The New Corporation: How 'Good' Corporations are Bad for Democracy*, New York, Vintage Books.

Bentham, J. (1789 [1879]) *An Introduction to the Principles of Morals and Legislation*, Oxford, Clarendon.

Boatright, J. (2003) *Ethics and the Conduct of Business*, Upper Saddle River NJ, Prentice Hall.

Bondy, K., Matten, D. and Moon, J. (2004) 'The Adoption of Voluntary Codes of Conduct in MNCs: A Three-country Comparative Study', *Business and Society Review*, Vol. 109, pp. 449–77.

Bowie, N. (1986) 'Business Ethics', in J. DeMarco and R. Fox (eds), *New Directions in Ethics*, New York, Routledge, pp. 158–72.

Christie, T. (2015) 'A Discussion of the Ethical Implications of Random Drug Testing in the Workplace', *Healthcare Management Forum*, Vol. 28, pp. 172–74.

De George, R. (1987) 'The Status of Business Ethics: Past and Future', *Journal of Business Ethics*, Vol. 6, pp. 201–11.

Dworkin, R. (1984) 'Rights as Trumps', in J. Waldron (ed.), *Theories of Rights*, Oxford, Oxford University Press, pp. 153–67.

Elliott, L. (2019) 'World's 26 Richest People Own as Much as Poorest 50%, Says Oxfam', *The Guardian*, 21 January, https://www.theguardian.com/business/2019/jan/21/world-26-richest-people-own-as-much-as-poorest-50-per-cent-oxfam-report (accessed 31 July 2022).

Fabre, C. (2000) *Social Rights under the Constitution: Government and the Decent Life*, Oxford, Oxford University Press.

Ferraro, F., Pfeffer, J. and Sutton, R. (2005) 'Economics Language and Assumptions: How Theories Can Become Self-Fulfilling', *Academy of Management Review*, Vol. 30, pp. 8–24.

Friedman, M. (1962) *Capitalism and Freedom*, Chicago, University of Chicago Press.

Friedman, M. (1970) 'The Social Responsibility of Business is to Increase its Profits', *The New York Times Magazine*, September 13, pp. 122–5.

Gunningham, N., Kagan, R. and Thornton, D. (2004) 'Social License Environmental Protection: Why Businesses Go Beyond Compliance', *Law & Social Inquiry*, Vol. 29, pp. 307–41.

Hayek, F. (1944 [1994]) *The Road to Serfdom*, Chicago, Chicago University Press.

Hinch, R. (2018) 'Chocolate Slavery, Forced Labour, Child Labour and the State', in A. Gray and R. Hinch (eds), *A Handbook of Food Crime*, Bristol, Policy Press, pp. 77–92.

Kahneman, D., Knetsch, J. and Thaler, R. (1986) 'Fairness as a Constraint on Profit Seeking: Entitlements in the Market', *American Economic Review*, Vol. 76, pp. 728–41.

Khurana, R. (2007) *From Higher Aims to Hired Hands*, Princeton, Princeton University Press.

Mistrati, M. (2010) *The Dark Side of Chocolate Child Trafficking and Illegal Child Labor in the Cocoa Industry*, Copenhagen, DR TV.

Mistrati, M. (2014) *Shady Chocolate Business*, Copenhagen, DR TV.

Morrison, J. (2014) 'Business and Society: Defining the "Social Licence"', *The Guardian*, 29 September, https:// www.theguardian.com/sustainable -business/2014/sep/29/social-licence -operate-shell-bp-business-leaders (accessed 30 June 2022).

Noonan, L., Tilford, C., Milne, R., Mount, I. and Wise, P. (2018) 'Who Went to Jail for Their Role in the Financial Crisis?', *Financial Times*, 20 September, https://ig.ft.com/jailed -bankers/ (accessed 5 July 2022).

Nozick, R. (1974) *Anarchy, State and Utopia*, New York, Basic Books.

Oxfam America. (2015) 'Lives on the Line', https://www.oxfamamerica.org/ livesontheline/ (accessed 15 July 2022).

Parker, M. (2002) *Against Management*, Cambridge, Polity Press.

Raz, J. (1984) 'On the Nature of Rights', *Analysis*, Vol. 93, pp. 194–214.

Roth, A. (2007) 'Repugnance as a Constraint on Markets', *Journal of Economic Perspectives*, Vol. 21, pp. 37–58.

Sandel, M. (2009) *Justice: What's the Right Thing to Do?* New York, Farrar, Straus and Giroux.

Searle, J. (1964) 'How to Derive "Ought" from "Is"', *Philosophical Review*, Vol. 73, pp. 43–58.

Singer, P. (1972) 'Famine, Affluence, and Morality', *Philosophy and Public Affairs*, Vol. 1, pp. 229–43.

Velasquez, M. (2012) *Business Ethics: Concepts and Cases* (7th Edition), New York, Pearson.

20 | Business and social exclusion

Caroline Shenaz Hossein

Introduction

Understanding how people participate in the business world is important. In Chapter 3, we explored how European countries extracted resources from the Global South as part of their own wealth accumulation. Cedric Robinson (1983) has shown that the dehumanization of certain groups of people will inevitably take place in order to exploit their labour in the capitalist system, labelling this phenomenon 'racial capitalism'. Similarly, Walter Rodney (1982) has illustrated that the underdevelopment of the Global South (along with its negative consequences for people of African descent) by processes of capitalist extraction and imperialism was not accidental. Despite these systemic harms, there are other ways of doing business and understanding its potential impact on the world. Thus when we look at social exclusion we must also explore the myriad of ways that people participate in the 'economy' on their own terms (see Gibson-Graham 1996, 2006; Hossein 2013, 2018; Roelvink et al. 2015).

Different crises (see Chapter 17) and forms of exclusion often push people to think of new ways of organizing the economy. Van Staveren (2015) argues that since the 2007–8 global financial crisis, many people have been exploring new ways to think about the economy to ensure that business is more embedded in social relations. The 2015 Greek financial crisis alerted citizens around the globe to the attitudes of business and government elites, and triggered action to reclaim the kind of markets people want to see in their societies. During the global pandemic (2020–) people around the world engaged in mutual aid groups to help one another during lockdowns and disruptions to trade. The police murder of George Floyd (May 2020) was the catalyst for Black Lives Matter protests around the world, protests which focused not only on the brutality of police violence toward Black communities (see Ransby 2018) but also on holding corporations accountable for their anti-Black racism.

In this chapter we want to examine some of the ways that people engage with business, both as workers and entrepreneurs in the Global South, and as racially marginalized groups in the Global North. For example, in

Rethinking Racial Capitalism Gargi Bhattacharyya (2018) pushes us to examine how excluded people create their own systems to make themselves free. While people commonly participate in capitalist markets as wage earners, they can also be producers, cooperators, members of labour unions or entrepreneurs. In the Global South, businesses often take the form of owner-operated legitimate but unregistered businesses, often very small in scale, that are part of the informal economy (see Chapter 22). These businesses can operate as sole-proprietorships but also as family-owned business and cooperatives. At times these businesses can provide the means for people to manage their exclusion from mainstream capitalist markets and create economic opportunities especially if they are following a cooperative model. In this chapter, we examine two ways of doing business: one that exploits and excludes the poor as workers; and another that can liberate them through some forms of self-employment. The question driving this chapter is: How can some forms of business be oppressive and other forms liberating? We want to stress that it is important to focus on how marginalized groups create alternative business opportunities, rather than simply see them as victims of capitalism.

As we've noted already (see Chapter 13), people's experience of business is different in different countries. Some countries have laws and regulations in place to manage diversity, equity and equality issues in the workplace, and others do not. It's important to note that discrimination in business affects people in all countries, although in different ways. For example, a person's identity (e.g. their social class, gender or race) can limit access to business resources, leading to the marginalization of certain groups in the economy and in the wider society (Hossein 2014b, 2015). This raises the issue of social exclusion. Yet, business can be liberating as well if it's people-focused (Gordon Nembhard 2011; Hossein 2016). At the global level, capitalist firms engage in exploitative employment practices, but at the small- and micro-business level, especially those that are member-owned, people can be viewed as creating and managing livelihoods on their own terms.

Definition: Informal economy

The informal economy is defined as a diversified set of economic activities, enterprises, jobs and workers that are not regulated or protected by the state. The concept originally applied to self-employment in small unregistered enterprises. According to Hart et al. (2014), the discourse on the informal economy can also include people in unprotected low-wage employment.

Source: Hart et al. (2014)

Key concept: Social exclusion

Social exclusion is defined as both the structure and processes of inequality among groups in society, and particularly inequality in the structural access to resources of those disadvantaged groups. In the book *Canada's Economic Apartheid*, Galabuzi (2006) argues that social exclusion refers to the inability of racialized Canadians to participate fully in society and the economy due to structural inequalities in access to social, economic, political and cultural resources.

Source: Galabuzi (2006)

In this chapter, as noted earlier, we examine two ways of doing business: as employees or as entrepreneurs. The examples consider the role of identities in business and how people react to systemic exclusion. For instance, it is important to look at diverse experiences, such as the cooperative enterprises of Canada's Indigenous people in the hinterlands or racialized women working as employees in an MNC in the Global South. In analysing business and social exclusion, we have to recognize that while mainstream business can be used as a tool to subjugate and control different social groups (e.g. racialized people, women), economically and politically, it can also be co-opted by marginalized people as a way to resist and counteract racialized capitalism (see also Chapter 21). Our objective in this chapter, then, is to consider how business can be simultaneously oppressive and freeing.

Identities are seldom analysed in mainstream business because markets are believed to be immune from racial, class and gender bias. By contrast, we locate the contextual environment and examine the identities of marginalized people, arguing that these do matter in market environments. Considering identities in business enables us to move away from a one-dimensional view of marginalized people as victims of an unsustainable economic system to seeing them as a group of people who resist oppressive economic models through their own forms of doing business. It is important to look at the innovative ways people engage in commerce to meet their livelihood needs and create a sustainable economic model.

Key discussion questions

- What is business exclusion? How can you distinguish it from social exclusion?
- How are people exploited as workers?
- What are some gender-specific risks in MNCs?
- How can the MDM theory explain social exclusion in Global South countries?
- Can business be viewed as a form of resistance for marginalized groups?

Untangling mainstream and critical perspectives

Modernization theory is a set of linear prescriptions that emanated from North American and Western European countries, implementing 'free' trade and 'free' markets under the guise of 'trickle down economics' (see Chapter 3). This enforced spread of capitalism by the Global North is associated with the 'Washington Consensus' (Williamson 1993), which we discuss in Chapters 13 and 14. Often associated with neoliberalism, the Washington Consensus shaped how the Global South was supposed to develop (Harvey 2007), as outlined in the case study of Indonesia and Chile. The Washington Consensus was based on the enactment of a series of fiscal reforms and structural adjustment programmes (SAPs) that were meant to set 'underdeveloped' countries on the right track to economic growth and prosperity. These reforms and SAPs were underpinned by an assumption that for the countries of the South to develop economically, they had to shift from being traditional and communal societies to more scientific, rational, secular and individualized societies.

The market fundamentalism promoted by the Washington Consensus has been disastrous for many countries around the world; the push for economic growth has come at a great cost. The negative effects have been particularly glaring in Southern countries in the aftermath of SAPs. Countries have adopted a pro-business system of low taxation, reduced welfare spending, privatization, trade liberalization and so on, which has had an adverse effect on vulnerable groups, especially women, elderly and children. SAPs totally ignore the complex social and historical terrain of the Global South, especially the experiences of enslavement and colonization that have instituted a colour-coded economic pyramid in which local elites (e.g. whitened elites through miscegenation [racial intermingling] or ethnic groups favoured by colonizers) inherited land, money and power at the expense of others (Thomas 1988).

Case study

Modernizing experiments: Indonesia Inc. and the Chicago Boys in Chile

The Global North's political and business elites 'tested' their economic reforms in countries like Indonesia and Chile.

The first major meeting to divide up the domestic economies of the Global South was in 1967 at a meeting in Switzerland. There, global capitalist elites decided how to parcel out key sub-sectors, such as banking, forestry, minerals and manufacturing in Indonesia. This meeting is commonly known as 'Indonesia Inc.', as political leaders as well as the Rockefeller Foundation, Lehman Brothers, Chase Manhattan Bank and international financial institutions (IFIs) met to determine the legal infrastructure for foreign investment in the country. This expansion of multi-national corporations (MNCs) into

---

the country was supported by Indonesia's president, General Suharto (1967–98). As a result of these investments, the Suharto family became one of the richest in Indonesia.

A few years later, another 'development' experiment was carried out in Chile after the 1973 overthrow of socialist president Salvador Allende by General Augusto Pinochet – supported by the US government. This is perhaps the most famous experiment of neoliberal 'reform', seen as a success story by many neoliberal thinkers. The experiment was led by Chilean alumni of the University of Chicago's Department of Economics who had returned home to try to implement neoliberal economic reforms. These men, who became known as the 'Chicago Boys', adopted the theories of Milton Friedman and other Chicago economists, and were able to implement these theories during Pinochet's authoritarian dictatorship (1973–90).

Both countries implemented a 'development' agenda that embraced an anti-state position favouring capitalist business models, which gave business owners the right to use labour and capital as they pleased with few impediments. The result of these 'modernizing' experiments has contributed to the exclusionary nature of business in these societies and elsewhere.

Source: *New Rulers of the World* (2001), fifty-three minutes, directed by Alan Lowery

As a result, business in many parts of the Global South has ended up controlled by local elites who exclude others from engaging in business. In her book *World on Fire: How Exporting Free Market Democracy Breeds Ethnic Hatred and Global Instability*, Amy Chua (2004) argues that the free-market mantra promoted by the Global North is dangerous because it does not consider this historical bias embedded in former colonized countries. Unrestrained capitalism manifests itself in a way that enables local elites in both business and politics to collude and manage investments to the exclusion of the indigenous masses. Chua (2004), a Filipina-American of Chinese ancestry, recounts a personal story in which servants in the Philippines slit her aunt's throat in an expression of ethnic hatred. Chua developed the concept of market-dominant minorities (MDMs) to understand these colonial histories, basing it on the observation that the elite business class is usually composed of a distinct racial or ethnic group. These political and economic elites collude with the IFIs and MNCs to reinforce existing inequalities in society. An example of MDM is the 250,0000 Lebanese that live in West Africa (The Economist 2011); rich Lebanese businesspeople have made payments to politicians like Sierra Leone's Siaka P. Stevens (1967–85) and Liberia's Charles Taylor (1997–2003) in exchange for exclusive rights to the diamond mines. The MDMs concept is useful because it helps explain how history has created a highly classed and racialized private sector in many countries around the world, where economic elites who are a distinct racial or ethnic group exploit the labour of the other racial or ethnic groups.

In contrast to critics like Chua, business professor C. K. Prahalad (1941–2010) argued, in his 2006 book *Fortune at the Bottom of the Pyramid: Eradicating Poverty through Profits*, that the private business sector can create economic opportunities for people in the Global South. According to Prahalad's 'bottom of the pyramid' (BOP) theory, engaging with the world's 4 billion poorest people as consumers could shift the poor upwards from the BOP, creating a range of business opportunities for the majority of people. The BOP theory is controversial as it illustrates how business can be used to promote the fortunes of the majority but ignores the structural inequalities embedded in a system. Prahalad (2006) claimed that multi-national businesses miss an opportunity when they discount the BOP and that the dominant logic of business has to change to work with businesses in the Global South. Many CEOs of MNCs do not see the poor as participating in the economy other than as beneficiaries of charity. Supporters of the BOP theory argue that it helps business to change their perceptions of the poor, highlighting how they are not only consumers but also producers and entrepreneurs.

Are global firms exclusionary or an opportunity?

Early development experiments in Indonesia (1967) and Chile (1973) – see case study – set in motion market fundamentalism for the Global South. Since then, MNCs have been on the move in search of cheap labour and inputs (see also Chapter 13). The Washington Consensus is firmly embedded in the South and in the IFIs, such as the World Bank, that promote market reforms. As a result, Southern countries compete among themselves and local elites strive to make their countries more appealing to foreign investors by lowering labour and environmental regulations (see Chapter 18), reducing tax levels and supplying cheap unskilled labour.

These development policies have embraced an anti-state argument and pushed capitalist business models that reinforce social divisions among people. This is particularly glaring in the Global South in the aftermath of SAPs imposed by IFIs. The negative effects of SAPs are not felt equally. For example, the market reforms of the 1980s required countries to adhere to a pro-business regime of low taxation, reduced welfare spending and the elimination of subsidies for things like fuel and food, which adversely affected the most vulnerable people, especially women and children. Market fundamentalism has ended up exacerbating historically rooted social conflicts. Issues of social exclusion are particularly well documented in the aftermath of SAPs. In her work, Oxford professor Francis Stewart (1991) has argued that women are the ones most affected by fiscal restructuring. Because of cutbacks to social services, women put extreme pressure on localized forms of social capital. In the aftermath of market reforms, women have the triple burden of work, family and community responsibility in order to fill in the gaps left by the withdrawal of government support (Stewart 1991). In her case study of Latin America, Molyneux (2002) also shows that responsibility for adjusting to restructuring falls most heavily on poor women, who have to figure out how to feed communities without their labour being compensated by the state or NGOs. For example, the poorest women are the ones who organize collectively on top of their paid workload to create soup kitchens or kitchen gardens in order to feed each other.

Key concept: Social capital as a contested concept

Social capital is a contested concept. It has been embraced by both the left and the right. Social capital represents human relationships either as personal 'assets' held by individuals or as social 'assets' held by social groups. It has been used to represent a variety of social phenomena, including social norms (e.g. the bonds that bind communities together), social networks (e.g. the linkages that bring diverse communities together) and social diversity (e.g. the differences between communities). Harriss (2002) in *Depoliticizing Development* points to the concept as an important tool of the World Bank in carrying out infrastructure and development projects in the Global South. While the concept has been criticized, it has also proved to be an influential idea that has been mainstreamed into government policies, business practices and the social economy (see Chapter 17).

Sources: Woolcock (1998); Harriss (2002)

Former Filipino president Ferdinand Marcos pushed women into precarious and dangerous work with the ultimate goal of increasing state revenues and his personal income (Pyle 2001). Women were forced into the informal economy as sex trade workers, domestics (e.g. nannies and maids) and factory workers. In the case of factory work, several studies have found that MNCs prefer young female workers in their twenties because they are viewed as compliant, docile, fearful of male authority and less likely to complain about wages, working conditions and long work hours (Stewart 1991; Pyle 2001). The mistreatment of the poor in MNCs value chains is well documented, and there is much debate about the benefits of MNCs to poor countries.

There is a counter perspective of MNCs, however, and it does not come from modernizers alone: critical feminists, particularly from the South, have also promoted the idea that MNCs can be beneficial to the people who secure employment through these firms. For the pro-market modernizers, MNCs are viewed as important investors in the poorest countries in the world. The argument is that MNCs not only create jobs but their presence also creates a demand for local value chains, thereby leading to the growth of locally owned subcontracting firms and scores of independent home-based businesses. Naila Kabeer (2004) questions liberal (Western) feminists who support the boycott of MNCs, maintaining that they can provide income and social benefits to working women in poor countries. A rush to regulate and boycott MNCs can have dire consequences for local economies, with damaging impact for the very people that liberal feminists intend to help. In countries where women have few opportunities due to tradition and customs that inhibit them from pursuing a career, these low-paying jobs provide them with a new form of confidence, status and leadership. The thinking here is that regulations to improve working conditions have to come from within a country in order to be effective. In a *New York Times* video, for example, Kalpona Akter, executive director of the Bangladesh Center for Worker Solidarity, argues that policymaking designed to improve the working conditions of people must come from inside the country, as the act of shaming international firms might deter them from investing in the country.

Short video: Local women speak out! – *Made in Bangladesh*

Some Bangladeshi women are not convinced that firms hiring four million people should be expelled from the country. This video clip (3.12 minutes) suggests that although women value the work they are doing, some of them agree there has to be legislation that also protects their rights as workers. In this short video, the journalists look at the conditions of female workers in garment factories in the wake of the 2011 fire at Rana Plaza, which claimed 1,100 lives. The debate remains over how to best regulate MNCs and local sub-contractors to ensure people do not lose their jobs.

Source: *New York Times* (2013). *Made in Bangladesh*: www.nytimes.com/video/world/asia/100000002231544/made-in-bangladesh.html?ref=asia (accessed September 2016)

Can business be a form of resistance? A critical perspective

In *The Great Transformation*, Karl Polanyi (1944 [2001]) argued that capitalist markets are not free or self-regulating (see Chapters 1 and 2). In fact, he argued that markets are socially constructed, especially by the state, to serve elite interests. Polanyi warned that privileging economic life over social life would be disastrous. He argued that it would lead to a social backlash, or 'double movement', as people would protest the social disruption caused by disembedding markets from society (see Chapters 16 and 17). This Polanyian perspective helps us to put the welfare of people before profit. The idea of 'putting people first' and markets second challenges the mainstream perspective that profit should override other considerations in business – see the discussion of shareholder primacy in Chapter 8, for example.

A contemporary example of this is Muhammed Yunus (2010), the 2006 Nobel Peace Prize winner, who questioned the role of banks in modern capitalism and set up the Grameen Bank three decades ago. 'Grameen' is a Bengali term for village. The aim of the bank was to put people first and to reorganize financial services in the form of group 'microbanking'. In his efforts to make microbanking socially inclusive, Yunus calls into question the kind of markets that exclude ordinary people from access to finance. Three decades after its inception, Yunus' microfinance movement, first energized in the South, proved that people-focused institutions can do banking differently, that is, through solidarity economics (see Chapter 22).

Despite positive experiences, however, commercialized microfinance has faced significant criticism for failing to offer actual alternatives to capitalism (see Roy 2010; Hossein 2014b, 2015). Feminist geographer Katharine Rankin (2001) was one of the first critics of microfinance, arguing that it is simply a strategy to make Nepali women 'rational economic actors' who fit into neoliberal economics. In her view, it did not change the systemic bias against poor women in society at all. While the 'Bangladesh Consensus', which was the South's response to the Washington Consensus (Roy 2010), failed to turn the tide of neoliberal politics, it offers an alternative vision of business that can be socially inclusive through a group model. As we detail in Chapter 22, the significance of the social economy (including nonprofits, cooperatives, self-help groups, associations, foundations etc.) demonstrates that business can be undertaken in ways to work for people.

These forms of alternative and cooperative economics were central concerns in the work of liberation scholars like Booker T. Washington, W. E. B. Du Bois and Marcus Mosiah Garvey, all three of whom are important but neglected theorists in the social economics of excluded people. Booker T. Washington (1856–1915) was born into slavery and rose to prominence as an African American leader, founding Tuskegee University. He strongly promoted the movement of Black people into trades and business. W. E. B. Du Bois (1868–1963) was the first African American to receive a PhD from Harvard University and co-founded the National Association for the Advancement of Colored People (NAACP). In *Souls of Black Folk*, Du Bois (1903 [2007]) showcased the business acumen of Africans and their concern for community. He also outlined the dislocation caused by African Americans' experience of enslavement, as well as the persistent and cruel forms of discrimination, exclusion and alienation in US society. In *Economic Cooperation among Negro Americans*, Du Bois (1907), through his concept of group economics, urged African Americans to draw on African traditions to create solidarity businesses. Finally, Marcus Mosiah Garvey (1887–1940) was a Jamaican-born moral philosopher and entrepreneur who put forward ideas of self-reliance in business for the African diaspora (Martin 1983). His theory of

Pan-African economic cooperation is followed by Black communities such as the Nation of Islam and Rastafarians.

Key thinker: Marcus Mosiah Garvey (1887–1940)

Marcus Garvey is an early example of a 'social entrepreneur' – someone who uses business in the pursuit of social goals. His press, Negro World, published articles that mattered to the disenfranchised African American community in the United States. He founded the Universal Negro Improvement Association (UNIA) and the African Communities League (ACL) to create one of the largest member-owned institutions for the African diaspora in the world. Garvey also founded a shipping firm, Black Star Line, through which he focused on maritime trade with Africa as well as cooperative-run laundries, restaurants and doll-making factories. The UNIA and ACL were created to uplift the lives of oppressed people through collective businesses. However, this idea of pursuing Black self-reliance and independence through business threatened white America, and Garvey was subject to economic sabotage and accused of mail-fraud by the US government.

Source: Martin (1983)

The goal of liberation theorists who advocate for inclusive markets is to co-opt business so that it creates opportunities for excluded and marginalized groups and allows these groups to seek freedom through economic independence in their own collective enterprises – enterprises that prioritize the needs of community – rather than simply working in white-owned businesses. It should be noted that Garvey, Du Bois and Washington were influenced by their own life experiences; and while they quarrelled with one another in terms of how to uplift an impoverished group, they all believed in diverse, alternative and cooperative economics.

Doing business in and for marginalized groups can be seen as a form of resistance to the negative impacts of capitalism, and it requires significant courage (also see Chapter 16). African American feminist economist Jessica Gordon Nembhard (2014) argued, in *Collective Courage: A History of African American Cooperative Economic Thought and Practice*, that economic sabotage, lynching and murder were very real threats that African Americans faced as they tried to create cooperative economies for themselves. One of the most dangerous of these was the Underground Railroad, which 'smuggled' hundreds of people out of slavery through informal collectives (Du Bois 1907). The Underground Railroad between America and Canada was a collective effort and a sharing of resources. Human rights activist and former slave Harriet Tubman was a remarkable heroine in this movement, assisting hundreds of slaves to freedom in Canada. African Americans and racialized people have been threatened since slavery, throughout the Jim Crow era, and into modern times, and the way people resisted oppressive systems was through self-managed cooperatives, but these institutions were (and still are) viewed as subversive.

Short video: Organizing cooperative businesses in the United States

America's Black citizens have endured violent attacks since slavery right up to the modern day. These racially marginalized people have been pioneers in the cooperative movement in the United States. In this interview from *The Laura Flanders Show*, City University of New York's (CUNY) Jessica Gordon Nembhard discusses the ways African Americans have engaged in both informal and formal collectives throughout history and into modern times, shaking up the idea that cooperatives originated in Europe.

Source: www.youtube.com/watch?v=_TVIghQMkBg#t=11 (accessed 23 October 2015)

Being an entrepreneur is not easy. Excluded groups in the Global South and North will turn to self-employment not only as a way to cope but also as a way to contribute to the business sector on their own terms (Knight 2004; Mirchandani 2002). Immigrant and diaspora groups also turn to entrepreneurship in order to improve their independence and economic well-being (see Chapter 15). Feminists have argued that social exclusion in business has prompted excluded people to create community economies, one such example being women workers in MNCs. Self-employment can also open up the economic possibility of determining one's own future. Here, we present three examples that illustrate the business exclusion of Haitians, Indigenous Canadians and people in the Global South, and how people react to such business exclusion.

First, the film *Poto Mitan: Haiti Women, the Pillars of the Global Economy* (2009) documents the lives of several Haitian women living in Cité Soleil (one of the largest slums in the Caribbean) and working in American sweat-shops for local subcontracting firms. These women rejected these low-wage jobs because they were precarious, unsafe, demeaning and lacked benefits and turned to self-employment. As outlined in Hossein's (2014a) work, Haitian women engage in collective commerce through the *caisses populaires* (credit unions) in order to support each other in business. They run their businesses out of their homes and in this way are able to take care of their children. While their incomes remain low, the women are no longer subject to harassment or maltreatment in the workplace. Moreover, they have the flexibility to engage in socially conscious-raising events that address poverty and gender-based violence in the community.

Second, in *Living Rhythms: Lessons in Aboriginal Economic Resilience and Vision*, Wanda Wuntunee (2010) describes the various ways Indigenous peoples in Canada pursue their economic livelihoods. Indigenous peoples, while one of the fastest growing racial groups in Canada, are plagued by poverty and social exclusion in the hinterlands and cities. In turning to business, some Indigenous peoples pursue profit, while others are more concerned with community well-being. The multifaceted ways people choose to do business illustrate how business can be liberating for some people – even if not for others, as we outline elsewhere in this book. In the empirical example later, we use Arctic Co-operatives Limited to show how group economics can help communities. For Indigenous Canadians, turning to business does not mean undermining social life, but finding a balance between respecting the social world and doing business (Wuntunee 2010; Southcott 2015).

Finally, in *Portfolios of the Poor: How the World's Poor Live on $2 a Day*, Collins et al. (2009) show that low-income people in Bangladesh, India and South Africa have complex financial lives with an array of devices to meet their economic needs, despite their financial exclusion. One of the most important financial supports for people who are excluded from mainstream business services is rotating savings and credit associations (ROSCAs) (Geertz 1962; Van Staveren 2015, Hossein 2016, 2018; Hossein and Christabell 2022) (see also Chapter 22).

Community economies have always been a part of our world and socially excluded people from businesses that work for them in spite of market fundamentalism (Gibson-Graham 1996, 2006; Roelvink et al. 2015; Hossein 2018). The most marginalized people rely on the support of friends and family to help them engage in entrepreneurial or personal projects. In this way, people are able to translate social capital – that is, their personal relationships, networks and contacts – into businesses aimed at caring for the well-being of people rather than profit alone.

Empirical example: The Arctic Co-operatives Limited, Canada

We draw on a specific example from Canada in order to illustrate this chapter's arguments that racially marginalized people can co-opt business to support their own lives and communities. The Arctic Co-operatives Limited (ACL), based in Manitoba, Canada, is an economic organization set up over fifty years ago to support the Inuit, Dene and Métis peoples. The following discussion is drawn from the Canadian Community Economic Development Network, an association of community groups and individuals.[1]

ACL is a service federation, owned and controlled by thirty-one Inuit and Dene community-based cooperative business enterprises located in Nunavut and the Northwest Territories. These cooperatives include retail stores, hotels, cable television operations, construction, outfitting, arts and crafts production and property rentals. The role of ACL is to coordinate resources, consolidate purchasing power and provide operational and technical support to the cooperatives. ACL enables local cooperatives to provide a wide range of services to their over 18,000 local member-owners in an economical way. ACL's democratic governance structure is designed to support the local ownership and control of each cooperative. Cooperative members take ownership in their local community business and have an equal share in the business affairs of the cooperative, as they adopt a 'one member, one vote' policy. Members are encouraged to participate in the operation of their cooperative by contributing ideas and making decisions on the policies and future direction of the cooperative.

For the Inuit and Dene peoples in Canada's Arctic, cooperation and collaboration are incorporated into the traditions and cultural contexts that frame everyday life. Survival in this harsh climate has always been a struggle, requiring informal family and group cooperation. As contact increased with Europeans, the former became aware of the cooperative business model and saw the fit with their own values and cultures. These early cooperatives were based on arts and craft production, fur harvesting and commercial fisheries, aspects of life important to Indigenous peoples.

In 1965, fourteen local cooperatives joined together with the government of Canada to form an Inuit art marketing organization – Canadian Arctic Producers. In 1981, two existing cooperative federations, the Canadian Arctic Producers Cooperative Limited and The Canadian Arctic Cooperative Federation Limited, joined together to form Arctic Co-operatives Limited (ACL). Founders had certain goals that they felt were best met by using the cooperative business model. For example, members did not want people from outside their communities coming in and establishing businesses to sell products and provide services, which would drain local income from the community and would not keep money circulating locally. It made sense to develop the services themselves co-operatively, and retain the profits from any businesses for their own opportunities and priorities. In this way, the profits could be used to develop new and better services and enterprises, which would create additional employment opportunities for both co-op and Indigenous members of the society.

The ACL symbolizes the importance of cultural preservation and the traditional values of cooperation and collaboration through business within northern communities. This cooperative business model has proven extremely successful. The ACL is an example of a cooperative business that hires 800 people and has revenues of all member businesses of nearly $179 million (as of 2009). It is an important story of Indigenous Canadians co-opting business to preserve culture and respect their social lives.

Conclusion

Business and social exclusion need not only concern the various ways in which market fundamentalism alienates people from their labour and lives. It is also important to understand that commerce, markets and business differ around the world (see Chapter 13). The Polanyi Institute at Concordia University in Montreal, Canada, is home to a group of community economy scholars who are interested in tackling cultural influences on markets and looking for business alternatives that are more amenable to human life. The Diverse Solidarities Economies Collective (DISE) is a group of feminist political economy scholars writing on new economies. Community Economies Research Network (CERN) is a global network of activists and researchers committed to publishing on diverse economies and to unravelling the idea that there is only one way to do business. People participate in markets in a variety of ways, as employees as well as cooperators and entrepreneurs (Gordon Nembhard 2011). In the globalization of extreme versions of free-market capitalism, it is worth noting that many business people are co-opting business concepts and models to not only resist corporate capitalism but also to pluralize the kinds of economic institutions we have in our world today in order to ensure we prioritize economic justice and social well-being.

In discussing business and social exclusion, this chapter introduced less well-known critical thinkers who have long argued for economic alternatives to business exclusion. These thinkers shed light on the Polanyian double-movements occurring in today's world, where people collectively organize counter-movements to show that business can be carried out in ways that are respectful of people. The ACL, an Indigenous cooperative, is an important example of a racially marginalized group creating a social-purpose business to share indigenous culture as well as to provide jobs for its people. Another positive contribution in business is made by the self-managed banking groups called ROSCAs, which people turn to and use alongside mainstream business services (Hossein 2013, 2016). People will opt out of commercial banking systems and participate in community-driven banking systems they know and trust.

By taking stock of the small things people do to resist mainstream business practices, we give power back to people, and by recognizing the diverse economies people come up with, we can correct the assumption that most people are simply passive victims of business and markets. The everyday counter-movements ordinary people are taking to protest mainstream capitalism are happening in different ways around the globe. The Poto Mitans in Haiti is a striking example of people's resilience in finding market alternatives. Collective economics speak to the many and diverse ways people will mobilize local resources to create people-oriented economic opportunities considerate of the community.

Suggested readings

- Chs 3 and 4, Galabuzi, G. (2006) *Canada's Economic Apartheid: The Social Exclusion of Racialized Groups in the New Century*, Toronto, Canadian Scholars Press.
- Ch. 1 Robinson, C. (2000) *Black Marxism: The Making of the Black Radical Tradition.* Second edition. London, Zed Press.
- Ch. 2, Gibson-Graham, J.K. (1996) *The End of Capitalism (As We Knew It): A Feminist Critique of Political Economy*, Oxford, Blackwell Publishers.
- Introduction, Gordon Nembhard, J. (2014) *Collective Courage: A History of African American Cooperative Economic Thought and Practice*, Pennsylvania, Penn State University Press.
- Ch. 1, Prahalad, C.K. (2006) *The Fortune at the Bottom of the Pyramid: Eradicating Poverty through Profits*, Upper Saddle River, NJ, Wharton School Pub.
- Introduction, Wuntunee, W. (2010) *Living Rhythms: Lessons in Aboriginal Economic Resilience and Vision*, Kingston, ON, McGill-Queens University Press.

Note

1   Canadian Community Economic Development Network: www.ccednet-rcdec.ca/CEDprofiles and www.arcticco-op.com/ (accessed June 2016).

Bibliography

Bhattacharyya, G. (2018) *Rethinking Racial Capitalism: Questions of Reproduction and Survival*, London, Rowman & Littlefield.

Chua, A. (2004) *World on Fire: How Exporting Free Market Democracy Breeds Economic Hatred and Global Instability*, New York, Anchor Books.

Collins, D., Morduch, J., Rutherford, S. and Ruthven, O. (2009) *Portfolios of the Poor: How the World's Poor Live on $2 a Day*, Princeton, Princeton University Press.

Du Bois W.E.B. (1903 [2007]) *The Souls of Black Folk*, Minneapolis, Filiquarian Publishing.

Du Bois W.E.B. (1907) *Economic Co-operation among Negro Americans*, Atlanta, Atlanta University Press.

The Economist. (2011) 'Lebanese in West Africa: Far from Home', 20 May. www.economist.com/blogs/baobab/2011/05/lebanese_west_africa (accessed 21 October 2014).

Galabuzi, G. (2006) *Canada's Economic Apartheid: The Social Exclusion of Racialized Groups in the New Century*, Toronto, Canadian Scholars Press.

Geertz, C. (1962) 'The Rotating Credit Association: A Middle Rung in Development', *Economic Development and Cultural Change*, Vol. 10, pp. 241–263.

Gibson-Graham, J.K. (1996) *The End of Capitalism (As We Knew It): A Feminist Critique of Political Economy*, Oxford, Blackwell Publishers.

Gibson-Graham, J.K. (2006) *A Postcapitalist Politics*, Minneapolis, University of Minnesota Press.

Gordon Nembhard, J. (2011) 'Micro-enterprise and Cooperative

Development in Economically Marginalized Communities in the USA', in A. Southern (ed.), *Enterprise, Deprivation and Social Exclusion*, New York, Routledge, pp. 254–76.

Gordon Nembhard, J. (2014) *Collective Courage: A History of African American Cooperative Economic Thought and Practice*, Pennsylvania, Penn State University Press.

Harriss, J. (2002) *Depoliticizing Development: The World Bank and Social Capital*, London, Anthem.

Hart, K., Laville, J.-L. and Cattani, A.D. (2014) *The Human Economy*, Cambridge, Policy Press.

Harvey, D. (2007) 'Neoliberalism as Creative Destruction', *The Annals of the American Academy of Political and Social Sciences*, Vol. 61, pp. 21–44.

Hossein, C.S. (2013) 'The Black Social Economy: Perseverance of Banker Ladies in the Slums', *Annals of Public and Cooperative Economics*, Vol. 84, pp. 423–42.

Hossein, C.S. (2014a) 'Haiti's *Caisses Populaires*: Home-Grown Solutions to Bring Economic Democracy', *International Journal of Social Economics*, Vol. 41, pp. 42–59.

Hossein, C.S. (2014b) 'The Exclusion of Afro-Guyanese in Micro-Banking', *The European Review of Latin America and Caribbean Studies*, Vol. 96, pp. 75–98.

Hossein, C.S. (2015) 'Government-Owned Micro-banking and Financial Exclusion: A Case Study of Small Business People in East Port of Spain, Trinidad and Tobago', *Canadian Journal for Latin American and Caribbean Studies*, Vol. 40, pp. 393–409.

Hossein, C.S. (2016) 'Money Pools in the Americas: The African Diaspora's Legacy in the Social Economy', *Forum for Social Economics* (forthcoming).

Hossein, C.S. (ed.) (2018) *The Black Social Economy in the Americas: Exploring Diverse Community-Based Markets*, New York, Palgrave.

Hossein, C.S. and Christabell, P.J. (2022) *Community Economies in the Global South: Case Studies about Rotating Savings and Credit Associations and Economic Co-operatives*, Oxford, Oxford University Press.

Kabeer, N. (2004) 'Globalisation, Labor Standards, and Women's Rights: Dilemmas of Collective (in)action in an Interdependent World', *Feminist Economics*, Vol. 10, pp. 3–35.

Knight, M. (2004) 'Black Canadian Self-employed Women in the Twenty-First Century: A Critical Approach', *Journal of Canadian Woman Studies*, Vol. 23, pp. 104–10.

The Laura Flanders Show. Interview with Jessica Gordon Nembhard. www.youtube.com/watch?v=_TVIghQMkBg#t=11 (accessed 23 October 2015).

Martin, T. (1983) *Marcus Garvey, Hero: A First Biography*, Dover, The Majority.

Mirchandani, K. (2002) 'A Special Kind of Exclusion: Race, Gender and Self-employment', *Atlantis*, Vol. 27, pp. 25–38.

Molyneux, M. (2002) 'Gender and the Silences of Social Capital: Lessons from Latin America', *Development and Change*, Vol. 33, pp. 167–88.

New Rulers of the World. (2001) Film: 53 Minutes. Prod. Alan Lowery.

New York Times. (2013) *Made in Bangladesh*.www.nytimes.com/video/world/asia/100000002231544/made-in-bangladesh.html?ref=asia (accessed September 2016).

Polanyi, K. (1944 [2001]) *The Great Transformation*, Boston, Beacon Press.

Poto Mitan: Haitian Women, Pillars of the Global Economy. 2009. Film: 60 minutes. Prod. Tet Ansanm.

Prahalad, C.K. (2006) *The Fortune at the Bottom of the Pyramid: Eradicating Poverty through Profits*, Upper Saddle River, Wharton School Pub.

Pyle, J. (2001) 'Sex, Maids and Export Processing Zones: Rules and Reasons for Gendered Global Production Networks', *International Journal of Politics, Culture, and Society*, Vol. 15, pp. 55–76.

Rankin, K. (2001) 'Governing Development: Neoliberalism, Microcredit and Rational Economic Women', *Economy and Society*, Vol. 30, pp. 18–37.

Ransby, B. (2018) *Making All Black Lives Matter: Reimagining Freedom in the Twenty-First Century*, Oakland, University of California Press.

Robinson, C.J. (1983 [2000]) *Black Marxism: The Making of the Black Radical Tradition* (2nd Edition), London, Zed Press.

Rodney, W. (1982) *How Europe Under-developed Africa*, Washington, DC, Howard University Press.

Roelvink, G., St. Martin, K. and Gibson-Graham, J.K. (2015) *Making Other Worlds Possible: Performing Diverse Economies*, Minneapolis, University of Minnesota Press.

Roy, A. (2010) *Poverty Capital: Microfinance and the Making of Development*, New York, Routledge.

Southcott, C. (2015) *Northern Communities Working Together: The Social Economy of Canada's North*, Toronto, University of Toronto Press.

Stewart, F. (1991) 'The Many Faces of Adjustment', *World Development*, Vol. 19, pp. 1847–64.

Thomas, C.Y. (1988) *The Poor and the Powerless: Economic Policy and Change in the Caribbean*, New York, Monthly Review Press.

Van Staveren, I. (2015) *Economics after the Crisis: An Introduction to Economics from a Pluralist and Global Perspective*, New York, Routledge.

Williamson, J. (1993) 'Development and the "Washington Consensus"', *World Development*, Vol. 21, pp. 1329–36.

Woolcock, M. (1998) 'Social Capital and Economic Development: Towards a Theoretical Synthesis and Policy Framework', *Theory and Society*, Vol. 27, pp. 151–208.

Wuntunee, W. (2010) *Living Rhythms: Lessons in Aboriginal Economic Resilience and Vision*, Kingston, McGill-Queens University Press.

Yunus, M. (2010) *Building Social Businesses: The New Kind of Capitalism That Serves Humanity's Most Pressing Needs*, New York, Perseus Book Group.

21 | Resistance and alternatives to corporate capitalism

Kean Birch and John Simoulidis

Introduction

The *autonomist* Marxist professor John Holloway (2005: 1) starts his book *Change the World without Taking Power* with the phrase: 'In the beginning is the scream. We scream'. He goes on: 'Faced with the mutilation of human lives by capitalism a scream of sadness, a scream of horror, a scream of anger, a scream of refusal: NO'. As a critic of capitalism, Holloway is concerned not only with dissecting capitalism and corporate power but also wants to think about resistance and revolution as ways to find alternatives that do not fall into the same trap as previous generations – a point to which we will return later. In particular, the emphasis he places in the title of his book on *not* 'taking power' reflects his concern that alternatives to capitalism simply replace one form of authoritarian or totalitarian political-economic regime with another one, as happened with the major socialist revolutions of the twentieth century. As Holloway (2005: 12) argues, the socialist countries that emerged in the twentieth century – like the Union of Soviet Socialist Republics (USSR) discussed in Chapter 10 and the People's Republic of China – have done 'little to create a self-determining society or to promote the reign of freedom'. Consequently, it is necessary to look beyond these examples in order to think about resistance and alternatives to capitalism and corporate power.

It is perhaps pertinent to start this chapter with the criticisms laid at the door of capitalism. While there are many well-known critics of capitalism, like Karl Marx from the nineteenth century and Karl Polanyi from the twentieth century, who we have already discussed in this book, there are many, many more we cannot cover in the space available. In light of this fact, we refer to a few recent examples here, especially people critical of the corporate form of power (or *corporate capitalism*). For example, the legal scholar Joel Bakan (2004, 2020) wrote a well-known book called *The Corporation* in the early 2000s, which was subsequently turned into a film of the same name. In this book, Bakan argues that the corporation is a 'pathological institution' because its organizational structure and governance compels people to act in ways similar to a psychopath. In the sequel to this book, which was also turned into a film, he argues that the new corporation is essentially the same as the old one, but a bit more 'charming': portraying itself as a socially responsible 'good corporate citizen'. However the 'good' corporate citizen is fundamentally bad for democracy since it is unaccountable to the public it serves and promotes corporate social responsibility as a weak substitute for public oversight and regulation. Others like Birch (2007) argue that the corporation is a 'totalizing institution' that colonizes other social institutions (e.g. family, school, community). As a result, corporate capitalism comes to infiltrate our lives in often insidious ways. The anthropologist David Graeber (2011) argues that informal, reciprocal and everyday economies are only transformed into formal markets, including capitalist ones, through state-led violence. Andreas Malm (2016: 14) argues that despite regular warnings from the Intergovernmental Panel on Climate Change, we have been carrying on the destructive 'business as usual' path of global warming, 'an economy of self-sustaining growth predicated on the growing consumption of fossil fuels, and therefore generating a sustained growth in emissions of carbon dioxide'. Finally, David Schweickart (2011) claims that the major social issues of our day – extreme inequality, unemployment, overwork, poverty, lack of real democracy and environmental degradation – are all connected to the institutions of capitalism. He argues that 'economic democracy' is a better and now realistic alternative, and for this reason, capitalism is no longer justifiable as an economic order.

As these ideas demonstrate, and as we illustrated in Chapter 12, there are many ways to criticize corporate capitalism; equally, there are many alternative visions, alternatives practices and alternative organizational structures to corporate capitalism (see Gibson-Graham 1996, and Chapters 15 and 22). The sociologist Erik Olin Wright (2016) divides the 'logics of resistance' into alternatives that involve 'taming', 'smashing', 'escaping' or 'eroding' capitalism. First, 'taming' involves working within capitalism through the development of political and policy strategies to ameliorate the worst impacts of capitalism (e.g. Keynesianism, social democracy). Second, 'smashing' relates to the revolutionary resistance engendered by capitalism (e.g. the Bolshevik revolution in Russia). Third, 'escaping' is closest to forms of economic democracy (e.g. cooperatives) we discuss in the next chapter. And finally, 'eroding' involves finding new ways of organizing the economy that gradually promote and support the emergence of a whole new economic system. As these four logics suggest, alternatives to capitalism and corporate power come in many shapes and sizes.

In this chapter, our aim is to consider both resistance *and* alternatives to corporate capitalism. We start with a history of resistance, stretching back in history to a range of examples like the seventeenth-century Diggers movement and the nineteenth-century labour movement. We then turn to contemporary forms of resistance, especially evident in the rise of the so-called anti-globalization movement, which is better thought of as the *global justice movement*. We then finish with a discussion of a range of alternatives to corporate capitalism, such as fair trade, local exchange trading systems and social economy – the last of these we discuss in more detail in the next chapter.

Key discussion questions

- Does capitalism automatically generate resistance?
- Are there key moments in the history of resistance to capitalism?
- What are the alternatives to corporate capitalism?
- What is the Global Justice Movement?
- Is fair trade an alternative to corporate capitalism?
- Can you conceive of a world without capitalism? What would it be like?

Resistance and revolution

History of resistance to capitalism. Ever since capitalism first started to emerge at the end of the medieval period, it has engendered criticism and resistance. As Karl Polanyi (1944 [2001]) noted, capitalism and capitalist markets are *instituted* rather than natural; that is, they are created through the transformation of existing social relations to force people to act in certain ways. For example, in the early days of capitalism people had to be forced to seek a wage for their labour by throwing them off the land which provided them with subsistence. This required the institution of private property and the institutional separation of the state from the self-regulating market, a separation so complex it could only be effected by the state itself (see Chapter 18). All elements of production, especially the 'fictitious commodities' of land, labour and money (which were 'fictitious' because they are not produced for sale on the market like 'real' commodities) had to be available on the market for sale (see Chapter 2). In order to be subject to market regulation they needed to have prices: rent, wages and interest. Yet the market posed a threat to the natural and social substance of the 'social fabric' of society. As a result, the social history of capitalism always involved a 'double movement' according to Polanyi (1944[2001]: 76) where 'the extension of the market organization in respect to genuine commodities was accompanied by its restriction in respect to fictitious ones'. The transformation of society that resulted from capitalism, especially the disembedding of the economy from society, led to a counter-movement as people sought to re-embed the economy in social relations.

An early example of this double movement is the resistance and response to the English enclosures movement that started in the fifteenth and sixteenth centuries. We have already discussed the enclosures in Chapter 2, but it is important to emphasize how significant it was in terms of the social dislocation it caused to peasants who were thrown off land they had used for centuries with no alternative means of subsistence. Resistance to enclosures was commonplace, with frequent riots during this period. However, more concerted and organized resistance arose during the English Civil War (1642–51) with social movements like the Levellers and, especially, the Diggers (Kennedy 2008). The Diggers were established in 1649 by Gerrard Winstanley as a religious political group that directly challenged the creation of private property through the enclosure of land. The Diggers, in particular, highlighted the exploitation of unlanded workers by land owners, arguing for a return to common ownership and working of land (Kennedy 2008). As such, they reflected the logics of 'escaping' and 'eroding' capitalism outlined by Wright (2016).

Other historical examples of resistance to capitalism include the emergence of the labour movement in the nineteenth century, particularly across the European capitalist heartland. The labour movement involved the collective and voluntary forms of social organizing to create organizations – especially trade unions – which were controlled by neither the government nor capitalist business. As such, they represent an example of the social economy, which we come back to in the next chapter. Such collective organizing and bargaining was often made illegal and harshly punished in countries like the UK, where the 1799 Combination Act banned trade unions; although these Combination laws were repealed in 1825, it was not until 1872 that trade unions were then legalized in the UK (Marx 1867 [1976]). Although associated with key revolutionary figures, who we discuss next, the labour movement would fall into the 'taming' capitalism logic of resistance (Wright 2016), since it has often focused on the need to improve working conditions and wages. That is not always the case, however, as we discuss next.

Definition: Trade union

A trade union is a collective and voluntary organization which represents the interests of workers in bargaining with employers and protecting workers' rights (e.g. health and safety, working conditions, labour organizing). Originally banned and repressed by capitalist countries when they first emerged in the eighteenth and nineteenth centuries, they were eventually legalized after years of struggle. In some countries (e.g. Germany, Japan), they were integrated in the management of the economy through particular forms of corporate governance or representation – see Chapter 4.

A number of political parties emerged directly out of this labour movement, including parties following socialist, communist and anarchist ideologies.

Despite their differences, these groups generally had a common goal in the elimination of private property and, consequently, of capitalist social relations. As such, they represent an example of the 'smashing' logic outlined by Wright (2016). The political parties that emerged from the labour movement were often at the forefront of resistance and revolution in Europe, including the 1848 Revolution in France that inspired Karl Marx and Friedrich Engels to write the *Communist Manifesto* (Marx and Engels 1848 [1985]). Subsequently, people like Marx, Engels and the anarchist Mikhail Bakunin helped to establish the International Workingmen's Association in 1864, bringing together socialists and anarchists from a number of European countries. Although the International eventually split as a result of disagreements between socialists and anarchists, it had an enormous influence on the world. A number of revolutions or political changes in the early twentieth century have their roots in these political movements. For example, socialist and communist parties came to power in a number of countries, including Russia (1917), North Korea (1948), China (1949), Vietnam (1954) and Cuba (1959) (Hobsbawm 1995). Despite achieving significant industrial and technological progress, however, these socialist regimes descended into totalitarianism, eradicating freedom and oppressing their people (Holloway 2005; Wright 2016).

Key thinker: Mikhail Bakunin

Mikhail Bakunin (1814–76) was a major anarchist thinker who lived at the same time as Karl Marx. Born in Russia, Bakunin spent much of his life travelling around Europe, supporting a range of revolutions or movements against capitalism. Arrested in 1849, Bakunin spent eight years in prison and was exiled to Siberia, from where he escaped in 1861. As an anarchist, Bakunin was committed to the idea that individual people are responsible for their own destinies, meaning that he rejected the ideas of Marx and others that history has an inevitability to it which leads to social change. One of his most well-known written works is the book *God and the State*, which was not published until 1882, six years after his death. In it, Bakunin rejects authority and hierarchy in all its forms, from the religious to the political.

Source: Introduction, by Paul Avrich, to *God and the State* by Bakunin (1970)

From social democracy to postcapitalism? While these autocratic and totalitarian regimes are not suitable visions for our futures, they represented enough of a threat to capitalist governments in the early- to mid-twentieth century to ensure that these governments sought to establish social safety nets for their citizens/subjects – another form of 'taming' capitalism in Wright's (2016) terms. The creation of welfare states followed on from attempts to create forms of social democracy in which capitalism was aligned with broader social goals like eradicating poverty, uncertainty and insecurity (Malleson 2014). As the dominant capitalist regime from the end of the Second World War until the 1970s, social democracy was underpinned by the economic ideas of John Maynard Keynes and the social and political philosophies of politicians like William Beveridge and philosophers like John Rawls. It is often associated with a so-called golden age of capitalism lasting from the end of the Second World War until the early 1970s (see Varoufakis 2011).

Since then, and as we have mentioned a number of times in this book, critical scholars have generally argued that we have entered a 'neoliberal era' (e.g. Harvey 2005). Neoliberalism is often seen as a return to nineteenth-century *laissez-faire* thinking, but it is better thought of as a combining of the state *and* market instead. Since the 1970s, for example, the state has not got significantly smaller in many countries in the Global North (Birch 2015: 158); in many cases, in fact, it has got considerably bigger. Neoliberalism has generated all sorts of resistance and is often blamed for the mess left by the 2007–8 global financial crisis. Our interest in this chapter, however, is not with neoliberalism *per se*. As we outline in Chapter 1 of this book, we think that the critique of and focus on free markets that underlies critical perspectives of neoliberalism often means that people miss or ignore how important business – which is, by definition, not a market – continues to be to any understanding of capitalism. Hence, this is why we focus on corporate capitalism in this chapter.

More recently, and with corporate capitalism creating all sorts of social, political, economic and ecological problems, several thinkers have begun to posit the idea that we are fast approaching the emergence of a 'post-capitalist' era – that is, the erosion of capitalism altogether posited by Wright (2016). Largely inspired by technological developments and their implications for the organization of the economy, people like Peter Drucker (1993), Jeremy Rifkin (2014) and Paul Mason (2015) have all argued that capitalism is facing a major challenge as the result of capitalism's internal contradictions in light of things like: the declining cost of production, the increasing consumption of information rather than material products, the rise of network technologies (e.g. Facebook, Twitter) and the profound changes these are having on work and workers. While the hyperbole around postcapitalism might be a bit rich in some cases, it is still worth considering these ideas and their implications to the future of capitalism as we will experience it in the twenty-first century. According to Mason (2015), for example, the oppression of workers that characterizes neoliberalism has stalled capitalism's dynamism. Moreover, the 'users' of digital services like Facebook actually create the content that makes the service valuable to other users (including advertisers), which means that the line between producing and consuming has actually become blurred due to the new technologies. We come back to some of these issues in Chapter 23, but wanted to raise them here as a potential trajectory for capitalism in the future.

Everyday alternatives to corporate capitalism

Tinkering around the edges or finding alternatives to corporate capitalism? While it is important to think big when it comes to imagining how the world could be otherwise, it is also important to bring ourselves back to the day-to-day world in which we live if we want to pursue those alternatives. As this book should have demonstrated already, many people have tried to find ways to tame the worst excesses of capitalism and corporate power. Many others have simply sought to sell it to us as the only political-economic system that works. This defence of capitalism is now a veritable industry; around the world there are thousands of think tanks (e.g. Fraser Institute, Canada), foundations (e.g. Coors Foundation, United States), policy networks (e.g. Atlas Research Network, United States), international fora (e.g. World Economic Forum (WEF), Switzerland), journals and magazines (e.g. *The Economist*), newspapers (e.g. *The Financial Times*) and much more besides, all directed at buttressing the supposedly unassailable logic and legitimacy of corporate capitalism. This defence goes back decades to books like Neil Jacoby's 1973 *Corporate Power and Social Responsibility*, which sought to counter a radical critique of capitalism in US public discourse (cited in Parker 2002: 177). Moreover, this defence of capitalism is well funded and institutionalized in university business schools, economics departments and other academic units. Much of it, from business ethics and CSR to *The Economist*, represents the problems of corporate capitalism as requiring only a little tinkering at the edges; they typically claim that nothing at the core of capitalism or corporate power is inherently problematic, only the most egregious actions of the worst outliers. It is notable that in the context of the multiple colliding pandemic era challenges of sustainability, inequality and technological change the WEF, an organization of global elites, announced the need for a 'Great Reset' of the global economy. The programme surprisingly questioned neoliberal policies and urged a transition from shareholder to 'stakeholder capitalism' (Schwab 2020). Nevertheless, some have raised the question of whether this commitment can be maintained in a serious way by placing corporations themselves and the 'privileged 1% or .001%' at the centre of these initiatives.

The problem is that business-led transformations of capitalism can only extend so far; taming capitalism only does so much, as Wright (2016) argues, especially when it comes to changing or challenging the inner workings or regulations of corporations and businesses. Here, as David Ciepley (2013) highlights, the private rules and laws of business still hold sway; for example, a business employer can determine what an employee has to wear (e.g.

uniform), how they have to work (e.g. labour process) and what they can say (e.g. discipline), no matter what the rules and laws are in wider society more generally. As such, things like freedom of speech do not apply inside the walls of capitalist business. Should we desire economic democracy or diverse economies, as promoted by the likes of Gibson-Graham (1996), then we have to find ways to go beyond this political-economic confinement. Despite what many people tell us, the brazen trumpeting of capitalism does not mean there are not many other ways to organize our economies and many alternatives to corporate capitalism we could pursue. For example, Parker (2002) provides a typology of protest, resistance and alternatives with many examples of each that we have adapted and updated here in Table 21.1. Parker's typology covers a range of activities, groups and structures, and we discuss several of them in more depth in the rest of this chapter.

Alternatives to corporate capitalism. In this section we are going to outline four alternatives to capitalism: (1) alternative production and trade, (2) alternative currencies, like local exchange trading systems (LETS), (3) alternative property systems, like open source and (4) alternative organizational structures, like economic democracy. Because we look at the last two in more detail in the next two chapters, we only provide a limited discussion of them here. We focus, therefore, more on the first two. It is important to stress that these four alternatives are not, by any means, the only or main alternatives to corporate capitalism in the world. There are many other alternatives, as writers like

TABLE 21.1 Resistance to Corporate Capitalism

Contestation and reform	Globalization from below	Delinking/relocalization
Fighting structural adjustment	Environmental	Anarchy
Peace and human rights	Labour	Eco-socialism
Land reform	Socialism	Small business
Fair trade	Anarchism	Food Sovereignty
Sustainable development	Anti-free trade	Indigenous Sovereignty
Anti-corporate	protests	Religious nationalism
Cyber-libertarian	Zapatista	Local alternative
Jubilee 2000	Greenpeace	organization
Amnesty International	Trade unions	Slow food
Peasants, squatters,	Political parties	Alternative food network
indigenous	Cooperatives	Local trading, community
Boycotts (e.g. Nike, Monsanto)	Occupy movement	credit
Hackers, open source		Anti-colonial, independence
		movement
		Religious fundamentalism

Source: Adapted and updated from Parker (2002)

Gibson-Graham (1996), Parker et al. (2007) and Parker et al. (2013) illustrate in their work. However, since we have limited space in a book like this, we choose to focus on a few examples. Finally, we should note that the anti- and alter-globalization movements, through venues such as the World Social Forum, have provided a global network for alternatives to the corporate capitalist organization of the economy. This was discussed at length in Chapter 17.

Alternative production and trade. Some scholars trace the historical origins of unfair trade to 1492 and European colonialism that has, 'for almost five centuries, shaped the lives and livelihoods of most of humanity' (Akram-Lodhi 2021). European colonial powers established a highly unequal global trading system. In the commercial period from the 1500s to early 1800s, 'company-states' like the Hudson's Bay Company, the Royal African Company and, most famously, the British East India Company were the agents of value extraction (Akram-Lodhi 2021). As the industrial economic structure in England changed, the economic needs of elite changed, and pressure was placed on the old colonial structure to change, too. Economic and colonial states needed their colonies to supply the means to complete the industrial revolution (like cotton from the United States) and also to provide a safety valve to absorb excess commodities and capital investments that could not be profitably employed in the Global North. Dominant forms of business-led globalization today, which the global justice movement seeks to challenge, are based on the idea of breaking down trade and investment barriers in order to encourage the supposed win-win benefits of international production and trade. However, these stated goals have rarely matched reality (Stiglitz 2002). Instead, multinational corporations (MNCs) have benefited from easier access to cheap labour and cheap resources in the Global South, as well as easy access to consumers in the Global North. As we have seen in Chapters 13 and 17, the advantages of liberalized global markets has been increasingly thrown into doubt by the disruption of trade and supply chains by global pandemics, geo-political conflicts and populist movements calling for greater economic nationalism.

Critics argue that unequal exchange continues to drive global inequality, uneven development and ecological breakdown. Economic growth in the Global North is still based on the exploitation of the Global South, with value being extracted through price differentials in international trade (Hickel et al. 2022; Cope 2019). It is, therefore, pertinent to consider whether there are any viable alternative forms of production and trade, since our daily purchases represent one area where we could make a difference in our everyday lives. One alternative is fair trade, which the World Fair Trade Organization (WFTO) – originally established in 1989 as the International Federation of Alternative Trade (IFAT) – defines as follows:

Fair Trade is a trading partnership, based on dialogue, transparency and respect, that seeks greater equity in international trade. It contributes to sustainable development by offering better trading conditions to, and securing the rights of, marginalized producers and workers – especially in the South. Fair Trade organisations have a clear commitment to Fair Trade as the principal core of their mission. They, backed by consumers, are engaged actively in supporting producers, awareness raising and in campaigning for changes in the rules and practice of conventional international trade.

As this definition illustrates, fair trade is an attempt to socially regulate markets by addressing historically unequal international trade relations, promoting social justice and environmental sustainability in global production. While it has shown some promise in doing so, it also faces some key challenges and contradictions. According to Raynolds and Greenfield (2015: 25), fair trade represents an example of Polanyi-like re-embedding of markets within social relationships: 'Infusing commodities with information regarding the people and places involved in production, fair trade seeks to "humanize" economic transactions and "shorten the distance" between producers and consumers'.

The institutional framework has shifted from the older fair-trade organization model (like the WFTO) to a newer yet rapidly growing Fairtrade certification model. The now-dominant fair-trade model was established in the late 1980s based on a formal process of certification and labelling for products sold by mainstream retailers. Coordinated by Fairtrade International, it aims to 'mainstream' fair trade by getting these products into supermarket shelves alongside conventional products rather than in sections reserved for speciality items. Today, it is estimated that the market for fair trade involves over 1.9 million farmers and workers and many millions of consumers worldwide (O'Brien 2019) and is growing rapidly (in part thanks to a successful marketing campaign linking fair trade and the UN Sustainable Development Goals). For farmers and workers in the Global South, the Fairtrade certification model requires that fair-trade producers are organized into democratic associations, uphold International Labor Organization standards and promote ecological practices. It also requires that importers buy from certified growers using stable contracts, provide credit and pay guaranteed prices and a social premium (fair-trade producers democratically decide how to spend this premium, but it has to be on projects to benefit the community).

The 'fair trade' movement – in opposition to notions of 'free trade' promoted by global financial institutions like the World Bank, IMF and GATT/WTO – has its origins in the mid-twentieth century and has a rather complicated history which we can only briefly sketch out here. According to Raynolds and Greenfield (2015), fair trade as we know it today evolved through a series of key historical moments. First, fair trade began in the aftermath of the Second World War with charities like Oxfam (UK) and Mennonite Central Committee (United States) importing craftwork from the Global South. Then it involved the establishment of alternative trading organizations like IFAT to enable producers from the Global South direct access to markets in the Global North without having to go through intermediaries like charities. Finally, it was driven by certain businesses (e.g. Co-operative Group, UK) in the Global North buying and selling fair trade branded products in their stores, as well as certification schemes like the International FAIRTRADE Certification Mark. Fair trade is now a major global phenomenon involving worldwide sales of US$9 billion in 2018 compared to US$6.3 billion in 2014, (Smithers 2014; Fairtrade America 2018), and there are numerous fair-trade products in the market, including food (e.g. bananas), beverages (e.g. coffee) and apparel (e.g. university-branded clothing).

Although it is possible to think of fair trade as an alternative to corporate capitalism, it has also been criticized on a number of counts for failing to really challenge corporate power (e.g. Fridell 2006). It is helpful to look at a specific example in order to unpack these criticisms. For example, Carroll and Buchholtz (2015: 317) discuss the international coffee MNC Starbucks as a business that has integrated 'ethical concerns into its corporate strategies', specifically through 'ethical' sourcing of their coffee and the purchasing of fair-trade coffee since 2000. While Starbucks claimed that 99 per cent of its coffee was 'ethically sourced' in 2020, this is based on the company's strategy of using its own CAFE standard. The proportion of certified fair-trade coffee it sells is in fact much lower (8.4% in 2013) and in 2022 the company announced it will reduce it further (Saker-Clark 2022). There are several important issues that this example, and others like it, raise for fair-trade. First, it is often difficult to differentiate the varied fair-trade value chains, meaning that fair trade can be easily diluted and co-opted as a brand through corporate-dominated licensing and retailing arrangements (Doherty et al. 2015). Second, it is evident that fair-trade principles often come into conflict with pricing decisions, with the former usually losing out to the latter (Fridell 2007). Finally, the participants in fair trade supply chains often have very different motivations, from creating new markets to transforming markets altogether (Jaffee 2014). How these divergent interests are managed is critical for ensuring that there is no compromise between ethics and market expansion (Renard 2005).

Alternative currencies: Local exchange trading systems. The third alternative is LETS. These are networks based on a local, often virtual, currency. LETS are typically small, with a membership in double figures, at most, a few hundred. Members buy and sell goods and services to and from one another. Often the items for sale are of a craft or hobby nature, though some members offer services which they also sell professionally on the formal market. LETS may be described as 'moneyless' to the extent that formal currency (e.g. dollar notes and coins) do not physically change hands; instead, a member's LETS account is credited (if they are a seller) or debited (in the case of the buyer) for the cost of the good or service exchanged; the transaction is recorded virtually by the system's administrator.

LETS often attract people from the alternative anti-capitalist and 'green' scene who wish to foster a local form of economy over which they have control. Members value the greater intimacy of exchanging with those in a community or neighbourhood, and they seek to reduce their reliance on corporations whose products are manufactured along supply chains which stretch across the world. Such local currencies have a long history (Peacock 2014), and many protagonists of LETS take inspiration from the impressive experiments with local money in the municipalities of Schwanenkirchen (Germany) and Wörgl (Austria) in the inter-war period. These experiments proved successful in getting unemployed people back to work, and involved not only private consumers and business but also local government. However, the Austrian Constitutional Court saw the issuing of an alternative currency as a threat to the central bank's monopoly on currency issue and hence the Wörgl experiment was declared unconstitutional in 1933; the experiment in Schwanenkirchen had already been outlawed in 1931.

The modern LETS movement was born in British Columbia in 1983. Few LETS today are borne of the economic hardship which gave rise to Schawankirchen and Wörgl, as many members of LETS, who are often well-educated, affluent and gainfully employed in the formal economy, seek an alternative economic lifestyle in LETS, rather than a way of earning a living. As a result, LETS rarely offer the poor and unemployed new avenues to make up for lost income from the formal economy (Peacock 2000). An exception is the Argentine barter network, Red de Trueque, the largest in the world, with hundreds of branches across the country. It was initiated in the 1990s in light of economic recession and involved between 2 and 3 million members.

Alternative business organization: Economic democracy. There is a growing interest in alternative forms of economic organization, which is often associated with the idea of the 'social economy' discussed in the next chapter. As an alternative to corporate capitalism, alternative business organizations are premised on a very different set of principles and structures, such as 'economic democracy' (Schweickart 2011). They are founded on the idea that the economy is always, and necessarily, embedded in social relations (Polanyi 1944[2001]; Gibson-Graham 1996; Amin et al. 2002). It might have made more sense to have called this book *Business in Society* to reflect this perspective. It is problematic to conceptualize the economy as distinct and separate from society because that would ignore the fact that our economic lives, livelihoods, choices, preferences and so on are profoundly shaped by our social, political and material circumstances: that is, our lives are patterned by centuries of inherited beliefs, habits and values. It is the reason that so many people spend so much money at certain events or times of the year, like birthdays, Christmas and other cultural moments. Thomas Malleson (2014) argues that taking on board these sorts of ideas means we can rethink our economies to promote *economic democracy* so that we can attain more control over the direction and shape of our working (and personal) lives. It is possible, from this viewpoint, to organize work differently so that we do not give up our rights as we currently do when we enter a capitalist corporation or business (see Ciepley 2013). There are many organizational examples representing this vision of economic democracy, which we discuss in more detail in Chapter 17. An example we include here is a case study of 'worker recovered enterprises' in Argentina.

Alternative property rights: Open source. Capitalist property regimes have gone through a major shakeout over the last few years as a consequence of social and technological changes, especially the rise of the internet, file-sharing, Web 2.0 and so on. As businesses, corporations and governments have grappled with the implications of these changes, they have promoted and supported increasingly stringent property rights, especially around intangible things like information and knowledge (Drahos and Braithewaite 2002). So-called intellectual property rights (IPRs) have been extended internationally by global governance institutions like the WTO. In response to the increasing privatization and commodification of knowledge, especially software, the open-source and open-access movements have sought to support free access to and exchange of knowledge and information (Wellen 2013). For example, the open source movement started in 1985 as a response to early attempts to make software code proprietary so that consumers could not alter it. Over time, the open-source movement has expanded to include new forms of open property rights (e.g. Copyleft), the support for open access to research (e.g. Science Commons) and challenges to corporate-dominated IP laws (e.g. Pirate Party, Sweden). For more on these issues turn to Chapter 23.

Case study

'Worker-recuperated enterprises' (or ERTs)

'Worker-recuperated enterprises' – or ERTs, derived from the Spanish *empresas recupera-das por sus trabajadores* – represent an example of an alternative business organization (see also Chapter 22). These ERTs emerged first in Argentina as a response to the 'neolib-eral' policies of the 1990s that saw much of the country's national industry sold off and the economy opened to foreign direct investment. This led to a high unemployment rate, increasing poverty and economic instability, which culminated in a full-scale economic crisis in 2001 marked by the largest sovereign-debt default up to that point in history. According to Kasparian (2021) the creation of ERTs was spurred by a 'crisis at the productive unit level' initiated by employers undermining the wage-contract through a variety of means such as 'wage cuts, arrears and partial payments, suspensions, bankruptcies followed by owner abandonment or fraudulent asset-stripping' (21). Since 2001, ERTs have spread to other countries in Latin America, including Uruguay, Brazil and Venezuela, and to countries of the Global North such as the United States, Turkey, Greece, Spain, Italy and France (Vieta 2021). However, ERTs still face many challenges given that they must work within the law and compete within capitalist markets. As such, ERTs still operate within a legal system which privileges private ownership and property rights.

ERTs are a strategy pursued by workers, primarily as a way to retain employment in factories and businesses that had gone bankrupt or been closed by their owners. While each factory or business has its own story, in general workers used the only resource left to them – their labour power – to restart the factories and businesses previously managed by private owners. According to Vieta, 'recent experiences with worker-recuperated firms in Argentina and elsewhere . . . [show that] recurrent structural crises of the capitalist system offer moments of rupture that can potentially become openings for new experiments with workers' control and self-management' (2021: xx).

Instead of a hierarchical, internal structure with a boss telling workers what to do, ERTs are organized and managed by the workers themselves based on the principles of self-reliance, direct democracy and horizontal organizing, where workers make decisions about production and management through general assemblies and democratic decision-making processes, rather than having instructions passed down through a chain of managerial command.

Argentina boasts the greatest number of ERTs with over 400 that employ almost 16,000 workers 'in sectors as diverse as printing and publishing, media, metallurgy, foodstuffs, construction, textiles, tourism, education, health provisioning, and shipbuilding' (Vieta 2021: 118). Measuring success is the source of some debate, as some prefer to focus on economic indicators such as productivity and growth, while others look at the promotion of social values such as 'solidarity and cooperative economics, community-focused development, and social inclusion' (Vieta 2021: 419). Some particularly successful examples of ERTs include FaSinPat – a name which is short for *Fábrica sin Patrones*, or a factory without bosses – a ceramics factory in western Argentina; IMPA, which is an aluminium products factory in Buenos Aires famous for its pioneering work in the movement and for its cultural centre and community-based high school courses, held symbolically in the old boss's office space; and Vio.me, started by workers inspired by the ERT movement in Argentina who converted a construction material factory that was abandoned by its owners in May 2011 to a factory for manufacturing soap. These types of ERTs tend to be deeply embedded in the communities; they are 'incubated cooperatives' as opposed to 'state induced' (Kasparian 2021). For a short introduction to worker-recuperated businesses with examples from around the world, see the documentary, *Own the Change: Building Economic Democracy One Worker Co-op at a Time* (2016) by GRITtv and the TESA collective.

Conclusion

In this chapter we have outlined the diversity and variety of resistance and alternatives to corporate capitalism. As we noted, resistance to capitalism has a long history, stretching back to its origins in the enclosure of land (see Chapter 2). Resistance has also entailed the development of everyday alternatives to corporate capitalism. In this chapter we outlined a few examples, including the global justice movement, fair trade, local exchange trading systems, economic democracy and the open-source movement. In the next two chapters we cover two key alternatives in more depth, the social economy and so-called 'sharing economy' businesses.

Suggested readings

- Ch. 1, Malleson, T. (2014) *After Occupy: Economic Democracy for the 21st Century*, Oxford, Oxford University Press.
- Peacock, M. (2014) 'Complementary Currencies: History, Theory, Prospects', *Local Economy*, Vol. 29, pp. 708–22.
- Malm, A. (2021) *How to Blow Up a Pipeline: Learning to Fight in a World on Fire*. London, Verso.
- Cheney, G. et al. (2023) *Cooperatives at Work*. Bingley (UK), Emerald.
- Wright, E.O. (2016) 'How to be an Anti-capitalist for the 21st Century', *Journal of Australian Political Economy*, Vol. 77, pp. 5–22.

Bibliography

Akram-Lodhi, A.H. (2021) 'Colonialism: How Unfair Trade Changed the World', in G. Fridell, Z. Gross and S. McHugh (eds), *The Fair Trade Handbook*, Halifax, Fernwood.

Amin, A., Cameron, A. and Hudson, R. (2002) *Placing the Social Economy*, London, Routledge.

Bakan, J. (2004) *The Corporation*, London, Random House.

Bakan, J. (2020) *The New Corporation*, Toronto, Allen Lane.

Bakunin, M. (1970) *God and the State*, New York, Dover Publications.

Birch, K. (2007) 'The Totalitarian Corporation?' *Totalitarian Movements and Political Religions*, Vol. 8, pp. 153–61.

Birch, K. (2015) *We Have Never Been Neoliberal*, Winchester, Zero Books.

Carroll, A. and Buchholtz, A. (2015) *Business and Society* (9th Edition), Stamford, CENGAGE Learning.

Chatterton, P. (2010) 'Do It Yourself: A Politics for Changing Our World', in K. Birch and V. Mykhnenko (eds), *The Rise and Fall of Neoliberalism*, London, Zed Books, pp. 188–205.

Ciepley, D. (2013) 'Beyond Public and Private: Toward a Political Theory of the Corporation', *American Political Science Review*, Vol. 107, pp. 139–58.

Cope, Z. (2019) *The Wealth of (Some) Nations: Imperialism and the Mechanics of Value Transfer*, London, Pluto Press.

Doherty, B., Bezencon, V. and Balineau, G. (2015) 'Fairtrade International and the European Market', in L. Raynolds and E. Bennett (eds), *Handbook of Research* on *Fair Trade*, Cheltenham, Edward Elgar, pp. 316–32.

Drahos, P. with Braithewaite, J. (2002) *Information Feudalism*, London, Earthscan.

Drucker, P. (1993) *Post-Capitalist Society*, New York, HarperCollins.

Fairtrade America. (2018, 29 October) 'Fairtrade Tops $9 Billion in Global Sales for First Time on 8% Growth', *GlobeNewswire*, https://www .globenewswire.com/news-release /2018/10/29/1638502/0/en/Fairtrade -Tops-9-Billion-in-Global-Sales-for -First-Time-on-8-Growth.html.

Fridell, G. (2006) 'Fair Trade and Neoliberalism: Assessing Emerging Perspectives', *Latin American Perspectives*, Vol. 33, pp. 8–28.

Fridell, G. (2007) *Fair Trade Coffee: The Prospects and Pitfalls of Market Driven Social Justice*, Toronto, University of Toronto Press.

Gesell, S. (1934) *The Natural Economic Order*, San Antonio, Free-Economy Pub.

Gibson-Graham, J.K. (1996) *The End of Capitalism (As We Knew It): A Feminist Critique of Political Economy*, Oxford, Blackwell Publishers.

Graeber, D. (2011) *Debt: The First 5000 Years*, Brooklyn, Melville House.

GRITtv and the TESA collective. (2016) *Own The Change: Building Economic Democracy One Worker Co-op at a Time*, https://www.youtube.com/watch?v =8G1-SYMatNc&t=12s&ab.

Harvey, D. (2005) *A Brief History of Neoliberalism*, Oxford, Oxford University Press.

Hickel, J. et al. (2022) 'Imperialist Appropriation in the World Economy: Drain from the Global South Through Unequal Exchange, 1990–2015', *Global Environmental Change*, Vol. 73, pp. 1–13

Hobsbawm, E. (1995) *Age of Extremes*, London, Abacus.

Holloway, J. (2005) *Change the World without Taking Power*, London, Pluto Press.

Jaffee, D. (2014) *Brewing Justice: Fair Trade Coffee, Sustainability, and Survival*, Oakland, University of California Press.

Kasparian, D. (2021) *Co-Operative Struggles: Work Conflicts in Argentina's New Worker Co-operatives*, Ian Barrett, trans., Leiden, Brill.

Kennedy, G. (2008) *Diggers, Levellers, and Agrarian Capitalism*, Lanham, Lexington Books.

Keynes, J.M. (1936 [1973]) *The General Theory of Employment, Interest and Money*, London, Macmillan.

Malleson, T. (2014) *After Occupy: Economic Democracy for the 21st Century*, Oxford, Oxford University Press.

Malm, A. (2016) *Fossil Capital: The Rise of Steam Power and the Roots of Global Warming*, London, Verso.

Malm, A. (2021) *How to Blow up a Pipeline: Learning to Fight in a World on Fire*, London, Verso.

Marx, K. (1867 [1976]) *Capital: Volume 1*, London, Penguin.

Marx, K. and Engels, F. (1848 [1985]) *The Communist Manifesto*, London, Penguin Books.

Mason, P. (2015) *Postcapitalism*, London, Allen Lane.

Nicholls, A. and Opal, C. (2005) *Fair Trade: Market-Driven Ethical Consumption*, London, Sage.

O'Brien, K. (2019, October 1) '25 Facts about Fairtrade', Fair Trade Foundation Media Centre, https://www .fairtrade.org.uk/media-centre/blog/25 -facts-about-fairtrade/.

Ostry, J., Loungani, P. and Furceri, D. (2016) 'Neoliberalism: Oversold?' *Finance and Development*, Vol. 53, pp. 38–41.

Parker, M. (2002) *Against Management*, Cambridge, Polity Press.

Parker, M., Fournier, V. and Reedy, P. (2007) *The Dictionary of Alternatives: Utopianism and Organization*, London, Zed Books.

Parker, M., Cheney, G., Fournier, V. and Land, C. (eds). (2013) *The Companion to Alternative Organization*, London, Routledge.

Peacock, M. (2000) 'Local Exchange Trading Systems: A Solution to the Employment Dilemma?' *Annals of Public and Cooperative Economics*, Vol. 71, pp. 55–78.

Peacock, M. (2014) 'Complementary Currencies: History, Theory, Prospects', *Local Economy*, Vol. 29, pp. 708–22.

Polanyi, K. (1944 [2001]) *The Great Transformation*, Boston, Beacon Press.

Raynolds, L. (2000) 'Re-Embedding Global Agriculture: The International Organic and Fair Trade Movements', *Agriculture and Human Values*, Vol. 17, pp. 297–309.

Raynolds, L. and Greenfield, N. (2015) 'Fair Trade: Movement and Markets', in L. Raynolds and E. Bennett (eds), *Handbook of Research on Fair Trade*, Cheltenham, Edward Elgar, pp. 24–41.

Renard, M.-C. (2005) 'Quality Certification, Regulation and Power in Fair Trade', *Journal of Rural Studies*, Vol. 21, pp. 419–31.

Rifkin, J. (2014) *The Zero Marginal Cost Society*, Basingstoke, Palgrave Macmillan.

Routledge, P. and Cumbers, A. (2009) *Global Justice Networks*, Manchester, Manchester University Press.

Ruggieri, A. and Vieta, M. (2014) 'Argentina's Worker-Recuperated Enterprises, 2010–2013: A Synthesis of Recent Empirical Findings', *Journal of Entrepreneurial and Organizational Diversity*, Vol. 4, pp. 75–103.

Saker-Clark, H. (2022, 17 February) *Starbucks Cuts Back Sale of Fairtrade Coffee in UK*, https://www.independent.co.uk/news/uk/starbucks-fairtrade-europe-middle-east-fairtrade-foundation-b2017451.html.

Schwab, K. (2020) 'Now is the Time for a "Great Reset"', in *The Agenda Weekly*, https://www.weforum.org/agenda/2020/06/now-is-the-time-for-a-great-reset/.

Schweickart, D. (2011) *After Capitalism* (2nd Edition), Washington, DC, Rowman & Littlefield Publishers.

Seoane, J. and Taddei, E. (2002) 'From Seattle to Porto Alegre: The Anti-neoliberal Globalization Movement', *Current Sociology*, Vol. 50, pp. 99–122.

Smithers, R. (2014) 'Global Fairtrade Sales Reach 4.4bn Following 15% Growth during 2013', *The Guardian Online*, 3 September. www.theguardian.com/global-development/2014/sep/03/global-fair-trade-sales-reach-4-billion-following-15-per-cent-growth-2013 (accessed September 2016).

Stiglitz, J. (2002) *Globalization and Its Discontents*, New York, W.W. Norton.

Varoufakis, Y. (2011) *The Global Minotaur: America, the True Origins of the Financial Crisis and the Future of the World Economy*, London, Zed Books.

Vieta, M. (2021) *Workers' Self-Management in Argentina*, Leiden, Brill.

Wellen, R. (2013) 'Open Access, Megajournals and MOOCs: On the Political Economy of Academic Unbundling', *SAGE Open*, Vol. 3, pp. 1–16.

Worth, O. (2013) *Resistance in the Age of Austerity*, London, Zed Books.

Wright, E.O. (2016) 'How to be an Anti-Capitalist for the 21st Century', *Journal of Australian Political Economy*, Vol. 77, pp. 5–22.

22 | The social and solidarity economy

Caroline Shenaz Hossein

Introduction

Billions of people around the world belong to institutions, both formal and informal, that are part of the social and solidarity economy (SSE). In the recent *Encyclopedia for the Social and Solidarity Economy* (UNTFSSE 2023), Jean-Louis Laville states that the SSE is a global phenomenon and that every place has a history of solidarity economies. The SSE's relevance in the world today stems partly from its development, as these economies were a response to ingrained inequalities and forms of exclusion in capitalist business and society (see Chapter 20). Some scholars (e.g. Amin 2009) have pointed out that these institutions arise out of economic crises, meeting the needs of their members and creators through genuinely democratic processes. The better we understand solidarity economies, the clearer it becomes that people around the world have engaged in them for pressing political, social and economic reasons.[1]

Within most countries in the Global North, the term 'social economy' is used to describe economies run by citizens. The social economy is defined as 'a bridging concept for organizations that have social objectives central to their mission and their practice, and either have explicit economic objectives or generate some economic value through the services they provide and purchases they undertake' (Quarter et al. 2018, 4). The social economy has also been described as the 'third sector' – that is, distinct from the public sector (the government) and the private sector (corporations and for-profit businesses).

Outside the Global North, however, this people-driven sector is more commonly referred to as the SSE (see Box 1). This term is more inclusive and acknowledges that people within the third sector have been excluded from interactions with the government and private sectors (Hossein 2018; Miller 2010). It includes many minorities and marginalized groups whose freedoms have been curbed by violence, systemic inequalities and entrenched forms of exclusion (Spade 2020). The SSE sector thus not only addresses economic wrongdoings in mainstream systems that conform to a capitalist (i.e. profit-driven) logic but also confronts systemic injustices such as racism, colonialism and many other forms of oppression.

People around the world engage in the SSE to support goals such as education, small enterprises, travel and even funerals. How many of us can say that they don't recall a parent or neighbour doing something for another family in exchange for small repairs, renovations or tax help? This type of bartering of services is an old system of community support. In the world at large, the business done through these types of exchanges is not formalized: that is, it does not have a 'price' and is not counted as economic production in the same way that wage labour or capitalist investment are (see Chapter 6). Yet SSE activities are hugely productive and valuable, creating vibrant community economies for people around the world (Gibson-Graham 1996, 2020). Drawing on theories such as that of *community economies*, this chapter will explore the history of social and solidarity economies, which have long been a part of human society despite their not being recognized by the economic mainstream. It will also look at the potential they hold for human cooperation, inclusion and development around the world.

Key discussion questions

- Why insert the word 'solidarity' in the social economy?
- What are community economies?
- How do excluded people organize solidarity economies?
- What kinds of social economy organizations are there?
- What characteristics define the social and solidarity economy?
- In what ways is the economy that we participate in also embedded into our society?

Humans as builders of solidarist systems

A core belief of those who study the SSE sector is that markets have always been a deeply embedded part of human society. In this sense, the economy is not separate from our social lives, nor has it ever been. In Chapter 6, we explored the work of Nobel Prize laureate Elinor Ostrom (1990) and her heterodox conclusion that human societies are inherently solidaristic. To really understand why solidarity matters, we must focus on the contributions made by people in other lands, exploring the worldwide use of the term 'SSE', its historical transformative consequences and its future potential.

The concept of collective action, as founded by Jessica Gordon Nembhard (2014), is a site of contestation for some groups. Gordon Nembhard (2014) argues that African Americans came together to pool goods and services because of the extreme exclusion and violence they endured in American society. The SSE, a treasure of our times, has been especially useful during periods of crisis and is of great value for our very survival.

Yet the SSE is still not viewed in the mainstream as a key feature in our world economy. In defining the economy, people usually equate it to big corporations and the drive for profits. However, this does not tell the full story of economic life. The SSE is part of our economy, and close study of it reveals that the economy is, in fact, very social. Austrian-born historian Karl Polanyi (1944 [2001]), author of the *Great Transformation*, exposed the fact that any effort to dis-embed the economy from society would lead to a 'double movement'. This movement is when people come together, in solidarity, to ensure the economy adheres to social norms and relations.

This concept of double movement is not new. Polanyi's work was inspired by the history of the Beninese people in West Africa. He wrote about the Kingdom of Dahomey as a place where economics and markets were intrinsically connected components of human life. Kenyan scholar Njeri Kinyanjui (2019) notes that the concept of Ubuntu ('I am because you are') has been a foundational part of the marketplace in many African countries. She argues that despite the growth thesis and other neoclassical economic ideas like *homo economicus* (see Chapter 5) imposed in her country, local economies are built on the values of Ubuntu and the practice of economic cooperation. The following video link portrays the Black Social Economy concept in the context of people of African descent cooperating in the market (see the next box). Here is a link to a short definition of the concept https://www.youtube.com/watch?v=8e2NRfEnoos

Key concept: The Black Social Economy

The concept of the Black Social Economy questions why Black and racialized people are excluded from the third sector when they go there seeking help and safe refuge. The Black Social Economy amplifies the many social and economic activities that people of African descent have had to undertake to survive. The Black Social Economy sheds light

In Canada, Nishnaabeg writer Leanne Betasamoke Simpson (2020) argues that extractive economics – involving industries such as mining, oil and gas and forestry – are vested in individualism and competition. These individualistic and extractivist values run contrary to the Nishnaabeg people's longstanding and traditional values of community well-being, unity and cooperation. Around the globe, Indigenous peoples, racial minorities, women and other excluded people understand that the SSE sector has always been a part of human society and not simply an 'alternative' to mainstream business and capitalism.

The SSE sector challenges the dominant definition of humans as money-focused self-interested individuals (see Chapter 5). Diverse forms of SSE reveal that people around the world are caretakers of the planet who prioritize community development and the sharing of resources (Ostrom 1990). The SSE provides a place for people to question the hegemony of the patriarchal and racist capitalist economic system by highlighting the central roles of identities and geography in shaping business in society (Yi et al. 2023).

Defining the social and solidarity economy

The SSE can be defined in both broad and specific terms. Starting broadly, Ethan Miller of the Community Economies Research Network (CERN) defines the solidarity economy as a 'movement of movements', a form of economics based on cooperativism, equity and social and economic democracy (2010: 3). Activist Emily Kawano (2021) defines the 'solidarity economy as a big tent that embraces many coexisting visions of democratic, post-capitalist economic systems'. That is, the SSE is the place of genuine democracy and a diversity of ideas. It is where economic transformations are more than people simply improving their position within their already existing socio-economic class.

The SSE focuses instead on shared goals and well-being for all. Key to the SSE is its global perspective, focused on both the Global South and other overlooked communities in the North (Laville 2023). Part of the goal of this chapter, and of SSE scholarship, is to reveal the breadth and importance of these often ignored, or even persecuted, social and economic forms of organization. For example, Gordon Nembhard (2014) explains that in the United States, people, particularly those living in crisis, have historically had to hide their social economies to survive because they would have been perceived as a threat to the dominant capitalist (and racist) economic culture.

The argument thus far shows that solidarity economies are rooted in the values of reciprocity, mutuality and cooperation. This diverse movement is focused on resistance to the neoliberal and patriarchal economic order (Bell et al. 2018). It is especially relevant to communities outside of the Global North, that address exclusion from formal systems through self-sufficiency, organization and sustainable growth. Furthermore, as Miller (2010) argues, the solidarity economy makes room for militancy and purposeful disruption to undo exclusionary economic systems.

Adding 'solidarity' to the social economy

For many, using the term 'social economy' does not adequately address excluded people who have had to struggle and fight for survival and their rights under racial capitalist environments. The addition of the term 'solidarity' acknowledges the need to build a just society. This is not just for those who have the wealth, security and privilege to experiment with the economic system, but for those who are forced to experiment because of powerful mechanisms of exclusion, oppression and exploitation.

Many argue that the social economy – without the solidarity component – has been 'mainstreamed' into government policy as a way to tidy up the failings of the system. Some even say it has been appropriated by corporations and other powerful actors to extend the neoliberal project (Graefe 2007; Bridge et al. 2009; Miller 2010; Birch and Whittam 2012).

The solidarity economy can be seen as made up of three distinct phases that apply to many different geographies: (1) awakening to a different vision of what we know to be the economy; (2) recognizing others as sharing a common vision and (3) cooperating, integrating and emerging our core human values in terms of how we engage with economics (Kawano 2021).

Figure 22.1 shows a Venn diagram of three circles representing an interactive social economy, according to Canadian scholars the late Jack Quarter, Laurie Mook and Ann Armstrong (2018). The diagram denotes the overlapping of the three sectors – the public, the private and the third sectors (or civil society groups). It shows that many types of SSE institutions, including self-help groups, mutual aid and informal cooperatives, would be located at the bottom of civil society in an area that does not interact with either the public or private sector.

Many women and racialized people do not interact with the state, private sector or even certain types of social economy organizations (e.g. nonprofits) because of racial exclusion (Spade 2020). Excluded people often turn to localized cooperatives and informal collectives like mutual aid, self-help and

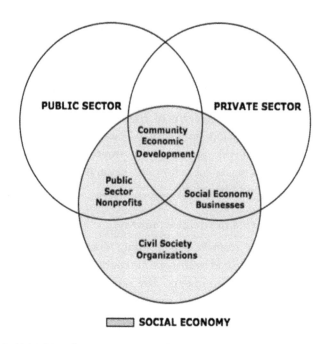

FIGURE 22.1 The interactive social economy. *Source*: Quarter, Mook and Armstrong (2018)

collectives to meet their needs, which means they aren't required to engage with the other two sectors.

The idea of the solidarity component of SSE emerged in the Global South, specifically in Latin America, to politicize the social economy and make it more inclusive for everyone. The World Social Forum, an annual meeting of civil society organizations, had its first meeting in Brazil (See box below). It is an important site for solidarity activists to convene and fight for better living standards instead of capitalist development (Kawano 2021, 2010; Gibson-Graham 1996). Adding solidarity to the social economy means choosing to fight against patriarchal and racist capitalist systems and to bring about change to the system.

Key example: The World Social Forum

In 2001 in Porte Allegro, Brazil, activists and civil society supporters decided that 'another world was possible'. At the World Social Forum, meetings are organized by civil society headers who push for serious debate of ideas and share experiences. These actors are opposed to neoliberal and imperialism. The forum is a globalized event and is non-denominational. It is a place where people everywhere come together to discuss issues. These meetings are focused on connecting people across different geographies and coming together globally.

Defining the actors in the social and solidarity economy

Some scholars have pointed out that the SSE can be hard to understand because of the diversity of actors that belong to it (Gibson-Graham and Dombroski 2020). Social economy books that map out the actors in the sector show that the practices, forms and types of organizations are constantly changing (Quarter et al. 2018; Hossein 2018; Amin 2009). Conflicts can sometimes occur between different parts of the sector because of this abundance of difference. In looking at the various practices and debates about the SSE, this chapter will highlight the diversity of practices, actors and ideas in the sector (Hossein and Christabell 2022; Quarter et al. 2018; Moulaert and Ailenei 2005; Birch and Whittam 2008, 2012; Bouchard 2010).

Actors in the SSE are distinct from those in the public and private sectors (see Table 22.1). While some actors are independent, others engage with the state and private sectors because they rely on a variety of income sources, such

TABLE 22.1 Social and Solidarity Economy Actors At-a-Glance

Types of actors	Main goal	Characteristics
Mutual aid and collectives (e.g. Quilombos, ROSCAs, self-helps groups, giving circles)	Self-determination	• focuses on self-help, liberation, reciprocity, and equity • active in the informal arenas • set against charity
Faith-based institutions (e.g. churches, mosques, temples)	Moral good	• built on specific religious beliefs or ideologies • depends on funding by believers
Nonprofits and charitable institutions (e.g. food banks, Aga Khan Foundation, Save the Children)	Helping people	• manages aid funds • relies on donors • makes moral judgements about beneficiaries in need of assistance
Cooperatives (e.g. credit unions, retail, worker coops, coop housing)	Member-owned and participatory	• developed out of the need for democratic decision-making in an institution • has voluntary membership • espouses equality among members
Social enterprises	Financial autonomy	• organized on cost-recovery mechanisms • balances social impact with earned revenue (e.g. sales that have a dual purpose of making money and meeting a social need)

Source: Adapted from the work by Quarter, Mook and Armstrong (2018)

as sales, subsidies, donors and grants. Some organizations rely on subsidies because they are running social programmes that require a lot of aid and investment, whereas other independent actors may refuse donations to avoid compromising their activism. In *Solidarity Not Charity*, Dean Spade (2020) shows how undocumented workers and immigrants are often socially vilified. But through mutual aid organizations, people can receive the assistance they need (see short video on this point: https://www.youtube.com/watch?v =rYPgTZeF5Z0).

Some SSE institutions are ancient: for example, mutual aid and self-help groups, informal banking cooperatives and religious institutions. Others are relatively new, such as microfinance institutions and social enterprises. A vast number of examples of SSE can be categorized through their actors, goals and structure across many geographical regions. For example, in Quebec, Canada, in the early 1900s the Desjardins *caisses populaires* (credit unions) were created to help the French-speaking and Catholic population, often excluded by the Anglo-Canadian banking system, to access small loans. A different example can be found in India, where the Self-employed Women's Association (SEWA), a trade union created to assist women working in the informal economy, is today a major movement with millions of members in self-help groups (Bhatt 2007).

Given the many versions of this type of economic organization, SSEs can be difficult to define. But many see this diversity as desirable, because people can choose the organizational form that works best for them and their communities. The pros and cons of this diversity are addressed in the class debate outlined in the Box below.

A class debate on the positives and negatives of the diversity of SSEs

The SSE has a lot of actors, making it difficult to understand what the SSE means. Discuss the positives and negatives of the sector:

Positives: The SSE creates space to develop a wide range of practices initiated by the people of those regions without any pressure to conform to a single idea of what the third sector should be. The SSE is people-focused, emphasizing social well-being and having a positive impact on society. This has led to liberation, increased rights and freedoms, creativity and citizen-led protest movements.

Negatives: Because the different actors within the SSE operate in separate spheres, they cannot always access the practices and solutions they need to achieve their ends. Further, certain actors may experience 'mission drift' from their original goals because they become focused on financial sustainability at the expense of these goals. As a result, some are coopted by the state and policymakers or business leaders. Others may be so intent on cooperating with the state or private sectors to secure funding that they don't engage in radical activism or genuinely seek to change the system.

Social and solidarity economy in action

Having defined the SSE and explored some of its goals and actors, we now examine how people can organize, theorize and create new politics to allow the SSE to thrive. Five types of actors make up the SSE: rotating savings and credit associations (ROSCAs), nonprofits, microfinance institutions, cooperatives and social enterprises.

Rotating savings and credit associations One of the oldest type of SSE actors are collectives known as ROSCAs. ROSCAs are mutual aid financing groups in which members share money according to an agreed-upon protocol. For example, in a group of twenty members, each member might contribute $100 per month to the group, for a total of $2,000, and then this lump sum is allocated to each member in turn. ROSCAs represent one of the earliest forms of finance: where people came together in a simple way to help each other to access monies and goods. In this way, people pooled money and engaged in financial collectives long before the idea of microfinance came into being. Today, ROSCAs continue to provide quick access to savings and credit for people, mostly women, who are excluded from formal banks (Ardener and Burman 1995). These actors are committed to values of trust, reciprocity and ground-up activism and development, and they have different methods and values than those of commercial microfinance (Hossein 2016). ROSCAs are a global phenomenon (Hossein and Christabell 2022).

Nonprofits and NGOs Nonprofits, also referred to as charities or NGOs, are another type of actor in the SSE sector. Nonprofits are businesses that don't aim for profit as their goal, and typically access subsidies to carry out social development work. Many nonprofits, including religiously motivated ones, participate in the SSE as a result of their beliefs and principles. For example, the Aga Khan Foundation, supported by Ismaili and Muslim donors, is a major non-profit working around the world to restore historical buildings, create educational museums and develop community. Nonprofits that focus on issues like alleviating poverty can run the risk of de-politicizing systemic issues. They can take the responsibility off the state and government of taking care of their citizenry. One example of this is in Haiti. Antony Loewenstein (2017), in *Disaster Capitalism: Making a Killing Out of Catastrophe*, explains how after the 2010 earthquake NGOs from the North turned Haitian people's suffering into a business. In the Global North, nonprofits increasingly have a for-profit business component to support their social goals. An example of this is Habitat for Humanity (Quarter et al. 2018).

Microfinance Many formal microfinance institutions are considered to be part of the SSE if they are concerned about their social impact and not solely about profit-making activities. If microfinance focuses on community well-being and control, then it has a significant role to play in the SSE (Quarter et al. 2018). Informal cooperative banks and ROSCAs were the pioneers of microbanking long before the 'microfinance revolution' began. In the 1970s, the Grameen Bank of Bangladesh was founded by the 2006 Nobel Prize laureate, Professor Muhammad Yunus, with the goal to create a bank for poor people. The organization of the Grameen Bank was similar to informal banking coops. These used the chit system, where women members were voluntarily organized into small groups and loans were allocated to each of the groups. While many have criticized the commercialized aspects of microfinance (Roy 2010; Rankin 2001), credit unions have also had some positive impacts on financial development (Hossein 2016; MacPherson 2010).

Cooperatives More than 1 billion people belong to formal member-owned cooperative institutions. Millions more engage in informal cooperatives, self-help groups and the commons. The International Cooperative Alliance (ICA) website defines cooperatives as autonomous associations of persons united voluntarily to meet their common economic, social and cultural needs and aspirations through jointly owned and democratically controlled enterprises (see also Gordon Nembhard 2014; Williams 2007). Cooperatives are guided by principles that distinguish them from commercial firms in that they emphasize accountability to members and must show concern for the community. Table 22.2 shows the seven cooperative principles of the ICA.

Cooperatives choose a 'one-member-one-vote' style of governance and are committed to building democracy by giving members the power to make decisions. This includes groups like workers, consumers or other people in the community, instead of exclusively shareholders.

Economist Curtis J. Haynes (2019) defines cooperatives as institutions that are concerned with economic justice, member engagement and human development as opposed to privatized ownership. A well-known example of a global cooperative firm is the Mondragon Cooperative Corporation in the Basque region of Spain. Born of exclusion and crisis, today it is a leading cooperative firm in household appliances and an actor in banking and education (Mollner 1984). Some argue that the cooperative movement owes its start and continued growth to the Global South (Williams 2007). According to the ICA, for example, India has the largest number of cooperatives in the world: one example of a major producer cooperative in India is Amul, a large milk and dairy business.

1. Voluntary and open membership
Cooperatives are voluntary organizations, open to all persons able to use their services and willing to accept the responsibilities of membership, without gender, social, racial, political or religious discrimination.

2. Democratic member control
Cooperatives are democratic organizations controlled by their members, who actively participate in setting their policies and making decisions. Men and women serving as elected representatives are accountable to the membership. In primary cooperatives members have equal voting rights (one member, one vote) and cooperatives at other levels are also organized in a democratic manner.

3. Member economic participation
Members contribute equitably to, and democratically control, the capital of their cooperative. At least part of that capital is usually the common property of the cooperative. Members usually receive limited compensation, if any, on capital subscribed as a condition of membership. Members allocate surpluses for any or all of the following purposes: developing their cooperative, possibly by setting up reserves, part of which at least would be indivisible; benefiting members in proportion to their transactions with the cooperative; and supporting other activities approved by the membership.

4. Autonomy and independence
Cooperatives are autonomous, self-help organizations controlled by their members. If they enter into agreements with other organizations, including governments, or raise capital from external sources, they do so on terms that ensure democratic control by their members and maintain their cooperative autonomy.

5. Education, training and information
Cooperatives provide education and training for their members, elected representatives, managers and employees so they can contribute effectively to the development of their cooperatives. They inform the general public – particularly young people and opinion leaders – about the nature and benefits of cooperation.

6. Cooperation among cooperatives
Cooperatives serve their members most effectively and strengthen the cooperative movement by working together through local, national, regional and international structures.

7. Concern for community
Cooperatives work for the sustainable development of their communities through policies approved by their members.

Source: https://www.ica.coop/en/cooperatives/cooperative-identity

---

Cooperatives: Economic Democracy in Action

The documentary film by Avi Lewis and Naomi Klein (2004) *The Take: Occupy, Resist, Produce* is a good resource for learning about worker cooperatives in Argentina (see also Chapter 21). It shows how workers fought to use the laws to be able to make use of abandoned factories and to create businesses that were controlled democratically by the workers for the good of community. This film is hosted on Films for Action free of charge. https://www.filmsforaction.org/watch/the-take-occupy-resist-produce/

Social enterprises Social enterprises are one of the newer forms in the SSE (Birch and Whittam 2008), and as such there is no consensus on their defining characteristics (Young Foundation 2012). The term 'social enterprise' exists on a continuum. On one end are organizations that focus on a social issue and use a business solution to solve the problem (e.g. Mohammed Yunus of the Grameen Bank, who is a social entrepreneur concerned about access to finance and created a bank for the masses). On the other end are social enterprises that have the goal of making money and that insert social objectives in less substantial ways.

These latter profit-oriented social enterprises are problematic within the SSE because they tend to focus mainly on making money (Peredo and MacLean 2006). As a result, their initial social goals are replaced by economic objectives. Nonetheless, important examples of social enterprises exist, such as A-Way Express Courier, 'a market-based entity founded and supported by a non-profit organization for the purposes of economically and socially benefiting persons on the social margins who are employed in or trained through the enterprise' (Akingbola 2015: 52).

Ethical solidarity and community economies

Economic geographers Katherine Gibson and the late Julie Graham argue that SSE thinking should resist taking sides in ideological debates. Their concept of the 'diverse economy' shatters old binaries and instead focuses on taking inventory of the vastly different ways people do business and engage in community-based economies around the world (Gibson-Graham 2006). The ideas of Gibson-Graham on the diverse economy are best argued in the book *Take Back the Economy* (Gibson-Graham et al. 2013), which provides a guide for how ordinary people can realize ethical and conscientious economies.

The authors call on us to take stock of these ethical coordinates in the community economy, some of which include (1) recognizing that the needs of people who feel threatened are met by an array of diverse economies (not just one arbitrary solution); (2) marshalling and distributing goods and services in ways to share the surplus among all in the community; (3) using goods in a way that is responsible towards the environment without levying blame on poor ethnic communities; and (4) activating the 'commons' (see Chapter 6) so that people share more with one another.

Figure 22.2 shows the well-known iceberg analogy, where the world economy is seen as the tip of an iceberg. The part that we see on the surface is the formal capitalist economy; but this is only a very small part of what the economy means to most people everywhere. The submerged part of the iceberg – the largest part of it, which is not visible to the eye of mainstream economics – is the living economy that we all belong to. Under the surface is a

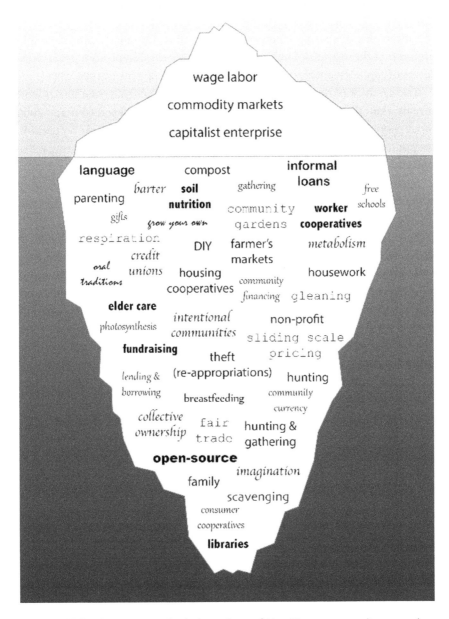

FIGURE 22.2 Diverse economies iceberg. *Source*: https://www.communityeconomies
.org/resources/diverse-economies-iceberg

371

medley of economic interactions (e.g. worker cooperatives, farmer's markets, fair-trade organizations and informal lending). These activities are rooted in the principles of sharing, common purpose and comradery. Gibson-Graham argues that these kinds of business operations are different from profit-driven forms of capitalist enterprise because of their ethical nature (1996, 2006).

Taking stock of the various kinds of SSE businesses that exist in our world reveals that they outnumber capitalist enterprises (Gibson-Graham 2006). Most people engaging in SSEs aren't doing it as a marketing or reputational ploy or to build a money-making empire. Instead, they are participating for the promise of transformative changes for their own well-being.

History provides many examples of people, especially those left out of formal systems, who engage in businesses that not only help them to survive but are also humane in their operations, allowing communities to thrive.

For example, Jamaican-born Marcus Garvey (1887–1940), founder of the Universal Negro Improvement Association (UNIA), emigrated to New York City and encountered racial discrimination that barred Blacks from opportunities. He thus campaigned for human rights and self-love among his community. One way to preserve the human spirit was to engage in Black-owned cooperative businesses (Lewis 1987; Martin 1976). The point here is that people of colour, like Garvey, were creating 'social enterprises' long before they had even been named as such.

A politicized solidarity economy

At the core of the SSE sector is conscious and political organizing. This means that people work together to transform society rather than accepting the patriarchal and capitalist society advocated by mainstream businesses. In the Canadian province of Quebec, for example, there is a long history of *économie sociale* (social economy) which has advocated for a politicized and citizen-led sector. Jean-Marc Fontan and Eric Shragge (2000) have argued that the SSE exists in deliberate forms of political action to make economic systems more cooperative in nature.

The SSE faces many challenges. One of these is the divergence between the Global North and the Global South in their ideas about reform and development (see Chapter 13). In the Global North, the social economy is often placed onto a continuum: on the one end, the social economy has a reformist view and collaborates with the state and private sectors, and on the other end, it is rooted in protests and social change. This political continuum is important for understanding the contested nature of the social economy. Pre-existing political beliefs often underlie the debates about what defines the social economy, what objectives it can achieve and how it should try to achieve those objectives.

In the Global South, and historically excluded groups in the Global North, the third sector is best represented by adding the concept of solidarity to the social economy, as discussed earlier. There are many innovative examples of this intentional addition. Many cases in Brazil, for example, show why solidarity is and has been important to the social economy for a very long time. Historical cases of the SSE in Brazil include the *Movimento Sem Terra* (Landless Workers' Movement), the *Quilombola* (Afro-Brazilian autonomous communities) and the Indigenous idea and practice of *Buen Vivir* (good living) (Silva 2023; Bohn and Grossi 2018; Dias Martins 2000). In the United States, Co-operation Jackson – a solidarity economy and network of cooperatives organized by African Americans in Mississippi – is a site of protest to build and fight against exclusion (Akuno 2017). Given the long and global history of these organizations, which come before a Eurocentric understanding of social economy, it seems clear that discussions about the third sector must now include SSE (Hossein and Christabell 2022; Laville 2023, 2010).

Conclusion

This chapter discussed the concept, practices and politics of the SSE. In many ways, the SSE can be considered an antidote to capitalism and capitalist business practices. SSE offers many ways for people and communities to organize people-centred businesses (Ilcheong et al. 2023). The SSE helps us to rethink both how the economy is defined and who its actors are. It offers many strategies and forms of organizing to provide individuals and communities with the resources, products and services they need to pursue the type of life they want. The SSE is founded on the principles of democratic control, self-determinism, mutualism, reciprocity, equity and autonomy, and in places where people make their livelihoods through both formal and informal institutions.

Suggested readings

- Ch. 1, Ardener, S. and Burman, S. 1995. *Money-Go-Rounds: The Importance of Rotating Savings and Credit Associations for Women.* Oxford, Berg.
- Haynes, C. (2019) 'From Philanthropic Black Capitalism to Socialism: Co-operativism in Du Bois' Economic Thought', *Socialism and Democracy*, Vol. 32, No. 3, pp. 125–45.
- Quarter, J. and Mook, L. (2010) 'An Interactive View of the Social Economy', *Canadian Journal of Nonprofit and Social Economy Research*, Vol. 1, No. 1, pp. 8–22.
- Spade, D. (2020). 'Solidarity Not Charity: Mutual Aid for Mobilization and Survival', *Social Text 142*, Vol. 38, No. 1, pp. 131–51.
- Yi, Ilcheong. (2023) *Encyclopedia on the Social and Solidarity Economy.* UNTFSSE. Choose any entry to learn about the SSE.

Note

1 This chapter draws on Hossein's paper on the solidarity economy currently
under review.

Bibliography

Akingbola, K. (2015) 'When the Business is People: The Impact of A-Way Express Courier', in J. Quarter, R.S. Ryan and C. Andrea (eds), *Social Purpose Enterprises: Case Studies for Social Change*, Toronto, University of Toronto Press, pp. 52–74.

Akuno, K. (2017) 'Build and Fight: The Program and the Strategy of Cooperation Jackson', in K. Akuno and A. Nangwaya (eds), *Jackson Rising: The Struggle for Economic Democracy and Black Self-Determination in Jackson, Mississippi*, Montreal, Daraja Press, pp. 1–20.

Amin, A. (2009) *The Social Economy: International Perspectives on Economic Solidarity*, London, Zed Books.

Ardener, S. and Burman, S. (1995) *Money-Go-Rounds: The Importance of Rotating Savings and Credit Associations for Women*, Oxford, Berg.

Banks, N. (2020) 'Black Women in the United States and Unpaid Collective Work: Theorizing the Community as a Site of Production', *Review of Black Political Economy*, Vol. 47, No. 4, pp. 343–62.

Bell, M.P., Leopold, J., Berry, D. and Hall, A.V. (2018) 'Diversity, Discrimination, and Persistent Inequality: Hope for the Future Through the Solidarity Economy Movement', *Journal of Social Issues*, Vol. 74, No. 2, pp. 224–43.

Betasamosake Simpson, L. (2020) *As We Have Always Done: Indigenous Freedom through Radical Resistance*, Minneapolis, University of Minnesota Press.

Bhatt, E. (2007) *We are Poor But So Many: The Story of Self-Employed Women in India*, Oxford, Oxford University Press.

Birch, K. and Whittam, G. (2008) 'Critical Survey: The Third Sector and the Regional Development of Social Capital', *Regional Studies*, Vol. 42, pp. 437–50.

Birch, K. and Whittam, G. (2012) 'Social Entrepreneurship', in D. Deakins and M. Freel (eds), *Entrepreneurship and Small Firms* (6th Edition), Maidenhead, McGraw-Hill, 105–23.

Birchall, J. (1997) *The International Co-operative Movement*, Manchester, Manchester University Press.

Bohn, S. and Grossi, P.K. (2018) 'The Quilombolas' Refuge in Brazil: The Social Economy, Communal Space and Shared Identity', in C.S. Hossein (ed.), *The Black Social Economy in the Americas: Exploring Diverse Community-Based Alternative Markets*, New York, Palgrave Macmillan, 161–86.

Bouchard, M. (2010) *The Worth of the Social Economy*, Brussels, Peter Lang.

Bridge, S., Murtagh, B. and O'Neill, K. (2009) *Understanding the Social Economy and the Third Sector*, London, Palgrave Macmillan.

Dias Martins, M. (2000) 'The MST Challenge to Neoliberalism', *Latin American Perspectives*, Vol. 27, No. 5 (September), pp. 33–45.

Fontan, J.-M. and Shragge, E. (2000) 'Tendencies, Tensions and Visions in the Social Economy', in E. Shragge and J. Fontan (eds), *Social Economy: International Debates and Perspectives*, Montreal, Black Rose, 1–15.

Gibson-Graham, J.K. (1996) *The End of Capitalism (As We Knew It): A Feminist Critique of Political Economy*, Oxford, Blackwell Publishers.

Gibson-Graham, J.K. (2006) *A Postcapitalist Politics*, Minneapolis, University of Minnesota Press.

Gibson-Graham, J.K., Cameron, J. and Healy, S. (2013) *Take Back the Economy: An Ethical Guide for Transforming Our Communities*, Minneapolis, University of Minnesota Press.

Gibson-Graham, J.K. and Dombroski, K. (2020) *The Handbook of Diverse Economies*, Cheltenham and Northampton, Edward Elgar Publishing.

Gordon Nembhard, J. (2014) *Collective Courage: A History of African American Co-operative Economic Thought and Practice*, University Park, Pennsylvania University Press.

Graefe, P. (2007) 'Social Economy Policies as Flanking for Neoliberalism: Transnational Policy Solutions, Emergent Contradictions, Local Alternatives', in S. Lee and S. McBride (ed.), *Neo-Liberalism, State Power and Global Governance*, Netherlands, Springer, 95–110.

Haynes Jr., C. (2019) 'From Philanthropic Black Capitalism to Socialism: Co-operativism in Du Bois' Economic Thought', *Socialism and Democracy*, Vol. 32, No. 3, pp. 125–45.

Hossein, C. (2016) *Politicized Microfinance*, Toronto, University of Toronto Press.

Hossein, C.S. (2018) 'Daring to Conceptualize the Black Social Economy', in C.S. Hossein (ed.), *The Black Social Economy in the Americas: Exploring Diverse Community-Based Markets*, New York, Palgrave Macmillan, 1–13.

Hossein, C.S. and Christabell, P.J. (2022) *Community Economies in the Global South: Case Studies about Rotating Savings and Credit Associations and Economic Cooperatives*, Oxford, Oxford University Press.

International Cooperative Alliance (ICA). 'Cooperative Identity, Principles and Values', https://www.ica.coop/en/cooperatives/cooperative-identity (accessed September 16, 2022).

Kawano, E. (2021) 'Imaginal Cells of the Solidarity Economy', *Non-profit Quarterly*, https://nonprofitquarterly.org/imaginal-cells-of-the-solidarity-economy/.

Kawano, E., Masterson, T. and Teller-Ellsberg, J. (eds). (2010) *Solidarity Economy I: Building Alternatives for People and Planet*, Amherst, Center for Popular Economics.

Laville, J.-L. (2010) 'The Solidarity Economy: An International Movement', *RCCS Annual Review*, Vol. 2, October, pp. 3–14.

Laville, J.-L. (2023) 'Origins and Histories of the SSE', in Y. Ilcheong et al. (eds), *Encyclopedia of the Social and Solidarity Economy*, Cheltenham and Northampton, Edward Elgar Publishing Limited in partnership with United Nations Inter-Agency Task Force on Social and Solidarity Economy (UNTFSSE). Open-access, https://www.e-elgar.com/textbooks/yi/.

Lewis, R. (1987) *Marcus Garvey: Anti-Colonial Champion*, Kent, Karia Press.

Loewenstein, A. (2017) *Disaster Capitalism: Making a Killing Out of Catastrophe*, New York, Verso.

MacPherson, I. (2010) *Hands across the Globe: A History of the International Credit Union Movement*, Victoria, TouchWood Editions.

Martin, T. (1976) *Race first : The Ideological and Organizational Struggles of Marcus Garvey and the Universal Negro Improvement Association*, Westport, Greenwood Press.

Martin, T. (1983) *Marcus Garvey, Hero: A First Biography*, Dover, The Majority.

Miller, E. (2010) 'Solidarity Economy: Key Concepts and Issues', in E. Kawano, T. Masterson and J. Teller-Ellsberg (eds), *Solidarity Economy I: Building Alternatives for People and*

Planet, Amherst, Center for Popular Economics, pp. 25–42.

Mollner, T. (1984) 'Mondragon: A Third Way', *Review of Social Economy*, Vol. 42, No. 3, pp. 260–71.

Molyneux, M. (1985) 'Mobilization without Emancipation? Women's Interests, the State and Revolution in Nicaragua', *Feminist Studies*, Vol. 11, No. 2, pp. 227–54.

Moulaert, F. and Ailenei, O. (2005) 'Social Economy, Third Sector and Solidarity Relations: A Conceptual Synthesis from History to Present', *Urban Studies*, Vol. 42, No. 1, pp. 2037–53.

National Cooperative Business Association (NCBA/CLUSA). '"The 7 Cooperative Principles" Slide', https://ncbaclusa.coop/resources/7-cooperative-principles/ (accessed August 14, 2022).

Ostrom, E. (1990) *Governing the Commons: The Evolution of Institutions for Collective Action*, Cambridge, Cambridge University Press.

Peredo, A.M. and MacLean, M. (2006) 'Social Entrepreneurship: A Critical Review of the Concept', *Journal of World Business*, Vol. 41, pp. 56–65.

Polanyi, K. (1944 [2001]) *The Great Transformation: The Political and Economic Origins of Our Time*, Boston, Beacon Press.

Quarter, J., Armstrong, A. and Mook, L. (2018) *Understanding the Social Economy: A Canadian Perspective* (2nd Edition), Toronto, University of Toronto Press.

Quarter, J. and Mook, L. (2010) 'An Interactive View of the Social Economy', *Canadian Journal of Nonprofit and Social Economy Research*, Vol. 1, No. 1, pp. 8–22.

Rankin, K. (2001) 'Governing Development: Neoliberalism, Microcredit and Rational Economic Women', *Economy and Society*, Vol. 30, pp. 18–37.

Roy, A. (2010) *Poverty Capital: Microfinance and the Making of Development*, New York, Routledge.

Silva, S. (Forthcoming, 2023) 'A Site of Contestation for Black Life: The Study of Quilombolas in the State of São Paulo, Brazil', in C.S. Hossein, S.W. Austin and K. Edmonds (eds), *Beyond Racial Capitalism: Cooperatives in the African Diaspora*. Oxford, Oxford University Press.

Spade, D. (2020) 'Solidarity Not Charity: Mutual Aid for Mobilization and Survival', *Social Text 142*, Vol. 38, No. 1, pp. 131–51.

The Take: Occupy, Resist and Produce. (2004). 'Documentary Film', Directed by Avi Lewis and Naomi Klein. Hosted on Films for Action, https://www.filmsforaction.org/watch/the-take-occupy-resist-produce/.

Thompson, J. and Doherty, B. (2006) 'The Diverse World of Social Enterprise: A Collection of Social Enterprise Stories', *International Journal of Social Economics*, Vol. 33, No. 5/6, pp. 361–75.

Williams, R.C. (2007) *The Cooperative Movement: Globalization from Below*, Farnham, Ashgate Publishers.

Yi, I., et al. (eds). (2023) *Encyclopedia of the Social and Solidarity Economy*, Cheltenham and Northampton, Edward Elgar Publishing Limited in partnership with United Nations Inter-Agency Task Force on Social and Solidarity Economy (UNTFSSE).

Young Foundation. (2012) 'Social Innovation Overview: A Deliverable of the Project: The Theoretical, Empirical and Policy Foundations for Building Social Innovation in Europe', *TEPSIE, European Commission*, 7th Framework Programme. Brussels, European Commission, DG Research.

23 | From sharing economy to surveillance capitalism

Richard Wellen, Kean Birch and Salewa Olawoye

Introduction

The internet and digital technologies are often portrayed as enabling the democratization of economic transactions and business. The best example of this tendency is the so-called sharing economy (Sundararajan 2016). This refers to digital platforms that have a business model which connects those selling products and services with buyers on the same platform. This model frequently sidesteps the rules which apply to conventional forms of business, management and work (Benkler 2006; Davis 2016; Srinicek 2017). Unfortunately, this vision of the sharing economy hasn't lived up to its name; instead, it has led to the dominance of digital platforms and intermediaries – including companies like Apple, Amazon, Google/Alphabet, Microsoft and Facebook/Meta – which make economic coordination more efficient but at the cost of reduced social accountability and increased market control (see Chapter 12). We find an example of such problems when we consider people working in the 'gig economy' who use platforms like Uber and are deprived of normal employment protections because they are considered to be 'independent contractors' instead of workers (Stanford 2017).

This chapter investigates the double-sided nature of the sharing economy, exploring the larger challenges of addressing the business and society relationship in an increasingly digital world. The very same forces that might enable a more horizontal and egalitarian sharing economy, providing opportunities for people to become independent producers and content-creators on, for example, YouTube or TikTok, have simultaneously increased the power of digital platforms and ushered in an era of precarious work and what Shoshana Zuboff (2019) calls 'surveillance capitalism'. By becoming the infrastructure of our daily lives, digital platforms are amassing ever-increasing hordes of our personal data that can be used to train algorithms to predict our actions and behaviours and, thereby, calculate the best way to get us to stay glued to our screens and to extract as much money from us as possible (Birch et al. 2021).

While highly personalized on-demand services may be welcome, many digital platforms have become powerful intermediaries and gatekeepers that cause harm to individuals, society and the environment through, for example, their capacity to escape regulations or sidestep the rules that other businesses must follow (see Bitcoin textbox). A clear example of these harms is the rise of disinformation and its impacts on our societies and politics. Companies like Facebook have enabled people to share their interests, interact with other like-minded people and build online communities; the downside of this is that they have also created virtual spaces for extremists to build communities propagating hate or for political operators to disseminate disinformation.

Case study: Digital currencies

'You can now buy a Tesla with Bitcoin'

On 24 March 2021, billionaire Elon Musk tweeted eight words: 'You can now buy a Tesla with Bitcoin'. This tweet in support of Bitcoin from the SpaceX CEO led to a spike in the price of the currency. Two months later, however, he rescinded this statement when he admitted to the contradiction of an environmentally friendly company accepting payment mined through excessive energy consumption, as documented by the University of Cambridge 'Bitcoin Electricity Consumption Index' (https://ccaf.io/cbeci/index). This retraction led to a 15 per cent drop in the price of Bitcoin. This plunge led to hundreds of billions of dollars in losses for Bitcoin investors and about $365 billion in the cryptocurrency market. One billionaire's tweet led to volatility that determined the direction of Bitcoins.

Bitcoin is a decentralized digital currency that was introduced in 2008 (Vranken 2017). It is stored in a publicly distributed digital ledger called a 'blockchain'. This blockchain is a connected body of data with information for each transaction used to identify the code for each exchange. Bitcoin transaction links can only be used once they possess a unique identifying code for each exchange. Since Bitcoins can be used for exchange, it raises the question, 'is Bitcoin money?' To address this, we first have to define money. Money is both 'a social construct used to form relationships and credit used to settle debt' (Olawoye-Mann 2021). It has three functions: (1) it serves as a medium of exchange – a means of settling debt, (2) as a unit of account – a means of measuring the worth of goods and services, and (3) as a store of value – used to accumulate wealth. Through its function as a store of value and a medium of exchange, Bitcoin is a unit of currency that has functioned as money. However, as a virtual currency it has no physical representation. There are no precious metals, governments or central banks to back it up. Private keys that are used to access their digital wallets can be lost, along with access to the Bitcoins contained within them. While Bitcoin and other cryptocurrencies are transparent, convenient and not exposed to typical exchange or interest rate volatilities, they are still highly volatile as seen through the effects of Elon Musk's tweets.

Sources: Vranken (2017), Olawoye-Mann (2021)

Commons-based economies

In Chapters 6 and 16, we discussed how private property and many of the institutions of capitalism are justified with reference to the 'tragedy of the commons'. According to Garrett Hardin's idea, commonly held resources which everyone has a right to use provide no incentive for individuals and organizations to protect and preserve those resources. Many subsequent thinkers have used Hardin's idea to support the idea that *only* private property rights will stop the 'tragic' over-use of resources. This logic has been used to justify the spread of new or stronger intellectual property rights – that is, patents, copyrights and trademarks – which many claim are necessary to incentivize people to invest in new technologies and innovations.

Hardin's logic, however, has not been universally accepted. By the late 1990s, many scholars writing about the internet and emerging digital technologies argued that these technologies enabled economic activity to be more decentralized and globally distributed, supporting more commons-based and cooperative alternatives to the conventional capitalist business models (Benkler 2016; Davis 2014).

One of the most famous examples of commons-based alternatives is the open-source software movement (Wellen 2013), which is responsible for successful computer software projects like the Linux operating system based on an open-access licence known as the 'GNU public licence'. Like other forms of intellectual property this licence restricts the use of the resource it governs, but it does so with a unique twist; it only allows cooperative and shareable uses and reuses (Weber 2004). The open-access licence itself requires future versions of the software to also be open and collectively 'shareable'. As a result, Linux has become a leading, freely accessible computer operating system created and maintained by an online community of volunteers.

The Linux operating system is perhaps the most well-known product that has been created and maintained under this open-access model of licensing. While Windows is still by far the dominant desktop operating system, Linux dominates among so-called supercomputers and is popular among professional developers. The success of Linux – and internet-based projects like Wikipedia – are examples of decentralized and collaborative ways of organizing economic activities, often with advantages over private property models. Wikipedia, for example, is a successful online encyclopedia run and produced by volunteers. The collaborative potential of these projects is based on the fact that ideas and information are inherently shareable since they are non-rivalrous, meaning they can be used simultaneously by many people (Xavier Olleros 2018). In the digital age, this model is particularly potent since ideas and information can be reproduced and distributed at near-zero marginal (i.e. additional) cost (Mason 2015).

The greater digital connectivity of the internet and especially Web 2.0 from 2000 onwards led to the rise of other collaborative practices like 'crowdsourcing', 'peer production' and the 'sharing economy' (Srinicek 2017; Sundararajan 2016). These different forms of production and sharing are based on the open, non-proprietary ownership rights discussed earlier. What they entail are forms of collective, communal activities that sit outside of formal market exchange (see Chapter 4). A number of critics of digital capitalism have argued that these forms of production help to radically alter economic and property relations, thereby challenging the standard conception that the private firm is the key organizational form in capitalism (e.g. Moulier Boutang 2011). These alternative forms are more than just possibilities, they may actually be more efficient because they enable the release of each individual's creativity rather than the subsumption of that creative potential to bureaucratic, corporate culture (see Malleson 2014).

Of course, despite the advantages of commons-based production there are still questions about whether its track record over the last decades demonstrates its potential to become a viable alternative to traditional business or to challenge capitalism. Some participants in the Linux project see themselves as part of the 'free software' movement which can challenge traditional business norms and practices. However, many Linux contributors still expect to receive indirect career and commercial benefits in the mainstream economy for being associated with the project (Shi 2014). Mainstream businesses benefit from using Linux for free, or from having Linux software experts on their staff (Papadimitropoulos 2020). Despite its idealistic origins the free software movement therefore shows how collaborative alternative models and mainstream models co-exist.

The promise of the sharing economy

As should be evident by now, the decentralizing and collaborative promises of digital technologies are often ambivalent and contradictory. The 'sharing economy' clearly exemplifies this contradiction. Early examples of the sharing economy included online peer-to-peer markets like eBay, though it is now usually associated with digital platforms like Uber, Lyft and Deliveroo (Sundararajan 2016). Ride-sharing platforms like Uber and Lyft enable users and drivers to connect with one another. Work and service platforms like TaskRabbit enable users to find people to do various tasks. The sharing economy comprises many other fields of work that can be disaggregated into granular contracts such as accommodation, massage therapy, delivery services, artwork and photography, cleaning, babysitting and so on. Because the exchanges of labour or services are now usually monetary in nature, scholars increasingly use the term 'gig economy' to refer to these activities (Sadowski 2020; van Doorn and Badger 2020; Gregory and Sadowski 2021).

The gig economy nonetheless has a sharing dimension to it, in that exchanges happen between peers rather than with a business. The businesses running the intermediary platforms of the sharing or gig economy charge fees for connecting users, often through the deployment of algorithm-driven matching models (Stanford 2017). As digital intermediaries these businesses can scale up rapidly and cheaply since they rely on digital technologies, and most of the assets being 'shared', like cars, tools or spare rooms, are owned by users or peers on the platform (Srinicek 2017).

Some observers praise these systems for pioneering a new and more democratic, collaborative and participatory economy (Sundararajan 2016). The new model is made possible by using digital technologies to lower the barriers to entry for self-directed work and to lower transaction costs in markets (see Chapter 7). Today, almost anyone can start their own short-term rental business or use social media to get paid for marketing products as an 'influencer' on TikTok or YouTube. No one participating on these platforms needs to be a credentialed expert or to move up the corporate ladder before contributing. These platforms allow you to monetize your car or apartment or turn your hobby as a photographer into a source of income in ways that simply weren't possible before. Thanks to customer ratings these platforms provide indicators of service reliability to buyers; for example, drivers on all the major ride-hailing platforms are rated by customers, and service quality is easily tracked by software, eliminating the need for expensive employee performance tracking which tends to translate into lower costs for consumers (Bieber and Moggia 2021).

These features are seen as realizing some of the utopian promises of digital technologies establishing new kinds of market opportunities for micro-entrepreneurs based on collaborative peer-to-peer relationships (Sundararajan 2016). Many platform workers enjoy the fact that they can work without a direct manager and need not be tied down by a single employer or long-term employment contract. Perhaps more importantly, gig workers can use their platform work to supplement their other work in an economy in which steady income in a single job or career may no longer be sufficient (Schor 2020).

Some people claim that the same algorithms that provide convenient and low-cost matching can also help to generate more sustainable patterns of consumption (Mi and Coffman 2019). For example, some might argue that Airbnb short-term rentals generate more sustainable resource use by ensuring that unused living spaces in expensive or desirable city neighbourhoods can be made available for rent. Likewise, ride-hailing platforms might ensure that personally owned cars spend less time sitting idle, making more efficient use of expensive urban space (Mi and Coffman 2019).

The costs of the sharing economy

In recent years critics have contested the claim that the sharing economy is a good way of addressing 'tragedy of the commons' forms of unsustainable resource consumption. Indeed, some researchers have claimed that peer-to-peer commerce actually promotes indulgent consumerism (Parguel et al. 2017). For example, there is evidence that ride-hailing services like Uber have reduced the demand for lower-emission public transit and have increased road congestion (Acquier et al. 2017). Likewise, Airbnb has been accused of promoting more short-term expensive rentals which have changed the character of neighbourhoods, reducing the stock of affordable housing by filling them with 'ghost hotels' purchased by investors (J. Schor 2020).

The 'digital cage' of gig work. When work is unbundled into commodifiable discrete tasks – through platforms like TaskRabbit – to allow flexible digital coordination, it has negative impacts on the lives of workers (Sadowski 2020). One area where this is especially the case is worker autonomy. While Uber drivers and other platform workers are free to reject rides or tasks and to set their own hours of work, these decisions end up having direct impacts on their personal ratings and, therefore, their capacity to earn on the platform (Rosenblat and Stark 2016). Moreover platforms increasingly use algorithmic processes to set prices, limiting the capacity of workers to control their work and earnings. Some researchers now speak of 'algorithmic domination' to describe the way that platform algorithms have replaced human managers to monitor work. Consumer rating systems are used to deactivate drivers or workers, with few if any opportunities for appeal (Tucker 2020; Muldoon and Raekstad 2022). In fact, many platforms do not disclose to workers the kind of data and rules that the algorithms use to allocate work or how service providers themselves are rated in response to searches and requests by customers (Vallas and Schor 2020).

There is also a larger social concern that as 'commodified' gig work and temporary contract work becomes more prevalent the resulting atomization and individualization means that workers lose access to many of the kinds of opportunities that organizations – including businesses – provide to workers to build their careers, like training and building networks (Anicich 2022). As a result, some work and service platforms can actually reinforce and amplify socio-economic inequalities since the success of each individual service provider depends on personal resources, such as owning a nice car or good tools or an apartment (Schor et al. 2020). In the words of Vallas and Schor (2020), platform work can be a 'digital cage' because the worker flexibility provided by platforms is often illusory, concealing the precariousness of their employment and lacking the social supports that are available through traditional organizations and employment relationships.

Regulatory issues with the gig economy. Perhaps the key social problem with the gig economy is that when work is assigned by platform intermediaries it creates regulatory gaps and 'grey zones' which allow risks to be shifted onto workers (Koutsimpogiorgos et al. 2020). For example, unlike regular employees, independent contractors lack access to workplace or statutory benefits such as unemployment insurance, public pensions, sick leave and vacation pay. Indeed, it is the ability to offload these kinds of costs – rather than the efficiency of the business model – that makes ride-hailing services like Uber cheaper than traditional taxis in many jurisdictions. The same applies to other gig platforms (van Doorn and Badger 2020). In fact, the business model of these platforms is often premised directly on exploiting these regulatory gaps, undermining collective attempts to organize work and employment (Sadowski 2020).

Policy case study

Regulating the gig economy

Unlike in North America, many EU countries provide some benefits and social insurance provisions for ride-hailing drivers, either as a matter of sectoral policy or because social supports like health care are provided by government rather than as employment benefits. In 2021 the European Commission issued a draft policy model for the gig economy that proposed a list of criteria that could be used to decide if platform workers should be classified as full employees with the right to join unions, earn a minimum wage and receive other public benefits (European Commission 2021). Another proposal aims to make the factors used by algorithms to rank, price and allocate work transparent. In Canada, Ontario's Labour Relations Board recognized that couriers working for the delivery service Foodora were not really independent contractors, as the company claimed, since their work is controlled by an app developed by the company. While the Board did not rule that Foodora was an employer, it nonetheless insisted that the company is more than a neutral intermediary between couriers and delivery customers, which meant that the couriers should be classified as 'dependent contractors'. It is noteworthy that after the labour ruling Foodora terminated its operations in Canada owing to the fact that couriers falling under this intermediate labour classification of 'dependent contractor' could soon have greater eligibility for unionization and other employee benefits (Tucker 2020).

In light of their contested and unsettled regulatory status and the growing recognition that they shift risks and costs onto workers and communities, ride-hailing platforms like Uber and Lyft and other gig economy businesses like Airbnb have devoted significant resources to lobbying governments to create or block regulations for the benefit of their business models (Vallas and Schor 2020). Politically, these firms have exploited the popularity of their convenient app-based and low-cost services to win over consumers as political allies in their campaigns against regulations and policies that would give platform workers more rights and higher pay (Rahman and Thelen 2019; Culpepper and Thelen 2019).

Solving the problems of the gig economy involves more than making regulatory changes; however, it also requires that existing social institutions, like trade unions, adapt and change. For example, even in those countries where independent contractors and gig workers have the right to be represented by unions, it's challenging to organize such a fragmented workforce. In some cases, unions have been reluctant to embrace platform workers since it could have the effect of legitimizing these non-standard precarious employment relationships (Jolly 2018). One alternative is to create worker-owned platform cooperatives (Scholz 2016). A growing 'platform cooperativism' movement has supported initiatives such as the worker-owned Driver's Cooperative in New York, which pays drivers more than Uber and Lyft (Conger 2021). Platform coops face the challenge of trying to provide better wages and working conditions in a sector where market success has often relied upon keeping labour costs low (Papadimitropoulos 2020). Successful worker-owned platform cooperatives remain relatively rare, since they are reliant upon financing from the gig-sector workers themselves, who often earn a low income (Bunders et al. 2022).

The rise of surveillance capitalism

Despite our focus thus far on the rise of the sharing or gig economy, the most powerful digital businesses are Apple, Amazon, Microsoft, Google/Alphabet and Facebook/Meta because of their control over the digital infrastructures that most of us depend upon in our daily lives. The business model for these Big Tech companies is based on collecting our personal and user data, often by providing us with free access to useful services like internet search or social media or app stores in exchange (Birch and Cochrane 2022). When accessing these supposedly free services, these Big Tech firms collect our personal and user data (e.g. purchases, websites visited, searches), which are trackable through ubiquitous online tracking technologies (e.g. cookies, 'like' buttons, device fingerprinting, IP addresses, application programming interfaces and much more). As a result, Big Tech learns everything about us; our habits, desires, preferences, relationships and even thoughts we are not always consciously aware of. This data can be used to train Big Tech's algorithms to better predict our interests and desires, which can be monetized by selling advertising, or making new products and services, or setting prices on the basis of our willingness to pay. A popular book by Shoshana Zuboff, Professor Emerita at Harvard Business School, refers to this new type of business model as 'surveillance capitalism' (Zuboff 2019).

Surveillance capitalism exemplifies the rent-seeking or rentiership pattern discussed in other chapters of this book (see Chapters 11 and 12). That is, it reveals an underlying business model that is concerned with controlling digital ecosystems and infrastructures rather than selling new products and services (Birch and Cochrane 2022). According to Zuboff, surveillance capitalism begins in the early 2000s when Google's management realized that they didn't have a way to monetize the company's free search service except by collecting more kinds of behavioural data about the search engine's users who could then be profitably targeted with advertising. Google's business model ended up driven by the need to make better predictions about people's desires and interests in order to draw more users to their ecosystem which, in turn, provided more value to advertisers. This gave rise to an imperative to develop a kind of cross-platform ecosystem of complementary apps and services such as Google search, Maps, Android mobile operating system and YouTube. The interplay between these services provided an even better way to extract personal and user data for training the predictive algorithms (Srinicek 2017; Lawrence et al. 2017).

Market power of Big Tech. As we discussed in Chapter 12, these Big Tech firms have reached their current size and scale as a result of network effects, which means that the value of their platform and its products and services increases as more people use it (Barwise and Watkins 2018). For example, the more buyers that Amazon attracts to its online marketplace the more likely it is that there will be more sellers to serve those buyers, which in turn makes it more attractive to more buyers. Likewise, as more people search on Google, it can collect more data to improve the relevance of its search results and other services, and therefore attract even more users. Added to the self-reinforcing impact of network effects is an additional advantage which we mentioned earlier in connection with commons-based and sharing models; namely, that these services, platforms and ecosystems provide users with low-cost means to participate in the economy.

This flexibility and convenience – much like gig work – looks like a great bargain but comes at a price. On the positive side of the bargain, an ecosystem like Amazon can provide even the smallest sellers of niche products with marketing opportunities and distribution channels they did not have under brick-and-mortar retailing. On the other hand, low-cost scaling and network effects have given Amazon enormous market power as a dominant shaper and controller of online commerce (Khan 2017). In this sense, Amazon does not just provide the marketplace but has become a gatekeeper that sets market rules, determining how consumer attention is directed or determining the degree to which sellers may or may not build their own relationship to customers (Legters 2022). Amazon's control and access to the user and commercial data from product sales allow it to learn consumer preferences. This gives the company the power to go beyond being a marketplace intermediary to being a market operator in its own right, creating Amazon-branded products to compete with the offerings of other sellers in their market. This practice has become the target of government regulators, who see it as an unfair use of its data-driven market power (House of Representatives 2020).

Big Tech's market power comes from extracting data from users in their ecosystems; Big Tech has considerable discretion over how much of the value created by that data is returned to users and what it can be used for. Hence, even when scale, personalization and cheap access improve the usefulness of digital technologies and ecosystems for users, the degree of unaccountable market power that Big Tech has acquired is problematic. Some thinkers have argued that the power that these surveillance capitalist firms possess is more 'extractive' than previous types of capitalism, labelling it 'technofeudalism' (Varoufakis 2021) to capture the fact that firms like Amazon are increasingly governing economic activity by controlling markets rather than competing in them. As a result, Big Tech has acquired a kind of private control and rule-making power over crucial social and economic infrastructures (Rahman 2017). Whether and how your product can be discovered on Amazon's marketplace, or if your content can be discovered through a Google search or on YouTube, is governed by opaque algorithms, application programming interfaces and other digital technologies controlled by these companies.

Responding to the social costs of surveillance capitalism. Critics have pointed to the social harms caused by Big Tech, especially threats to the quality of public information and the amplification of extremism. For example, social media like Facebook, TikTok and Twitter use algorithms to analyse and aggregate data from the postings, videos and online reactions of their users. This enables them to create profiles of users and then to filter and recommend material they think those users will like. Unfortunately, these algorithms are designed to increase user engagement, since advertising is their prime source of revenue, which means they reinforce user prejudices rather than challenge them.

Social media has given people more control over the types of information they receive than was possible in the era of pre-digital media. It also enables civic, democratic and social justice groups to organize in ways not possible before. However, this unprecedented level of networked connectivity can also be exploited through personalized ratings, recommendations, filters and, ultimately, advertising (Zuboff 2019). Algorithmic filtering and personalization selectively place emphasis on information and content that appeals to our pre-existing interests and beliefs, leading to what has commonly been known as 'filter bubbles' or 'echo chambers' (Lauer 2021). So, while Facebook, Google, and other social media may have added to the diversity of our information choices, they have also made it easier to spread disinformation at a scale larger than was possible with traditional media like newspapers.

The question of how to address these social harms – and how to regulate Big Tech – has been the subject of controversy. For example, some have argued that the social harms caused by Big Tech can be addressed by curbing their monopoly power or breaking them up (Khan 2017; US House of Representatives 2020). However, as a number of scholars have argued, breaking up companies like Facebook/Meta or Alphabet/Google would not change the nature of the business model founded upon the monetization of user data (Pistor 2020; Birch and Cochrane 2022).

Aware of the public scrutiny of their social role and power, Big Tech firms support 'self-regulation', recruiting workers to police harmful or extremist content (de Streel et al. 2020). Social media sites like Twitter and Facebook now regularly post warnings or even place outright bans on certain users or types of content. Perhaps the most ambitious policy of self-regulation is Facebook's maintenance of an independent Oversight Board of experts to give advice and make decisions on content moderation cases. Although the Oversight Board has independent decision-making authority over cases, it has no power to influence issues of Facebook's platform design or algorithmic processes that amplify harmful content in the first place (Bell 2021). Another example is the EU's new Digital Services Act, which is expected to be implemented by 2024 and aims to hold Big Tech accountable for eliminating harmful or illegal content on their platforms. The Act would subject digital platforms to public scrutiny by requiring transparency about how their algorithms work and by mandating independent annual audits about the systemic risks posed by those algorithms (Satariano 2022).

Exploiting users and their content. As we have seen, one of the key features of Big Tech's market power is that users and other content providers share their data for free with platform owners, while the platform itself has wide discretion over how much of the value generated by that data is returned to users. There have been varying approaches to analysing this issue and recommending policies to address it.

Critics of digital capitalism argue that when we interact with platforms, we should really think of ourselves as 'prosumers' – effectively online workers/ producers – since so much of our consumption and online activity generates value for platform owners (Moulier Boutang 2011; Marazzi 2011). Consequently, the platform's free appropriation of our 'user-generated content' can be seen as another form of exploited labour (Humphreys and Grayson 2008).

Taking a more liberal-market approach (see Chapter 13), Posner and Weyl (2018) argue that because digital platforms use our data and social media posts without our consent, we should have property rights over our data since it is created by us. According to Viljoen (2021), though, this liberal-market perspective assumes that property rights are the best way to deal with the problem. Viljoen argues that this ignores the fact that data is produced by users collectively and is therefore best thought of as a social and public resource. For example, when TikTok's algorithm recommends a video for me the decision it makes is not only a result of what I allowed the platform to learn about me but about what the platform learned from the behaviour of many others (like me). Meaningful data rights and fairness would require not just individual bargaining power, but rather collective democratic mechanisms for determining how data can or should be used to influence, sort and categorize us (Viljoen 2021).

Empirical example: The digital disruption of the newspaper industry

Big Tech's impact on the newspaper industry has become a major focus for regulators in many countries. For example, the rise of digital platforms has been associated with a decline in advertising revenues supporting journalism and the production of news, both of which play important public functions in society. Studies show that from 2005 to 2020 annual newspaper advertising revenue in the United States fell from $49.4B to $8.8B (Barthel 2021). This is because Facebook and Google have increasingly become for many the preferred content-discovery intermediaries for news and the best way for advertisers to reach information audiences. At the same time, these platforms are the leading online advertising brokers due to their control of our data and online ad exchanges. This transfer of advertising revenues from news organizations to digital intermediaries has led to a crisis for the journalism profession and has created 'news deserts' in communities that have lost local newspapers.

Aware of criticism about their market power, the large digital platforms have responded by developing grant programmes to fund news and journalism initiatives, such as the Meta/Facebook Journalism Project and the Google News Initiative. However, there is not yet any indication that these initiatives will restore the media industry. Seeking a more systemic solution, some countries like Australia and Canada have brought in government mandates requiring Big Tech intermediaries to share advertising revenues with news producers when their journalistic content is featured on Big Tech platforms. Despite its aims, this policy has been criticized for subsidizing and favouring established media companies without promoting innovative digital alternatives (Bossio et al. 2022).

Conclusion

The complexity and ambivalence of business transformations in the digital age are a challenge for those trying to develop critical approaches to understand these changes and for those developing policies and alternatives to address them. Commons-based economic alternatives such as open-source software, Wikipedia and platform cooperatives indicate some pathways towards a more collaborative economy, but the impact of these initiatives has been overshadowed by new types of socially unaccountable corporate power in the gig economy and surveillance capitalism. In particular, economies of scale in a data-driven economy make it possible for some firms to become *de facto* gatekeepers over key social and public infrastructure in ways that were not possible with earlier forms of corporate power (Madiega 2020). In addition, new types of digital intermediaries appear to circumvent traditional frameworks for regulating business. Old regulatory frameworks and institutions for addressing the needs of workers may no longer be adequate when gig economy platforms unbundle and commodify work into granular tasks, thereby doing away with the traditional employment relationship. Similar problems of social accountability emerge as more of us receive our news from platforms such as Google and Facebook, which shape, but don't produce, the content they recommend and filter.

References

Acquier, A., Daudigeos, T. and Pinkse, J. (2017) 'Promises and Paradoxes of the Sharing Economy: An Organizing Framework', *Technological Forecasting and Social Change*, Vol. 125, No. July, pp. 1–10, https://doi.org/10.1016/j.techfore.2017.07.006.

Anicich, E.M. (2022) 'Dehumanization Is a Feature of Gig Work Not a Bug', *Harvard Business Review*, https://hbr.org/2022/06/dehumanization-is-a-feature-of-gig-work-not-a-bug.

Barthel, M. (2021) *Six Key Takeaways about the State of the News Media in 2020*, https://www.pewresearch.org/fact-tank/2021/07/27/6-key-takeaways-about-the-state-of-the-news-media-in-2020/.

Barwise, T. and Watkins, L. (2018) 'The Evolution of Digital Dominance: How Ann Why We Got to GAFA', in M. Moore and D. Tambini (eds), *Digital Dominance: The Power of Google, Amazon, Facebook and Apple*, Oxford, Oxford University Press, pp. 21–49.

Bell, E. (2021) 'Facebook Has Beefed Up Its "Oversight Board," But Any New Powers Are Illusory', *The Guardian*, 14 April, https://www.theguardian.com/commentisfree/2021/apr/14/facebook-has-beefed-up-its-oversight-board-but-any-new-powers-are-illusory.

Benkler, Y. (2006) *The Wealth of Networks*, New Haven and London, Yale University Press.

Benkler, Y. (2016) 'Peer Production, the Commons, and the Future of the Firm', *Strategic Organization*, 1–11, https://doi.org/10.1177/1476127016652606.

Bieber, F. and Moggia, J. (2021) 'Risk Shifts in the Gig Economy: The Normative Case for an Insurance Scheme against the Effects of Precarious Work*', *Journal of Political Philosophy*, Vol. 29, No. 3, pp. 281–304, https://doi.org/10.1111/jopp.12233.

Birch, K., Cochrane, D.T., and Ward, C. (2021) 'Data as Asset? The Measurement, Governance, and Valuation of Digital Personal Data by Big Tech', *Big Data and Society*, Vol. 8, No. 1, pp. 1-15, https://doi.org/10.1177/20539517211017308.

Birch, K. and Cochrane, D.T. (2022) 'Big Tech: Four Emerging Forms of Digital Rentiership', *Science as Culture*, Vol. 31, No. 1, pp. 44–58, https://doi.org/10.1080/09505431.2021.1932794.

Bossio, D., Flew, T., Meese, J., Leaver, T., and Barnet, B. (2022) 'Australia's News Media Bargaining Code and the Global Turn Towards Platform Regulation', *Policy and Internet*, Vol. 14, No. 1, pp. 136–50.

Boutang, Y.M. (2011) *Cognitive Capitalism*, Cambridge, Polity.

Bunders, D.J., Arets, M., Frenken, K. and De Moor, T. (2022) 'The Feasibility of Platform Cooperatives in the Gig Economy', *Journal of Co-Operative Organization and Management*, Vol. 10, No. 1, p. 100167, https://doi.org/10.1016/j.jcom.2022.100167.

Conger, K. (2021) 'A Worker-Owned Cooperative Tries to Compete with Uber and Lyft', *New York Times*, May 21.

Culpepper, P.D. and Thelen, K. (2019) 'Are We All Amazon Primed? Consumers and the Politics of Platform Power', *Comparative Political Studies, January*, 001041401985268, https://doi.org/10.1177/0010414019852687.

Davis, G.F. (2014) *Corporate Power in the 21st Century. April*, 1–31.

Davis, G.F. (2016) 'What Might Replace the Modern Corporation? Uberization and the Web Page Enterprise', *Seattle University Law Review*, Vol. 39, pp. 507–19.

de Streel, A., Defreyne, E., Jacquemin, H. and Ledger, M. (2020) *Online Platforms' Moderation of Illegal Content Online Law, Practices and Options for Reform*, https://www.europarl.europa.eu/RegData/etudes/STUD/2020/652718/IPOL_STU(2020)652718_EN.pdf

European Commission (2021) *Proposal for a Directive of the European Parliament and of the Council on Improving Working Conditions in Platform Work*, https://ec.europa.eu/commission/presscorner/detail/en/ip_21_6605.

Gregory, K. and Sadowski, J. (2021) 'Biopolitical Platforms: The Perverse Virtues of Digital Labour', *Journal of Cultural Economy*, Vol. 14, No. 6, pp. 662–74, https://doi.org/10.1080/17530350.2021.1901766.

Humphreys, A. and Grayson, K. (2008) 'The Intersecting Roles of Consumer and Producer: A Critical Perspective on Co-production, Co-creation and Prosumption', *Sociology Compass*, Vol. 2, No. 3, pp. 963–80, https://doi.org/10.1111/j.1751-9020.2008.00112.x.

Jolly, C. (2018) 'Collective Action and Bargaining in the Digital Era', in M. Neufeind, J. O-Reilly and F. Ranft (eds), *Work in the Digital Age: Challenges of the Fourth Industrial Revolution*, London and New York, Rowman and Littlefield.

Khan, L.M. (2017) 'Amazon's Antitrust Paradox', *Yale Law Journal*, Vol. 126, No. 3, pp. 710–805.

Koutsimpogiorgos, N., van Slageren, J., Herrmann, A.M. and Frenken, K. (2020) 'Conceptualizing the Gig Economy and Its Regulatory Problems', *Policy and Internet*, Vol. 12, No. 4, pp. 525–45, https://doi.org/10.1002/poi3.237.

Lauer, D. (2021) 'Facebook's Ethical Failures Are Not Accidental; They are Part of the Business Model', *AI and Ethics*, Vol. 1, No. 4, pp. 395–403, https://doi.org/10.1007/s43681-021-00068-x.

Lawrence, M. and Laybourn-langton, L. (2018) *The Digital Commonwealth: From Private Enclosure to Collective Benefit*, IPPR, http://www.ippr.org/research/publications/the-digital-commonwealth.

Legters, B. (2022) 'Brand Loyalty in the Digital Age: The Battle for Customer Attention', *Forbes*, June 3.

Madiega, T. (2020) *Regulating Digital Gatekeepers Background on the Future Digital Markets Act* (Issue December), https://www.europarl.europa.eu/RegData/etudes/BRIE/2020/659397/EPRS_BRI(2020)659397_EN.pdf.

Malleson, T. (2014) *After Occupy: Economic Democracy for the 21st Century*, Oxford, Oxford University Press.

Marazzi, C. (2011) *The Violence of Financial Capitalism*, Cambridge, MA, MIT Press.

Mason, P. (2015) *Postcapitalism: A Guide to Our Future*, New York, Farrar, Straus and Giroux.

Mi, Z. and Coffman, D.M. (2019) 'The Sharing Economy Promotes Sustainable Societies', in *Nature Communications* (Vol. 10, No. 1). Nature Publishing Group, https://doi.org/10.1038/s41467-019-09260-4.

Muldoon, J. and Raekstad, P. (2022) 'Algorithmic Domination in the Gig Economy', *European Journal of Political Theory*, https://doi.org/10.1177/14748851221082078.

Olawoye-Mann, S. (2021) 'Towards a Harmonious View of Money: The Nigerian Experience', *Journal of African Studies and Development*, Vol. 13, No. 4, pp. 115–123.

Papadimitropoulos, V. (2020) 'The Commons: Economic Alternatives in the Digital Age', in *The Commons: Economic Alternatives in the Digital Age*, University of Westminster Press, https://doi.org/10.16997/book46.

Parguel, B., Lunardo, R. and Benoit-Moreau, F. (2017) 'Sustainability of the Sharing Economy in Question: When Second-Hand Peer-to-Peer Platforms Stimulate Indulgent Consumption', *Technological Forecasting and Social Change*, Vol. 125, pp. 48–57, https://doi.org/10.1016/j.techfore.2017.03.029.

Pistor, K. (2020) 'Rule by Data: The End of Markets?', *Law and Contemporary Problems*, Vol. 83, No. 2, pp. 101–124.

Posner, E. and Weyl, E.G. (2018) *Radical Markets: Uprooting Capitalism and Democracy for a Just Society*, Princeton, Princeton University Press.

Rahman, K.S. (2017) 'The New Utilities: Private Power, Social Infrastructure, and the Revival of the Public Utility Concept', *Cardozo Law Review*, Vol. 39, pp. 1621–89.

Rahman, K.S. and Thelen, K. (2019) 'The Rise of the Platform Business Model and the Transformation of Twenty-First-Century Capitalism', *Politics and Society*, https://doi.org/10.1177/0032329219838932.

Rosenblat, A. and Stark, L. (2016) 'Algorithmic labor and Information Assymetries: A Case Study of Uber's Drivers', *International Journal of Communication*, Vol. 10, pp. 3758–84.

Satariano, A. (2022) 'E.U. Takes Aim at Social Media's Harms with Landmark New Law', *New York Times*, 22 April, https://www.nytimes.com/2022/04/22/technology/european-union-social-media-law.html.

Sadowski, J. (2020) 'The Internet of Landlords: Digital Platforms and New Mechanisms of Rentier Capitalism', *Antipode*, Vol. 52, No. 2, pp. 562–80, https://doi.org/10.1111/anti.12595.

Scholz, T. (2016) *Platform Cooperativism: Challenging the Corporate Sharing Economy*, New York, Rosa Luxemburg Stiftung.

Schor, J. (2020) *After the Gig: How the Sharing Economy Got Hijacked and How to Win it Back*, Oakland, University of California Press.

Schor, J.B., Attwood-Charles, W., Cansoy, M., Ladegaard, I. and Wengronowitz, R. (2020) 'Dependence and Precarity in the Platform Economy', *Theory and Society*, Vol. 49, No. 5–6, pp. 833–61, https://doi.org/10.1007/s11186-020-09408-y.

Shi, T. (2014) 'Mainstreaming, Counter-Co-Optation, and Depoliticization by a Counterculture', *Journal of Marketing Development and Competitiveness*, Vol. 8, No. 3, pp. 107–20.

Srinicek, N. (2017) *Platform Capitalism*, Cambridge, Polity Press.

Stanford, J. (2017) 'The Resurgence of Gig Work: Historical and Theoretical Perspectives', *Economic and Labour Relations Review*, Vol. 28, No. 3, pp. 382–401, https://doi.org/10.1177/1035304617724303.

Sundararajan, A. (2016) *The Sharing Economy: The End of Employment and the Rise of Crowd-Based Capitalism*, Cambridge, MA, MIT Press.

Tucker, E. (2020) 'Towards a Political Economy of Platform-Mediated Work', *Studies in Political Economy*, Vol. 101, No. 3, pp. 185–207, https://doi.org/10.1080/07078552.2020.1848499.

Vallas, S. and Schor, J.B. (2020) *Annual Review of Sociology*, https://doi.org/10.1146/annurev-soc-121919.

van Doorn, N. and Badger, A. (2020) 'Platform Capitalism's Hidden Abode: Producing Data Assets in the Gig Economy', *Antipode*, Vol. 52, No. 5, pp. 1475–95, https://doi.org/10.1111/anti.12641.

Varoufakis, Y. (2021) 'Techno Feudalism ids Taking Over', *Project Syndicate*, 28 June, https://www.project-syndicate.org/commentary/techno-feudalism-replacing-market-capitalism-by-yanis-varoufakis-2021-06.

Viljoen, S. (2021) 'A Relational Theory of Data Governance', *The Yale Law Journal*, Vol. 131, No. 2, pp. 573–654.

Vranken, H. (2017) 'Sustainability of Bitcoin and Blockchains', *Current Opinion in Environmental Sustainability*, Vol. 28, pp. 1–9.

Weber, S. (2004) *The Success of Open Source*, Cambridge, MA, Harvard University Press.

Wellen, R. (2013) 'Open Access, Megajournals, and MOOCs: On the Political Economy of Academic Unbundling', *SAGE Open*, Vol. 3, No. 4, pp. 1–15, https://doi.org/10.1177/2158244013507271

Xavier Olleros, F. (2018) 'Antirival Goods, Network Effects and the Sharing Economy', *First Monday*, Vol. 23, No. 2, https://doi.org/10.5210/fm.v23i2.8161.

Zuboff, S. (2019) *The Age of Surveillance Capitalism: The Fight for a Human Future at the New Frontier of Power*, New York, Public Affairs.

24 | Conclusion

Business and the Challenges Ahead

Richard Wellen and Sonya Marie Scott

The goal of this book has been to explore the relationship between business and society in several ways. We have introduced foundational concepts and critical perspectives and have shown how these foundations illuminate controversial issues regarding the role of business in a changing world. Throughout we have seen how the relationship between business and society is multifaceted, requiring us to come to terms with major issues in politics and economics such as climate change, global equity and the new types of corporate power and influence. In this conclusion we'll take the opportunity to discuss the complex and often contradictory relationship between business-led social responsibility and the challenges presented by climate change and global inequality.

Let's start with a key theme of corporate and business governance: Can business be held to standards of social responsibility? If so, how might this be accomplished? Chicago School economist Milton Friedman famously argued that business managers are ultimately responsible for their company's financial bottom line instead of social concerns ('The Social Responsibility of Business is to Increase its Profits', 1984). When he identified the pursuit of profit as the social responsibility of business, he meant to defend several aspects of the then-ascendant neoliberal model which placed a priority on markets as solutions to many social problems previously addressed by the welfare state (Chapters 1, 4, 9, 13, 15, 17 and 20). Part of Friedman's argument was formulated in terms of principal-agent accountability: the job of the managers of corporations is to be accountable to shareholders who ultimately care about the firm being as profitable as possible (Chapters 8–12). Yet the point of Friedman's chapter was not just to argue that managers as 'agents' are doing their job properly when they look out for the interests of their financially self-interested 'principals'; he also wanted to provide support for the idea that when businesses are profit-driven rather than motivated by social causes, the result will be better for society. This idea reaches back to the classical liberalism of Adam Smith and his conception of the invisible hand (see Chapter 5).

The neoliberal model has certainly dominated economies of the Global North over the past three decades. And yet it is notable that the idea that the core tenets of neoliberalism – that is, that it is a socially optimal system which justifies market-oriented solutions and the primacy of shareholder interests – have been questioned by many in recent years, including prominent business leaders who have publicly argued in favour of the social responsibility of business to a variety of stakeholders (Chapters 11, 12 and 23). Leading heterodox economists like Mariana Mazzucato (2018), Marilyn Waring (1999) and others have pointed out that the belief that economic value is reflected in market prices is responsible for many problematic policies and practices that obscure the benefits of public investment and publicly controlled enterprise (see Chapters 6 and 18). Both Mazzucato and Waring also argue that the legacy of market fundamentalism can be found in our adherence to conventional value indicators like GDP which are unable to measure values such as human well-being, equity, environmental progress and community goods. In 2019, the increasing salience of these critical perspectives led the Business Roundtable (BRT), a lobbyist organization composed of the top CEOs in the US business community who advocate for business interests, to declare the importance of business commitment to the well-being of stakeholders (Harrison et al. 2020). This reversed the BRT's 1997 statement proclaiming that the 'paramount duty' of business is to serve the interests of shareholders.

Perhaps the most high-profile and increasingly controversial institutional proponent of 'stakeholderism' today is the World Economic Forum (WEF). This organization is composed of leading business elites and politicians and is funded by the world's largest corporations. The WEF holds an annual high-profile meeting in Davos, Switzerland, where CEOs, politicians, civil society groups and academics convene to discuss major economic issues of the day, including market and business trends, geopolitics and environmental issues. What's particularly striking is that the leadership of the organization and its main publications and speakers have become increasingly committed to questioning the neoliberal consensus. Klaus Schwab, the executive chairman of the WEF has called for a 'Great Reset' – that is, a transition to a new type of capitalism where the corporation is understood to be a 'social organism' and not just a 'commercial entity'. He calls for a full rejection of neoliberalism on the grounds that '[f]ree-market fundamentalism has eroded worker rights and economic security, triggered a deregulatory race to the bottom and ruinous tax competition, and enabled the emergence of massive new global monopolies' (Schwab 2020).

Many of the WEF's recent publications appear to be open to transformational change. For example, as the 2022 spike in energy costs led to soaring profits for energy companies the WEF published several articles calling for taxes on these windfall profits. These reports recommended that these windfall tax revenues be used to fund investments in decarbonizing the economy and assisting low-income countries most affected by climate change as well as supporting people unable to pay for rising energy prices.[1]

However, some have criticized the WEF's preference for 'multistakeholder governance', where business would be expected to contribute to social issues by partnering with NGOs and where governments and organizations like the UN would operate more like a public-private partnership (Gleckman 2018). Heterodox critics (see Chapter 14) believe that this is a way of privatizing governance since organizations like the WEF often see corporations with governance mandates as an alternative to democratic governments and regulatory oversight of business. While social responsibility (Bakan 2020) and green capitalism (Buller 2022) have become central to the public profile of business advocacy organizations, these groups are silent about the economic democracy alternatives (worker cooperatives, social and solidarity economy organizations, organized labour) surveyed in this book (see Chapters 15, 20, 21, 22 and 23). There is also very little accounting for the role that those who have been historically excluded from economic power and decision-making ought to play in setting the agenda for the world's most powerful corporations (see Chapters 3, 15 and 20). It is not surprising that neither the WEF nor the BRT has proposed policies for limiting the degree of power corporations have in the political sphere nor do they propose changing how corporations are governed so that 'stakeholders' like workers and those affected by business decisions have a role in making those decisions. This raises concerns about whether the movement for making business more 'responsible' is really an opportunity to avoid the more ambitious goal of making the economy and its institutions more democratic and inclusive. Those who are more cynical about corporate philanthropy have pointed to the way in which this proactive corporate approach is intended to curtail the scope of state regulation and intervention and increase their own market positions in so doing (Tusikov 2016). While business leaders may indeed be motivated by a genuine concern about issues like climate change and economic inequality, this does not imply that business should not have greater accountability to stakeholders in the way it defines these social issues and shapes the process for addressing them.

There is perhaps no contemporary issue that does more to reveal the importance of social responsibility than climate change (see Chapter 16). We have discussed some of its devastating consequences to both human and non-human life and are now witnessing the effects on the Global South in the form of natural disasters such as droughts, floods, increasingly volatile storms and rising water levels. In August and September of 2022 there were historic floods in Pakistan which claimed 1,700 lives (including at least 550 children), displaced 8 million people, wiped out core infrastructure and led to historic levels of disease and food insecurity (UN News 2022). The World Bank (2022) assessed the flood damage at US$14.9 billion, with many billions more needed for reconstruction and building future resilience. Also, in August and September of 2022, there was a historic level of drought in Southern China, which led to extremely low water levels that shut down important trade routes along the Yangtze River to manufacturing centres, affecting the circulation of goods and the production of hydroelectric power (Bradsher and Dong 2022). There is no doubt that these new volatile climate realities affect the entire global community. There is also no doubt that geopolitical power and global inequality demand that we consider the disproportionate burden of this new reality on countries in the Global South, coupled with the fact that most of the emissions that have contributed to this warming stem from the high consumption patterns of those in the Global North.

Such themes were the topic of the international climate conference COP27, hosted in Egypt in 2022. Particularly salient was the demand for climate equity and climate reparations, that is, the demand that nations which have disproportionately contributed to carbon emissions through high levels of industrial production and consumption contribute concrete resources to countries who have contributed very little to climate change yet nonetheless suffer its consequences to devastating effect. Climate conferences such as COP27 can be traced back to the First Earth Summit held in Stockholm in 1972 (Jackson 2007), evolving throughout several decades into sites where global goals around the reduction of emissions and other environmental protection measures were written into legally binding international agreements such as the Kyoto Accord (1997) and the Paris Agreement (2016). These conferences and agreements serve as an interesting counterpoint to the WEF. At times the same issues are raised – including the increase in stakeholder-oriented business models that take environmental consequences into effect – and at times a stark contrast emerges between the goals of multinational business, no matter how progressive the social mandate, and environmental protection in general.

Climate activists have been clear for years that, without systemic changes, measures to achieve the targets and goals to reduce carbon emissions and fossil fuel dependence will be woefully inadequate at stemming the environmental damage of climate change. Of particular note are those involved in the global youth movement for climate action – often associated with activists such as Greta Thurnberg of Sweden or Vanessa Nkate of Uganda, though Nkate has spoken of the exclusion and marginalization faced by young climate activists from the Global South and from racialized minorities in the Global North (Evelyn 2020). Demonstrations in September of 2019 – named *The 2019 Climate Strike* – took place across the globe and presented a rallying cry for governments and large business to take seriously the need to fundamentally alter our emissions records and economic systems. While the Covid-19 pandemic prevented similar protests in the subsequent years, these issues continue to manifest with every natural disaster linked to climate change and with every WEF and climate conference which brings such issues to the limelight. Indigenous climate activists have also made the world stage with reports of melting ice and changing landscapes from the Arctic regions. For example, Sheila Watt-Cloutier, a Canadian Inuk human rights and environmental activist, has argued that climate change is an infringement on human rights (2015). This is because emissions from industrial production and consumption have had a destructive impact on the landscapes and natural habitats where many Inuit and northern Indigenous communities have hunted and fished since time immemorial (see Chapter 1). Changes to the fundamental ways of living and surviving are raising serious questions about the fate of certain communities in precarious environmental settings. The grim reality of these issues can be quite overwhelming and has even resulted in a certain form of climate nihilism – or feeling of futility and meaninglessness – among many young people living in postmodern societies (Chapter 1). While this is understandable, it's also helpful to look at what can be done and the ways in which economic thinking can change to promote a healthier and more sustainable future.

Let's start with the idea of the *necessity for continuous economic growth* – one of the core assumptions about the economy and business that has played a role in global over-production and over-consumption of fossil fuels and other non-renewable resources. The idea of growth is baked into the very core of economics and economic policy today. If you hear that 'the economy isn't doing well' what this tends to mean is that rates of growth (and as a result, rates of profit) are either low or negative. We all know that a recession is a bad economic sign, because it means that there is a net reduction in economic indicators over the course of two-quarters (i.e. over six months). When there is an economic crash or depression, economists often focus on how we ought to recover from this injury to the economy by increasing growth. And yet this idea is relatively new in our collective history, linked to the rise of capitalist production and profit-oriented economic activity. Towards the end of the Great Depression of the 1930s in the United States, economist Alvin Hansen (1939) coined the term 'secular stagnation' to describe a sick recovery from a profound economic crisis (Chapter 17). The recovery was 'sick' because rates of growth within the economy were not picking up fast enough (i.e. they were stagnant), putting into question the fundamentals of the system. Likewise, in 2013, five years after the 2008 global financial crisis (GFC), Larry Summers – a prominent economist and advisor to various US presidential administrations – publicly revived the term raising alarm that the recovery from the GFC was based on financial speculation and not on productive market foundations (Summers 2014). Given the shocks of the pandemic and the subsequent period of global inflationary pressures, the idea that a consistent rate of growth must be maintained is questionable not only because of the implications for the climate but also because of its many cyclical disruptions. This leaves us with an important set of questions. Is there really a tradeoff between environmental well-being and economic well-being? Are growth and ever-increasing rates of profit necessary for economic and social well-being? How do orthodox economists reconcile continuous and unlimited growth on a planet with limited resources?

One answer to these questions has emerged in the debate on *decoupling*, which refers to the ability of an economy to 'grow', while not using increasing levels of material and energy resources at the same time (UNEP 2014). Initiatives such as the Green New Deal (See Chapter 16) in the United States have relied upon such concepts and promoted business and economic strategies that allow economies and industries to grow while decreasing resource consumption and carbon emissions. The model of green growth relies heavily on innovations and technologies – as well as supporting policy initiatives – that allow energy generation and production to proceed with far less resource consumption, waste and environmental harm (Zenghelis 2019). Efforts to make initiatives such as the Green New Deal a legislative reality have been met with a large degree of business resistance, however, despite the public claims that corporations are committed to the environment and multi-stakeholder concerns (Milman 2021).

Even in the academic sphere, where business doesn't tend to define the issues, critically minded researchers and observers have disagreed on the solutions to many of today's most pressing social and environmental problems. To start with a model which closely resembles the ideas put forward in the Green New Deal, let's look at the green growth paradigm. Dimitri Zenghelis is a prominent economist in the UK who advises on climate policy. He warns that one way or another, the human community will be forced to embrace 'decarbonization', or the reduction of emission of carbon into the environment as a result of human economic activity:

> Mankind will either manage the transition to net zero carbon emissions
> proactively by transitioning the economy, or nature will do it for us,
> by depopulating and deindustrialising the planet. Put another way,
> the fastest and the slowest global economic growth paths will both be
> low carbon. The growing realisation that the low-carbon transition is
> inevitable, and that it will be most effective if managed early rather than
> postponed, is changing the lens through which global climate policy is
> viewed. (2019: 55)

According to the green growth school, however, such a move need not be as economically catastrophic as it might sound. Instead, it can bring about corrections to market failures (i.e. cleaner air, less environmental volatility and many other climate benefits), increased economic activity through innovation of green technologies, and increased productivity with less resource use. It appears to be the best of all possible world but requires, quite crucially, large corporations to commit to a rather extensive shift in their strategies of production, distribution and resource use. The fear of a short-term cut to profitability and existential threat to fossil-fuel-dependent industries (such as oil and gas extraction and mining) are enough to disrupt the possibility of this transition in the short and medium terms, though advocates like Zenghelis say that these fears can be overcome by showing how the advantages of system-wide commitments to proactive changes may actually be cost-saving (Zenghelis 2019).

Many heterodox scholars are also critical of the green growth movement, arguing that the concept of decoupling is too optimistic about technological fixes and still relies far too heavily on businesses motivated by profit and on maintaining levels of consumption that most in the Global North have come to associate with the good life (Hickel and Kallis 2019). The degrowth movement instead proposes that we must fundamentally reorient our understanding of economic well-being and challenge the idea that growth is a measure of economic health or progress. Economic anthropologist Jason Hickel (2021) argues that although it might seem paradoxical, shrinking our economies is the primary way towards a prosperous future. This approach requires a recognition that the obstacle to change is not that business lacks sufficient social responsibility or ecological strategies, but rather that the very goals of capitalism run into conflict with environmental well-being. In order to sustain human communities and begin to put the brakes on irreversible climate catastrophe, argues Hickel, we have to go to the root assumptions of the capitalist system, replacing a focus on profit, mass extraction and financial efficiency with a focus on slow, subsistence-oriented and diversified systems of production. The capitalist imperative to continually grow the economy may seem reasonable at first glance – most put the ideal growth number at around 3 per cent per year – but as Hickel points out, this leads to exponential growth, which means that 'the economy churns through more energy, resources and waste each year, to the point where it is now dramatically overshooting what scientists have defined as safe planetary boundaries with devastating consequences for the living world' (2021, np). This also raises issues of inequality as well, both in absolute terms (human activity means the decimation of entire species of plants and animals) and in human terms (the Global South bears the burden of the consumption of the Global North, thus worsening inequality).

In capitalist economies (as we know them) business firms are strongly driven to try to sell as many products and services as possible as profitably as possible and also to support public policies that assume that economic growth is the best foundation for achieving social progress (Wiedmann et al. 2020). It therefore isn't hard to see why the degrowth movement is unappealing to the leaders of business today, even to those embracing stakeholderism over shareholder primacy. No matter where one falls on the green growth versus degrowth debate, the urgency of climate change means that we must ask some serious questions about the future of capitalism, business, and the planet itself. Throughout this book we have seen a variety of approaches that help us understand how we got to this stage of capitalist development with its many fundamental theoretical and practical challenges. From the early enclosure movement in England (Chapter 2) to the global spread of capitalism through the slave trade and colonial endeavour (Chapter 3) to the rise of the modern corporation (Chapters 7 and 10) and its spread across the globe as the dominant business form (Chapter 12) the extraction and consumption of resources have been at the core of the dominant economic model. Despite many theories that challenge this model (Chapters 6, 19, 22 and 24), and despite many efforts to regulate and govern business in order to reign in the market failures inherent to our contemporary capitalist order (Chapters 12, 14 and 18) we are still standing in the face of a crisis of epic proportions. Indeed, the recent turn away from globalization in the face of increased transnational tensions and competition (Chapter 13) may make it more difficult to convince nations to cooperate on problems like climate change which are inherently global. On the other hand, perhaps increasing comprehension of the nature of the crisis will boost popular support for transformational, cooperative and sustainable business alternatives (Chapters 15, 20, 21 and 22) that would be more conducive to the long-term well-being of humans and all other species of the planet.

Note

1 See, for example, the following publications from the WEF: 'Tax fossil fuel profits to counter climate crisis: UN chief' (23 September 2022) and; 'How windfall taxes could bolster efforts to reach net-zero' (7 October 2022).

Bibliography

Bakan, J. (2020) *The New Corporation*, Toronto, Penguin Random House.

Bradsher, K. and Dong, J. (2022) 'China's Record Drought is Drying its Rivers and Feeding its Coal Habit', *The New York Times*, 29 August, https://www.nytimes.com/2022/08/26/business/economy/china-drought-economy-climate.html (accessed November 2022).

Buller, A. (2022) *The Value of a Whale: On the Illusions of Green Capitalism*, Manchester, Manchester University Press.

Evelyn, K. (2020) '"Like I Wasn't There": Climate Activist Vanessa Nkate on Being Erased from a Movement', *The Guardian*, 29 January, https://www.theguardian.com/world/2020/jan/29/vanessa-nakate-interview-climate-activism-cropped-photo-davos (accessed November 2022).

Friedman, M. (1970). 'The Social Responsibility of Business is to Increase its Profits', *The New York Times*, 13 September, https://www.nytimes.com/1970/09/13/archives/a-friedman-doctrine-the-social-responsibility-of-business-is-to.html (accessed November 2022).

Gleckman, H. (2018) *Multistakeholder Governance and Democracy: A Global Challenge*, New York, Routledge.

Hansen, A. (1939) 'Economic Progress and Declining Population Growth', *American Economic Review*, Vol. 29, pp. 1–15.

Harrison, J.S., Phillips, R.A. and Freeman, R.E. (2020) 'On the 2019 Business Roundtable "Statement on the Purpose of a Corporation"', *Journal of Management*, Vol. 46, pp. 1223–37.

Hickel, J. (2021) *Less is More: How Degrowth will Save the World*, New York, Random House.

Hickel, J. and Kallis, G. (2019) 'Is Green Growth Possible?' *New Political Economy*, Vol. 15, pp. 1–18.

Jackson, P. (2007) 'From Stockholm to Kyoto: A Brief History of Climate Change', *UN Chronicle*, https://www.un.org/en/chronicle/article/stockholm-kyoto-brief-history-climate-change (accessed November 2022).

Mazzucato, M. (2018) *The Value of Everything: Making and Taking in the Global Economy*, New York, Public Affairs.

Milman, O. (2021) 'Apple and Disney among Companies Backing Groups against US Climate Bill', *The Guardian*, 1 October, https://www.theguardian.com/us-news/2021/oct/01/apple-amazon-microsoft-disney-lobby-groups-climate-bill-analysis.

Schwab, K. (2020) 'Post-COVID Capitalism', *Project Syndicate*, https://www.project-syndicate.org/commentary/post-covid-capitalism-great-reset-by-klaus-schwab-2020-10 (accessed November 2022).

Summers, L. (2014) 'US Economic Prospects: Secular Stagnation, Hysteresis, and the Zero Lower Bound', *Business Economics*, Vol. 49, pp. 65–73.

Tusikov, N. (2016) *Chokepoints: Global Private Regulation on the Internet*, Oakland, University of California Press.

United Nations News (2022) 'Pakistan Floods: Six Month Wait for Water to Recede, Warn Relief Agencies', 20 September, https://news.un.org/en/story/2022/09/1127051 (accessed November 2022).

UNEP. (2014) 'Decoupling 2: Technologies, Opportunities and Policy Options', in E.U. von Weizsäcker, J. de Larderel, K. Hargroves, C. Hudson, M. Smith and M. Rodrigues (eds), *A Report of the Working Group on Decoupling to the International Resource Panel*, Paris, France.

Waring, M. (1999) *Counting for Nothing: What Men Value and what Women are Worth*, Toronto, University of Toronto Press.

Watt-Cloutier, S. (2015) *The Right to Be Cold: One Woman's Fight to Protect the Arctic and Save the Planet from Climate Change*, Minneapolis, University of Minnesota Press.

Wiedmann, T., Lenzen, M., Keyßer, L.T. and Steinberger, J.K. (2020) 'Scientists' Warning on Affluence', *Nature Communications*, Vol. 11, pp. 1–10.

World Bank. (2022) 'Pakistan: Flood Damages and Economic Losses Over

USD 30 Billion and Reconstruction Needs Over USD 16 Billion - New Assessment', October 28, https://www.worldbank.org/en/news/press-release/2022/10/28/pakistan-flood-damages-and-economic-losses-over-usd-30-billion-and-reconstruction-needs-over-usd-16-billion-new-assessme (accessed November 2022).

Zenghelis, D. (2019) 'Securing Decarbonisation and Growth', *National Institute Economic Review*, Vol. 250, pp. 54–60, https://doi.org/10.1177/002795011925000118 (accessed November 2022).

Index

www.ingramcontent.com/pod-product-compliance
Ingram Content Group UK Ltd.
Pitfield, Milton Keynes, MK11 3LW, UK
UKHW020652280225
455688UK00004B/97